Broadcasting Modernism

UNIVERSITY PRESS OF FLORIDA
Florida A&M University, Tallahassee
Florida Atlantic University, Boca Raton
Florida Gulf Coast University, Ft. Myers
Florida International University, Miami
Florida State University, Tallahassee
New College of Florida, Sarasota
University of Central Florida, Orlando
University of Florida, Gainesville
University of North Florida, Jacksonville
University of South Florida, Tampa
University of West Florida, Pensacola

UNIVERSITY PRESS OF FLORIDA

Gainesville/Tallahassee/Tampa/Boca Raton/

Pensacola/Orlando/Miami/Jacksonville/

Ft. Myers/Sarasota

BROADCASTING MODERNISM

EDITED BY

DEBRA RAE COHEN

MICHAEL COYLE

& JANE LEWTY

Copyright 2009 by Debra Rae Cohen, Michael Coyle, and Jane Lewty
Printed in the United States of America on recycled, acid-free paper
All rights reserved

14 13 12 11 10 09   6 5 4 3 2 1

Frontispiece and part titles: Library of Congress, LC-M32-7235

LIBRARY OF CONGRESS CATALOGING-IN-PUBLICATION DATA
Broadcasting modernism/edited by Debra Rae Cohen,
Michael Coyle, and Jane Lewty.
p. cm.
Includes bibliographical references and index.
ISBN 978-0-8130-3349-5 (alk. paper)
1. Radio and literature. 2. Modernism (Literature) 3. Radio authorship. 4. Radio plays—History and criticism. 5. Radio broadcasting—History—20th century. I. Cohen, Debra Rae. II. Coyle, Michael, 1957– III. Lewty, Jane.
PN1991.8.L5B76   2009
809.'91129–dc22   2008052384

The University Press of Florida is the scholarly publishing agency for the State University System of Florida, comprising Florida A&M University, Florida Atlantic University, Florida Gulf Coast University, Florida International University, Florida State University, New College of Florida, University of Central Florida, University of Florida, University of North Florida, University of South Florida, and University of West Florida.

University Press of Florida
15 Northwest 15th Street
Gainesville, FL 32611-2079
http://www.upf.com

CONTENTS

Acknowledgments vii

Introduction: Signing On 1
Debra Rae Cohen, Michael Coyle & Jane Lewty

PART I MEDIUM & METAPHOR

1 Inventing the Radio Cosmopolitan:
  Vernacular Modernism at a Standstill 11
  Aaron Jaffe

2 Wireless Ego: The Pulp Physics of Psychoanalysis 31
  Jeffrey Sconce

3 Marinetti, *Marconista*: The Futurist Manifestos
  and the Emergence of Wireless Writing 51
  Timothy C. Campbell

4 "Masters of Sacred Ceremonies": Welles, Corwin,
  and a Radiogenic Modernist Literature 68
  Martin Spinelli

5 Flying Solo: The Charms of the Radio Body 89
  David Jenemann

PART II PRESSURES & INTRUSIONS

6 Gertrude Stein and the Radio 107
  Sarah Wilson

7 The Voice of America in Richard Wright's *Lawd Today!* 124
  Jonah Willihnganz

8 Annexing the Oracular Voice:
   Form, Ideology and the BBC   142
   Debra Rae Cohen

9 Desmond MacCarthy, Bloomsbury, and the Aestheticist
   Ethics of Broadcasting   158
   Todd Avery

10 "We Speak to India": T. S. Eliot's Wartime Broadcasts
   and the Frontiers of Culture   176
   Michael Coyle

PART III NEGOTIATIONS, TRANSACTIONS, TRANSLATIONS

11 "What They Had Heard Said Written":
   Joyce, Pound and the Cross-Correspondence of Radio   199
   Jane Lewty

12 "Speech Without Practical Locale":
   Radio and Lorine Niedecker's Aurality   221
   Brook Houglum

13 Materializing Millay: The 1930s Radio Broadcasts   238
   Lesley Wheeler

14 Updating Baudelaire for the Radio Age: The Refractive
   Poetics of "The Pleasures of Merely Circulating"   257
   J. Stan Barrett

15 I Switch Off: Beckett and the Ordeals of Radio   274
   Steven Connor

Bibliography   295

Contributors   317

Index   319

ACKNOWLEDGMENTS

This volume had its origins in a seminar at the annual meeting of the Modernist Studies Association in Birmingham, 2003. During preregistration, the seminar filled quickly; when it met, there were almost as many auditors as official participants. Discussion was lively and continued in various locations for the next two days—and nights. Over the next two years, at academic venues ranging from the Popular Culture Association, to the International T. S. Eliot Society and the International James Joyce Symposium, to the Cultural Studies Association, to the meeting of The Space Between on "Technology, Media and Culture," we witnessed an upsurge of interest in "the forgotten medium." And so, this volume appears in the wake of some five years of excited talk and exchange. Our special thanks go to early voices whose work does not appear in this volume: Stuart Christie, Ben Friedlander, Marty Boyden, Diana Collecott, Hiroshi Muto, Marguerite Rippy, and the late Burton Hatlen. Thanks, too, to some of our friends and colleagues whose apparently inexhaustible willingness to hear us brainstorm proves them as dedicated a set of listeners as any late-night call-in show could boast: Robert Brinkmeyer, David Chinitz, Kevin Dettmar, Andrew Gibson, Jean-Michel Rabaté, Wade Geary, and Kara Rusch.

We're grateful to the anonymous press readers of the manuscript for their insightful and practical suggestions, and to the Departments of English at Colgate University and the University of South Carolina for the timely financial support that enabled us to complete the last stages of manuscript preparation. For her help with the bibliography, a tip of the hat to Jahnelle McMillan, and for his exemplary work on the index, another to Bob Ellis. Our project editor, Jacqueline Kinghorn Brown, and copy editor, Patterson Lamb, proved helpful and responsive. Finally, for having been tuned-in nearly from the get-go, we thank our energetic editor at University Press of Florida, Amy Gorelick.

Some material in *Broadcasting Modernism* has appeared in print before, and we thank the publishers mentioned below for their permission to use this work: Chapter 3, "Marconi, *Marconista*," is an abridged version of a chapter from Timothy C. Campbell's *Wireless Writing in the Age of Marconi*, copyright 2006 by the Regents of the University of Minnesota, reprinted by permission of the University of Minnesota Press. A version of Chapter 9, "Desmond MacCarthy, Bloomsbury, and the Aestheticist Ethics of Broadcasting" was published in Todd Avery, *Radio Modernism: Literature, Ethics, and the BBC, 1922–1938* (Aldershot: Ashgate, 2006); it is reprinted here with kind permission of the publisher. Chapter 11 is a version of Sarah Wilson's "Gertrude Stein and the Radio", *Modernism/Modernity* 11.2 (2004): 261–78, © The Johns Hopkins University Press, reprinted with permission of the Johns Hopkins University Press. Chapter 13 comprises material reprinted from Lesley Wheeler's "Edna St. Vincent Millay's Performance of Presence," in *Voicing American Poetry: Sound and Performance from the 1920s to the Present*, copyright © 2008 by Cornell University, used by permission of the publisher, Cornell University Press.

Broadcasting Modernism

Introduction

Signing On

DEBRA RAE COHEN, MICHAEL COYLE & JANE LEWTY

In the 1920s and 1930s, radio was indeed "in the air." Its rapid growth from a point-to-point medium to a worldwide communication network in the course of a mere decade ensured that radio quickly became a mighty element of what educator J. E. Barton called in a broadcast the "bottleneck age [where] a hundred new currents of thought, and a hundred new habits of life, have been poured . . . with a disconcerting suddenness that has no parallel" (412). Commentary at the time about the social effects of the medium was at once celebratory and cautious. Take the example of E. B. White: when Harold Ross began publishing *The New Yorker* in 1925, he announced that "it is not edited for the old lady in Dubuque." Priding itself on a certain cosmopolitanism, the magazine published serious (though not necessarily Modernist) writers—writers such as White, who for many years anonymously contributed the "Talk of the Town" column. In his column for May 21, 1938, White observed that radio "has immensely accelerated culture in that it has brought to millions of people, in torrential measure, the distant and often adulterated sounds of art and life. But it is still an open question whether this mysterious electrical diffusion has been a blessing to man, who appears at the moment to be most unhappy about nearly everything" ("Comment" 13). "Coming from the skies"—in torrents—radio seemed to White to threaten all before it, its unifying capacities as unsettling as they were desirable. In the words of another reviewer, C. DeLisle Burns, "bridging the gap may be only increasing the tendency to fight on the bridge. . . . The more you know of other people, the more you may dislike them" (77).

White's almost casual comment suggests several important things more: first, that even popular writers not much interested in the avant-garde were alive to the impact of radio on culture; second, that this impact was in fundamental ways *instrumental* in the ongoing shaping of what we have learned to call Modernism/modernity; third, that the deep ambivalence marking contemporary response to the medium itself was an index of its inescapability.

But what White heard so clearly grew faint over subsequent decades, and in the heyday of "High Modernist" scholarship went more or less ignored by literary scholars. In the early twenty-first century, however, Modernist Studies are increasingly in conversation with the strategies, tactics, and concerns of cultural studies. Scholars have essayed such topics as the marketing of Modernism, the institutions of Modernism, or the relations of polite to popular discourses. Collectively, these new conversations are remapping and reshaping what we conceive of as "Modernist" and suggesting new ways of estimating the enduring presence of Modernist values. The increasingly pressing question for us is how forms of literary production relate to other forms of cultural production. That question, as regards radio in particular, is complicated by several factors. Radio was, at the outset and by definition, an especially ephemeral medium, incapable of inscription. Little effort was made to preserve the content of broadcasts, even once the technology existed. The very lack of an archive, the dissipation of waves in space, makes it almost impossible to reconstitute that very radio *presence* that so fundamentally marked the decades of the 1920s and 1930s.

Moreover, in those decades, radio was not understood in the same terms it is today. Contemporaneous commentators argued the value of radio for the promotion of "serious" culture, but there was at least such an argument to be made. In our time, by contrast, the fortunes of radio are greatly diminished. What was in the Modernist era the newest and most compelling of modern technologies—awesome in the true sense of the word—today serves mostly to dispatch sporting events, create opinion forums ("talk radio"), serve advertisers, promote the music industry, or, sometimes, rerun old radio shows from the days when radio *was* dominant. The unprecedented power of radio in its time is almost impossible to overstate; its presence intermittently ebbed and flowed as direct subject matter, as a platform for artistic expression, or as a subliminal force shaping the dynamics of Modernist textualities.

Many of the key figures of Modernism quite self-consciously wrote *for* radio, thinking as they did so about the special requirements of the medium and about how those requirements must necessarily change the ways they organized and presented their work. Eliot, Woolf, Pound, Orwell, Beckett: all wrote work especially designed for a radio audience. But beyond this kind of work, which arguably could be seen as ancillary to the work that made their reputations, writers and poets of the Modernist period, as the essays in this volume demonstrate, found their very sense of the artist's mission reshaped by the cultural project of radio.

Before evaluating the nature of "broadcasting" as an ordered cultural practice, however, it is necessary to be aware of its meaning. The agency of "broadcasting" encompasses all technologies, including the written word. It is a term that implies free character, used, for example, by Walt Whitman in *Leaves of Grass* to describe the arbitrariness of nature: the "broadcast doings of day and night." The notion of the written word as a transgressive signal, circulating at random beyond its original context, has been dealt with in classic texts such as Walter Ong's *Orality and Literacy*, Marshall McLuhan's *The Gutenberg Galaxy*, and Friedrich Kittler's *Discourse Networks 1800/1900*. A persistent image in the last is that of the "deathly still room" where the pen "scratches without preliminary speech and so without a soul" (183), blankly etching something inarticulate, something that is, in a sense, white noise. The act of receiving any written word is to succumb to a peripheral entity who imagines an audience before, during, and after the words are consigned to paper. In a Socratic sense, writing produces a negative effect, scattering, rolling, and throwing voices in a pretense of mutual exchange when it is, in fact, a broken dialogue. Media are the means by which interaction is hopefully facilitated and improved; yet charges of inauthenticity were leveled at every communication device prior to the advent of radio, such as the printing press and the phonograph, all of which claimed to duplicate and distribute the indicia of human presence.

Radio was present even where it was absent, which is, of course, the paradox at the very heart of the medium. Despite its precise reproduction and breathtaking range, radio opened up a void. To scatter words abroad in space, either through auditory sign or lonely inscription, serves as a reminder of the absent other, as well as of the dissolving of the individual into massed ranks. When ritualistically facing the radio itself, positioned in the corner of every living room, one would have been implicitly aware, in the words of Leo Lowenthal, that the broadcast designed "especially for you" meant "all of you" (544).

This paradoxical pervasiveness has been figured in a number of contradictory ways since the advent of wireless. Indeed, Carolyn Marvin has posited that the pattern for the complex metaphorics of the response to broadcasting—on the level of the body, the community, and the larger world—was laid down even earlier, in reaction to nineteenth-century developments in electricity. As Jeffrey Sconce has detailed, such early conceptions of wireless tied it to the occult, with writers like Villiers de l'Isle Adam seeing it as a means of recapturing "dead voices, lost sounds, forgotten noises, vibrations lockstepping into the abyss" (10). In 1922, as the BBC first formed as a company, W. H. Worrell enthused that radio is "apparently supernatural . . . affording a change from the regularity of nature and of average human experience" (70). As late as 1930, socialist Upton Sinclair—not a writer ordinarily associated with occult musings—proposed that, "the human brain is a storage battery, capable of sending impulses over the nerves. Why may it not be capable of sending impulses by means of some other medium, known or unknown? Why may there not be such a thing as brain radio?" (193). Such ideas perhaps informed the early celebration of voices in the air as both means to and expression of social unity, the sense that broadcasting unites people with "a consciousness of kind" (Cantril and Allport 18). Certainly, the rhetoric of John Reith, first director-general of the BBC, partakes of the spiritual even as it posits wireless as a mechanism for constructing citizenship and facilitating the seamless operation of national and international advancement. As he wrote in 1924, "the message of peace on earth, proclaimed in the first Christmas to a few shepherds, can reach the hearts of all men of goodwill. . . . [This benefit is] neither merely national nor international but supra-national" (*Broadcast* 222). For Reith, radio facilitates the Arnoldian pursuit of perfection.

These similar rhetorics fueling disparate agendas, all founded in electrical-magical thinking and a sense of radio's occult power, demonstrate the complexity with which the metaphorics of radio carry, in Marvin's terms, "the freight of social fantasy" (233). Ideological commitments in and of themselves seldom determine attitudes toward radio. No one would accuse Filippo Tommaso Marinetti of being, like Sinclair, a socialist, or like Reith, an Arnoldian, but, in his 1933 manifesto, "La Radia," he and Futurist co-conspirator Pino Masnata celebrated what they saw as the liberatory powers of the air. Their manifesto was free of the doubts that would trouble White. Radio was, they declared, free from the "rancid sentimentalism" of the cinema and would abolish "the audience as self-appointed judging mass systematically hostile and servile always against the new" (266, 267). Marinetti and Masnata saw radio as, in some senses, dismantling the very unity that other proponents used to celebrate radio—and yet they, too, regarded radio as defining a new era.

In Marinetti and Masnata's model, radio represented a liberatory absence of the sentimental. But what struck them as liberation struck other observers, like E. M. Forster, as loss. Marinetti and Masnata constructed themselves as part of a new Futurist elite and understood the eradication of traditional constraints as a step toward the unleashing of potential power. But for the English Forster, the destruction of the sentimental and its implicit appreciation of loss was a sign of a new and unsettling omnipresence, and the pervasiveness of voice portended claustrophobia. In his *Commonplace Book*, Forster worried that "wireless etc. abolishes wavings of handkerchiefs, etc. Death the only farewell surviving. We do not get away from each other as we did" (38). The aestheticism in Forster's handkerchiefs also shows up in more materialist farewells. The vision of radio as unifying, shared by observers as disparate as Virginia Woolf and John Reith, could be and was construed in more threatening terms, as the specter of social control, or (as with White) the looming homogenization of mass culture. Indeed, the vision turns nightmarish when linked to the advent of fascism, as in the proliferating megaphones in the writings of W. H. Auden and Christopher Isherwood, and culminates in the über-Modernist critiques of the Frankfurt School, especially Horkheimer and Adorno's attack on "the Culture Industry." Bertolt Brecht, who came to disagree with other Marxist writers about the value of radio, nevertheless stated in 1927 that "everyone justifies the shameful results of radio so far by pointing to its 'unlimited possibilities,' and so radio is a 'good thing.' It is a very bad thing" (qtd. in Cory 345).

These constructions of what Timothy Campbell terms the "radio imaginary" (xiii)—that is, the metaphoric models that were deployed to summarize the relations between technology and community—did not, in other words, merely compete. We can now see how they worked instead in creative tension to shape the culture of modernity and played out those tensions in Modernist texts on the levels of both content and form. It's not just that writers argued among themselves about what radio augured but that within individual careers, coteries, and texts these individual models jostled and combined in fruitful ways. For Virginia Woolf, wireless was at once the means to erase national division and "a mere travesty and distortionment" (*Letters* 146); even Adorno, as David Jenemann observes in his essay here, construed the power of the radio voice as both intrusive and uncanny. Indeed, the uncanniness of radio, as Steven Connor's essay in this volume makes clear, is in large part adumbrated by its contradictions: it is both everywhere and only perceptual and interior, at once figurable as intimate and impersonal.

The tripartite structure of this volume responds to and elucidates the informing tensions of the radio imaginary. Part One, "Medium and Metaphor," comprises five essays that treat the potency of radio as an idea and the importance of those ideas themselves in shaping Modernist production. We conceive of "Modernist production" in broad terms that reflect the recent scholarly recognition of Modernism*s*—the perception that "Modernism" was not (and is not) monolithic, playing out everywhere in the same ways at the same time to the same ends. To move forward from this recognition, "thick descriptions" of Modernist culture (to borrow Clifford Geertz's phrase) must be inseparable from analyses of Modernist artifacts and texts. The essays in this section thus examine models of the radio imaginary in contexts from pulps to philosophy. Part Two, "Pressures and Intrusions," considers wireless influence on the text in variously particular cultural contexts. By juxtaposing and historicizing the commercial American and noncommercial British models of broadcasting, these essays underscore their divergent specificities and cultural effects. Part Three, "Negotiations, Transactions, Translations," offers individual case studies of important and influential Modernist figures ranging from Ezra Pound and James Joyce in Modernism's first wave, to Wallace Stevens and Lorine Niedecker somewhat later. Collectively, *Broadcasting Modernism* endeavors both to theorize and to historicize the relation of changing literary forms to the emergent forms associated with radio; that the case studies cover three generations is important since it enables the scrutiny of a half-century of evolving relations among models of radio. The structure of our volume places these case studies in the context of the earlier two sections, tracing the influence of metaphoric models of radio and its historical circumstancing on the works of individual Modernist practitioners.

Whereas what might be termed the "sonic presence" in Modernist literature has been noted by a number of recent critics,[1] no volume to date has claimed for its focus the centrality and indeed inescapability of radio as a feature of the Modernist landscape. That this should be so even as our picture of the relations between elite and popular culture becomes ever more nuanced is a matter of concern. Even in the recent studies that have provocatively tied new technologies to the Modernist body and senses, radio remains the invisible medium. For the most part, such studies have understandably taken the lead of Walter Benjamin's "The Work of Art in the Age of Mechanical Reproduction" (1935), privileging technologies of reproduction over those of transmission. Consequently, although it has long been a truism that film helped shape the Modernist novel, that the gramophone and the typewriter left their imprint on its musculature (or that the line of Modernist poetry was inconceivable without the typewriter), radio has been as ephemeral historically as were its original productions, so pervasive as to be overlooked.

Radio Studies per se is a well-established field, but it has thus far remained the province of social scientists. To date, there are no book-length studies of radio from a theorized position in literary studies apart from the work published by contributors to this volume.[2] Existing publications in this field tend to focus on the social history of sound and media, as in Emily Watson's *The Soundscape of Modernity*, Jeffrey Sconce's *Haunted Media*, and John Durham Peters's *Speaking into the Air*, or to read the effects on narrative of the panoply of modern technologies, as in Cecelia Tichi's *Shifting Gears*, R. L. Rutzky's *High Techne*, Lisa Gitelman's *Scripts, Grooves and Writing Machines*, Sarah Danius's *The Senses of Modernism*, and the works of Friedrich Kittler, *Discourse Networks 1800/1900* and *Gramophone, Film, Typewriter*. Key to other relevant publications has been the growth of "sound theory," much of which focuses generally on the cultural poetics of sound and the relationship of the senses to mechanically reproduced sound. The most significant works here are those by Douglas Kahn (*Noise Water Meat*) and our contributor Steven Connor (for instance, *Dumbstruck*). None of these works, nor the only two salient collections on sound theory, *Wireless Imagination*, edited by Kahn with Gregory Whitehead, and *Sound States*, edited by Adalaide Morris, explicitly pinpoint the Modernist era, when both radio and the reactions to it emerged.

The authors in our volume argue not only that broadcasting activity mattered to a wide range of literary figures but also that the Modernist project was enabled and often inspired by various aspects of wireless communication. As Jane Lewty has proposed, "The creative process of any writer during this time was affected by the surround-sound of context, or, rather, the colonization of daily life by radio" (150). Radio did more than change expectations for literary work, did more than merely publicize literary work, did more than obtrude itself as theme: it exerted pressure on textual and even generic forms. Radio changed the relation of authors and poets to their work; it transformed readers into audiences, and in doing these things it served as a catalyst for the reconfiguration of the relations between writers and readers that is so important a part of the Modernist project.

Notes

1. See especially Cuddy-Keane and Beer.
2. See Campbell and Avery.

PART I MEDIUM & METAPHOR

CHAPTER 1

Inventing the Radio Cosmopolitan

Vernacular Modernism at a Standstill

AARON JAFFE

> People think that science is electricity, automobilism, and dirigible balloons. It is something very different.... It is the genius of knowledge vivisecting the vital genius.
> —Remy de Gourmont, *Promenades philosophiques*, 1902

Two vital geniuses. One emergent avant-garde. The first genius, a foreign patrician well-connected to the British ruling class, wages a massive PR campaign in early twentieth-century London. Appropriating, coordinating, and synthesizing the work of others, he finds rapid, transnational, and culturally transformative success, builds an institutional apparatus, and in the process turns himself into a name brand. Later, in the thirties, he is disgraced by his unsavory political entanglements: celebrity avant-gardist turned fascist yes-man. The second, also an outsider, has more obscure origins but also has some success promoting, organizing, and drawing capital to the rival New York side of operations. His genius—if not his business acumen—is more vital. Yet, in the process, he too becomes a name brand. His eventual demise is only slightly less ignominious than the first's: largely forgotten in the forties, this avant-gardist turns pigeon-feeding crank with an infatuation for death rays and UFOs.

I am writing here of neither Futurists nor Vorticists—not psychoanalysts, not political revolutionaries—not strictly speaking, at least. Instead the two traveling avant-gardists, the transcendent, self-vivisecting foreigners making beachheads in the economic and cultural capitals of the Anglo-American world, are the "inventors" of radio, Guglielmo Marconi and Nikola Tesla. Although Marconi and Tesla frequently provide codicils to the heroic lists of the good and great at the service of science and progress, their identities are much more unstable, hybridized, and, for that matter, modern than is usually appreciated. Above all, the pair were practitioners of a rhetoric of invention akin to what Gregory Ulmer has called "heuristics"—a Modernist discursive vernacular that not only speaks for their obvious self-fashioning as technologists, capitalists, and publicists but also helps account for the centrality in praxis of their capacities as autodidacts, polymaths, and aesthetic, literary, and political aspirants. Above all, Marconi and Tesla were engaged in an archly Modernist struggle of hyperbolic self-definition against other inventors, patent-holders, and, ultimately, each another, a struggle for prestige and patent rights that helped institute the incipient promotional rhetoric of radio as a paradigm of modern self-hood in an age of increasing technological and economic displacements.

Let us turn, then, from representations of radio culture in canonical Modernism and the work of Modernists broadcasting on the airwaves to the links between the first promoters and ideologists of the radio medium and the ideological dimensions of the mass communication technology in its proto-forms. In 1887, Heinrich Hertz demonstrates the existence and propagation of electromagnetic radiation by building an instrument to produce electromagnetic waves, a transmitter-oscillator, and an instrument to detect them, a receiver-coherer. He is reputed to have said upon this occasion: "I don't see any useful purpose for this mysterious, invisible electromagnetic radiation" (Harrison 155). During the thirty or so years to follow when this mysterious, invisible radio-medium is thinkable—but thinkable otherwise before broadcast programming takes hold as a dominant application—its existence provides vital Modernist geniuses of all vivisections with enormously productive and inventive energies. By 1927, Bertolt Brecht describes radio as an "antediluvian invention": "As far as radio goes," he writes, "I immediately had the frightful impression that it was an unbelievably ancient apparatus, long ago forgotten in deluge" (37). For Brecht, radio had resolved itself into the bourgeoisie's megaphone and a technique of mass consumption: "Later generations would have the opportunity to marvel how a certain caste was able to tell the whole planet what it had to say and at the same time how it enabled the planet to see that it had nothing to say" (38–39).[1]

Now that radio is all but forgotten—Clear Channel, XM satellite radio, podcasting, and WiFi notwithstanding—we can begin to remember something more obvious in its early history: what radio designates, once upon a time, at least, is not sound but something like light, invisible light, frequencies in the electromagnetic spectrum that can not been seen with the unaided eye. Before physicists hypothesized wavelike particles, before the term "radio" came to name a thing that emits sounds and sundry programming content, this much was known: radio radiates. Unlike visible light, however, this radiant energy depends on extrasensory instrumentation to be perceived. By filiation, "radio" recalls "radiance," "light shining with diverging rays; hence, brilliant light, vivid brightness, splendour." The *Oxford English Dictionary (OED)* gives a Shakespearean example: "In his bright radience and colaterall light, must I be comforted." More germane still is the newer word "radiation": "the emission and diffusion of heat-rays. Now, the emission of energy of any kind in the form of rays or waves, esp. electromagnetic waves." The *OED* puts the term "radio" at the turn of the twentieth century. In particular, this dominant sense from 1906: "The transmission and reception of radio-frequency electromagnetic waves, esp. as a means of communication that does not need a connecting wire." Only later (tagged by the dictionary in Modernism's *annum mirabilis* 1922, incidentally) does the word acquire the sense of "organized wireless broadcasting in sound; the sound broadcasting network or service as a whole; sound broadcasting considered as a medium of communication or as an art form." Daniel Tiffany is one of the few in Modernist studies to make the connection between radio and Modernism explicit in terms of what he calls its "nonvisual image": "a radiological medium that veers between verbal and visual 'frequencies' . . . rooted in the assumption that [Modernist poetics] entails a mediation of visuality simply by its displacement of the image concept into a verbal medium" (21). Unlike Tiffany, I put the emphasis on radiant mediation—and not radiant mediation as it bears on the Modernist verbal icon but rather as it radiates authorship invisibly as a medium of invention: an "un-visual" transmission to a proliferating array of passive receivers.[2]

In the assorted writings and promotional activities of Marconi and Tesla, there is compelling case for elective—or should I say, electromagnetic—affinities between the temporal and spatial implications of wireless transmission across national borders and international waterways (as "invented" by Marconi and Tesla) and the creation of an impossible cosmopolitan ideal for the Modernist author-function. I am less interested in the respective contributions of these radio-Modernist inventors to technology or technique than, first, their rhetorical and ideological contributions to establishing the cultural preeminence of radiant technologism as a "mass mediaura," to cite Samuel Weber, and, second, their tacit and explicit theorizing this technology as a Modernist vernacular, to echo Miriam Hansen on early cinema. Simply put, Nikola Tesla's "Problem of Increasing Human Energy" (1900) and Joseph Conrad's "Preface" to *The Nigger of the "Narcissus"* (1897) have more in common than you think, and, preeminently, the commonalties depend on a shared sense of a radiant modernity at work in and through the dynamics of the intersubjective transmission and reception of invention.

Answering the question of who invented radio is like answering who invented Modernism. The difficulty in the search for a single responsible agent lies in neither prize being precisely technics—not technology nor technique, respectively. Unlike a seed-drill, a thing for which we can point to one Jethro Tull in a certain year in a certain workshop in a certain corner of Berkshire, both radio and Modernism are decidedly products of—and in turn productive of—spatial dislocation and temporal transience.[3] In fact, both are more akin to media than technics: bundled technical ideas made material and institutional in a regulative (but not constitutive) communicative practice. Here, competing claimants and matters of patent dispute are both beside the point and symptomatic of the historical controversy about authorship made famous by poststructuralism. Radio and Modernism are, in other words, beyond the prerogatives of author-inventors. Instead, names like Marconi and Conrad, Tesla and Eliot signify emergent medial practices, to put a somewhat different spin on Foucault's formula about the founders of discursivity, applied technologists at work upon a scene of media transience.

In "Tradition and the Individual Talent," Eliot comments upon the poststructuralist author-function controversy *avant la lettre* by means of his famous "finely filiated platinum" analogy. Unbundling "the man who suffers" from "the mind which creates," in effect, he dispenses with the constitutive features of the romantic authorial ideal (specifically, that authors express their personal emotions through their art) while tacitly retaining its regulative logic (that authors are instruments of transcendent valuation). Though the catalytic agent, the pure substance of the artist's mind, passes through reaction unchanged and unabsorbed, its agency is nevertheless realized by enabling the process. Eliot's catalytic metaphor comes not from the so-called pure science of academic scholarship but from the applied science of engineering, more specifically, the burgeoning field of chemical engineering. He could have easily selected from the expansive repertoire of electrical engineering: aerials, antennae, beams, detectors, operators, receivers, coherers, transmitters, emitters, oscillators. The artist works as extrasensory apparatus—not a person precisely but a technical thing for realizing a technical medium. The reification is evinced not only by his framing analogy but also by his use of the relative pronoun "which" rather than "who"—the man who suffers, the mind which creates. Authorial agency, then, represents not so much a feature of superlative subjectivity but a functional close-up manifestation of the distant and far-off. Dispossessed of the sufferings of his "private mind," having escaped personality, the mind of Eliot's mature author comes to emit the zeitgeist instead, the "mind of Europe—the mind of his own country" (*Selected Essays* 3–11). Transmitting over the horizon, the radio-Modernist plots in this manner a phantasmal escape through the imagined hazards of the present literary parochialism into the cosmos of transhistorical valuation.[4]

Marconi, the Human Beat Box

To learn more about radios, I built one of my own—or, I should say rather, two.

The first lesson learned about radios is that two different technologies are involved, receivers and transmitters. The lesson is, of course, obvious to anyone who ever listened to a radio yet never transmitted a signal: the knobs and dials of radio reception belong to the hands of the many, the mode and means of its transmission are controlled by the hands of the few. Crucially, in radio's prehistory, before programming is regularized or indeed even imagined, numbers of receivers and transmitters have more parity. And at radio degree zero, there's only Tesla's set-up tuning in to the big nothingness of interstellar background noise and Marconi's ambition to commercialize a technology that transmits information without wires beyond the horizon.

Building simple radio receivers and transmitters is surprisingly easy. The former is a storied school science project. The latter is a celebrated if risky means for do-it-yourself culture-jamming: transmission as transgression. Instructions are readily available for both right now on the Internet. Download at your leisure. Aside from a few special electronic components, more about which later, all you really need is a soldering iron, some solder, a few spools of copper wire, and some household junk (a ballpoint-pen sleeve, a cardboard mailing tube, scrap wood, a battery, and an old telephone receiver).

Having done my research and compiled my shopping list, I go to Radio

Shack to look around. The retail chain, now specializing in consumer electronics goods (radio-controlled vehicles, speaker wire, cell-phone plans) seems an apt place to begin my project: "You've got questions, we've got answers." Founded in Boston in 1921, right before broadcast programming takes off, it begins existence as a mail-order supplier for shipboard radio operators and experimenters, professionals and amateurs alike (Farman). Despite its current status as a grazing station for the technologically overfed, it remains a trusty repository of raw electronics components in sorted bins: enamel coated magnet wire, soldering irons, wire strippers, alligator clips, diodes, audio output transformers, generic circuit boards, and 9–volt battery snaps.

My second lesson in radio building comes from an act of terminological recovery, the forgotten history of the phrase "radio shack." Formerly jargon for the stick-built, tarpaper structures precariously holding Marconi's wireless sea telegraphy prototypes on the decks of ships, the term eventually comes to name the ship's communication command center: "radio shack," the one-room enclosure behind the bridge, the workplace where radio operators dwell with their transmitters, receivers, components, and other equipment (Harris; see also figure 1). Attached, aerialed, antennaed, and, inevitably, at risk—among the choicest targets for incoming attack—the shack itself is a large, ontologically unstable radio-set: a portable laboratory cum war-machine. However marginalized and subordinated, this space serves as an uneasy workshop of interiors and exteriors, tinkering and programming, casting out and pulling in, up-close and far off, to and from. Later, in the era of shortwave "ham," "radio shack" names the hidden interior stores situated in basements, attics, garages, or backyard sheds where hobbyist-tinker-programmer plays amateur-experimenter.

Bruno Latour's concept of "black-boxing" usefully names the discursive imperative by which, in his words,

> scientific and technical work is made invisible by its own [promotional rhetorical] success. When a machine runs efficiently, when a matter of fact is settled, one need focus only on its inputs and outputs and not on its internal complexity. Thus paradoxically, the more science and technology succeed, the more opaque and obscure they become. (*Pandora's Hope* 304)

In a sense, "black-boxing" explains the end-user's phenomenological situation in which technologies are routinized and made normative "no matter how controversial their history, how complex their inner-workings, how large the commercial or academic networks that hold them in place" (Latour, *Science in Action* 3). As opposed to black-boxing, which treats input and output as already reified and aestheticized surface phenomena at the exterior interface, radio-shacking, to coin a phrase, insists on the messy, work-network of the transient insides: inner workings, fluxing bodies, modifying components, selecting input, and programming output. To radio-shack means to touch the workings of an application with a specific communicative ambition. Transmitter, receiver, antennae, ground, operator, programmer: in here, at the scene of the invention of approximate proximity, social action happens at a distance. The third lesson isn't merely to open the black box and peek under the hood: it takes us inside the radio prototype to unbundle the component dreamwork.

Having failed to interest the Italian military in his work, Marconi travels to London in 1896, British mother in tow, pursuing patents and commercial fortunes. In his luggage the experimental radio-telegraphy equipment is packed, secreted, and secured, following longstanding habit for his prototypes, in a specially fabricated protective box. Inevitably this box rouses the suspicious of British customs officers. Prying it open, they face its unfa-

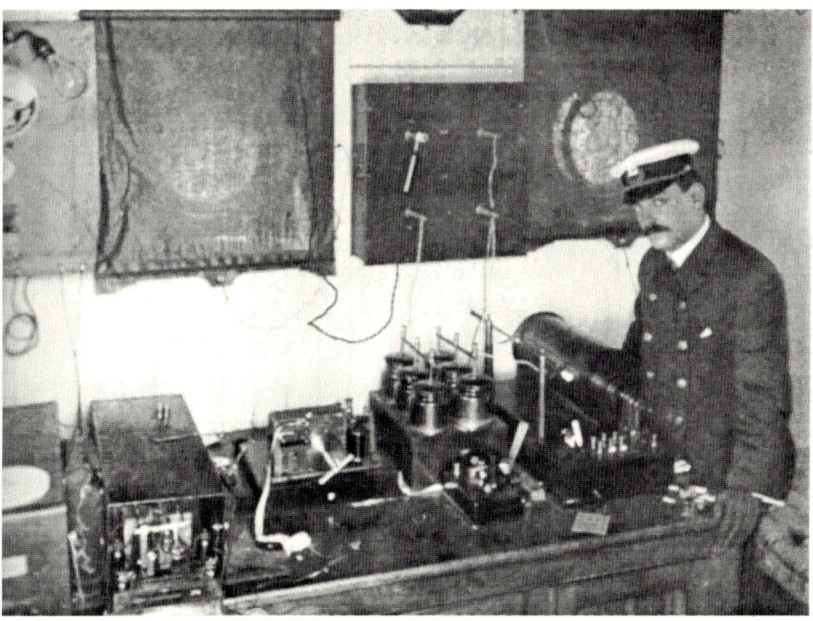

"The Marconi Man and His Instruments." *The World's Work*, February 1904. Public domain.

miliar-looking techno-viscera: wires, screw-clamps, spark-coils. Some kind of futuristic assassination device, perhaps? Eventually it clears, though not before invasive uncomprehending fingers (luckily, *no* bomb) damage its contents beyond repair (Masini 66–67).[5]

Marconi's work provides an instructive instance of the way Latour's "black-box" effect bears upon the rhetoric of invention. Just as Marconi's habitual boxing of prototypes neatens up, packages, licenses, hides, and, in a sense, jointly aestheticizes and reifies the disarrayed inner workings of his work for end-users, so too the application itself "black-boxes" the scientific work, influence networks, and research controversies of others. About this, Marconi is clear:

> I was fairly well acquainted with the published results of the work of the most distinguished scientists who had occupied themselves with the subject of electric waves; men such as Hertz, Branly, Lodge, Righi and many others. . . . much criticism was leveled at me . . . because in my early experiments, I used a form of oscillator which had been devised by [Righi] and which itself was a modification of Hertz's oscillator. By availing myself of previous knowledge and working out theories already formulated, I did nothing but follow in the footsteps of Howe, Watt, Edison, Stephenson and many other illustrious inventors. I doubt very much whether there has ever been a case of a useful invention for which all theory, all the practical applications and all the apparatus were the work of one man. (Qtd in Masini 48–49)

The points of emphasis are telling, especially what they reveal about a rhetoric of invention in radio Modernism. Marconi presents himself not as an author of "pure" scientific knowledge but as a mere reader of its literature review. He fashions himself, in other words, as an applicant of pure science on instrumental technology. Unlike the work of scientists Hertz, Branly, Lodge, and Righi, the work of the inventor does not occupy itself with the subject of knowledge in some noninstrumental sense. It makes its appeal not with claims to originality as a function of its position in the scholarly apparatus but with innovation as objective means. Here, Marconi identifies the hidden technical practice of pure science as his influence network, Augusto Righi's incremental modifications to Heinrich Hertz's oscillator. Marconi is simply the first to recognize that this apparatus (of scientific knowledge) is a media transmitter in all but name. The different modification of the apparatus that makes the difference turns not on the incremental apparatus but on the differential application. The death of the scientist-author effects the birth of the technologist-transmitter.

Marconi's work-network nods respectfully to the scholarly achievements of scientific discovery, conceived as properly application-less, but simultaneously pirates its apparatus, adapting it to a precedent technology pregnant with extant applications, telegraphy with wires. Supporting Armand Mattelart's thesis that "communication serves first of all to make war," radio is first conceived by Marconi as telegraphy improved for modern warfare: wireless telegraphy imagines sending code over the horizon to naval ships at sea and mobile armies in far-flung theaters (xiii). Thus, young Marconi's first love, according to his biographer, is none other than an old telegraph: a used piece of equipment purchased to un-box, dismantle inner-workings—and practice Morse code. In fact, at least in the early years of the project, the notion of the telegraph—transmitter and receiver of code bundled together—encapsulates Marconi's vision for radio *tout court*. Arguably, his claim to radio innovation rests with reading Hertz's technical apparatus for probing the electromagnetic spectrum as a kind of wireless telegraph—a means of sending and receiving information through electromagnetic fields. It is thus fitting that the first code sent over the horizon, radio's first program, so to speak, is a sequence of letters: H-E-I-N-R-I-C-H H-E-R-T-Z (Harrison 154). The credit for this goes not to Marconi but to Alexander Popov, but the point remains: the technologist makes the medium speak. Indeed, it speaks the scientist's name but speaks it ironically: the founder of its discursivity has founded a promotional machinery, a communicative application for credit-taking. To say that Marconi—or, for that matter, Hertz, Tesla, Popov, Branly, Bose, Lodge, Fleming, Fessenden, DeForest, or Armstrong—invented radio is not to say he did so *ex nihilo* but instead that his name became "black-boxed" with a certain modification of the application's component configuration.

Going wireless, I found out, requires a lot of wire.[6] To build a "simple crystal radio," I need a wire coil, an antenna, a ground wire—not to mention, my first cheat, a whisker-thin wire encased in a specially ordered germanium diode. First, the wire coil. I tightly wind an entire spool of enamel coated magnet wire, wire against wire, around a section of mailing tube. The rest of the rudimentary receiver consists of two capacitors: an antenna, 50 feet of insulated wire threaded up a tree to a third-story attic window; and a ground, more insulated wire extending from my receiver down to a cold-water pipe touching the ultimate ground, the earth itself. With the help of a germanium diode (the "crystal" in question, a signal detector that sorts out the distorting alternations of an electromagnetic signal), this air-cored coil inductor and capacitors form a resonant circuit, storing radio energy for me to tap with an old telephone handset (my second cheat). The historical terms for this process of signal reception are evocative: to receive a radio signal is called cohering or condensing it. Radio-shacking success: I am inside the apparatus homing in far-off signals from earth. Before J. C. Bose invents the solid-state diode in 1901, which Marconi subsequently incorporates, Marconi and others employ a device called a coherer for this function (a glass tube containing various loose metal filings or liquid mercury). With my receiver up and running, a fourth radio lesson, one about electromagnetic radiation Hertz would no doubt appreciate: my radio receiver is powered wirelessly and without batteries by the very radio-energy it detects. It runs and is run by the broadcast from a distant Gospel AM station.[7]

Do-it-yourself radio transmission—remote propagation of radio-energy through the electromagnetic spectrum—is another thing altogether.[8] Technically, the key component for a simple transmitter is an oscillator, an electromagnetic beat box. This much hasn't changed since Hertz's oscillator, except now in the age of semiconductors and micro-electronics a 1 MHz oscillator suitable for AM transmission is about the size of a Chiclet and only slightly more expensive. Cheap and easy though it may be to "radio-shack" a transmitter, putting one to use invites specific forms of legal jeopardy. Transmitting without a license is expressly forbidden by this and most governments. Interfering with legal transmissions is riskier still. "Jamming [U.S. right-wing broadcaster] Rush Limbaugh," as in Jerod Pore's apt example, "is a guaranteed ticket to jail (unless you build a disposable transmitter and leave it broadcasting from someplace you never plan on being again)" (27). Frankly, for some, bristling at the late assertion and defense of private property rights by the State, the transgressive impetus of "liberating the airwaves" (couched in the discourse of squatter's rights and just commons) is verily staked on its spatialized metaphorics.

The frequency allocation of the radio-band is tightly regulated because the spectrum, as such, is finite. With the exception of some shortwave public access, citizen band (i.e., CB), and the legacy of the public bands at the low end of the radio dial, it has been sold off to the highest bidder. In 1899, the only thing Tesla finds with his 200-foot antenna is the rhythmic pulse of interstellar background noise (Simons 346). In 1906, the International Radiotelegraphic Convention, held in Berlin, establishes cooperative standards of frequency allocation among countries for regulating use of the airwaves to foster effective radio-telegraphy at sea. In 1934, the Federal Communications Commission is set up to regulate broadcasting in the United States. Other nation-states follow suit, some following the United States after World War I with a private-enterprise model, others like Britain (for a time at least) sponsoring a public broadcasting model, and still others like France maintaining a public-private hybrid (Mattelart 63–64). Thereafter, the spectrum is sectioned off into discrete subparcels. Present FCC diagrams resemble *Broadway Boogie Woogie*. Anyone radio-shacking together a transmitter must reckon with the priority of this map, which amounts to a political map of the police state of invisible exteriors, the electromagnetic spectrum as a nonmaterial, always already thoroughly policed communication medium.

The last lesson of radio-shacking: the subjective transformation of space it affects rests at the crux of a radio-Modernism. In *Mapping World Communication*, Mattelart (after Paul Virilio) observes that the first wave of new technical communication networks, from the pre-electric, semaphore telegraph of the eighteenth century to the "rail model" dominant in the nineteenth century, play out first in terms of the administration and standardization of time—not least, for the mode of production in terms of labor time and the invention of leisure as mass desideratum (22–23). The second wave, the emergence of telecommunications in the late nineteenth century, is linked to a subsequent project of mastering space, understood, in certain terms, as closing distances from transmitters (formerly producers) to receivers (formerly consumers). Radio-Modernist reception, as Mattelart's subtitle puts it, comprises a sequential and ironic triad: war, progress, and culture. Ascendant metaphors in this incipient spatializing language include spatial representation, spatial rights, access, enlargement, horizons, perspective, circulation, room, territory, frontiers, beacons, concentration, homelessness (37–39).

MC Tesla

In 1900, the year before Marconi sends a radiotelegraphic transmission across the Atlantic with much fanfare, Nikola Tesla publishes an article called "The Problem of Increasing Human Energy" in *Century* magazine. A decidedly eccentric piece, aimed at general readers and crammed with astonishing scientific and scientist claims from the bodily necessity of vegetarianism to the technological requirements for perpetual peace, it programs a visionary playlist for radio, far beyond the imaginary limits of Marconi's improved telegraph, including notions of radar, wireless telephony, and wireless power transmission. Most remarkably, it advances a theory of radio from which the human actor's very mind and body are transformed, the human collective augmented en masse by the radiant transmission of intelligence through the electromagnetic medium. The prolific inventor thus heralds, in his words, the coming of teleautomata and a world wireless web.

The publication follows numerous stunning technical—and, indeed, promotional—successes by Tesla. In addition to inventing the alternating current induction motor, he is responsible for black-boxing the electric power grid as we now know it: bundling technologies that not only made alternating current the dominant standard worldwide, a world wire web, but also made obsolete the direct current system of his early nemesis Edison. The so-called Tesla patents, sold to Westinghouse Electric for a lump sum with no royalties, allowed electricity to be sent long distances. The funds from these activities—supplemented by venture capital from curious backers like J. P. Morgan—in turn allowed Tesla to set up a series of lavish laboratory showplaces, modeled, it seems, on the Edisonian precedent, Menlo Park. If the germ of Marconi's work came via an apprehension of a nascent telegraphic apparatus in Hertz's electromagnetism workshop, Tesla's teleautomatics begins with a vision of the promise of a total electric grid—power stations and pylons beyond every horizon enveloping the planet.

In 1898, Tesla patents a "Method of and Apparatus for a Controlling Mechanism of Moving Vessels or Vehicles" (U.S. patent #613,809). That same year, he unveils the "self-acting engine" publicly in the form of a radio-controlled "crewless boat" before a crowed house in Madison Square Garden (Tesla 19, Seifer 193–203). Outfitted with steering and signaling systems, set loose in a large water-filled tank, the vehicle obeys directions shouted from the crowd: go left, go right, stop, reverse. Even more astounding is its uncanny ability to answer the questions directly from the crowd with its flashing lights. Instead of drawing the audience's attention to the miracle of a remote transmitter, Tesla encourages the belief—a form of black-boxing, to be sure—that the boat is controlled by raw mind power, much to his discredit in the electrical engineering community. We should not simply chalk this performance up to poor business judgment or ill-conceived publicity—"misguided showmanship," one of his biographers calls it (Lomas 158).

A more apt charge is misunderstood showmanship. For Tesla, there was, after all, no deceptive intent in so framing the demonstration: his point is that the boat *is* controlled by mind power, if not telepathy precisely. It is (or better, he is) a teleautomaton, a thing moving under its own power (-automaton) operating at a distance from itself (tele-). That Tesla billed his device with this name should have alerted audience members to the storied tradition of the automaton, a machine built, as the *OED* puts it, "to simulate the actions of living beings." The legacy of spectacularly exhibited, simulated life forms provides a kind of parodic inversion of the rhetoric of technology seen in Latour's black box: artfully lifelike exteriors concealing (and inevitably channeling attention to) the mechanisms of interiors, sophisticated clockwork, or, in the case of a frequent hoax, actual human beings hidden inside. In Tesla's case, simply put, the human inside is hidden, elsewhere, at a distance. Before the discourse of automata takes on the specter of the proletarian menace with the advent of the robot (in Karel Capek's play *R.U.R.* in 1920), it is linked to the uncanny in a more general form. Think here of the mechanical love-object in E. T. A. Hoffmann's supernatural tale "The Sandman," the source of Freud's formulation, or Walter Benjamin's cryptic reference to the chess-playing automaton uncannily operated by "a little hunchback" in the first of his "Theses on the Philosophy of History" (*Illuminations* 253).[9]

The "self-acting engine" episode receives a prominent place in Tesla's *Century* article. It includes photographs of the device and, crucially, a painstaking discussion of the exhibition and its subsequent misunderstanding, which has, he writes, obscured "the great force of the underlying principle" of intelligent teleautomata. In his words, the teleautomaton is not to be understood as a mere "automobile torpedo" but rather

> a machine capable of acting as though it were part of a human being—no mere mechanical contrivance, comprising levers, screws, wheels, clutches, and nothing more, but a machine embodying a higher principle, which will enable it to perform its duties as though it had intelligence, experience, judgment, a mind! . . . A machine having all the bodily or translatory movements and the operations of the interior mechanism controlled from a distance without wires. ("The Problem" 8–9)

Tellingly, the first of the four qualities, intelligence, is also Tesla's preferred word for radio-transmission over alternatives such as signals or information. Whereas mere "movement" designates animation, automation, bare life in its most minimal definition, intelligent human being and intelligent electromagnetic oscillation alike share in "complex movement." In fact—and here perhaps he tries even his most credulous supporters—it soon becomes apparent that Tesla views himself, and indeed every intelligent being, as a kind of teleautomaton:

> I am an automaton endowed with power of movement, which merely responds to external stimuli . . . and thinks and acts and moves accordingly. I remember only one or two cases in all my life in which I was unable to locate the first impression which prompted a movement or a thought, or even a dream. . . . long ago, I conceived the idea of constructing an automaton which would mechanically represent me, and which would respond, as I do myself . . . to external influences. (9)

If the automaton isn't hiding inside, it's hiding somewhere else. Because Tesla himself, *ego scriptor*, is removed from his own intelligent stimuli—the inventive input influencing his movements, thoughts, dreams comes in from somewhere else, outside and afar—he is, by his own definition, a teleautomaton.

Significantly, for Tesla, the human—considered from a totalized perspective—is always directed by some kind of remote control, be this "ignorance, stupidity, . . . imbecility, . . . visionariness, insanity, self-destructive tendency, . . . religious fanaticism," or other impetus (7). The historically freighted word *mass* obtains a specific, now lost, technical reference for Tesla and his contemporaries that merits some unpacking. For modern science, he writes, "the sun is the past, the earth is the present, the moon is the future. From an incandescent mass we have originated, and into a frozen mass we shall return" (1). "Man," too, is "a mass urged on by a force," but "not an ordinary mass, consisting of spinning atoms and molecules, and containing merely heat-energy":

> He is a mass possessed of certain higher qualities. . . . His mass . . . is being continuously exchanged, new taking the place of the old. Not only this, but he grows, propagates, and dies, thus altering his mass independently both in bulk and density. What is most wonderful of all, he is capable of increasing or diminishing his velocity of movement by the mysterious power he possesses by appropriating more or less energy from other substance, and turning it into motive energy. (2–3)

For Tesla, then, *mass* functions less as a figure of the amassing, undifferentiated crowd than as a kind of mythopoetics for the efflorescent human medium, mass understood as a summing (and summoning) of the collective movements of teleautomata, transmitters and receivers, yielding radio-augmented inventive and illuminative energies—not singly filamented incandescence, but florescence (an appropriate term given Tesla's role in inventing filament-less light), phosphorescence (light without heat), radio-luminescence.

In effect, Tesla achieves much the same sense of "mass" that Weber locates in his gloss on Benjamin's use of the term. Weber writes:

> Nothing could seem more dated [in Benjamin's "Artwork" essay] than [its] heavy-handed notion of "mass," which reeks of the collectivist discourses of the Thirties. And yet, the work returns sufficiently in this and other late texts of Benjamin to suggest that he, for his part, did not consider it to be as inert as it might seem today. . . . Whatever else is meant by "mass" in his writings, it entails a dynamic element that demands attention. Mass movements are the result, or rather, the corollary, of that movement of *detachment*, *ablösen*, that marks the decline of aura. For aura relates to mass not just as uniqueness does to multiplicity but also in spatial terms as a fixed location does to one that is caught in an incessant and complex movement. (84–85)

One frequently overlooked aspect of Benjamin's famous essay "The Work of Art in the Age of Mechanical Reproduction" is the fact that the media technology driving many of its claims is not only film but also radio. Specially significant here is Benjamin's preference, well noted by Weber, for the radio term "Aufnehme," or reception, for consumption, and "Aufnehmer," or receiver, for consumer (a point obscured in Harry Zohn's translation, which variously uses cognates of "behold" or "listen") (83). The technological reproduction of the experience of artwork takes place in an efflorescence of receivers. As it takes on, in Weber's phrase, a "massive, mass-like character," Tesla's incandescent origin, like Benjamin's aura, becomes filament-less, distant, devoid of an organizing, unique singularity, "a *de-piction* of distancing and separation" repeatedly experienced up close, in the most individuated and intimate of interior spaces, for example, before the radio box in the living room (84, 87).

DJ Konrad Korzeniowski

Joseph Conrad's much discussed preface to *The Nigger of the "Narcissus"* (1897) supplies, among other things, components for radio-shacking the unconscious of radio-Modernism, another pre-figurative dream for Modernist invention cast in incipient language shared by Marconi and Tesla. The preface's foundational claim in Modernist aesthetics and its importance as a statement of Modernist pictorialism tend to obscure its investments in a particular discursive transition between two metaphorical repertoires of technical invention, incandescence and efflorescence. Of the two, incandescence—the language of Edison's light, as Charles Bazerman describes it—comes first for Conrad, defining the condition of the work of art in "a single-minded attempt to render the highest kind of justice to the visible universe, by bringing to light the truth, manifold and one, underlying its every aspect" (xxxix). In fact, incandescence supplies the very framework for the famous opening comparison between scientist and artist. Before the substance of Conrad's comparison is made, Edison is there flipping the switch, as it were, illuminating the bulb's filament for mass visitation of his workshop.

For Conrad, the distinctiveness of the scientist's appeal, the prestige of it, follows from the conspicuous and authoritative display of public work—the public display of science at work, the saturnine body public touring the laboratory for leisure. Scientists, he writes,

> speak authoritatively to our common-sense, to our intelligence, to our desire of peace or to our desire of unrest; not seldom to our prejudices, sometimes to our fears, often to our egoism—but always to our credulity. And their words are heard with reverence, for their concern is with weighty matters: with the cultivation of our minds and the proper care of our bodies; with the attainment of our ambitions; with the perfection of the means and the glorification of our precious aims. (xxxix)

What this account is not is the usual, unambiguous narrative of the heroic scientist as the agent of social progress. It certainly begins with familiar, unmistakably progressive self-acting engines (common sense, intelligence, desires for peace or improvement) but then moves to modes of impetus with more ambiguous value (prejudice, fear, egoism, and credulity). The switch from the unequivocal to the equivocal properties of the light-bringing happens about the archly Conradian word "unrest." It also echoes his change in emphasis from concerns of the singular site of transmission—here filament becomes antenna—to the decidedly multiple sites of reception. The appeal of the scientist is, it seems, to be weighed *en masse*, in its massed claims about proper uses for gray matter and for those bodies that matter, the body public. The appeal is also amassed—or totalized—on the multitude, the undifferentiated "masses" massing, exercising their right to indolent leisure, while captive to the filament in the laboratory (xxxvi). The perfection of mass means, the glorification of mass aims, puts the receiver at a certain but immeasurable distance removed from the light-bringer—indeed from the very visibility of enlightenment. It is no less than the invention of consumption as an activity of laboring classes.

It is, as Conrad says, otherwise with the artist. Modern artists sit alone in ill-lit quarters, studios, and garrets, unnoticed, away from the spectacle of the laboratory ("the obscure lives of a few individuals out of all the disregarded multitude of the bewildered, the simple and the voiceless"). Although the artistic credo begins in common cause with the conspicuous-making properties of incandescence, it ends making an appeal to another type of credulity, credulity before technical invention. This appeal, I submit, calls to account not so much the artist's interior life (the representative unconsciousness and the vanguard of the impressionist subject) but rather the artist's role as a transmitter and ultra-sensitive receiver of invisible, filament-less, and temporally penetrating light. In short, radiant cosmos becomes cosmopolitan radiation—spanning Tesla's still hypothetical world wireless web from every "place of splendor" to every "dark corner." By super power stations of extension, the invisible medium is efflorescent on the bewildered and voiceless: "the subtle but invincible, conviction of solidarity that knits together the loneliness of innumerable hearts: to the solidarity in dreams, in joy, in sorrow, in aspirations, in illusions, in hope, in fear, which binds men to each other, which binds together all humanity—the dead to the living and the living to the unborn" (xl). This cosmic radiation, inventive and luminescent energy radiant in the world, however inconspicuously, figures as cosmopolitan radiation. It is not filamented around the public display of an inventor-artist but beamed, emitted, transmitted from the transmitter through a medium more like the electromagnetic spectrum than phlogiston or luminescent ether.

In so many words, Radio Free Conrad:

> the appeal of one temperament to all the other innumerable temperaments whose subtle and resistless power endows passing events with their true meaning, and creates the moral, the emotional atmosphere of the place and time. Such an appeal, to be effective, must be an impression conveyed through the senses; and, in fact, it cannot be made in any other way, because temperament, whether individual or collective, is not amenable to persuasion. (xli)

Conrad's transmission is not sent with telephonic point-to-point precision but dispersed, or broadcast, through the medium and as the medium ("It sounds far off . . . and is heard only as a whisper, often incomprehensible, but at times, and faintly, encouraging"). Somehow it thus reinvigorates language:

"the light of magic suggestiveness . . . brought to play for an evanescent instant over the commonplace surface of words." Similarly, it somehow reinvigorates human solidarity: "a single-minded attempt of that kind . . . shall awaken in the hearts of the beholders that feeling of unavoidable solidarity; of the solidarity in mysterious origin, in toil, in joy, in hope, in uncertain fate, which binds men to each other and all mankind to the visible world" (xlii). These powers depend on a particular experience of close-up distance, an un-visual image of proximity becoming approximate.

In the final section of the preface, Conrad emphasizes the spatializing implications of this broadcast from transmitter to receivers using a peculiar example:

> Sometimes, stretched at ease in the shade of a roadside tree, we watch the motions of a labourer in a distant field, and after a time, begin to wonder languidly as to what the fellow may be at. We watch the movements of his body, the waving of his arms, we see him bend down, stand up, hesitate, begin again. It may add to the charm of an idle hour to be told the purpose of his exertions. If we know he is trying to lift a stone, to dig a ditch, to uproot a stump, we look with a more real interest at his efforts; we are disposed to condone the jar of his agitation upon the restfulness of the landscape; and even, if in a brotherly frame of mind, we may bring ourselves to forgive his failure. (xliii)

Benjamin sets a remarkably similar scene in his "Artwork" essay as he defines "aura" as "the unique phenomenon of a distance, however close it may be": "If, while resting on a summer afternoon, you follow with your eyes a mountain range on the horizon or a branch which casts its shadow over you, you experience the aura of those mountains, of that branch" (*Illuminations* 222–23).[10] The fixed point of reference, Weber notes, is what holds the ever transient aura in time and place—is what closes the distance of the mountains and the branch and sets them before the alert receiver. What remains of aura, one might ask, for Conrad's laborer in the distant field?

The message of Conrad's allegory is that the manual exertions of the laborer received from afar, from the vantage of leisure, are only of diversion: "stretched at ease in the shade of a roadside tree, we watch the motions of a labourer in a distant field, and after a time, begin to wonder languidly as to what the fellow may be at." In effect, he draws on three factors of radio communication: first, the jar of agitation (or movement); second, the landscape (or the phenomenon of distance as a space of dispersal); and third, the roadside tree (or the site of leisure). Initially, because of the narrative framework, it appears that the artist is, yet again, playing the romantic part of the sensitive instrument—for tree, read antenna or receiver—homing in on the pictorial frequencies of the landscape at work. Yet, what soon emerges is that both the site of the tree and the second person narrative frame represent an audience structure, and it is the frustrated worker in the distant field, the transmitter in the example, who represents "the workman of art." The figure of the radio-Modernist is but a fitful and weak transmitter sending from afar fitful oscillations destined for what's at best a poor, unenergetic reception: "Art is long and life is short, and success is very far off. And thus, doubtful of strength to travel so far, we talk a little about the aim—the aim of art, which, like life itself, is inspiring, difficult—obscured by mists" (xliv)

Notes

1. For the host of ways Brecht's diagnosis remains remarkably prescient, see Streeter.

2. This chapter was completed before the appearance of Timothy C. Campbell's superb *Wireless Writing in the Age of Marconi*, which offers, among other things, a subtle synchronic reading of the emergence of a Marconian media ecology, focusing on wireless transmission.

3. On this point, especially Benjamin's notion of origin as transience, see Hanssen, 19ff.

4. For an expanded discussion of this cultural matrix, see my *Modernism and the Culture of Celebrity*.

5. Back in 1896, Marconi's British contacts arrange an audience for him with Sir William Preece, the chief engineer with the Royal Mail. He brings a new apparatus, the successor to the one damaged upon his arrival. A post office functionary records the encounter in the following terms:

> The young foreigner . . . had with him two large bags. . . . The contents of these bags were placed on the table and seemed to consist of a number of brass knobs fitted to rods, a large spark coil and some odd terminal, but most fascinating of all a large-sized tubular bottle from which extended two rods. So far as could be seen, these terminated inside the bottle on two discs, very closely together. Between them could be seen some bright filing or metal particles. This immediately took the Chief's eye and was obviously, by the careful way it was handled, something of great importance and certainly of particular interest. (Qtd. in Masini 71)

6. One need not be a technological determinist to appreciate Mattelart's point about imperial fortunes linked to cornering raw materials for making rubber encased copper wire.

7. During World War II, soldiers set up rigs much like mine, so-called foxhole

radios, and used rusty razor blades and pencil points as signal detectors and bayonets as grounds.

8. See Dery on the subculture associated with this activity.

9. Benjamin's black-box, the chess-playing automaton as exterior phenomenon, is likened to "historical materialism," the historical driver, the imperative of which being that it "must win all the time." The secret of the puppet's sham success is the work(ing) of the actually living engine(s) imprisoned within, made "wizened" and "invisible" but also strictly instrumental by the spectacle. Here, radio-shacking takes on a theological-messianic character. Like Tesla, the inevitable human inside is always elsewhere.

10. Weber's more evocative translation: "On a summer afternoon, resting, to follow a chain of mountains on the horizon or a branch casting its shadow on the person resting—that is what it means to breathe in the aura of these mountains—of this branch."

CHAPTER 2

Wireless Ego

The Pulp Physics of Psychoanalysis

JEFFREY SCONCE

A brilliant professor addresses his class on the mechanics of the soul. Establishing narrative and scientific premise as quickly as possible, he states, "All the known powers of the universe . . . are forms of vibration." A student writes in his notebook, for redundant expository emphasis, "Powers = vibrations. Soul = ditto." Most of the students are bored, but a young lady in the front row shivers as if "drawn to the edge of the abysmal unknown." The professor goes on to describe an elaborate device that will one day "capture the soul" by transcribing these vibrations, adding finally, "the rule of the world will be in the hands of the man who invents the soul machine" (Oliver 744). After class the professor asks the young lady in the front row, the beautiful Myra, to visit his lab, for he has, incredibly, already invented "the soul machine." Feeling they are already greatly "in sympathy," he hopes Myra will assist him in the "greatest discovery of all time" by agreeing to have her soul erased and replaced with his own. If she agrees, her will, desire, and memory will be completely obliterated in order to become "the new diaphragm," a blank slate for receiving the Professor's imprinting commands. "The final object of the machine is to place my desires—my best and worthiest desires, please God!—into the world, and make it better," he explains. Frightened, but hopelessly in love (as empirically detected by an "affection meter" on the machine), Myra agrees to the plan—but only if the Professor will first take her out for a long romantic afternoon. Once her will and memory are erased, she reasons, he will at least remember her as her former self. Later, back from their afternoon by the river discussing "music, pictures, and books," the soul transcription begins—but in the process, a tremendous explosion destroys the machine and knocks the Professor unconscious. When he awakes, Myra is indeed under his complete control—all vestiges of her former self are lost. Seeing what he has done, the Professor is tormented by guilt and grief. Finally, Myra calls him aside and reveals she was only pretending to be an erased soul under his control. She devised the plan while the Professor was unconscious so that he might be taught a valuable lesson. "There is a soul machine," she tells him at last. "It is called love."

Owen Oliver's short story of 1911, "The Soul Machine," is typical of many fantastic tales of the era that employed variations of wireless technology to explore occult mysteries of consciousness, will, and telepathic contact. As modernity's most recent and certainly most miraculous of telemedia to suggest a radical splitting of consciousness from the body, wireless no doubt struck many as a type of "soul machine," a mystical device that seeded the ether with disembodied voices and spectral presences. Rudyard Kipling's 1901 story, "Wireless," remains the best known and most influential of such tales, connecting Marconi's wondrous invention with possibilities of "mental telegraphy" in a story that would establish many of the conventions of this popular subgenre for the next thirty years.[1] Such speculation was more than a convenient literary conceit. During the first three decades of the new century, as wireless itself moved from nautical technology to amateur novelty to the institution of broadcast radio, numerous scientists, philosophers, and psychologists explored the still ambiguous boundary between psychic phenomena and a unified theory of electricity, magnetism, waves, fields, ether, and consciousness. As late as 1925, psychic researcher Sir Oliver Lodge continued to promote a comprehensive theory of the ether as a medium spanning the material and spiritual worlds, even as Einstein's quantum physics displaced this invisible medium from the realm of science to that of poetry. "The Ether of Space is a theme of unknown and apparently infinite magnitude," wrote Lodge in the aptly titled *Ether and Reality*. "By a kind of instinct, one feels it to be the home of spiritual existence, the realm of the awe-inspiring and the supernal." And yet, as the physicist Lodge quickly reminded the giddily mystic, "the Ether is a physical thing" (173).[2]

This "kind of instinct" for the ethereal, both literary and scientific, goes a long way toward providing a historical context for understanding "The Soul Machine," at least in terms of motivating its fanciful invention of a device that might transcribe, transmit, and even bulk erase the "vibrations" of the human soul. But there is another current running through Oliver's story, one less pronounced perhaps, yet no less imprecated in modernity's occult interest in secret agencies and invisible powers. As a diagnostic tool of the ego, psychoanalysis also promised to map the occluded mysteries of the self, presenting in its levels, energies, and flows its own form of half-understood "soul machine." And as in the metaphysical science fiction attending the spread of wireless, the popular lore of psychoanalysis also routinely trafficked in a metaphysical occult—imagining messages disembodied from a volitional "self" coursing their way through a medium every bit as mysterious and ineffable as the ether—the Freudian Unconscious. The "soul machine" proper—that strange vibrating contraption in the Professor's basement capable of transcribing, transmitting, and erasing the human ego—operates as a curious fusing of these two technologies of dislocated identity, a concrete mechanical emblem to bridge the mysterious mediums of ether and unconscious.

The most prominent link between wireless and psychoanalysis, its chief avenue of conceptual exchange, was through the science of telepathy. As an interstitial transmission thought to emanate somewhere between "ether and reality," telepathy promised for some fifty years to provide a long-suspected and long-hoped-for integration of physical, psychological, and spiritual phenomena. In this respect, telepathy can be seen as the third and perhaps even dominant science of occult communications intertwined with the simultaneous growth of wireless and psychoanalysis in the early years of the century. The following pages look more closely at these telepathic exchanges, especially as this occult braiding of radio, telepathy, and psychoanalysis became more prominent in the wake of World War I. Much like the growth of Spiritualism in the wake of America's Civil War, the incalculable loss of the Great War provoked a resurgence of interest in a variety of occult phenomena.[3] And in much the same way that the telegraph became central to nineteenth-century occultism, wireless figured significantly as an uncanny presence in this postwar imagination. "Nor is there much doubt as to the origin of this trend," wrote Freud of the era's "occult revival." "It is a part expression of the loss of value by which everything has been affected since the world catastrophe of the Great War, a part of the tentative approach to the great revolution towards which we are heading and of whose extent we can form no estimate; but no doubt it is also an attempt at compensation, at making up in another, a supermundane, sphere for the attractions which have been lost by life on this earth" ("Psychoanalysis and Telepathy" 177). Having astutely historicized postwar occultism, Freud nevertheless embarked in the 1920s on what would become the most paranormal phase of his career, beginning with the odd companions of 1919, "The Uncanny" and *Beyond the Pleasure*

Principle, and progressing through a series of essays that considered possible relationships between psychoanalysis and telepathy. While Freud rarely wrote about technology directly, his most famous comments limited to the "prosthetic gods" section of *Civilization and Its Discontents* (38–39), this postwar work on telepathy placed psychoanalysis in implicit dialogue with wireless as the era's other mysterious new science of occult agency and communication. Underlying all of these phenomena—psychoanalysis, telepathy, wireless—was a shared foundation in *energetic* speculation about the transference of thought, an attempt to explain seemingly occult phenomena in the air and in the mind through the language of scientific naturalism.

Quantum Cathexis

Battles over the status of telepathic phenomena had shadowed Freud's entire professional career. Any bid to create a science of the mind, neurological and/or psychoanalytic, had to contend in some way with this highly visible controversy, a conceptual struggle that even in the twenties still remained within the boundaries of mainstream scientific conjecture. Perhaps hedging his bets until all the science was in, Freud's writing on telepathy was notoriously conflicted, even as it gradually moved from suspicious rivalry to a more deliberate inscrutability. Thus, in the unpublished paper of 1921, "Psychoanalysis and Telepathy," the as-yet unconvinced Freud regarded recent popular interest in the occult as a noxious irritant, grouping it with the insubordination of his new adversaries Jung and Adler. "We do not seem destined to work in peace on the development of our science," he complained of this assault on his science (177). A year later Freud was more coy on the topic: "You will learn nothing from this paper of mine about the enigma of telepathy; indeed, you will not even gather whether I believe in the existence of 'telepathy' or not" ("Dreams and Telepathy" 197). "The Occult Significance of Dreams" (1925) saw Freud move one step closer in indulging the phenomenon: "One arrives at a provisional opinion that it may well be that telepathy really exists and that it provides the kernel of truth in many other hypotheses that would otherwise be incredible" (127).[4] Finally, in 1926, the year of his seventieth birthday, Freud had apparently become convinced—personally if not publicly—of telepathy's reality. "If anyone should bring up with you my Fall from grace," he wrote to colleague Ernest Jones, "just answer calmly that my acceptance of telepathy is my own affair, like my Judaism and my passion for smoking, etc., and that the subject of telepathy is not related to psychoanalysis" (*Complete Correspondence* 597). Having in his career described "omnipotence of thought" as a neurotic mode of infantile regression, having textually diagnosed Daniel Schreber's telepathic horrors as psychotic paranoia, and having as recently as 1919 praised colleague Victor Tausk's work on the telemechanic delusion of "influencing machines," Freud in the mid-1920s was nevertheless prepared to consider telepathy as science rather than as symptom.[5]

Freud's motivation in embracing telepathy has been the cause of much speculation, and has made these once esoteric and long marginalized portions of the Standard Edition increasingly central to recent studies of psychoanalysis. Whatever the source of Freud's ultimate conversion, a significant foundation for such belief can be found in the alliance between psychoanalysis and psychic research in theorizing the electrical economies of the mind and brain. Science had known since the experiments of Galvani that the body's nervous system was in some sense an "electrical" network, an association that proved vital in making early techno-occult connections between telegraphy and Modern Spiritualism.[6] As Roger Luckhurst documents in his history of telepathy, many prominent physicists of the late nineteenth century turned to electrical induction to explain mind to mind contact as only one of several physical "inter-phenomena" wholly consonant with the principles of scientific naturalism, a material theory of the occult that provided a crucial theoretical cornerstone for all subsequent psychic research.[7]

The conduction and induction of energy was no less central to the speculations of Freud, who, like the proponents of psychical research, was careful to position his seemingly occult interests within the realm of objective science. While psychic research moved toward the mysterious physics of induction to theorize telepathy, psychoanalysis remained true to its roots in the more conductive forces of cathexis, an economic theory of neural binding and discharge discussed at length in Freud and Breuer's pathbreaking volume *Studies on Hysteria* (1892) and theorized in meticulous detail in Freud's "Project for a Scientific Psychology" (1895). Following closely after Freud's work in the histological dissection of nervous tracts under arch-mechanist Ernst Brücke, this important early work founded psychoanalysis on the "principle of constancy"—a belief that organisms work toward "pleasure" by eliminating the disturbing excitations of displeasure (Solms 14). And in placing the "principle of constancy" at the heart of psychoanalysis, Freud was wholly in keeping with Victorian theories of the nervous system as circuitry seeking proper balance. George Beard's study of 1881, *American Nervousness*, was particularly influential in advancing such a model of energetic reserves, regulated stability, and the lamplight of the mind. "When new functions are interposed in the circuit," he wrote, "there comes a period, sooner or later, varying in different individuals, and at different times of life, when the amount of force is insufficient to keep all the lamps actively burning." Beard foresaw a dim future—literally—for a generation of neurasthenics unable to cope with the accelerating irritants of modernity. "Those that are weakest go out entirely, or, as more frequently happens, burn faint and feebly—they do not expire, but give an insufficient and unstable light—this is the philosophy of modem nervousness" (99). In his physiological contribution to *Studies on Hysteria*, Breuer made a very similar argument about the "abnormal excitability" of the hysteric's nervous system, a circuit Breuer also chose to characterize in terms of telephones, lamps, and other electronic wonders. Later in the essay Breuer invokes the metaphor of "short-circuiting" in describing hysteria, an over-charging of a weak wire that burns out normal connections. Finally, going to the metaphorical well a third time, Breuer writes somewhat defensively, "I shall scarcely be suspected of identifying nervous excitation with electricity, if I return once more to the comparison with an electrical system" (203).

Breuer's desire to distance himself from the electrical metaphor, even as he uses it once again, speaks to the ambiguous conflations inherited by Freudian cathexis. The nervous system (and by extension the psyche) is not *literally* an electrical system—and yet it operates in every way as if it were a wired network of flowing electrical energy (the mysterious forces $Q\,/Qh$ in the "Project").[8] Freud was thus true to neurology, psychic research, and psychoanalysis when he accepted as a matter of course that the passivity of sleep, a time of lower (and thus less "positive") activity in the brain (as well as the ego's most undefended moment), would naturally create "favorable conditions for telepathy" ("The Occult Significance of Dreams" 135–41).[9] By 1925, the time of this essay, Freud believed he had even located the exact transmission point of telepathic phenomena, one that again must be seen in terms of cathexis and energy transfer. "On the basis of much experience I am inclined to draw the conclusion that thought transference . . . comes about particularly easily at the moment at which an idea emerges from the unconscious, or, in theoretical terms, as it passes over from the 'primary process' to the 'secondary process'" ("Occult Significance" 89). True to the often paranoid obsessions of psychoanalysis, Freud and his followers came to be concerned with telepathy as manifest chiefly at the moment of analytic countertransference. This was the explicit topic of Helene Deutsch's paper of 1926, "Occult Processes Occurring during Psychoanalysis," and speaks to what John Forrester describes in *The Seductions of Psychoanalysis* as the discipline's fascination with "leaked communication." "Once the psychoanalytic situation has been conceptualized as a semipermeable discursive membrane," writes Forrester, "telepathy becomes a threat to that situation. The aim of the rules of analytic discourse is to regulate the flow across the membrane; telepathy represents a direct threat to this attempt at discursive regulation" (251).

Particularly sensitive to such "leakage," the Hungarian analyst Istvan Hollos took a most active interest in studying telepathic countertransference, proposing, after Freud, that these telepathic exchanges almost always involved a message "connected with a wish which is not yet in a state of repression, but is in the process of being repressed" (Devereux 200). Working in dialogue with an unnamed physicist, Hollos proposed a neurological theory that blended the Freudian thesis on primary and secondary processes with foundational speculation on telepathic induction some fifty years previous. The result was a kind of *quantum cathexis*, a process wherein psychic material, much like electrons, gave off energy when "jumping levels," in this case between the orbitals of the primary and secondary process. At the heart of the theory was the inductive biophysics of "crossed nerve bundles," nodal points in the nervous system capable of transferring impulses through inductive association rather than conductive networking. "There is a genuine logical nexus between the explanation of the crossing of nerve bundles by means of 'neuromotor induction' and the induction process of the unconscious," argues Hollos. "In other words, this theory implies that if an intraindividual nerve induction exists, then an interindividual one may also exist" (Devereux 201). During his period of public indecision on the topic, Freud often argued that psychoanalysis had little to say about the demonstrable reality of telepathic thought but could be of value in subjecting allegedly telepathic material, like dreams, to rigorous analytic dissection. But this disavowal, unblocked by Hollos's intervention, denied a material theory of telepathy already implicit in the energetic foundations of the Freudian project. Psychoanalysis *could* in fact locate the telepathic wave: physically as a type of "Qh-spark" set loose during cathexis, and situationally as an unconscious transmission from a "repressing" analyst to the contemplative and thus receptive mind of the reclining analysand.

Anxious Stimulation

In 1926, the same year that Freud confessed his ultimate "acceptance" of telepathy to Ernest Jones, empirical verification of mind to mind contact, mediated through the transfer of electromagnetic energy, appeared finally to be at hand in a series of experiments by Professor Ferdinando Cazzamali, a neurologist at the University of Milan. Cazzamali, noted the *New York Times* in its coverage "treated the human brain as a broadcast station" in order "to see what radio signals sent out by the brain could be picked up by delicate radio receivers" ("Human Radio Emanations" 27). Cazzamali's experiments depended on "highly excitable persons as subjects" who, once under hypnosis, emitted signals "at the extremely low wave length of from four to ten meters," sounds that were "similar to wireless signals, but were often accentuated until they resembled whistling or the tones of a muted violin" (27).[10] Playing on the decade's growing popular fascination with broadcasting, the reporter noted that the difficulties presented to Cazzamali in his experiments were almost identical to the main challenge facing the homebound wireless enthusiast—electrical interference. Despite such difficulties, the *Times* reporter believed the results to be encouraging enough to proclaim, "the scientific study of thought transference has suddenly become respectable" ("Radio's Aid" 3).

The respectability of such research was no doubt greatly enhanced by the world's newfound ability to sit near a radio in the living room and hear voices emanating from across the nation and even around the globe; or, just as often, to listen to the otherworldly swirls of static and interference that seemed to hold these voices hostage in the ether. While wireless had long existed in the public consciousness as an abstract concept, the 1920s saw the actual dissemination of radio as a broadcast technology in the home. Before the war, wireless had been primarily a point-to-point concern generally confined to shipping interests, the military, and a limited number of amateur operators. Broadcasting itself, pioneered in large part by the prewar networking activities of the amateurs, quickly achieved corporate and governmental codification in the early and mid-1920s as the United States and Europe negotiated how this new practice, wholly unforeseen a mere decade earlier, would be regulated.[11] The founding of the BBC in the United Kingdom (1922), and NBC and CBS in the United States (1926 and 1927, respectively) signaled a new soundscape for the young medium. Gone were the prewar pleasures of amateur "DX-fishing," wherein a cadre of wireless enthusiasts searched the airwaves to make distant two-way contact, replaced instead by the national blanketing of regularly scheduled unilateral broadcast entertainment.[12] In a variety of forums, this new sonic environment met with great resistance, provoking anxieties about the scope of networked power, the dangerous influence of institutional forces beyond the home, and the new threats bound to living in a world of inescapable global interconnectivity. And just as quickly, the uncanny power of the medium fused with a concern over the power to manipulate the personal and social by external forces. Experimenters such as Cazzamali only confirmed that the spark of life, as a spark, could easily be drained, implanted, short-circuited, and otherwise perverted and diverted from its normal channels—in the air and in the body.

Standing at the frontier of such speculation, pulp writers of the 1920s and 1930s also considered the wireless forces that might link telepathy, psychic energy, and the mysterious dimensions of the human ego. Whereas Freud, Deutsch, and Hollos concentrated on the cathected arc lamp binding analyst and analysand, pulps like *Weird Tales* and *Astounding Stories* pondered the larger implication of a world bound by the "free discharge" of consciousness as radiophonic energy. Tom Curry's "The Soul Snatcher" (1930), for example, opens with yet another of the era's overreaching professors rationalizing that a man killed in one of his wireless "soul transfer" experiments might have been "the Lindbergh of the Atom . . . hailed as the first man to travel through space in invisible form, projected on radio waves" (103). The story itself concerns the professor's efforts, at the request of a distraught mother, to save a young man on death row accused of killing the professor's unlucky atomic Lindbergh (who at this point has vanished into thin air). The professor agrees to use his technology to effect a kind of jailbreak, first switching egos with the young man and then switching bodies. In a testament to the frequently inelegant exposition of pulp fiction, the professor tells the mother, "I shall first switch our egos, or souls, as you say: Then switch the bodies. It must always take this sequence: why, I have not ascertained. But it always works thus" (105). Narratively, of course, it must "always [work] thus" so that the professor, in the tale's climax, can find his ego trapped in the young man's body (which, in turn, remains trapped in jail!) while the young man's ego can transmigrate into the body of the professor back in his lab. A technical complication (yet again!) prevents the final exchange of bodies, and so the jailed professor, unable to convince anyone of what has actually happened, goes to his death (as the young man) in the electric chair. This Cartesian horror story ("I think, but somehow I still am not") proved compelling enough to be adapted for the screen in 1936 as the rather unfortunately titled *The Man Who Changed His Mind*, an RKO release starring Boris Karloff.

Curry's story speaks to the confusion facing science fiction writers of the period who sought to untangle metaphysical soul, psychoanalytic ego, and bioelectric self. Just what is "snatched" in Curry's story, and if not immanent to the body, where is it? Brain exchange stories were as old as *Frankenstein*, of course, which in its own time captured the speculative energy attending Galvani's discoveries about organic currents. The added dimension of "The Soul-Snatcher" is that of the ego converted to and transmitted by invisible electromagnetic wavelengths, a marvel that equates wireless not only with the confusing possibilities of a "leaky" ego but also with an electrical essence at the core of consciousness itself. Transplant stories, in their crude equation of self with the dull organ meat of the brain, lack the ability of the wireless story to locate "self" as a dynamic flow of invisible energies housed yet somehow independent of the physical body's conductive networks, a position not unlike the critical shift in psychoanalysis from physiological to psychological etiology, from wiring to ideation. As Janet Oppenheim notes in her history of psychical research, the "independent existence of mind" was equally important to psychical research. "Whether dubbed mind, soul, spirit, or ego . . . such an entity distinct from brain tissue was requisite to rescue man from a state of virtual automatism, a mere bundle of physical and chemical properties" (205). The ultimate "horror" in Curry's story, of course, is in imagining the fate of incarceration in the wrong "brain tissue," energy in the wrong battery, a most literal splitting of ego and corporeal self that leads to the disassociative panic of considering the larger physics binding self and body, mind and brain, ego and electricity.

Just as radio evoked anxieties over distant control and loss of self, the psychoanalytic idea that "messages" in the form of repressed desires and traumas might speak from elsewhere in the mind could be every bit as unsettling, suggesting a similar disassociation between imagined self, or ego, and the rest of the famous iceberg submerged deep in the unconscious. Playing on these mysteries even as he hoped to diffuse them, James Oppenheim titled his 1923 layman's guide to psychoanalysis *Your Hidden Powers*, introducing his lessons by asking readers: "Why does radio interest you?" The answer, for Oppenheim, was that radio promised to make people happier, their lives more wonderful. "But suppose someone came to you and said: 'Science has discovered something greater than radio. It has made a discovery in human nature. It is discovering you'" (1). The key to one's "hidden powers," of course, was psychoanalysis. "Perhaps you have heard of it," continues Oppenheim in his rhetorical dialogue with the reader. "Perhaps you have dismissed it as some new cult, some form of religion, something to do with spiritualism, or what is called the 'occult.' It is none of these" (4). So deep, apparently, were the popular associations of psychoanalysis and the supernatural, Oppenheim felt obligated to assert a final time that Freud's work, though it dealt with the "hidden," was not a product of occult mysticism. "I merely want to point out that true scientists have made these discoveries in exactly the same way scientific discoveries have always been made," he writes, as if both radio and the dreamwork had issued from the labs at RCA (5).

Exploiting this energetic fog, William Rouse's story of 1921, "The Dead Man's Thoughts," presents a particularly suggestive melding of emotional and technological transference of power. The story opens with a poor but happy newlywed couple receiving a surprise visit from the bride's former suitor, a brilliant scientist who vanished shortly before the couple's wedding and has been missing for three months. After giving his blessing to the young couple, the scientist describes his current research project. "I shall be able to demonstrate in the laboratory exactly what 'stuff dreams are made of,' and the minds that dream them, and the bodies that carry the minds," he boasts, adding "no thought, no feeling, is ever manifested save as the result of physical force" (642–43). Months later, a telegram arrives announcing the scientist's untimely death. Knowing the couple would be too proud to accept money from his estate, the dead scientist instead offers them the free use of his home so that the husband can complete his studies without financial strain. He asks only that Phyllis, his former love, will place fresh roses in the study every afternoon in his memory. The couple accepts the offer and moves in for the winter. Over the following weeks, Phyllis becomes increasingly depressed, no doubt in part because the roses she leaves each day in the study die each morning before dawn. Theories of ghosts and hauntings are considered, but eventually the husband discovers a letter explaining an elaborate revenge plot afoot in the house. "The thought of death has its own ethereal vibration," explains the scientist in this letter from beyond the grave, "Hate also travels by vibration. . . . More than Marconi did for telegraphy I have done for the conscious transmission and direction at will of thoughts and emotions" (649). The husband reads on to discover that an apparatus has been concealed in the study where Phyllis goes each day to replace the roses, a device that broadcasts "thoughts of suicidal despair" (powerful enough, apparently, to drive even nonsentient flowers to their death!). After saving Phyllis from an impending suicide attempt, he breaks through the wall and uncovers the device, "a mass of delicate and intricate apparatus from which countless antennae arose." He empties a revolver into the machine, and suddenly feeling "happier than he ever had before," returns to attend to the still shaken Phyllis.

As the story of a living dead man who seeks to eliminate all traces of desire, to destroy himself and the young lovers who look forward to a life of home, hearth, and family, "The Dead Man's Thoughts" is uncannily evocative of Freud's perplexing essay of 1920, *Beyond the Pleasure Principle*. Like countless other pulp tales of the era, Freud's stimulating theory of "traumatic neurosis" also presents an extraordinary account of an energetic self negotiating the anxious challenges presented by a world of energetic threats. In Rouse's tale, life, romance, and Eros "win" in the end, as they must, but only after the reader is allowed to revel in Phyllis's strange affinity for an affectless quiescence lurking beyond the normative confines of domesticated sexuality, an extinguishing yet perversely alluring force of the mind made manifest in the waveforms of a secreted machine. Freud's postwar need to think "beyond" pleasure and the principle of constancy, meanwhile, staged a similar confrontation between the sexual instincts and the organism's seemingly uncanny desire to return to a state of absolute peace, a biological oblivion that preexisted the endlessly anxious stimulation that is (modern) life. Rouse employs a quite literal *deus ex machina* ending to produce a secreted technology behind this radiophonic siren song of the void. Freud's reveal from the psychic "beyond," meanwhile, is the negating power of the "death drive."

Such thematic similarities between "The Dead Man's Thoughts" and *Beyond the Pleasure Principle* suggest shared conceptual frameworks and common discursive horizons; that is, Rouse and Freud, publishing these works within a year of one another, channeled voices of scientific and psychic intuition in different languages for different audiences (and with vastly different impacts).

Of course, throwing Rouse's tale of energetic despair into the same discursive pool as Freud is to also link *Beyond the Pleasure Principle* to the conventions of contemporaneous pulp fiction (or at least pulp science). While this may seem glibly scandalous, it is worth noting just how skeptical, even playful, Freud himself was in conjuring this realm at the occult border of known psychoanalytic theory. "What follows is speculation, often far-fetched speculation, which the reader will consider or dismiss according to his individual predilection," he writes. "It is further an attempt to follow out an idea consistently, out of curiosity to see where it will lead" (*Beyond* 17). Acknowledging this aleatory aspect of the essay, Jean Laplanche calls *Beyond the Pleasure Principle* "the most fascinating and baffling text of the entire Freudian corpus," describing Freud himself as "profoundly free" and "audacious" in its writing (106). Laplanche finds the essay itself to be "only sporadically and superficially subordinated to logical imperatives," adding "the holes in the reasoning constitute so many traps; the sliding of concepts results in blurring terminological points of reference; the most far-reaching discussions are suddenly resolved in the most arbitrary manner. If one resists the inherent movement of the text," he warns, "one may derive the impression that every question in it is poorly posed and in need of reformation" (107). If we do not accede to Freud's stylishly inconsistent logic, in other words, we are likely to confuse him with Hugo Gernsback, the great patriarch of the pulps and the author of the equally loopy piece of energetic speculation, *Ralph 124c 41+*.[13]

Ostensibly inspired by the clinical experience of traumatized veterans compulsively reliving moments of battlefield stress, the real protagonist of *Beyond the Pleasure Principle* is Freud's famously embattled vesicle, "a living organism in its most simplified form . . . susceptible to stimulation" (28). Employing a still influential Victorian doctrine of recapitulation, Freud locates the origins of consciousness in the nervous fate of our single-cell ancestors. Bombarded by external stimuli, Freud postulates, the vesicle would develop a "crust which at last will have been so thoroughly 'baked through' by stimulation that it would present the most favorable possible conditions for the reception of stimuli" (29). Herein lie the evolutionary origins of the sense organs—eyes, ears, and suggestively, the antennae that "are all the time making tentative advances toward the external world and then drawing back from it." Freud's distracted, even besieged vesicle—a type of flotsam flâneur—becomes the foundation for the essay's subsequent "free associations." And in these prehistoric musings, Freud provides an evolutionary precursor to the "over-taxed" subject so central to other sociobiological accounts of nervous modernity. Echoing Breuer's echoing of Beard, Freud proposes of his anxious vesicle, "*Protection against* stimuli is an almost more important function for the living organism than *reception of* stimuli" (30). Fast-forward through millions of years of homological thinking and Freud, in a rather deft rhetorical move, makes this single-celled organism a spatial metaphor for all human perception/consciousness (the system *Pcpt-Cs*). And yet, though ensconced behind an armature of ever more elaborate and specialized defenses, modern consciousness would appear no less melancholy and tenuous than the protoplasmic ancestor Freud describes with such pathos: "This little fragment of living substance is suspended in the middle of an external world charged with the most powerful energies; and it would be killed by the stimulation emanating from these if it were not provided with a protective shield against stimuli"(30). Freud then adapts Breuer's psychic economies to adhere *beyond* the pleasure principle, and in the process, casts modern man's consciousness as a type of "capacitor," one that must survive the withering assault of external stimuli even as it must also negotiate the "unshielded" influence of internal energy. Overwhelmed from the outside by a traumatic breach, consciousness must respond through strategies of mastery, retroactively making the cathected investments necessary to guard against such intrusions (i.e., anxiety). Overwhelmed from the inside, consciousness must project the threat to the external world, opening the door for various neurotic dysfunctions. Thus does consciousness itself appear to spring from a constant "re-wiring" of psychic energy born of a perpetually paranoid state of energetic danger, stretching from anxious beginnings in the Archean sea all the way to the "shell shock" of World War I.

Given the shared interest of wireless pulp and occult Freud in telepathic energy as an electronic index of hidden powers and secret pathways, small wonder that they might echo one another in such speculation. Indeed, it is not difficult to see how the era's pulp fiction, with its own "free associations," "blurring of terminological points of reference," and lack of "logical imperatives," also busied itself with the great postwar task of thinking through mankind's seemingly self-evident instinct for death. While Freud looked backward to evolution for his energetic theory of the anxious subject, pulp writers employed futuristic wireless stories about the telepathic disruption of space and time as their chosen means for capturing the growing external threats of modern consciousness. Such stories implied that radio, by expanding the encrusted "shell" of the human psyche around the world, only extended the potential for accelerated and more devastating traumatic intrusions as listeners found themselves unwillingly conscripted into broadcasting's ethereally collective mind. In "The Night Wire" (1926), for example, a lone wireless operator begins receiving sporadic messages that a deadly fog is enveloping a remote Mexican village. Consistently interrupted by interference and failed transmission links, the messages gradually make it clear that the fog is slowly expanding to cover the entire earth and will eventually kill every living soul on the planet. There is no escape—the wonder technology of wireless providing only a type of impotent clairvoyance of the shock yet to come. This new and unprecedented source of anxiety—the ability to hear the step-by-step narration of one's own impending annihilation—was a truly unique gift of wireless modernity, a feature exploited most famously in Orson Welles's infamous Halloween presentation of *War of the Worlds* on CBS radio in 1938.

The desire (and dread) of foreseeing trauma before it had a chance to breach the walled defenses of the electronic psyche was also a central concern in stories of wireless time displacement. Most famously introduced in H. G. Wells's novella, *The Time Machine*, the possibilities of time travel quickly found their most plausible presentation in the allied mysteries of wireless transmission. While sending an actual body through time and space seemed wholly incredible, the ability to hear or see across space and time seemingly remained at the fringes of theoretical possibility. John Pierce's story "Pre-Vision," for example, found its inspiration in an actual news clipping from a 1924 issue of *The Physical Review* on the possible subatomic foundations of predetermination. The tale begins with a scientist inventing a televiewer that can screen events from the future. Testing his quantum theory of "anticipated potentials," the scientist's first experiment reveals a future moment in the lab with the scientist unconscious on the floor. Seconds later an explosion hurls a vacuum tube into the man's forehead, knocking him out cold. After his recovery at the hospital, a second experiment in quantum Calvinism shows the scientist in the lab arguing with someone, a shadowy figure who soon collapses. "Doesn't this thing show anything but accidents?" wonders the exasperated scientist. Inevitably, his friend visits for a demonstration of the machine and in a heated argument over the ethics of the device collapses from a heart attack. A third "pre-vision" shows the scientist's girlfriend, angry that he is persisting in these experiments, running out into the street to be hit by a car. This time, however, the scientist is able to intercede and saves her by throwing himself in front of the moving vehicle. Waking up again in the hospital, his thoughts turn a final time toward his strange invention seemingly capable of only channeling anxiety from the future. "Was the machine a thing of evil, that it prophesied only ill?"

An even more literal expression of radio as an oppressive blanket of impending "evil" could be found in Eric Frank Russell's story, "The Great Radio Peril," a tale that linked the inescapable omnipresence of the wireless signal with the battered psychic defenses of the body politic. After the nations of the world cannot cooperate on shared broadcast standards, the world devolves into a wireless shouting match. A year later the world's crops begin to fail, leading to widespread famine and riots. Rumors circulate that the increased wireless signal is behind the crop disaster, a proposition accepted by some scientists and rejected by others. Mass hysteria takes over, however, when a left-leaning farmer in Wyoming tells his own story of crop failure, all because his metal barn constantly resonates with the signal of nearby station WHFS. "What sort of country was this, anyway, when a feller's wheat got electrocuted every time some fat capitalist sprayed the air with a tooth-paste ad?" (53). Soon vigilante groups are destroying the world's transmitters, including a reenergized Ku Klux Klan sweeping through and destroying the broadcasters of the American south. The crops return the following year, although it is never made entirely clear whether radio was indeed responsible for the catastrophe.

Playing with the sci-fi idea of wireless signals eating away at the cellular structure of the world's crops, Russell's radio story is really more concerned with the possibilities of wireless eating away at the public's brains. Highly contemptuous of the new mass audience created by radio, Russell's story is, somewhat ironically (but quite typically), an archly mass-elite critique of the popular appearing in one of the popular's most denigrated of media—the lowly pulp. When the attempt to negotiate new radio standards among the nations fails, for example, Russell describes a bored press and audience quickly moving on to a new topic of all-consuming interest—Italian sextuplets. In language somewhere between Wilhelm Reich's *Listen Little Man!* and a Z-grade zombie movie, Russell writes, "The little man who served behind a counter, piloted a brewer's dray, or rushed to catch the eight twenty-five to the office each morning, was forced to surrender his views anent radio and take an interest in what the sextuplets were fed upon, how they were given it and who gave it 'em" (48). Later, once the famine has passed and the anti-radio hysteria has subsided, the public turns its attention to a Soviet scientist who "dumbfounded biological circles by successfully crossing a dog with a goat" (55). Russell concludes his tale of wireless idiocy with a queer turn toward self-reflexive cynicism, one presumes, about his own place in this fictional wireless universe. Summing up a world returned to normal, he writes, "An obscure author tore up his thirtieth rejection, started afresh and wrote a story telling how Martians resembling pink spiders wiped out the world with a giant transmitter directing its beam through interplanetary space. The story was kicked out—without regrets." As Russell concludes, "The world had had quite enough of radio"(55). The ending remains ambiguous, however, in that it is unclear whether the world has had "enough of radio" itself or enough of an obsessive dialogue about the dangers of transmitting invisible energy, be it by pink spiders, soul snatchers, fascist dictators, clairvoyant televisions, sleepy psychoanalysts, or the secreted fortress of one's own "hidden powers."

Beyond Space and Time

In one of the most interesting passages in *Beyond the Pleasure Principle*, Freud detours from his account of his vesicle's anxious evolution to wax philosophical in a fleeting but suggestive encounter with Kant. Freud pauses to consider an idea that he admits "must sound very obscure" (32): namely, the premise that time and space are, following Kant, "necessary forms of thought," inasmuch as they provide consciousness with another type of protection against indiscriminate stimuli (31).[14] The connection here, only hinted at by Freud, with other accounts of modernity's radically changing experience of time and space is as fascinating as it is "obscure." Inasmuch as his theory hinges on the idea of overtaxation, perhaps Freud suspected, like so many other commentators on modernity—then and now—that even the fundamental bulwarks of time and space were increasingly inadequate as encrusted defenses for the modern subject. This would be especially true in an age when technologies like wireless were thought to have such a transformative impact on the experience of being in the world, a thesis adopted within modernity itself and foundational in almost all subsequent accounts of the era.[15] Marshall McLuhan certainly echoed such sentiments a half-century later in his canonical work, *Understanding Media*, a study that either through unconscious channeling or egregious plagiarism revisits *Beyond the Pleasure Principle* with minimal distortion. "With the arrival of electric technology, man extended, or set outside himself, a live model of the central nervous system itself," McLuhan wrote:

> To the degree that this is so, it is a development that suggests a desperate and suicidal autoamputation, as if the central nervous system could no longer depend on the physical organs to be protective buffers against the slings and arrows of outrageous mechanism. It could well be that the successive mechanizations of the various physical organs since the invention of printing have made too violent and overstimulated a social experience for the central nervous system to endure. (43)

Do we experience space and time differently, more nervously, than the "pre-modern?" Only someone with a real time machine can answer that question definitively. Certainly, the period's convergence of interest in telepathy suggests an anxious impulse to re-theorize self, space, and time through a new vocabulary of invisible power. Wireless, telepathy, and psychoanalysis, after all, provided crucial intersections for imagining not only the possibilities of occult agency and invisible communications but also the secreted wellsprings of power itself in its many guises. From Freud to philosophy, spiritualism to science, pulps to politics, the discourses of modernity explored this allusive conflation of electrical, social, and personal power, displacing theories of information, transference, and control from one realm to the other. Haunting both Freud and the pulps was the implication that an energetic self in a world of accelerating energetic danger risked energetic dissipation and dissolution, that electromagnetic powers might figure prominently in the negotiation of personal and social powers. Thus, the very same ether that held so much wonder and transcendental possibility for figures like Lodge, a spiritual scientist who adamantly refused to give up his nineteenth-century paradigms of a benevolent unifying force, became in the twentieth century an anxious repository for invisible energies and atomizing threats.[16] Ego, meanwhile, formerly a self-evident fortress of the self, became in the age of Freud no less precarious as an object fashioned by occult force, to the point that Freud himself worried that its energies might leak out at the threshold of the crucially insulating moment of repression. Perhaps little more than an electronic trick, consciousness as the foundation for self found itself, much like its protoplasmic ancestors, resisting a world of perpetually threatening and quickly accelerating stimuli. As invisible communication, finally, telepathic power provided a profoundly influential avenue for theorizing, in science and in fiction, the electromagnetic pathways that might bind brain and radio as receivers, mind and transmission as electrical inscriptions.

Which returns us a final time to Freud, telepathy, the origins of consciousness, and his famously irritated vesicle. In his final essay on telepathy, "Dreams and the Occult," Freud implicitly returned to our evolutionary ancestor, who, just as it created consciousness itself through the constant management of bombarding stimuli, may have also have had a hand (or cilia) in creating the foundations of telepathy. Considering the evolutionary origins of telepathic contact, Freud echoes the logic of *Beyond the Pleasure Principle* by writing, "one is led to a suspicion that this is the original, archaic method of communication between individuals and that in the course of phylogenetic evolution it has been replaced by the better method of giving information with the help of signals which are picked up by the sense organs" (55). Telepathic power, in other words, is the fundamental wellspring of all subsequent manifestations of power, be they electrical, psychical, or political, a suspicion Freud confirms by conjecturing that telepathy "might have persisted in the background and still be able to put itself into effect under certain conditions—for instance, in passionately excited mobs" (55). It would be difficult to provide a more concise image of modernity's scientific and superstitious obsession with the anxieties of invisible power, the nervousness at the core of wireless and psychoanalysis. In Freud's scenario, telepathy, a by-product of consciousness, which is itself a by-product of nervous irritation, lies as a dormant transmitter in the human mind until those moments when struggles over power become most naked. Having earlier noted telepathy's affinity for the inter- and intrapersonal power exchanges of analytic repression and transference, Freud in the 1930s relocates such energetic radiation of biosocial influence to the mob, the mass, the body politic. In the process, he asks us to reimagine Gustave Le Bon's influential work on "the crowd" as the story of a primordial energy binding "the popular mind," an occult analogue of the "great radio peril" that threatens to join forces in overthrowing the structures of self, reason, and democracy. In so doing, Freud follows a similar trajectory in the interests of the pulps, from the occasional "snatched soul" and individuated control beam to a mass mind subject to external energies, powers, and control. But like all good pulp writers, Freud wanted to leave his readers intrigued by such prospects rather than simply terrified. "All this is still uncertain and full of unsolved riddles," he writes, "but there is no reason to be frightened by it" (55).

Notes

1. For a more detailed analysis of this genre, see my chapter "The Voice from the Void," in *Haunted Media*.

2. For a more complete account of the ether in cultural history, see Milutis.

3. World War I produced a number of popular studies concerning psychic and occult contact. Hereward Carrington's *Psychic Phenomena and the War* (New York: Dodd and Mead, 1918) compiled, with little attempt at verification, psychic incidents associated with the Great War. More poignant and widely read was Sir Oliver Lodge's *Raymond; or, Life and Death* (London: Methuen, 1916), a book based on mediumistic contact with Lodge's son, Raymond, who died in battle in 1915.

4. In the same essay, Freud pays tribute to the magnetic powers of his own mind, noting, "I have often had the impression, in the course of my experiments in my private circle, that strongly emotionally colored recollections can be successfully transferred without much difficulty" (127).

5. Freud discusses "omnipotence of thought" and "magical thinking" at length in "Totem and Taboo." For his analysis of Schreber, see "Psycho-Analytic Notes on an Autobiographical Account of a Case of Paranoia (Dementia Paranoides)." For Freud's obituary of Victor Tausk, see "Victor Tausk." Tausk's study, "On the Origins

of the Influencing Machine" (1918), has been reprinted many times, most recently in *Incorporations*, ed. Jonathan Crary and Sanford Kwinter.

6. See Sconce, "Mediums and Media," in *Haunted Media*, 21–58.

7. Luckhurst 75–92. Alex Owen argues that many involved in the Victorian occult revival, while suspicious of the soulless materialism of "scientific naturalism," were nonetheless invested in a "rational" inquiry into psychic and spiritual phenomena (1–16).

8. Interestingly, some sixty years after Breuer's disavowal that psychic and electrical energy appear to be the same thing, James Strachey introduced a similar word of caution in presenting "Project for a Scientific Psychology" in the Standard Edition. "There is a risk that enthusiasm may lead to a distortion of Freud's use of terms and may read into his sometimes obscure remarks modern interpretations that they will not bear." A footnote informs the reader this distortion involves "a supposed reference to electricity in the Project" (SE [1]: 293). This admonition is particularly perplexing given that Strachey, only one page earlier, enthusiastically supports the idea that the "Project" might anticipate recent work suggesting "the human nervous system may be regarded in its workings as similar or even identical with an electronic computer" (292).

9. He repeats this claim in "Dreams and the Occult," 37.

10. For a full account of Professor Cazzamali's findings, see also "Says Human Brain Emits Radio Waves," and "Radio's Aid Is Invoked to Explore Telepathy."

11. The definitive history of this transition remains Susan Douglas's *Inventing American Broadcasting*.

12. For a more detailed discussion of the cultural implications of this move toward network broadcasting, see Sconce, *Haunted Media* 92–123.

13. *Ralph 124c 41+: A Romance of the Year 2660* was originally published serially in *Modern Electrics* in 1911, and then collected and reprinted in *Amazing Stories Quarterly* (Winter 1929). Most recently, the book has been reprinted by the University of Nebraska Press (2001).

14. One cannot help but be struck here by the post-Lacanian literature in schizophrenia that approaches the disease precisely as a breakdown in signification, and thus time and space, leaving the subject unable to restrict and process incoming stimuli. This, of course, is the hallucinatory sense of the perpetual present elaborated on by Fredric Jameson in his work on postmodernism. See *Postmodernism, or, the Cultural Logic of Late Capitalism*.

15. One of the most influential accounts of this thesis remains that of Kern.

16. For an influential account of the relationship between "live" broadcasting and disaster, see Doane.

CHAPTER 3

Marinetti, *Marconista*

The Futurist Manifestos and the Emergence of Wireless Writing

TIMOTHY C. CAMPBELL

In a history of twentieth-century encounters between literary Modernism and turn-of-the century communication technologies, Marinetti's Futurist manifestos occupy a singular role. For Douglas Kahn and Gregory Whitehead, much of the manifestos' significance resides in Marinetti's conception of a wireless imagination (*immaginazione senza fili*) and the term's capacity to chart "sonographic resonances" among voice migrations, phonography, and noise in a modern media ecology (x).[1] For Jeffrey Schnapp, Marinetti's wireless imagination, when seen in conjunction with other technologies developed during the second industrial revolution, opens up cognitive possibilities, making "thinkable" new forms of literary expression (154). The term does double duty, capturing locally the possibilities one communication technology, wireless telegraphy, offers Modernism while embodying more generally the features of early twentieth-century encounters with technology.

Given the privileged position of the manifestos and the wireless imagination for many writings on sound technologies and literary production, it is surprising therefore that the details of Marinetti's interaction with wireless technology remain unscrutinized. The reasons, having much to do with the conflation of the machine with communication technologies, I have discussed elsewhere.[2] Consequently, for all the emphasis on Marinetti and his wireless imagination, the actual parameters of his interaction with wireless telegraphy and later radio remain largely unknown.[3] It is precisely to these encounters that I turn in the following pages.

To situate Marinetti in a larger context of wireless listening and writing, my itinerary opens with an examination of the principal details of wireless telegraphy circa 1912 (a date that marks the publication of Marinetti's most important statement on the wireless and aesthetics in the "Technical Manifesto of Futurist Literature"). Recuperating the details of wireless invention in the figure of Guglielmo Marconi, I begin by focusing on the wireless medium itself as well as the principal features of the wireless operator, or *marconista*, as he was known in Italy. The wireless listener not only demonstrates a remarkable virtuosity in hearing the dots and dashes of Morse Code out of the static but also in writing down these messages. The coupling of writing to an acute sense of hearing underscores the differences with his predecessor, the telegraph operator, and later the radio engineer. This crucial point—that the *marconista* symbolically captures the dots and dashes moving across the ether—will mark the contours of Marinetti's engagement with the wireless in the Futurist manifestos.

After outlining the technical characteristics of the wireless operator and the nature of the wireless transmission, I turn to the "Technical Manifesto of Futurist Literature" and its enmeshment in wireless listening and writing. I argue that Marinetti's literary appropriation of wireless's practices in words in freedom (*parole in libertà*) and wireless imagination (*immaginazione senza fili*) is sparked by his prior transformation into a *marconista*. Where before Marinetti depends upon an outdated lyrical I (*io lirico*) for poetry, he now simulates a wireless receiver that converts the sights and sounds of modern life into writing. Turning next to his "Answer to Objections," his rejoinder to criticism that greeted the publication of the "Technical Manifesto," I show how Marinetti's wireless imagination denies its Romantic lineage, becoming instead a dictating machine whose transmissions to the medium Marinetti have little to do with sense. Following this line of inquiry leads me to argue for a rubric of wireless writing in which a number of modern writers work.

Wireless Writing: Instructions for Use

The details of the invention of wireless telegraphy are well known. Although many contributed to the emergence of wireless telegraphy (Maxwell, Hertz, and Tesla, to name the most decisive), the name of Guglielmo Marconi is most often associated, rightly or wrongly, with its invention.[4] Beginning with a series of experiments in 1895, Marconi essentially produced a variation of the telegraph without the wires (captured in the Italian *telegrafia senza fili* and the German *die drahtlose Telegraphie*), which relayed signals tapped at a transmitter to a receiver using Morse code. Aided crucially by James Clerk Maxwell's theory of electromagnetic radiation published in 1865 and by Heinrich Hertz's experimental proof of the existence of radio waves in 1888, better known as Hertzian waves, Marconi recognized in these early sound waves the possibility for sending messages (marconigrams, as they were known in the United Kingdom) using Morse code. He did so by utilizing primitive circuits and galvanic batteries to set up "spark-gap transmitters" that sent very weak electromagnetic waves to receivers that consisted of iron filings. These iron filings "cohered" or "discohered" depending upon the reception of the Hertzian wave, thus marking the dots and dashes of Morse code. Equally noteworthy were his antenna designs, his arrangements of circuits, and the introduction of the ground-plane, or grounded vertical antenna for wireless transmission and reception. Of singular importance, however, was Marconi's discovery that long waves followed the curvature of the earth; in practice this meant that the Marconi receiving unit need not be in the transmitter's line of sight. And so Marconi was the first to transmit wirelessly across, over, and around all obstacles simply by using the earth (Aitken 192–93). Despite these advances, the first wireless was limited by the weakness of its signals until a method could be found to amplify them at the receiving end or to increase the power of the signal at the site of transmission. The successful resolution of these problems took another twenty years and a world war to overcome.

What then are the principal characteristics of the wireless transmission at the time Marinetti invokes them in 1912? Most significant is the weakness of the wireless transmission vis-à-vis the telegraph. Given the power constraints of the spark transmitter, Marconi came quickly to depend upon the acoustic properties of the ear and in particular its capacity for sound recognition. Where, for instance, the Morse telegraph had depended upon machines that inscribed dots and dashes onto tape, the Marconi-wireless (as it was first called) included a headset and inscription tools (pen and paper) that the *marconista* would use to write down the sounds that were faintly echoing in the receiver. Therefore, the demands upon such a listener went well beyond anything required of the telephone or telegraph operator.

The following account from one of Marconi's own wireless-operators (the singular Marconi *marconista*) spells out the device's chief differences from old-fashioned telegraphy:

> Instead of interpreting the dots and dashes of the telegraphic alphabet from the Morse machine's strip of paper, now the so-called dots and dashes were listened to with a telephonic headset. After some practice, one could transcribe the meaning instantaneously on a piece of paper. At that moment the real and true wireless operator was born, the one we see today with his headset, ready to spring to another's aid, one with his apparatus, having the possibility of concentrating his hearing on a given signal and tonality and to distinguish it rationally from the atmospheric discharges and other transmissions; to perceive very weak waves augmenting consequently the distances of communication. A Morse machine could never do all that. It required a strong signal without interference and discharges of any sort in order to work. Otherwise it did not work or it would spit out a strip muddled with indecipherable dots and dashes. (Landini 51–52)[5]

Aside from its more melodramatic features (linked with the fame accrued the wireless thanks to its role in salvage operations for the *S.S. Titanic*), the passage captures well the principal features of the wireless and its operator. The wireless differs from the telegraph both in its instantaneous transcription of dots and dashes into written signifiers on the page (thanks to its exploitation of human hearing) and in the heightened amount of noise out of which the wireless operator must pick out meaningful signals. Meaning in wireless communication occurs therefore as the result of an acoustic selection by its *marconista*: what cannot be written down does not count as a meaningful message. The contrast between wireless and telegraph operators emerges clearly here: the wireless couples a hand that writes with an ear that has been trained to capture acoustic data out of a noisy channel. Put differently, where the telephone and telegraph construct an interface between the headset and body, the wireless does so among a headset, a body, and paper. Taken together, these elements form not only a communication system but an information system as well, since acoustic data are received and then symbolically processed in writing. The result, as Marconi's *marconista* recognizes, is both impressive and worrying: a medium without wires that allowed for almost instantaneous communication across the globe; and a greater identification between apparatus and user (the passage's "one with his apparatus") that looks forward to the more severe couplings of the contemporary cyborg.[6]

Marinetti, Marconista

This admittedly brief preface to wireless invention provides an important context for understanding its later appearance in the Futurist manifestos. It is by now commonplace when speaking of the interaction between technological and organic communication systems to see mutual inspiration at work between them—media affected "not just the way people wrote and communicated but the way they perceived their own minds and bodies" (Otis 182). Naturally, Marinetti's manifestos are little different—the industrialized makeover of the human body and psyche is on display on every page. But rather than confirming what Marinetti himself admits to, I want to pose a different question in the pages that follow: what happens when a poet—and Marinetti had confirmed himself previously as a French poet long before the publication of the manifestos—simulates wireless practices, turning himself into one of the period's many *marconisti*? What are the effects of reproducing or reenacting the technical processes of a communications technology that trains a listener not only in how to hear but also in how to process sounds? And more crucially, what are the results when media have been transposed and sound has been assaulted as a complex of data that was previously impossible to put into writing?

No manifesto invokes the wireless and its operator more than the "Technical Manifesto of Futurist Literature." There, in one of the more oversized manifestos (nine pages), Marinetti elaborates a model of modern writing deeply indebted to the wireless specifications I noted above. Opening famously with a scene of dictation between a biplane propeller and its pilot and passenger, Marinetti first inscribes the wireless in an acoustic scene. The would-be pilot sits atop the gas cylinder and tunes his hearing to the sounds of the propeller behind him. What he writes at that moment and what follows, he tells us before proceeding to his bolded letters and mathematical signs, is the transposition of the sounds of the propeller into the medium of writing: "This is what the whirling propeller told me, when I flew two hundred meters above the mighty chimney pots of Milan" (84).[7] Marinetti takes dictation from the propeller and so puts into practice one of the key Futurist tenets of the manifesto outlined in paragraph 11: "To listen to motors and to reproduce their conversations" (88). That a propeller's dictation is a condition for the production of the manifesto points to a first level of media connectivity between Marinetti's ear and the transmitting propeller. Marinetti becomes a medium for the propeller's transmissions and begins bracketing data flows: a selection from the propeller's sounds results.

Crucially, nowhere does Marinetti write down in the manifesto the real sounds of the propeller (he would do so for artillery barrages later the same year in *Zang Tumb Tumb*). Instead, he attempts to elaborate a relation among the sound of the propeller, the hearing he is practicing, and a mode of writing that can register those sounds on paper. Two concepts, or more precisely, a condition for literary production and a mode of association, help pinpoint the engagement between the propeller and Marinetti in the manifesto. The first, words in freedom (*parole in libertà*), register in script the dictations sound machines such as the propeller make to the writer. The second, the wireless imagination (*immaginazione senza fili*), refers to the Marconi-wireless, the telegraph without wires (*telegrafia senza fili*), though Marconi nowhere receives credit. It is the principal medium through which Marinetti receives the sounds of the propeller and by extension those of modern life. Both appear in the densest section of the manifesto and only after Marinetti has established the conditions for transposing noise into writing.

Leaving the wireless imagination in reserve momentarily, what distinguishes words in freedom as a writing practice? As Marinetti sees it, words in freedom are capable of registering the sounds of modern life as manifested by what he calls "objects in freedom" (*oggetti-in-libertà*):

> The man sidetracked by the library and the museum, subjected to a logic and wisdom of fear, is of absolutely no interest. We must therefore drive him from literature and finally put matter in his place, matter whose essence must be grasped by strokes of intuition, the kind of thing that the physicists and the chemists can never do.
>
> To capture (*sorprendere*) the breath, the sensibility, and the instincts of metals, stones, wood, and so on, through the medium of free objects (*oggetti-in-libertà*) and whimsical motors. To substitute for human psychology, now exhausted, the lyric obsession with matter. ("Technical Manifesto" 87)

The passage lays out starkly the differences between literature and a new category, one obsessed with the possibilities opened by objects in freedom (translated unfortunately as "free objects" above) and a new mode of hearing sounds. Hearing for Marinetti is linked to isolated episodes of intuition in which these same objects in freedom are caught via a process he calls "to capture" (*sorprendere* in the original). The verb appears whenever Marinetti instructs his readers on how to engage the movement of objects and so we should be attentive to its meaning. Literally, *sorprendere* is defined simply as *prendere dal di sopra* (to take from above), which in turn has come to mean "to capture suddenly, especially when attempting something dishonest" (Cortelazzo 1232). The reference to Marinetti's vantage point high above Milan in a plane is clear enough, but it also points us in the direction of the kind of recording that Marinetti is at that moment himself practicing. Listening to the propeller, Marinetti captures its respiration, its sensibility and its instincts as he later puts it, not by a direct transposition of the sounds but rather through a process of *sorprendere*. What form this and the "strokes of intuition" (*colpi d'intuizione*) may take remains unclear, although he indicates that listening to objects in freedom and subsequently transposing them into writing will rid us of literature. Where before there was a rotten human psychology, now there will be a "lyrical obsession of material" (84).[8]

The relation between wireless simulation and Marinetti's literary experiments becomes clearer at this stage. Words in freedom register the sounds of objects in freedom, the nonhumanized matter of modern life deanchored from a human psychology. The term "words in freedom" first appears near the end of the "Technical Manifesto," though Marinetti has previously revealed its major components in paragraphs eight and nine:

8. There are no categories of images, noble or gross or vulgar, eccentric or natural. The intuition that grasps them has no preference or *partis pris*. Therefore the analogical style is absolute master of all matter and intense life.
9. To render the successive motions of an object, one must render the *chain of analogies* that it evokes, each condensed and concentrated into one essential word. (86, emphasis in original)

Marinetti sets up a duality between "categories of images" and "chains of analogies," two seemingly different registers with which intuition maintains a relationship. For its part, intuition both perceives the successive movements of an object in motion, and necessarily gives (*bisogna dare*) the chain of analogies that the object evokes. A previously encoded version of the real, a visual category with the reference to images, gives way before an auditory process based upon a calling forth (*evoca*) that is finalized in another symbolic encoding, more condensed and essential than its predecessor. Intuition dictates in both cases, but only in the latter does the registration more closely correspond to the real. In the widening space granted his words in freedom, Marinetti will draw upon the wireless to describe the mode of hearing and the writing he has in mind.

What are the principal features of these words? Fundamentally, words in freedom are tasked with carrying information in a world of moving objects that sound. This accounts for the sheer randomness that governs Futurist syntax, the dispersal of nouns as they arise, and Marinetti's strategy highlighted in the manifesto's opening paragraph: "One must destroy syntax and scatter one's nouns at random, just as they are born" (84). Along the same lines, Marinetti's instructions to the Futurist *in potentia* may be read as a command to write down the sounds that matter makes and to record the data flow of objects that sound. The possibility that the sounds never cease or that the data flow of objects in freedom and the medium of writing (not to mention poetry) may be incompatible are issues I will return to momentarily. Second, words in freedom are charged with marking sounds (typically in onomatopoeia). Where the *marconista* decodes the dots and dashes of Morse code in writing, however, Marinetti assumes something like a sonic-sphere in which objects continually sound. But the resemblance with the *marconista* is apropos: the task of the budding Futurist will be to turn himself into a writer/listener who, with some effort, hears not only the sounds these objects are making but will also render them symbolically on the page. The result is less a writer in the traditional sense than a body that writes down the endless sounds of endless movement.

Guiding Wires

Inserted between the sounds of modernity, the propellers and automobiles that dot the manifesto's landscape and the body that registers their movement is the wireless imagination (*immaginazione senza fili*). That the term still resonates today, eighty years after its introduction, testifies to Marinetti's extraordinary grasp of a publicist's vocabulary.[9] Unfortunately, the nebulous nature of the concept and the short space Marinetti devotes to it in a manifesto dedicated to technology and literature require that we proceed carefully. The reference to wireless imagination appears only once and then in no seeming relation to what follows:

> Together we will invent what I call the "imagination without strings" [*l'immaginazione senza fili*]. Someday we will achieve a yet more essential art, when we dare to suppress the first terms of our analogies and render no more than an uninterrupted sequence of second terms. To achieve this we must renounce being understood. It is not necessary to be understood. Moreover we

did without it when we were expressing fragments of the Futurist sensibility by means of traditional and intellective syntax. (89, emphasis in original)[10]

The formulation is odd, especially considering what we know of imagination and the wireless. On the one hand, introducing the wireless seems natural enough in a paragraph that concerns the more essential nature of accelerated transmissions. Indeed, in most early accounts of the wireless, the fantasy of weightless material is obsessively repeated: in often gripping fashion many Marconi biographies detail the birth of the wireless and how Marconi himself had done away with heavy matter.[11] The passage is keyed therefore not only by a distrust of wires but also by a fantasy of mental telepathy, in which the lack of wires signals a stronger connection. Put somewhat differently, wires weigh down lines of communication. Marinetti echoes these considerations in the manifesto, equating greater distance between analogies with more solid relationships between them:

> In this there is *an ever-vaster gradation of analogies*, there are ever-deeper and more solid affinities, however remote. Analogy is nothing more than the deep love that assembles distant, seemingly diverse and hostile things. An orchestral style, at once polychromatic, polyphonic, and polymorphous, can embrace the life of matter only by means of the most extensive analogies. (85, emphasis in original)

The greater the distance between signifiers, the more solid the resemblance. On the other hand, Marinetti is taking dictation from a propeller, the fragments of which appear in their traditional syntactic accoutrements. He repeatedly urges his readers to "introduce three elements into literature that have been neglected," the first of which is noise (*rumore*) (88). The difficulty, it would appear, lies in speaking of imagination in the same vein as dictation and the writing down of sounds. Two questions follow: who or what dictates to Marinetti when a wireless imagination is engaged in registering the sounds of modern life; and what would a nondictated and hence purely inspired cultural product of imagination look like?

For the answer, I want to turn to Marinetti's "Risposte alle obiezioni" ["Answers to Objections"], for there in his transformation into a proper *marconista* he displays the corporal changes that wireless writing enacts on its human component. In response to our first question on the origin of the transmission, Marinetti is uncertain; he hedges his bets by coupling the creative spirit with a lucid will:

> Every creative spirit can confirm during the work of creation that intuitive phenomena combine themselves with logical intelligence. It is therefore impossible to determine exactly the moment in which unconscious inspiration ends and lucid will begins. Every now and then this latter one suddenly generates the inspiration, other times rather it accompanies it. ("Risposte alle obiezioni" 56)[12]

Inspiration arises unconsciously with a marked lucidity or intuition produces a hallucination that is the first act of poetic production. Afterward, a pen marks down in words what imagination has produced. Such a formulation recalls poetry's role within a conception of the Romantic imagination. Writing of Romanticism and the discourse network of 1800, Friedrich Kittler equates imagination with poetry thus: "It is precisely the translation of other arts into a nonmaterial and universal medium that constitutes poetry. This medium is variously labeled fantasy or imagination. Imagination generically defines all the arts, but it specifically defines one highest art. Only poetry can claim 'the imagination itself, that universal foundation of all the particular art forms and the individual arts' as its proper material" (*Discourse Networks* 113).

On a first reading, poetry also claims Marinetti's notion of imagination as its proper material, for the manifestos never refer explicitly to writing as a medium. Marinetti joins the larger realm of the creative spirit, itself an unrecognized dictating machine of poetry, with intuition and wireless imagination. A century before, poetry was both the primary medium for imagination and the generator of flights of fancy. Essentially, Marinetti substitutes a previously hallucinating Romantic imagination with a creative spirit called a wireless one and so discloses the relationship of poetry and imagination that Kittler describes so acutely above. Indeed, with the introduction of the wireless imagination, Marinetti gestures toward a radically different form of literary production based on the dictation of objects in freedom to a writing hand. The premise is that poetry now transposes a propeller's sounds.

The consequences of reading Marinetti's wireless imagination as a dictating machine are significant. Most important, we may wish to reconsider enlisting Marinetti in the ranks of the denigrators of vision sketched by Martin Jay and others.[13] Those discussions fail to locate in a sustained and systematic way the cause of Marinetti's heightened auditory sensibility (and simultaneous downgrading of vision) in a simulation of wireless practices. Furthermore, they fail to see the connection between intuition and dictation and the implicit command of a wireless imagination to associate (condensed) words to perception. It isn't that Marinetti is somehow less visual or more auditory but rather that both the auditory and the visual are merely data flows in a system in which a wireless imagination (call it intuition or the creative spirit) dictates the sense perceptions of objects that sound in the real.[14]

Entropy and the Wireless Transmission

How exactly does a wireless imagination work? For all the fanfare surrounding it and the words in freedom in the "Technical Manifesto," Marinetti is short on details. Only in "Answers to Objections" do we discover that simulated wireless practices detach heads and limbs from the operator's body:

> After many painful and unrelenting hours of work, the creative spirit is suddenly free of the weight of all obstacles, and becomes, in some way, the prey of a strange spontaneity of conception and execution. The hand that writes seems to detach itself from the body and freely stretches itself from the brain, which, also in some way has been detached from the body, becoming air-borne. It looks down on the unexpected phrases that take leave of the pen with an awesome lucidity. (56)

The wireless uncouples the subroutines of writing by forcing the creative spirit, what Marinetti displaces metonymically with intuition or imagination, out into the open as a dictating, sense-registering machine. After several difficult hours of "unrelenting work," Marinetti's spirit tires of swimming against the current and moves in a more congenial direction, where it becomes prey to a strangely spontaneous combination of conception and execution. A relation emerges between the writing hand cut off from a controlling consciousness, a detached brain armed with visual recognition capacities ("looks down . . . from above with an awesome lucidity"), and an unmentioned third term, the missing, dictating wireless imagination.

The suggestion of a circuitous relation points us in the direction of the second law of thermodynamics for an explanation of how a simulated wireless works. The law states that in any interaction in which energy is exchanged, the amount of thermal energy convertible to mechanical energy is diminished. In such interactions, entropy—a measure of unusable energy—increases.[15] In other words, when you do a job, a part of the energy is expended as loss or entropy. In the 1950s, a number of theorists, most notably Claude E. Shannon, extended entropy from its thermodynamic manifestation to what we know today as modern information theory. In Shannon's classic definition, entropy measures "how much information may be communicated and with what degree of fidelity, within certain constraints such as the amount of energy available in the communications system and the strength of any intrusive undesired signal (noise)" (Schachterle 190).

One of the first to recognize the importance of Shannon's work was Jacques Lacan. Writing within the context of Freud's pleasure principle, he makes clear the connection between entropy and the machine.

> Mathematicians qualified to handle these symbols locate information as that which moves in the opposite direction to entropy. When people had become acquainted with thermodynamics, and asked themselves how their machine was going to pay for itself, they left themselves out. They regarded the machine as the master regards the slave—the machine is there, somewhere else, and it works. They were forgetting only one thing, that it was they who had signed the order form. (83)

Of course, no textual justification exists for labeling Marinetti as the unconscious master of the machine described by Lacan; if anything, the manifestos continually celebrate signing off on the order form. For instance, consider the following from another Futurist manifesto: "Hence we must prepare for the imminent, inevitable identification of man with motor, facilitating and perfecting a constant interchange of intuition, rhythm, instinct, and metallic discipline of which the majority are wholly ignorant, which is guessed at by the most lucid spirits" (Marinetti, "Multiplied Man" 91). In the ever-shortening distance between man and machine, the wireless serves as a means for facilitating the incessant exchange of intuition and rhythm between man and motor (aeroplane, automobile) that is finalized in the "inevitable identification" of both.[16] Framed against the backdrop of identification, Marinetti's wireless imagination registers real sounds and then translates them into their phonemic, alphabetic equivalencies. After he begins simulating a wireless receiver in his brain, there will be another source of information concerning the transmission standards of the human.

But let's return to entropy and the wireless. Once we recognize the circuit between the machine and its user, we immediately find ourselves in the realm of energy.

> Now, this fact turns out to have a considerable importance in the domain of energy. Because if information is introduced into the circuit of the degradation

of energy, it can perform miracles. If Maxwell's demon can stop the atoms which move too slowly, and keep only those which have a tendency to be a little on the frantic side, he will cause the general level of the energy to rise again, and will do, using what would have degraded into heat, work equivalent to that which would have been lost. (Lacan 83)

The passage requires elaboration. Where a circuit runs between machine and user, it will by necessity show a degradation of energy, a loss, what Lacan via Shannon calls entropy. If it is somehow possible to introduce information into the circuit, information understood as that which makes a difference (Lacan offers the classic example of Maxwell's demon able to stop slower atoms from moving), the energy level rises because what would have been lost previously due to entropy (heat) has now been converted into work.[17] Something similar happens in the "Technical Manifesto," where the wireless inserts itself in the circuit between man and machine, specifically the transmitting propeller, and introduces a singular kind of information; namely, that intuition or the creative spirit can take dictation over long distances when a certain speed is maintained between a writing hand and a recently transformed wireless imagination. An accelerated transmission between hand and imagination converts energy previously lost into words in freedom, information for short. Yet information ought not to be confused with meaning—that is, the difference between what one could say and what one does say; instead, it measures "one's freedom of choice when one selects a message. The greater the entropy, the greater the freedom of choice and the greater the overall information that may be communicated" (Weaver 8).

It is difficult to underestimate the importance of this piece of information for a history of the wireless. Words in freedom—the condensed output of the *marconista* that registers objects in freedom—results from the introduction of information that limits (or extends, depending on one's point of view) what is experienced and written down to associations that can keep up with the infernal wireless command to exchange, incessantly, sense perceptions for their scripted form. A tentative history of the wireless and Marinetti's role therein will view the manifestos and more particularly words in freedom as exhibits of entropy and then show how the various descriptors associated with Marinetti's poetic output (nihilistic, antagonistic, unreadable) are conditioned primarily by a forgetting of technical media, in this case the wireless and the role they play in the emergence of words in freedom.

Twenty-First Century Wireless Writing

I opened this essay by noting the pivotal role Marinetti and the Futurists play in twentieth-century histories of sound. As important as those contributions are, a closer examination of the intricacies of Marinetti's interaction with wireless telegraphy suggests that we reconsider enlisting Marinetti among the modern aficionados of sound. For Marinetti, the acoustic and visual properties of objects matter only to the degree he can associate them symbolically in writing. To do so, however, he transforms himself into a species of *marconista* circa 1912, simulating the effects of wireless technology on his own body, and in the process inventing a wireless imagination and words in freedom. Like that of the period's other wireless operators, Marinetti's technological virtuosity will be measured in the number and arrangement of words captured on paper.[18] In the process, the manifestos provide us with technological standards for writing and more specifically poetry, toward the establishment of recording thresholds for capturing the sights and sounds of objects that move.

Reading Marinetti as *marconista* and the Futurist manifestos as primers on wireless practices has a number of important implications. First, by placing the wireless at the heart of Futurist poetic production, we move beyond the limited perspective that inscribes the wireless as simply one more theme in a constellation of modern themes in the manifestos. Instead, we will want to ask how the manifestos make manifest (if I may be allowed the pun) modalities of wireless communication. Second, we will want to ask what other figures of heroic Modernism articulate similar perspectives on the wireless and writing. Here in particular I have in mind Ezra Pound (and to a lesser extent Wyndham Lewis), especially the procedure Pound uses in Cantos XVIII and XIX of registering symbolically the voices of the dead and living as if they were simply overheard or transmitted badly. Enrolling Pound as a later *marconista* might better account for the oft-noted affinities between Futurism, Imagism, and Pound's production, circumventing the anxious idea of influence, under which Pound himself suffered vis-à-vis the Futurists. Finally, by returning our attention to the details of wireless invention as they play out in the manifestos, we may in fact be better able to locate our own present moment of wireless connectivity and how it mirrors an earlier wireless age. One wonders how, for instance, recent textual forms, be they the traditionally print-based or digital, account for, reproduce, and narrate the increasing role of wireless technology in the present media ecology. How is the heightened connectivity of wireless media made contingent on culture and the symbolic order that precedes it? A number of contemporary artists are exploring these questions in their works, providing the coordinates for a future mapping of wireless media.[19] Reading Marinetti in conjunction with their imagined responses, we can perhaps begin to make out the figure of the contemporary *marconista*.

Notes

1. See in this regard Helleman and Blum. For my use of the term "media ecology," see Johnston, "Mediality" and "Friedrich Kittler."

2. Campbell, *Wireless Writing in the Age of Marconi*.

3. Margaret Fisher's recent examination of Ezra Pound and Marinetti is the exception.

4. The history of wireless invention remains contested. Some, notably Friedrich Kittler, insist on the role of Adolf Slaby, while others, including Margaret Cheney, award Nikola Tesla the distinction of having first transmitted wirelessly; still others argue for British scientist David Edward Hughes. Thus, writing in February 1901, Tesla claimed to have invented his own system of telegraphy without wires as early as 1893, two years before Marconi. Hughes, for his part, had apparently constructed a portable wireless transmitter in London as early as 1879, almost a decade before the discovery of Hertzian waves. Without rehearsing the various claims to the wireless mantle here, what seems clear is that a number of figures contributed decisively to the emergence of the wireless before Marconi: Heinrich Hertz's monumental discovery in 1888 that sparks could be employed to generate electromagnetic waves (soon known as Hertzian waves); Edouard Branly's experiments in 1890 demonstrating the effects of electric charges on metal filings in test tubes; Oliver Lodge's proof that Branly's tube could detect Hertzian waves; and Hughes, Tesla, and Slaby. All of which is to say that Marconi was not the first to transmit wirelessly. Crucially, however, Marconi did extend the range of the wireless transmission well beyond his predecessors, transmitting wirelessly across the Atlantic in 1901, while perhaps more importantly successfully marketing his wireless to British scientific authorities. See Weightman, especially 93–99, from which I have drawn here. For Slaby's claims, see Kittler, *Gramophone* 94–96. Margaret Cheney presents her case for Tesla in *Nikola Tesla: Man Out of Time*. For general histories of wireless invention, Aitken offers the best account of the wireless and the scientific research that preceded its development. More recently, Hong brilliantly reads the specifications of early wireless technology and individual contributions.

5. Unless otherwise indicated, all translations are my own.

6. The seminal account of the cyborg is of course Haraway's "A Cyborg Manifesto." For a recent compelling reading of the cyborg and immunity, see Roberto Esposito, *Immunitas*.

7. Cf. Russolo's "The Art of Noise (Futurist Manifesto 1913)": "Let's walk together

through a great modern capital, with the ear more attentive than the eye, and we will vary the pleasures of our sensibilities by distinguishing among the gurglings of water, air and gas inside metallic pipes. The rumblings and rattlings of engines breathing with obvious animal spirits, the rising and falling of pistons, the stridency of mechanical saws, the loud jumping of trolleys on their rails, the snapping of whips, the whipping of flags" (7–8).

8. It is of course tempting to read Marinetti's conclusion as either a conceit or more Futurist posturing. Should we take him at his word, however, then his lyrical obsession with matter would demonstrate that with the growth of wireless media, knowledge, aesthetics, and literature count for less. "Be careful not to force human feelings onto matter," he writes on the next page. In its place, information comes to the fore as that which makes a difference, information about matter, "its different governing impulses, its forces of compression, dilation, cohesion, and disaggregation, its crowds of massed molecules and whirling electrons" (87). Marinetti has no need of literature as it fails to record adequately the movements of matter.

9. See Salaris and Rainey's discussion of futurist publishing.

10. The English translation of *l'immaginazione senza fili* as "the imagination without strings" is unfortunate as it obscures the invocation of Marconi's *telegrafia senza fili*. For this reason, I have chosen to refer to the term as "wireless imagination."

11. Consider this description of Marconi's first wireless transmission: "And at that moment a rifle shot reverberates beyond the celestial hills, extending to the Reno Valley. The young hero seemed to say, 'Away with wires, away with heavy matter; all I need is the electric pulse for transmitting what is in the head and heart.' Marconi cries out: 'The wave went through, it went through, Mother, Father!' And he throws himself to his knees in an irresistible impulse of gratitude to the Supreme Author of all things" (Landini 22).

12. Arguably more significant than even the "Technical Manifesto" itself, this rejoinder has yet to be translated into English. All translations of the "Risposte" are thus my own.

13. See Jay, *Downcast Eyes*; for a survey of Italian commentary, compare Contini, *Letteratura* 666–68 and "Innovazioni"; Mengaldo, *Il Novecento* 206–10; Binni, *La poetica del decadentismo italiano*; and Bo, "La nuova poesia." A useful summary of Futurist commentators may be found in "Futurismo."

14. Jeffrey T. Schnapp offers a reading of visual perception in the manifesto, framed by the impact of aviation on the collective imagination: "It is under the aegis of this mechanized human type . . . that I now wish to turn away from the 1912 manifesto's musings on the transfiguration of matter towards what was earlier defined as their visual counterpart, a *poetics of image-streams* (emphasis mine) associated with aviation's impact on the faculty of sight" (165–66). He goes on to examine "networks of perceptual and/or intuitive strings" envisaged by flight plans and wireless telegrams, but never makes explicit the nature of the wireless medium that successfully picks up the propeller's transmission (165).

15. See Lance Schachterle's essay on Thomas Pynchon for a succinct history of the term; I am indebted to him for the following section.

16. At this point, it only seems fair to recall Marshall McLuhan's insight into the workings of media, which the wireless and its inflected writing continue to confirm: "For each of the media is also a powerful weapon with which to clobber other media and other groups. The result is that the present age has been one of multiple civil wars that are not limited to the world of art and entertainment" (McLuhan, *Understanding* 20–21).

17. One of the best histories of Maxwell's demon is Clarke; see too Goldman; Hayles, *Chaos Bound*, especially chapter 2; and Levine.

18. Twenty years later in "La radia," Marinetti continues to maintain this critical stance, arguing that radio should return to its wireless origins, mimicking his own registration of sounds into writing. In such a scenario the distinction between living beings and matter collapses: "4 The reception amplification and transfiguration of vibrations emitted by living beings living or dead spirits of dramas of wordless noise-states 5 The reception amplification and transfiguration of vibrations emitted by matter Just as today we listen to the song of the forest and the sea so tomorrow shall we be seduced by the vibrations of a diamond or flower" (Marinetti, "La radia" 267).

19. Janet Cardiff's recent exhibit at the Castello di Rivoli in Turin deeply engages a wireless sonority (Janet Cardiff, *A Survey of Works Including Collaborations with George Bures Miller*, Turin, Italy, May 21–August 31, 2003). See too media artist Paul DeMarinis's recent explorations of the implications of twentieth- and twenty-first-century wireless voice transmissions. A sampling may be found at http://www.well.com/~demarini/.installations.html.

[CHAPTER 4]

"Masters of Sacred Ceremonies"

Welles, Corwin, and a Radiogenic Modernist Literature

MARTIN SPINELLI

> It is a theater which eliminates the author in favor of what we would call, in our Occidental theatrical jargon, the director; but a director who has become a kind of manager of magic, a master of sacred ceremonies. And the material on which he works, the themes he brings to throbbing life are derived not from him but from the gods. They come, it seems, from elemental interconnections of Nature which a double Spirit has fostered.
> What he sets in motion is the MANIFESTED.
> —Antonin Artaud

8 May 2005 marked the sixtieth anniversary of what is probably the second most famous broadcast in the history of American radio, Norman Corwin's *On a Note of Triumph*, commissioned for and broadcast on VE (Victory in Europe) Day. Various commemorative events were planned, including an inevitable "re-creation." When the public radio producer with the rights to produce that re-creation asked me for advice on how to approach his project I suggested that the literal restaging of the original script which he had in mind might not be the best route. I proposed instead a program that grappled with some of the loose themes and modes of expressions in the original (the costs of war, the debate between intervention and isolation, the

aestheticization/anti-aestheticization of conflict, etc.) in a more contemporary setting, perhaps even utilizing the current war for source material. After a moment's hesitation he assured me that his production was going to be completely "modern" (using the latest digital recording tools, working with computer music, etc.) but that his desire was to be as faithful as possible to the original script. There is a difference, however, between restaging a radio script and re-creating a broadcast event: the former defines radio as a material product, a document or a recording while the latter describes radio as a synthesis among producers, broadcast institutions, and audiences, in short, as a relationship.[1]

The single most famous broadcast in the history of American radio, the 1938 CBS/Orson Welles/Mercury Theatre on the Air production of *War of the Worlds*, is famous precisely because it activated (or stumbled onto) a new manifestation of the radio relationship. Because of my emphasis on the radio relationship, literary-radio theoretical models with roots in theatrical/dramatic scholarship are often more helpful than those with roots in poetics. To that end, this essay occasionally uses Artaud's aborted broadcast of *Having Done with the Judgment of God* and his earlier investigations into the Theater of Cruelty as points of reference. Reading the achievements and the shortcomings of Artaud's work in the context of the other two broadcasts—particularly his uses of glossolalia and aggressively abstract voice/language play organized under his larger project of engendering a psychological catharsis in his audience—assists my claim that innovation in this relationship is the distinguishing feature of a radiogenic Modernist literature rather than solely an experimental formal quality at the level of word or sound.[2]

While previous studies of *War of the Worlds* have been successful in describing the extent of the panic and the nature of the response in particular individuals, no sustained attempts have been made to describe the causes of those effects in Modernist, or even in simply "literary," terms. The situation is similar with *On a Note of Triumph*. Reviews in the immediate wake of the broadcast and Corwin biographies decades later have settled for describing it as a moving social statement or a historic monument to be cherished. This essay attempts to redress the balance by offering for the first time sustained and thorough close readings/listenings of each of these broadcasts, and by doing so in Modernist literary and theatrical terms. But while Artaud's Theater of Cruelty is used as a template for analyzing and delineating much of the Modernist character and appeal of these other two broadcasts, the circuit of appreciation is reciprocal: the studies of the accomplishments of *War of the*

Worlds and *On a Note of Triumph* suggest explanations for Artaud's limited success (on both radio and the stage) in mobilizing in his audiences the shock, catharsis, and transformation described as his explicit goal in his essays and letters. While each of these three broadcasts takes a different mode of audience address, has a different approach to the vernacular, and makes use of different radio framing strategies, their combined study illuminates a Modernist radiophony in which a participatory relationship is central.

Artaud's November 1947 radio piece, *Having Done with the Judgment of God*, is emblematic of so much of his work: it was innovative at the level of language and pure sound, a Modernist reinvention of primitive ritual, a material witness to the cruelty of early twentieth-century asylums, and above all a *cri* (scream) aspiring to Modernist subjectivity. It was also canceled the day before it was scheduled to be broadcast because it was deemed too anti-Catholic and anti-American for the listening public, given only a private audition at a theater in February 1948, and only broadcast on French radio a quarter century later.[3] In short, it was a theoretical triumph but a theatrical failure. While this cannot be said of the other broadcasts, Artaud's work here is particularly useful in beginning to articulate specific facets of radiogenic Modernist literature's relationship to and transformative effect on its audience. Further, his clearly stated means to that end—the ritual use of language beyond or before meaning and the voice's ability to defamiliarize language—are the beginnings of a serviceable taxonomy for describing the more recognizably Modernist turns in other broadcasts.

War of the Worlds

War of the Worlds begins, traditionally enough, with an unadorned announcement that the "Columbia Broadcasting system and its affiliated stations present Orson Welles and the Mercury Radio Theatre on the Air in *The War of The Worlds* by H. G. Wells" (00:01).[4] Welles was then introduced as the star, and by 00:40 he had begun narrating what could have been a very straightforward retelling of the Wells story, then forty years old: "We know now that in the early years of the twentieth century this world was being watched closely by intelligences greater than man yet as mortal as his own." While under the microscope, humanity scurried about its business unaware; at this point Welles's voice gives only the slightest indication of foreshadowing that within this very mundane nature of bourgeois humanity lies its downfall. This scene of placid American life takes its first interesting turn at

02:08 when "on this particular October thirtieth" "business was better, the war scare was over, sales were picking up" and "the Crossley service estimated that thirty-two million people were listening in on radio." Present in this picture of complacency—so often the expressed target of Modernist assaults—is the scene of listening to the radio. Here the formal frame of Welles narrating a story recedes, a radio announcer's voice is faded up, and listeners entered the play-within-the-play (the radio-program-within-the-radio-program).

The mention of the "Crossley service" is interesting in that it foregrounds for a moment the frame and squarely locates the listener of the Mercury Theatre's broadcast within the narrative: thirty-two million people were listening to their radios one October 30th, which is exactly the situation of the audience of the Mercury broadcast. In Borgesian fashion, the listener is in the story (and also identified with the very "normal" listening public presented). But this device also offers two oppositional modes of listening: the listener is invited to project him- or herself from a detached and objective position outside the frame to a more experiential position within it—from witnessing the ritual to participating in it. Alternatively, the listener has been reminded of the situation of listening to the radio and all of the semantic work that he or she does regularly in that situation to complete the circuit of radio meaning. The choice is between immersion and self-conscious reflexivity. In either case, what is momentarily brought to the fore is the experience of listening to the radio; it is a story about the radio relationship. The audience within the narrative is there throughout the whole of the play, a silent character witnessing its own destruction with no lines but seated just in front of the ears of the Mercury broadcast listeners.

The stage thus set, listeners are met with a weather report stating that "a slight atmospheric disturbance of undetermined origin is reported over Nova Scotia" (2:27). The announcer then hands off to the Meridian Room in the Hotel Park Plaza where listeners are to be entertained by Ramón Raquello and his orchestra, and after several seconds of music the announcer returns to introduce properly the orchestra and song. Several seconds later (3:43), the first "special bulletin" is aired from "the Intercontinental Radio News" which reports several explosions observed on the surface of Mars having happened some minutes ago and plumes of hydrogen gas moving toward Earth with great velocity. The trope of the special bulletin is extremely important in context. While relatively new in the evolution of radio news, it was becoming a more regular feature: a month earlier America seemed on the cusp of war with Germany in the wake of the Munich Crisis. Hitler's demanding of

Britain and France that Germany be allowed to annex a part of Czechoslovakia caused numerous interruptions to regular programs (Blue 8–9).[5]

After more music, a connection is made with a mobile unit interviewing Professor Richard Pierson of the Princeton Observatory (Welles's second role) for his assessment of the explosions on Mars (06:12). True to the radio journalism style of the day, the reporter, Carl Phillips, describes the scene in the observatory and overplays the tension, saying that Pierson may be interrupted during the interview as he is "in constant communication with the astronomical centers of the world." Pierson dismisses the predisposition toward alarm and explicitly chides the popular belief in life on Mars, saying "the chances against it are a thousand to one." The voice of authority, a staple of radio news and information programming then and now, is here invoked to calm fears and allay anxiety.[6] An examination of the use of this voice of authority provides insight into the Mercury Theatre's degree of sophistication in understanding the radio relationship. *War of the Worlds* anticipates its audience's complex appreciation of radio semantics; in fact, it anticipates an oppositional reading: when voices of authority go through the trouble of trying to allay fears and discourage speculation there is often good reason for concern. Calming thus invokes its opposite, panic. This structure coincides with another recognizable radio trope: the reporter's role in overdramatizing an event (which might indeed be a nonevent even within the frame of the narrative) to keep listeners tuned in. When these two apparently competing structures collide, the audience, capable of reading each quite well, is left in a state of uncertainty. It is this kind of uncertainty that traditionally draws in a listener and instigates a heightened engagement with a radio program, a curiosity about what is going on that might allow a listener to the Mercury broadcast to slip into the frame and become the more vulnerable listener within the narrative.

At this moment, outside the frame, on another network, something relevant was happening. On NBC, the first segment of *The Edgar Bergen-Charlie McCarthy Show* (the popular ventriloquist show and most listened-to program on radio that year) featuring the dummy Charlie was coming to a close, and some light singing was being offered; listeners spun their dials to see what else was available. Hadley Cantril's study estimates that 12 percent of McCarthy's audience moved over to the *War of the Worlds* broadcast.[7]

Without the benefits of the initial framing and the initial announcement that the broadcast was a dramatization, the likelihood of being taken in by it becomes a degree more possible. The Mercury Theatre accessed this reality by pirating a vernacular, by utilizing, in a completely blank way, existing and familiar radio semantic structures. This is language gaming not with the intrinsic value of words but with larger linguistic/meaning systems. Some reviewers, however, chose to locate the cause of the panic not in the verisimilitude of the broadcast-within-the-broadcast but in a defect in the audience. Writing three days after the event in her *New York Tribune* column, Dorothy Thompson takes issue with the specific argument of deception-by-dial-surfing: the dramatization was not "in the least bit credible, no matter at what point the hearer might have tuned in" (qtd. in Koch 92). Thompson says that Welles and the Mercury Theatre are not to be blamed; their project was so masterfully enacted that they should be awarded medals for exposing "the incredible stupidity, lack of nerve and ignorance of thousands," for demonstrating that Americans are no more immune to radio propaganda than Germans, and for exposing an undue faith in the credibility of radio news.

More charitably than Thompson, I chose to locate the achievement of *War of the Worlds* in the broadcast's understanding and appropriation of radio vernacular and the context of the given radio listening experience. Radio was an unimpeachable vehicle for important announcements; the reworking of that expectation in a piece of radio literature constitutes the success of *War of the Worlds* as a piece of Theater of Cruelty and the numbers collected by Cantril describe the extent of that accomplishment. Between four and nine million people heard the broadcast—Cantril places the figure at six million—with at least one million of them having been in some way disturbed by it (47–56).[8] A qualitative assessment of the specific responses describes individuals reporting hearing news of the invasion on other stations, some being literally sick in bed for days after the broadcast (Cantril 50–51), and even an attempted suicide (Koch 23).

Dance music, at this point in the broadcast, is offered from various metropolitan hotels, interrupted by reports confirming explosions on Mars and then a meteorite landing on a farm in Grovers Mill, New Jersey. Phillips the reporter says it took him and Pierson ten minutes to make the journey from Princeton (11:09), but less than two minutes of listening time have elapsed since they were last heard at the observatory. As Phillips provides "a word picture of the scene," it is interesting to note that the relatively poor (by today's standards) quality of the radio and recording equipment of the time makes the scene changes from indoor to outdoor seem less artificial and more plausible. The resistance in the technology of the era, the noise and the nontransparency, makes this part of the broadcast more believable. Information occluded or lost in transmission is then filled in by the listener and arguably heightens the experience of the radio relationship.

At this point, another instantiation of the radio relationship is acted out in the broadcast itself. The farmer in whose field the meteorite landed, Mr. Wilmuth, says that he was listening to the radio "and that professor fella was talkin' about Mars" when he was interrupted by the meteor (12:49). While he is saying that he was "half dozin'" and only "listenin' t' the radio kinda half-way," Phillips (as any good radio journalist would) urges him to get to the point and tell us what he saw; Wilmuth says he did not see anything, but he heard something, a hissing which he then recreates for the microphone. Wilmuth is then interrupted as listeners are enjoined to hear the hum emanating from the meteorite-cylinder. Wilmuth the ear-witness to the dramatic event is less significant than Wilmuth the surrogate listener: he is both listener in the play (listening to the radio about events on Mars) and also the listener to the Mercury Theatre's radio program. The Mercury Theatre's picture of their imagined audience is not at all flattering: Wilmuth does not know how to speak to a microphone and has to be coached; he was listening to the radio half asleep and is perhaps dreaming the nightmarish events occurring; he hems and haws and has to be somewhat rudely interrupted by Phillips for more pressing matters. He is not "media savvy" in any sense, and it is precisely a lack of savviness that caused the distress in the wake of the broadcast. The "average listener" presented here in Wilmuth is a reminder of the frame, of the broadcast-within-the-broadcast, but is also the target for the Mercury Theatre. This is not a person given respect or worthy of admiration; it is instead a person in need of an epiphany yet incapable of an epiphany on his or her own. The broadcast might even be read as intended for two audiences simultaneously: the audience of real Wilmuths who will be fooled, and an audience of cognoscenti for whom the audience of real Wilmuths is part of the entertainment.

At this point in the broadcast-within-the-broadcast (15:30) the limits of plausibility (even within its historical context) are tested. After Pierson describes the metal of the cylinder as "extra-terrestrial," one end of it unscrews and Phillips describes a black Martian as large as a bear, with tentacles for arms and a V-shaped mouth complete with dripping saliva. Yet at this moment of high fantasy, judicious efforts to maintain the frame are undertaken: as listeners had come to expect, the covering of live news events is often fraught with technical difficulties, and for Phillips to get a better view of the

Martian he has to make some equipment changes and unplug his microphone. After half a minute of the regularly scheduled music program, the broadcast returns to Phillips, who asks if he is "on" and sounds a bit flustered. Death and destruction due to the Martian heat ray soon follow. Phillips's last words are "It's coming this way now. It's about twenty yards to my right"; his last word is truncated and then there is complete silence. After a few seconds, an announcer matter-of-factly apologizes: "Due to circumstances beyond our control we are unable to continue the broadcast from Grovers Mill" (18:39) and listeners are once again returned to the continuing music program. In short order, another scientist dismisses any connection between the explosions on Mars and the events at Grovers Mill; the explosions, he says, are just random volcanic activity. While the scientific community, the government (23:40), and CBS (at 23:20 it turns over its airwaves to the state militia "to serve in the public interest") are asserting their impossible control over the escalating situation, the listeners (the silent ones inside the broadcast-within-the-broadcast and their doubles immersed in the Mercury Theatre's production) again cannot help but feel the panic implied in the appeals for calm. After listeners learn that the Martians have temporarily retreated into their crater, CBS reestablishes contact with the mobile unit on the scene and with Pierson "by direct wire." As with Wilmuth previously, in an effort to reassert plausibility listeners hear amateurish feedback and microphone handling noise as Pierson, presumably on his own, picks up the story from the scene with some scientific conjecture about the heat ray. Soon the cylinders start to walk, a national emergency is declared, the Martians use poisonous gas, communication lines are cut, more cylinders land, and the broadcast starts to resemble a more conventional radio drama. While the pretense of "special wires" is evoked again at 32:33 to maintain a semblance of the original frame, the transitions from scene to scene feel more like filmic cuts than they do like journalistic handoffs (far more elaborate rituals in 1938 than today).

By 34:32 the broadcast seems to be originating from "Langham Field" (evoking the real "Langley" airfield) rather than studios in New York, and the audience is eavesdropping on various communications between bases and pilots without any real fixed focal point; amid vague reports of carnage and black gas, the audience loses contact with them almost as quickly as their voices appear. There is, at this point, only the residue of a frame remaining and the audience is (or so it is expected) completely immersed in the narrative. At 36:32 the drama returns to "Broadcasting House" in New York

City where a radio announcer atop the roof describes bells pealing to warn people to evacuate and recounts the destruction of the army. As he reads a bulletin about cylinders falling all over the country, he says, "This may be the last broadcast," and distant sound effects fill the brief silence until the audience hears him collapse. Then (40:15) a pilot's voice, appropriately filtered to sound like air traffic communication, says these last lines before a long silence: "2X2L calling CQ New York. Isn't there anyone on the air? Isn't there anyone on the air? Isn't there anyone? 2X2L . . ."

It is as if radio itself is reflexively broken: it cannot communicate, it cannot help, it cannot save (even itself); it has been reduced to one slightly anxious voice out in the ether. Radio is here a cry out to an audience expecting a good story, but that desire for an immersive experience in a good story is made the target of the broadcast's cruel hoax. It is as if *War of the Worlds* has negotiated a way out of the paradox of all representation, the conundrum of the spectacle: typically the more complete the spectacle, the less opportunity for imaginative engagement, while the greater the opportunity for imaginative engagement, the less complete the spectacle. In practice, *War of the Worlds* constructs a nearly perfect spectacle to fuel imaginative engagement and its real world dramatic momentum; it requires that a spectacle be generated only to critique engagement with the spectacle. Therein lies its cruelty. The absorption so expertly cultivated in *War of the Worlds* is then exposed as problematic, as empty, and even dangerous; an audience sits and listens as its world is destroyed and then is sent screaming and "rending garments" out into the streets by its faith in traditional radio language.[9]

At 40:45 a new announcer, wholly outside of the story, reminds anyone in doubt that, "You are listening to a CBS presentation of Orson Welles and the Mercury Theatre on the Air in an original dramatization of *The War of the Worlds* by H. G. Wells." After an intermission, listeners are again reminded that they are listening to a dramatization, the music swells ominously and the story picks up with Pierson describing his encounters and travails in his diary (occasionally in a more poetic than vernacular style)[10] before the Martians are wiped out by naturally occurring invisible microbes. Listeners hear his encounters with characters, and the music is no longer the music of a faux dance orchestra but the emotive bridges familiar to radio drama; the original frame is gone and what remains is a relatively traditional radio play. But it is the frame to which we should return to expand our understanding of Modernist radiogenic literature.

Its success is due largely to the unique communicative characteristics radio offers to literature. In other (primarily visual) media, a 1930s audience would have always been struck by the material presence of the communication apparatus: they would have chosen to sit in a seat in a cinema, opened a particular book, or put on a record; and with these actions and the given scenes of consumption in mind it would have been impossible to completely forget the media/literary frames of these experiences, no matter how absorbing the story. On radio, however, the frame can more readily be forgotten or even missed entirely. As is obvious here: the narrative frame is an audience listening to the radio on a particular day, identical to the experience of the actual intended audience.

In the end, it was this frame, this play-within-a-play structure, which proved most threatening to institutional power. In perhaps the truest testament to the program's assault on conventionality, its literary device was perceived almost instantly as a danger to civil authority and control: commentators' and politicians' ire and attention were focused precisely on the appropriate framing of different radio genres of communication and the demonstrated ability of literature to disrupt those distinctions—news was to sound like recognizable news and drama was supposed to sound like recognizable drama. In the wake of the broadcast, for example, CBS banned the use of the play-within-the-play device from all its future radio dramas. The *New York World Telegram* called on all stations to demarcate news and fiction clearly, effectively cordoning off drama to prevent this disruptive radio moment from ever happening again (Koch 94, 17). For perhaps the first time in American history the intelligentsia were calling for legislation to ban a particular literary device: Heywood Broun, in his *Variety* column of November 2, felt that modes or registers of listening should not be tampered with, saying that the sanctity of radio forms and listeners' assumptions about them "should not be disturbed even for innocuous or comic effect" (Koch 91). After its own review of the script and the broadcast recording, the FCC mandated that all fictionalized news within radio drama be preceded by a special disclaimer, and in response to these concerns the networks made sure that nothing of the kind was ever repeated and dramatizations of news broadcasts were expressly forbidden.[11]

On a Note of Triumph

Artaud asked many things of the theater, including that it "bring to all of us a natural occult equivalent of the dogma in which we no longer believe"

(*Artaud on Theatre* 131). In radio he might have found an ideal medium for his ritual without religion as it (and the ear before it) had a perceived connection to the supernatural.[12] However, his proposed incantations required a degree of initial participation on the part of his audience, which he had difficulty realizing due in part to his resistance to familiar semantic structures and vernacular language. Yet the participation hoped for by Artaud and the audience's role in semantic work are at times so profound for him that through them a kind of "magic identification is made: WE KNOW IT IS WE WHO ARE SPEAKING" (67).

This magic identification, this realization of the "we who are speaking," has been regarded as the most striking achievement of *On a Note of Triumph*. In the broadcast, Corwin uses language that strikes a balance between representation and innovation often organized in the nonstructures familiar to stream-of-consciousness writing. From his start at CBS in 1938, Corwin had been cultivating a characteristic style through the *Columbia Workshop* and other venues open to experiment. His efforts to develop a literary form unique to (popular) radio were generally supported by CBS, and in 1939 he was the sole respondent to a CBS memo challenging its writers to produce material designed to make its audience more "radio conscious" (Bannerman 44–45). Corwin's resulting piece, *Seems Radio Is Here to Stay*, was introduced by the announcer as "an original verse brochure" and explores numerous radiogenic tropes and devices: radio as a simultaneously individual and collective experience—"You wonder at the pronoun *we?*"; the expressive sounds of the technology of radio itself—oscillators varying pitch and rhythmic pattern; the serendipitous quality of radio programming—"Were you expecting us?"; radio's time shifting omnipresence—"good evening or good afternoon, good morning or good night"; the disembodied voice in narrators' self-consciously but inexplicably disappearing and being replaced by new narrators; recording's uncanny ability to reanimate the voices of the dead; and above all (and most important as a precursor for *On a Note of Triumph*) radio's technological ability (embodied in Corwin's metonymic trope of "the microphone") to transport a listener across space and time instantly to any destination.[13]

Corwin's best-known pieces were hybrid in genre and often described as drama with "a brisk documentary mode of expression" (Bannerman 7). More than thirty million people—more than half the country's population— heard his sesquicentennial anniversary hybrid program on the Bill of Rights, *We Hold These Truths*, which coincided with the start of the war. On the morning of May 8, 1945, President Truman announced the end of the war in Europe to the largest single radio audience ever then recorded, and *On a Note of Triumph* was first broadcast that evening.[14] The listening figures are important for two reasons: first, they complicate the familiar narrative of Modernism's occasional feud with populist or "mass" culture (Corwin's work demonstrates that their was a large and receptive audience for radio literature with a significant degree of formally innovative material and unfamiliar semantic turns); and second, the possibilities for toying with the relational network of radio are greater with a larger audience.

If the Mercury Theatre belittled its audience through the figure of Wilmuth, Corwin exalts his audience from the first lines by invoking and cultivating a myth of the heroic American Everyman and inviting identification with him: "Take a bow, little guy. / The superman of tomorrow lies at the feet of you common men of this afternoon" (00:33).[15] The narrator's repeated address to "you" floats throughout the broadcast from being directed at the soldiers, to being directed at the 1945 listener, to being directed at some future audience or beneficiary of this particular moment in history.[16] Shortly, this proposed "you" begins to take on international dimensions as the focal point of the broadcast ranges across the world. A sense of a collective project builds momentum as attention travels from America to Poland to Greece to Scandinavia, stopping at places that sound intentionally "foreign" to an American ear (and difficult for an American mouth to pronounce) like "Dnepropertrovsk." At 8:20, as the narrator Martin Gabel details the celebrations happening in parks in the urban centers of the United States and Europe, the multilingual names of those parks run together to create the impression of one single polyglot location for the festivities. The effect is both to locate the audience in a global scene or consciousness and to mobilize in them a global imagination.

While international accents and vernaculars often accompany this movement from place to place, American vernaculars are regularly deployed as a counterbalance to Gabel's stentorian and commanding oration. At 3:30 his somewhat fustian tone is unexpectedly deflated by the folk song "Round and Round Hitler's Grave." At first, it is tempting to read this essentially populist expression of victory about dancing on Hitler's grave as a complete rejection of Modernist language use if not also the principles of innovation and novelty—indeed, much of the broadcast might be read as a condemnation of Modernist ideals embodied in the figure of the German superman—but Corwin maintains a fine line between involving a mass audience through the use of familiar language and forms and reinventing or reframing them in a manner more concerned with literary radio experimentation. At the moment, for example, when the folk song verges on (what certainly seems to a twenty-first-century ear) repetitive silliness, Corwin manages to give it an injection of gravitas and intrigue by having it translated and performed first in Serbian, then Danish, then Greek. While the original English performance cultivated a response to something provincial, kitschy, and ultimately simplistic, the translations that follow (a genuine affront to the ear) jar the listener into an appreciation of the precise opposite: the global/universal, the linguistically novel, and the complex. While one language, or even language in general, is initially unable to embody or enact the ineffable sentiment of the moment, the mixing of four languages makes a better attempt.

In Corwin's initial investigation into the creative/Modernist dimensions of radio space in *Seems Radio*, unique radio expressive modes and characteristics are presented in almost catalogue form, listed for their own sake as a kind of primer for radio literature. In *On a Note of Triumph*, these characteristics are integrated into a much larger project of meditating on the war. At the first presentation of the German prisoner, for example, Corwin makes the microphone itself something of a co-narrator for the story with its own abilities and intentionality. The prisoner is set in front of the microphone and it is that microphone that serves as our explicit guide to his rise to power: "It was 1933. / The mike, reversible, goes back to it" (15:20 and 452). The microphone, metonym for the entire structure and apparatus of radio (technological and semantic), not only takes history forward in time but also transports the listener back in time twelve years.

Prior to the introduction of the microphone the "ear" had been positioned as a pivotal figure, self-consciously foregrounded as the organ through which the listeners' own meditation should happen: "take your good ear out of low range" to filter out the cheering of crowds, to tune it in to the "intonations of wind and water" on a plane's route to the continent (with sound effects preempting the words). At 10:03, the ear is introduced to the "modest voice, as sensible and intimate to you as the quiet turning of your own considered Judgment," of the soldier whose questioning loosely structures the next fifty minutes; at this point listeners are enjoined to "Close your eyes and concentrate and listen." While the story may unfold in language, and while the language is often deployed in familiar linguistic constructions (such as instructions to listen and metaphors about listening), the piece instigates (or hopes to instigate) a *sensual* meditation on the world, extremely resonant with a

Modernist theatrical experience. With the entry of the prisoner, the medium for this sensual mediation is transposed from the ear to its technological extension: radio. The microphone becomes the conduit through which the physical and intellectual landscape of the war is experienced, as in "Now if you will permit us to move the mike along, being careful not to trip either over the rubble of treaties or the ruins of Rotterdam" (20:43 and 456).

Expanding and integrating another radio literary trope first explored in *Seems Radio*, the microphone reappears at 43:48 to collapse geographical space into radio space: "We hoist our microphone again, fifty feet higher than Everest" and follow it as a guide to the ongoing Pacific front of the war. In what might sound today like a slightly quaint literalization of radio's powers, the microphone explicitly pulls both the narrator Gabel and the audience up to address a pilot flying West; he and Gabel share a congratulatory word over the ambience of the engines about the end of the war in Europe. From there the radiogenic experience of the folding of time and space becomes more palpable and exciting: "Look below you now—sunlight fretting the surface of the sea. / ... In a flicker, banks of cumulus ahead now fall behind; / Leagues rush past; noonday is caught up with." And then, "in our mike sight," Gabel and the audience see below a fleet of ships and descend to speak with a ship's engineer. As this scenario unfolds, it is eventually implied that the listener is holding the microphone; this metaphoric involvement in the actual physical production of the broadcast mirrors the larger radio relationship: "Now hoist you up and overboard, and dive with your equipment well in hand, / Into the sea and under it. .... / Unreel the cable of this mike and light your head lamp, for we're diving deeper" (46:07). In these lines there is both a desire to invite, but also an attempt to force, a specific kind of audience engagement. Again the "you" is present all the way down to the bottom of the sea where the listener holding the microphone tries in vain to communicate with dead sailors on a sunken submarine. In the script for *On a Note of Triumph*, however, the broadcast "you" and "your" were originally "we," "us," and "our."[17] This change is further evidence of Corwin's efforts to project his listener into the broadcast, into the theatrical experience. This projection, however, happens here metaphorically using ideas and images readily available to the listener through years of media coverage of the war. If other Modernist approaches ran the risk of alienating an audience, at moments like this one Corwin runs the risk of impoverishing an imaginative engagement through kitsch. Corwin, however, may have been aware that he was straining against the limits of this radio metaphor within the broadcast, and the radio relationship is also occasionally represented as fraught and unsettling. At 18:43, for example, a German not affiliated with the party is executed for listening to British radio; he protests on his way to the guillotine that he does not even own a radio.

Corwin knew, as did Artaud, that the self-consciously theatrical presentation of reality often made its essential cruelty more palpable and transformative. The narrator Gabel describes the invasion of Poland in theatrical terms:

> Extra—double feature—Austria and Anschluss:
> And the corpses of the suicides of gay Vienna are sanitarily disposed of.
> Darkness rising: pageants and parades: drapes and flags and searchlights and the goose-step
> Next week umbrella dance at Munich—Salomé bearing the head of John the Czech.
> And coming soon, too soon, Lavish Spectacle—Millions in the Cast—
> Curtain Going Up—
> POLAND DEVOURED BY LIGHTNING AND LOCUSTS IN EIGHTEEN DAYS.(19:35 and 455–56)

This is uncannily troubling because it confronts the listener with an aestheticization of war that invokes its opposite. Through the spectacle-ized representation of the cruelty of the invasion here (and in the media coverage of the war that Corwin was referencing), the broadcast draws an attention to the linguistic tropes and framing devices of that spectacle. Seeing the spectacle *as spectacle* demands an awareness of the brutality outside of the frame. The effects of theatrical representation as more troubling than its reality are felt again at 22:00, when the fall of France is presented as a scene in a play.

Perhaps the most explicit point of overlap between *On a Note of Triumph* and the Theater of Cruelty comes in the approach to the ritual dimension of theatrical language. Incantation-like language is ubiquitous in *On a Note of Triumph*, first appearing clearly at 05:50 in an address to "the God of Wrath." In this first of a number of thinly veiled prayers for retribution against the German people, a minister begins by enacting call-and-response with his congregation, followed by a rabbi's sermon about tyranny, power, and freedom, and finally a bishop and priests in a cathedral chanting in Latin. The implicit but unmistakable indictment of the German people and leadership in the minister's section transforms into a more cerebral meditation on the war in the rabbi's section and ultimately resolves in the much more opaque

Latin. This movement from the specific to the generalized bridges the gap between the clear vernacular expression (a Modernist straw man) and the transformative power of word sounds not explicitly connected to familiar linguistic systems (a Modernist protocol). The move to Latin invokes sensations beyond language, but this is done only after those sensations are prompted in very familiar language. Here Corwin again negotiates between vernacular language as an entrée for a large audience and linguistic innovation as a point of departure for imaginative engagement, if not catharsis.

On a Note of Triumph reasserts its ritualized tone in Corwin's final prayer to the "Lord God of trajectory and blast" (54:26 and 483–84). Soft organ music develops a quieter churchlike atmosphere as snatches of a wartime vernacular and popular imagination are presented in a slightly stylized format that clearly aspires to the category of poetry: swords are made into plowshares, God is entreated to let dead soldiers witness hungry children now eating eggs and drinking orange juice, and "freedom has withstood the tyrant." It pleads for peace and returns to the figure and interests of the common man:

> Lord God of the topcoat and the living wage . . .
> Do bring sweet influences to bear upon the assembly line:
> Accept the smoke of the milltown among the accredited clouds of the sky: . . .
> Lord God of test tube and blueprint . . .
> Appear now among the parliaments of conquerors and give instruction to
>   their schemes:
> . . . Sit at the treaty table and convoy the hopes of little peoples through
>   expected straits,
> And press into the final seal a sight that peace will come for longer than
>   posterities can see ahead.

In 1945, critical opinion about these lines was decidedly mixed. At the most basic level there was tremendous debate about how to categorize the broadcast. Corwin, long acknowledged as a "radio poet" (Bannerman 4), himself refused to call the broadcast poetry (1945: 7). The *New York Times* had similar difficulty and chose to describe the broadcast as belonging to "radio's strange ethereal regions" requiring "interpretations dissimilar to those in [other] media" (Jack Gould x5.1). Perhaps the most productive approach to questions of the literary status of *On a Note of Triumph* and the cultural category of the poem is simply to refocus attention onto the radio relationship. To do this requires that we should again look past the volume of response to study the response qualitatively. Sociocultural assessments of *On a Note of Triumph* were far more prevalent than literary ones; it was hailed both as a stirring expression of the zeitgeist and a message from the moment to future generations. *Newsweek* called it elegant propaganda rather than art (Bannerman 154), and in other popular periodicals it was variously "one of the high-water marks in radio listening" (*Variety*); "as idealistically disturbing as a bomb" (*Toledo Blade*); and "something for all of us to hear at frequent intervals, for our own good and for the good of the country" (*Akron Beacon Journal*) (Corwin, *Untitled* 535–42). So correct was the sentiment and so powerful its incantations that the Army required all German prisoners of war to listen to a translation of the broadcast in German in the hope of transforming fascist minds. Not surprisingly, this experiment was met with resentment and occasional laughter (Blue 330; Bannerman 161). This outcome serves to reiterate that in order for radio projects to have the cathartic effects described and desired by Artaud, they must begin with an understanding of their audience's cultural outlook; they must inhabit, in a significant way, the cultural spaces of their listeners.

But it was precisely a cloying attachment to the audience's cultural outlook that the sole self-consciously literary review of *On a Note of Triumph* chose to criticize. In an October 1945 article called "Radio Plays as Literature," UCLA professor of English William Matthews said of Corwin, "He has an alert, ranging, fertile mind, and restless energy. But it is a mind that usually finds its place in the first of the bandwagons" (41–42). Addressing the difference between effective popular/vernacular expressions and aesthetic value, Matthews says that while he agrees with them, "antifascist, pro-democratic, pro-Common Man pronouncements do not necessarily constitute good literature." His comments point to a (possibly reductive but not wholly incorrect) assessment of the tension between innovation and cultural resonance in many Modernist literary radio projects: intense commitment to linguistic innovation alienates then bores, while intense commitment to vernacular expressions satisfies then bores. *War of the Worlds*'s successful navigation through this dilemma was due to innovation with the radio frame rather than with radio language. There is a particular shortcoming in Matthews's review that is worth mentioning, as it is also a pitfall for many contemporary scholars of broadcast literature: the review addresses only the published book version of *On a Note of Triumph*, not its broadcast or its recording, then available (42). For Matthews, how something read on the page was explicitly the test of good literature. So while he can easily criticize Corwin for pilfering from Ogden Nash and John Donne, he cannot appreciate the intimacy of the "ear work" accomplished, nor is he positioned to appreciate the aural/ritual effects that might happen exclusively in sound/listening. In fact, much of the work of this period *reads* quite badly—quite (to use Matthews's word) "undergraduateish"—but can *sound* quite engaging. Matthews's approach denies the specificity of the radio relationship (which must include the social-linguistic context and importance of the day) and cannot help but lead to disappointment. Hence, he cannot appreciate its innovative performative qualities and its complex use of sound, its Modernism in the ear.

Those who listened to *On a Note of Triumph* as a radio broadcast were fairly consistent in their assessment of its radiophonic qualities, even if they did not praise its poetry. Gould is a case in point; while he too found much of the broadcast "strangely disappointing," he does praise it for its "fresh and experimental radio writing. . . . The transition from the whining sirens over London to the gaiety of the Berlin cafes was extraordinarily effective radio theatre" (x5.1). But again, it is ultimately work with the radio relationship that I wish to foreground as the most important marker of Modernist radiophony. Even though the transformation which attended *On a Note of Triumph* was the shedding of tears rather than the "rending of garments" of *War of the Worlds*—it is less cruel, inviting more an epiphany than a catharsis—it does successfully enact the radio relationship through its invocation of a healing sense of collective destiny in the midst of fresh memories of the war.

Following Cantril's lead, most latter-day radio scholarship has cast *War of the Worlds* and *On a Note of Triumph* as sociopolitical phenomena, as parables about the function of broadcasting in American civil society. Around *War of the Worlds* this writing is cautionary and admonishing; Jeffrey Sconce, for example, in his *Haunted Media*, reads *War of the Worlds* as an extraordinary moment in the history of *noncommunication*, a frightening reminder of the failed Brechtian promise for a utopian radio of multilateral speech (113). While not at all inaccurate, such readings often underestimate both the resilience of audiences and the cruel power of radio. By extrapolating a theory of broadcasting from Artaud read through *War of the Worlds* and *On a Note of Triumph*, it is possible to articulate a species of Modernist radio experiment as working not *on* its audience but *with* its audience. In addition to being pivotal moments in the study of the radio relationship, these two broadcasts also spawned threads of radio experimentation still being developed by innovative radio practitioners. Far from ending the possibilities for the radio prank, *War of the Worlds* ushered in radio's trickster aesthetic in both high and low cultural spheres.

In his *Pressures of the Unspeakable*, Gregory Whitehead presented himself to/through the ABC in Australia as the director of the International Institute of Screamscape Studies and, with the collusion of people on the inside, set up a phone recording system at the ABC to collect samples of the "Australian screamscape." Listeners (some of whom had deduced it was a joke, some of whom took it very seriously) called in and left their screams with brief explanatory messages. At the end of the project "Dr. Whitehead" presented and analyzed his findings on one of the ABC's most important interview programs. He has since repeated this performance on various other stations and networks around the world. In a more populist (if also harsher and more derisive) interpretation of the radio relationship, *The Phil Hendrie Show* toys with listener expectations every night on KFI in Los Angeles and on a few other stations around the United States. Hendrie initially appears as a fairly typical right-wing talk show host with a regular stable of "guests" from the southern California area. The ruse here, however, is that while the callers are real, the guests are fake, invented and voiced by Hendrie the host. With truly admirable technical skill he flips between his role as journalist/interviewer and his voicing of a politically incorrect restaurateur or a vacuous TV news anchor or a morally stunted high school football coach. While his performance is flawless, dry and utterly believable, he will often begin his show by stating that his program is not real; yet those who believe themselves to be the audience of the program call in with self-confident questions and heartfelt outrages while another audience lurks and laughs in silence.

The slightly schizophrenic juxtapositions of voices in *On a Note of Triumph* have also left their mark on subsequent generations of radio voice montage. In its multilingual transitions, language often rematerializes back into sound. These moments of instability between the language mode of speech perception and the sound mode of perception are precursors of the multivoiced radio literary strategies taken up later by Glenn Gould in his famous radio journey *The Idea of North*, and more earnestly (and digitally) by Christof Migone in his *Hole in the Head*, an attempt to re-create for broadcast "ecrit brut" or the writings of the clinically insane.

All of these innovations happen, and could only happen effectively, within an understanding of a radio context. My ultimate contention then is that traditional analyses of broadcasts like *War of the Worlds* and *On a Note of Triumph* as sociopolitical events, and (conversely) other broadcasts as merely literary documents preserved on tape, have occluded their importance as genuinely innovative radio happenings that define a new species of radio art as occurring only incidentally in sound or the broadcast voice. Instead, this is an art that resides much more prominently in the space between the producer, the institution, and the listener, the space of the radio relationship.

Notes

1. For a more detailed discussion of the notion of radio as a relationship, listen to my *Radio Radio* program with Gregory Whitehead (available online at www.ubu.com/radio). I am indebted to him for an appreciation of this relationship.

2. As substantial studies of Artaud's radio work and Theater of Cruelty have been undertaken elsewhere (most importantly for my purposes is Weiss, *Phantasmic Radio*), I have refrained for issues of space from including all the relevant material here.

3. Weiss 12–13 and *passim* includes a substantive close listening of *Judgment* and its related audio material as well as a close reading of the written text and supporting documents.

4. The time code in the full-hour broadcast will be cited rather than the pages in the script as there are minor differences between the script and the broadcast, and the audience experienced the latter, not the former.

5. These preoccupations were so prominent in the minds of the listening public that one woman, in a post-panic interview, reported that she thought it was the Germans who had destroyed New Jersey (Cantril 53).

6. Similarly, later in the broadcast (27:04) the secretary of the interior appeals for calm after the Martians have killed more than 6,000 militia in New Jersey and asks for faith in God and faith in the military.

7. Cantril notes that other audience surveys showed that up to 19 percent of McCarthy's audience switched over to *War of the Worlds*. On a typical night, McCarthy's share of the audience was 34.7 percent while the Mercury Theatre garnered only 3.6 percent (82–83).

8. Cantril's study suggests that the highest rates of outright belief in the Martian invasion occurred among the poor, the poorly educated, and listeners in the South (59–68). There has been speculation, however, that the panic was not as extensive as originally believed. Welles himself initially cited a newspaper vendetta against radio for poaching its advertising as hyping the story (Welles and Bogdanovich 19). In addition, the radio historian Susan Douglas suggests that the irresistible lure of great headlines exaggerated accounts of the panic and drove up the number of newspaper stories about the event to 12,500 in the weeks that followed (*Listening In* 165).

9. Later in life, Welles, in his own dramatization (if not exaggeration) of the panic, described the events that ensued after the broadcast in quasi-biblical terms: "Six minutes after we'd gone on the air, the switchboards in radio stations right across the

country were lighting up like Christmas trees. Houses were emptying, churches were filling up; from Nashville to Minneapolis there was wailing in the street and the rending of garments" (Welles and Bogdanovich 18).

10. At 54:08, empty city shops are "displaying mute wares to empty sidewalks."

11. For more detail, see Douglas (*Listening In* 165) and Cantril (vii).

12. Respected newspaper editor Martin Codel writes of radio's "occult powers" (xi) as late as 1930; Douglas writes of the "radio séance" (*Listening In* 46–51); Schmidt talks about Feuerbach's connection between the ear and religion (xv).

13. The full script is available in Neil Strauss's *Radiotext(e)* (137–46).

14. In the immediate wake of the broadcast the CBS offices in New York received several thousand congratulatory calls; the originating studios of KNX, Hollywood, received more than 1,600 calls; more than 4,000 cards, letters, and telegrams arrived; and the editors of *Billboard* described it as the best radio program they had ever heard (Bannerman 158).

15. Time-coded citations refer to the audio recording of *On a Note of Triumph* widely available on cassette and CD. Where required, citations to the printed text refer to the script published in Corwin's *Untitled and Other Radio Dramas*. All line breaks and capitalizations come from this text.

16. Corwin endeavors to create a sense of this broadcast as an audio time capsule. At 2:50 the listeners are instructed to clip the last communiqué from Allied high command to give to their children; and at 4:45 the program is offered as a kind of channel marker in a historic consciousness: "Size up the day and date. / Look in on prayer and thanksgiving, song and laughter dated Planet Earth, May 1945" (*Untitled* 444).

17. The script has the line: "Now we hoist us up and overboard, and dive with our equipment well in hand" (475).

[CHAPTER 5]

Flying Solo

The Charms of the Radio Body

DAVID JENEMANN

> . . . ich fliege allein in einem apparat ohne radio.
> —Bertolt Brecht, *Der Flug der Lindberghs*

In *Current of Music*, his long-unpublished volume on radio broadcasting, Theodor W. Adorno describes the uncanny, animist power of the radio voice that terrifyingly infiltrates the listener's private space:

> The isolated listener definitely feels overwhelmed by the might of the personal voice of an anonymous organization. Second, the deeper this voice is involved within his own privacy, the more it appears to pour out of the cells of his most intimate life; the more he gets the impression that his own cupboard, his own phonograph, his own bedroom speaks to him in a personal way, devoid of the intermediary stages of the printed word; the more perfectly he is ready to accept wholesale whatever he hears. It is just this privacy which fosters the authority of the radio voice and helps to hide it by making it no longer appear to come from outside. (114)[1]

Writing sometime between 1938 and 1941, while serving as musical director for the Princeton Radio Research Project (PRRP), Adorno attributes to the radio broadcast the power not only to take over the body of the listener but also to give life to the material objects of the bourgeois home. The resulting phantasmagoria of talking cupboards and bedroom furniture holding their cellularly innervated owners in thrall sits uncomfortably between a Merry Melodies cartoon and the dystopian science fictions of the period. But the extremity of Adorno's image should not mask its import; while the radio might create automata out of household objects, it also installs a machinelike consciousness in the mind of the listener. The cupboard, the phonograph, and the listener are hence caught up together as one monstrous radio body.

To pursue this idea a little further, let us consider not a sound but an image: an old, upright telephone sits on a table in front of a window. The window's shade is half drawn, and its cord mirrors the one that connects the telephone's receiver to its mouthpiece. In the half-obscured window, a vague reflection can be seen, ghostly and insubstantial compared to the mechanical solidity of the telephone and the finality of the shade. The reflection is of a human figure, but its head has been cut off by the shade and the top of the frame. Consider the image further: with its clean lines and solid colors, one might initially mistake the image for a photograph. But look closer. In fact the image is a skillful rendering done in conté crayon, gouache, and pencil.

What I am describing here is the seminal precisionist work by the American artist Charles Sheeler, his 1923 "Self Portrait." In many ways, Sheeler's painting stands as an emblematic Modernist image of the tenuous relationship between the subject and its machine-age objective conditions. The corporeal human "self" alluded to in the title[2] recedes into the hazy glass background, its decapitated head at once emasculating the painter and consigning it to anonymity. In place of the human figure one would expect in a self-portrait, we have the upright (and unavoidably phallic) certainty of the telephone, which now stands both in front of and for the absent artist. It is a clever painting, because in foregrounding the telephone, Sheeler suggests one of the paradoxes of Modernism: increasingly the mechanical body supersedes the human one. The "ear" and "mouth" of the telephone are far more powerful than that of their human operator, able to extend to the farthest regions of the planet at impossible speeds. Lifting the telephone receiver, like pulling the window shade, would suggest a capitulation of the subject to the mechanical object, an effacement. And yet the telephone nevertheless depends on that human operator's agency to achieve its impossible feats. The receding reflection and the concrete telephone serve as mutually mediating yet interdependent antipodes that together, in their early twentieth-century context, form an even then no-longer-new type of mechanized human being. The telephone's user gives life to the instrument at the same time that his own life is mechanically transformed. The strength of Sheeler's work depends on the way that the formal strategies of "Self Portrait" reproduce and affirm the contradictions of its content. The photographic realism of precisionism is an illusion, the work of an artist whose intense labor has been poured, contradictorily, into the effacement of that labor. Individuating, "painterly" techniques give way to the demands of realism. In "Self Portrait," Sheeler disappears into the mechanical precision of his own work in much the same way that the telephone user has to immerse himself in the mechanism for it to become expressive. Yet in both the painting and the creation of the painting, the ghost of a superannuated subject remains, haunting and troubling the mechanisms with which he has destroyed himself.

Sheeler's painting, a mute image that nonetheless speaks of the possibilities and challenges of mediated sound, embodies the dialectical problem facing modern subjects, who, with the rise of visual and auditory transmissions technologies (film and television, phonograph and radio), were increasingly confronted by the possibility that their technological innovations might overrun them, destroying subjectivity altogether.[3] If Modernism is, at least in part, concerned with the increasingly vexed interface between humanity and technology and the accompanying anxiety that what is "human" has been irrevocably transformed by humanity's machines, Sheeler's painting suggests a possible way out of this conundrum, albeit a perhaps unpalatable one for those who cling to the hope of a transcendent and free-willed subject. What "Self Portrait" suggests is that it is only through a resignation to the realities of technological mediation, through willing self-negation, that the subject has the possibility of maintaining some kernel of its humanity. In this regard, Sheeler's painting anticipates Adorno's aesthetic theories, particularly as they deal with radio broadcasts. Adorno, like Sheeler, suggests that in modernity, perhaps the best way to escape the subjective domination of the individual in conditions of administered, mechanized life is not through resistance but through resignation. Radical alterity, if such a thing could be said to figure into Adorno's thinking, would be a function of subjective dissolution more than it would be a product of decisive political resistance. Thus, typically, in a letter to Thomas Mann, Adorno wrote that one must recognize "the power of determinate negation as the only permissible figure of the Other" (*Notes to Literature* 18). And as in the "Self Portrait," for Adorno more often than not the space for this working-out of the subject's thoroughgoing dissolution was not in the political arena but in the production of cultural and aesthetic objects.

Hence, I would like to keep Sheeler's "Self Portrait" in the background when considering some of Adorno's responses to radio broadcasting, for it is clear, when examining Adorno's theoretical output, that he recognized the potentials and pitfalls of the broadcast medium in much the same way that

Sheeler imagined the telephone. Further, Adorno acutely understood that the radio offered to subjects the possibility of new types of bodies and new forms of subjectivation, but ones that carried with them the threat of capitulation to authoritarian aims.

The choice of a picture of a telephone to begin this essay on radio is a deliberate one, because for Adorno, the radio marks at once an advance on the telephone's technological innovations while at the same time displaying a shift toward authoritarian tendencies with regard to intersubjective communication. Whereas the telephone is limited in the range of its communication possibilities (person-to-person rather than mass dissemination), broadcast radio forecloses the potential for two-way communication. This foreclosure is one of the fundamental precepts of "The Culture Industry" essay, in which technological innovation leads to an internalization of oppression and consumerist logic on the part of the audience:

> Technical rationality today is the rationality of domination. . . . Any need which might escape the central control is repressed by that of individual consciousness. The step from telephone to radio has clearly distinguished the roles. The former liberally permitted the participant to play the role of subject. The latter democratically makes everyone into listeners, in order to expose them in authoritarian fashion to the same programs put out by different stations. No mechanism of reply has been developed, and private transmissions are condemned to unfreedom. (Horkheimer and Adorno 95–96)

Although Adorno doesn't deny the plethora of options on the radio, even in the early days of AM, he sees individuality as foreclosed by the fact that all of the programs did exactly the same things. Even though NBC and CBS were in the 1930s and 1940s producing programs such as *Art for Your Sake* and *Music and You,* as well as touting their commitment to "Broadcasting in the Public Interest" both in congressional hearings and publicity manuals, listeners were in fact asked to adapt their listening tastes to a standardized range of programming that denied the possibility of rejoinder.

Until recently, Adorno's pessimistic diagnoses of the audience's internalization of authoritarianism would have lent themselves to the widely held notion that Adorno was merely a European intellectual elitist, enamored with "serious" music and unfamiliar with both the material practices and the historical development of radio and American musical forms, particularly jazz. In the last few years, however, that situation has begun to change, in no small part due to the rediscovery and critical reassessment of the richness of Adorno's radio writings, which culminated in the massive *Current of Music*.[4] When Adorno came to America as an exile in 1938, he was asked by the director of PRRP, the sociologist Paul Felix Lazarsfeld, to answer the question, "How can good music be conveyed to the largest possible audience?"—using the principles of empirically driven administrative research (Adorno, "A Social Critique" 208–17). As Adorno and Lazarsfeld both later acknowledged, Adorno was uniquely unsuited to empirical research and was profoundly suspicious of a methodological principle that treated any phenomenon like audience responses undialectically, that is, apart from the overall network of social and economic relations.

That Adorno's uneasy relationship with PRRP and his impatience with the fact-finding and focus groups colored his early American writings is abundantly evident even in those texts that are not about radio per se. Consider the first page of the well-known "Fetish Character" essay (1939), where Adorno makes a point of drawing attention to audience research as part of radio music's problem: "If one seeks to find out who 'likes' a commercial piece," he writes, specifically targeting the methods of PRRP, "one cannot avoid the suspicion that liking and disliking are inappropriate to the situation, even if the person questioned clothes his reaction in those words. The familiarity of the piece is a surrogate for the quality ascribed to it. To like it is almost the same as to recognize it" ("On the Fetish Character" 288). Here, as elsewhere, Adorno stands firm on the idea that in the face of administered culture, subjective judgments of taste are increasingly suspect. Could listeners, who heard the same range of "plugged" songs, Adorno asked, legitimately be expected to distinguish their likes from those of the programming experts?

While he may have disagreed with Lazarsfeld and his colleagues at PRRP, it is also clear from Adorno's radio writings that what he took from that experience was a thoroughgoing understanding of how radio worked as a total enterprise. Hence, in the late 1930s and early 1940s, Adorno took "the radio" to be not simply a broadcast, an industry, a technology, or an audience but a cultural form that incorporated each of these elements in a contradictory, ever-changing whole. This uneasy body, which Adorno terms radio's "physiognomy," had many corporal members—its listeners, its practitioners, its technicians—but it tended to speak with one voice, the voice that came out of the radio box. The term "physiognomics" is a problematic one, reflecting both superannuated psychological principles (the unconscious could be written on the body) as well as unsavory links to eugenics and other anthropometric studies that sought, with racialist agendas, to essentialize certain bodily characteristics. Adorno was sensitive to these problems, yet nevertheless insisted on the value of the term "physiognomics" as a metaphor: "Radio and the sound which we receive over our radio sets are not a human face. To apply the term, physiognomics, to a study of the phenomena presented to us by radio seems to be of purely metaphorical value, if any." But that metaphor has a certain cachet when thinking about the way that radio, as a mass medium, articulated a body of listeners around a single pole. Thus, Adorno explains, "This question is not purely terminological. It involves the relation between this study and the individual sciences of psychology, technology and sociology. Roughly speaking, we insist upon the physiognomic approach because the phenomena we are studying constitute a unity comparable to that of a human face" (*Current of Music* 76–77).

This face, Adorno insisted, purported to speak with one irreproachable voice, and this voice, with its apparent, unmediated closeness to the listener, is what gave the radio the illusion of an anthropomorphically coherent body. This illusion was, to Adorno's mind, important because it had material effects on the listening audience: "In a society which has as gross a veneer of 'appearance' as ours, it is just as important to study the mechanism which produces the 'illusion' as it is to discount it. That is why our method takes the illusion of the 'radio voice' so seriously and suggests research into it on a larger scale. In our study, the 'illusionary' character of the 'radio voice' plays as important a role as its 'reality'" (*Current of Music* 85). Clearly, Adorno's theoretical approach far overreached PRRP's need to discover how to deliver good music to the beleaguered "Midwestern farmer," the ostensible beneficiary of its research. Indeed, the genuinely populist aims of PRRP, were thoroughly undermined by Adorno's holistic approach. On the one hand Adorno refused to accept that the "likes" and "dislikes" of the audience could be legitimately measured apart from a context in which radio functioned as a social agency that dictated those likes and dislikes as much as it provided them. On the other hand, he was keen to point out that by virtue of the technological limitations of the radio, even what purported to be "good" music was reduced to a series of mixed-down, recognizable, classical "hits" that functioned in exactly the same fashion as did popular music. Adorno saw the radio as a collectivizing agent with unsettling authoritarian overtones that functioned in part by isolating individuals from one another yet making them feel as though they were a part of a greater whole. By speaking to individuals as individuals, it nonetheless reduced them to passivity and objecthood. "As paradoxical as it sounds," Adorno wrote, "the authority of radio becomes greater the more it addresses the listener in his privacy. An organized mass of listeners might feel their own strength and even rise to a sort of opposition" (*Current of Music* 114).

There is ample evidence that there was a concerted effort on the part of the networks to minimize opposition to their programs and their advertisers, in part by cultivating the illusion that the radio was not so much a technological, yet ultimately rational, marvel, but rather a magical box providing direct access to the phantoms of the ether, wonderland, and, ultimately, to God. In radio productions like *Seems Radio Is Here to Stay* (CBS 1939), which claimed explicitly that the radio was able to channel the ether and thus all of history, as well as in publicity manuals, with titles like *Alice in Sponsorland* (NBC 1941), *What Goes on Behind Your Radio Dial* (NBC 1942), and *The Word of God* (NBC 1941), NBC and CBS sought to obscure the technological and economic intricacies of mass, network broadcasting (then little more than a decade old), in favor of the illusion that the broadcast was at once unimpeachably authoritative, magically efficient and deeply personal. The networks, it would seem, were just as committed to claiming they could make the bedroom furniture talk as was Adorno.[5]

Adorno's theories, which suggested that good radio essentially couldn't exist as long as the radio as an institution was organized in its then-current form, clearly antagonized his fellow PRRP researchers, who included Frank Stanton, soon to be president of CBS. Through his holistic approach to "the radio," Adorno implied that the institution itself was inherently authoritarian; when the Rockefeller Foundation funding for the project was renewed, Adorno's music section was pointedly disbanded, and he was left with many of the components of *Current of Music* in inchoate form.

Nevertheless, as Robert Hullot-Kentor writes, Adorno, in his contact with American radio broadcasting, diagnosed a fundamental change in human experience. "No one had previously considered that the nature of the person could be so transformed historically that culture would become inadequate to humanity. . . . Whereas culture presupposed an autonomous individual, the contemporary American had been so overwhelmed by real and constant anxiety, has been so broken in on by heteronomous forces, that this autonomy and its capacity for involvement with extramental reality could no longer be presumed" ("Right Listening" 191–92). For readers of Adorno's radio theories, the question would therefore seem to be how radio listeners—and for that matter radio practitioners—could shake off the shackles of "unfreedom" and transform the logic of authoritarian communication into something that provided the possibility of a rejoinder Adorno himself insists was foreclosed. If the radio created new forms of bodies, how could those bodies turn, Golem-like, against their creators and overwhelm the authoritarian voice that was altering human interactions at a "cellular" level?

Adorno was hardly the first to ask this question, nor, *pace* Hullot-Kentor, was he the first to imagine the revolutionary possibilities inherent in the technological union of human beings and their radio anodynes. Indeed, the notion that electronically transmitted sound necessarily expanded the parameters of what it meant to be human goes all the way back to Edison and the origins of recording technology. "After all," Douglas Kahn writes, "Edison developed his philosophy and his status as an expert on the afterlife only after his body had techno-melded with the mediational properties of the phonograph, becoming a quasi-body which could better commune with ghosts.... People expected to hear dead voices played back through this half-man, half photograph, this machine that could die, a man that contained voices of the past" (Kahn, "Death" 76–77).

But while images of phono- and radio-graphically enhanced human subjects abound in Modernism,[6] a look at even a single example of these avant-garde experiments with the radio body reveals why Adorno felt that an adequate reply to broadcasting conditions had yet to be developed. Bertolt Brecht's 1929 radio play, *Lindbergh's Flight: A Radiolehrstück for Boys and Girls*, offers a potentially progressive integration of listeners and radio broadcasts while purporting to give to the audience the voice Adorno later would claim was denied them. In *Lindbergh's Flight*, Brecht sought to wrest the audience from its complacency as well as its isolation by having listeners perform the leading role—that of Lindbergh—as a collective, speaking with and back to the radio, which was to broadcast sound effects and the musical score by Kurt Weill and Paul Hindemith. "In Brecht's conception for the piece," Mark Cory explains, "Lindbergh's struggle against the elements and against his own fatigue was not to be understood as a triumph of one individual but rather as a collective triumph of the human spirit" (345). The audience was, in Brecht's didactic conception, to serve as both learner and teacher simultaneously. "Consequently the boys and girls in his idealized audience were to recite the part of airmen, learning by their participation the important lessons of overcoming fatigue and adversity" (345).

Brecht's radio play was indeed radical in its conception. As Mark Silberman claims, "He was not only thematizing the radio in a broadcast presentation but suggesting how the medium itself can transform social communication through its technological advantage: the ear is to become a voice" (Brecht 41n). The problem with this reimagined radio broadcast in practice, however, is that in giving voice to the audience members and making them active parts of the radio body, the play nevertheless transforms them into an undifferentiated mass, each playing out the same script. Brecht was, of course, well aware of this contradiction and strove to defend his concept by arguing that what the chorus of radio participants represented was the disciplined, revolutionary class, taking over the means of production as embodied by the radio. "The increasing concentration of mechanical means," he insists, "call[s] for a kind of *rebellion* by the listener, for its mobilization and redeployment as producer." That rebellion, Brecht argued, demanded that the listener accept the dialectical proposition that "this exercise helps to teach discipline, which is the basis of freedom" (40).

However, in the exchange between isolated consumption and disciplined production, Brecht runs the risk of winding up by accident where, before him, the Futurists traveled by design—namely, to the point where the body of the radio functioned as an emblem of fascist aesthetics. Brecht seems to recognize this, and ultimately acknowledges that *Lindbergh's Flight* is destined to be a failure, not because of the eventually revealed unsavory politics of its title character[7] but because the mechanism whereby the play would truly serve its didactic purposes and the mass could actually participate requires the unlikely collusion of the same state the play ultimately hopes to transform. "Thus," Brecht writes, "*Lindbergh's Flight* has no aesthetic and no revolutionary value independent of its application, and only the state can organize this. Its proper application, however, makes it so 'revolutionary' that the present day state has no interest in sponsoring such exercises" (40). This resignation on Brecht's part returns us to Adorno's claim that no mechanism of reply had yet been developed to counteract the cycles of participation, subsumption, and domination on the part of the radio experience. Whereas in Lindbergh's Flight, the audience as a collective Lindbergh could sing, "ich fliege allein in einem apparat ohne radio" ["I'm flying alone in an airplane (*apparat*) without a radio"], the reverse is in fact true: the individual audience members, singing tonelessly to their script, are alone with their radios without a mechanism (*apparat*) to transport them to the collective revolution Brecht envisions.

How then does Adorno envision a solution to the authoritarian effects of radio broadcasting and the "physiognomy" its voice helped animate? This is a vexed question for Adorno scholars, as throughout his career he maintained a near-allergic reaction to offering plans for resistance to the culture industry and its assault on individuality. To tell individuals how to defy one dominating logic was to subject them to yet another one, and Adorno's suspicion of didacticism as yet another form of authoritarianism was a central component in his long-running disagreement with Brecht's theatrical methods. Nevertheless, while working for PRRP, Adorno did offer a number of tentative suggestions for how radio might transform itself into a truly liberatory and participatory medium. Most of these suggestions, which appeared in a 161-page memo to PRRP entitled "Music in Radio" (1938), were outlandish and unworkable, even as they reflected Adorno's conception of the radio as a multifaceted social form. These ideas ranged from redesigning the radio box so it looked more like a machine and less like a tabernacle to sending out teams of researchers to sit with listeners while they experienced different versions of musical performances. True to Adorno's aversion to providing definitive solutions that would undermine the readers' capacity to think and create for themselves, these suggestions for the most part don't survive in the manuscript of *Current of Music*. However, at one point in the section on "Radio Physiognomics," Adorno does offer an open-ended suggestion that there may be means of combating the "pseudo-immediacy" of the radio with a more genuine one: "We shall have to discuss this possibility in the *Music Study* in its proper place. It is the problem of combining electrical musical instruments with radio. Both tendencies, as much as they appear to be opposed—the objectivation of radio phenomena by broadcast records and the breaking down of its reification by 'playing on the radio' as electrical instruments suggest—coincide in one decisive element" (*Current of Music* 128).

While Adorno does not rejoin the issue of "playing on the radio" in *Current of Music*, it is clear from the "Music in Radio" memo that what Adorno had in mind were the possibilities embodied by the theremin. By functioning as both transmitter and receiver and through theoretically transforming the radio itself into an instrument, thereby overcoming the problems Adorno identified with music's mediation and manipulation, the theremin enabled Adorno to envision a music that could truly transcend historical and technological contingencies and achieve a "utopian" Hegelian synthesis. "Very bluntly," Adorno continues, "this might even lead to the disappearance between so-called subjective and objective elements of sound with the achievement of definite perfection of mechanical instruments, and specifically, its immediate application to radio" ("Music in Radio" 152).

Adorno was not alone in noting this liberatory aspect of the instrument, and even a cursory overview of news accounts of Leon Theremin's early performances suggests the enthusiasm and amazement listeners had for this new technology. In December of 1927, the *New York Times* reported that Theremin's accomplishment was perhaps on a par with Lindbergh's from earlier that same year. "New York will soon be stirred by the radio invention which has taken Paris by storm," the report from France begins. "Since the revelation of the possibilities of music from ether waves, Paris, artistic and intellectual, mundane and technical has talked of little else. What can happen when the imagination of Paris is sympathetically aroused was shown in the case of Lindbergh" (Birkhead n16).

With the theremin's integration of performer and instrument and its much-touted ability to transcend spatial constraints via the ether, the liberation of musical experience became a function of electronic transmission, in a sense relying on the mechanism to escape from mechanization. The utopian nature of this free movement corresponds with Adorno's ideas regarding radio physiognomy, but was also in keeping with Theremin's own early support for the communist revolution and the vision of a truly classless society (and its therefore theoretically mobile population). As Theremin's student, Lydia Kavina, suggests, through this synthesis the theremin exceeded other electronic instruments precisely because it gave free rein to the human aspect of music-making:

> Its emphasis is not on the employment of a variety of colors, but rather on conveying the emotions. The theremin, unlike its computerized cousins, is played spontaneously. In this sense, it has much more in common with traditional instruments than with a synthesizer: its music is created by the musician, not by the instrument itself. (Kavina 52)

In a very real way, therefore, with the theremin the performer quite literally became a radio body, integrated into the mechanism while it transmitted and received, animating the sounds from the ether through the movement required to make it sing. For Adorno, the broadcast radio's "physiognomy" is ultimately the sound of alienation and a false consciousness of unity, where "the radio would represent the listener's ears being conquered by capitalist society in the form of the microphone, which has now become a sort of social substitute for the ear itself" ("Music in Radio" 126). The technological innovations of the theremin, on the other hand, offered the possibility of radio's return through the sound machine to the realm of the completely human.

But even at the time Adorno wrote those words, the potentials embodied by the theremin had become passé, and the technological innovations of the instrument had stalled. Just as Brecht's didacticism offered no guaranteed resistance to authoritarianism, Theremin's innovations offer no necessary defense against subsumption under the aegis of capitalism. Indeed, despite the enthusiasm for Theremin and his instrument when they initially arrived in the United States, within months of his debut the fad was already fading, as evidenced by the unenthusiastic review from 1928 titled, with palpable ennui, "'Music from Ether' Again." Here, the description of Theremin waving his hands in the air to draw sound from his instrument makes him sound like a cheap parlor magician, whose tricks have gone stale. "The program, in large part," the reviewer continues, "repeat[s] that given hitherto" (21). As if to confirm the image of Theremin as a huckster, as well as the notion that the instrument is no more liable to escape the logic of reification than any other radio broadcast, a 1932 Christmas ad for Gimbels in the *New York Times* features a photograph of Theremin dramatically raising his arms in front of the instrument. But despite the dramatic pose Theremin strikes, what the ad reveals is that in a few short years Theremin had been reduced from performing on the stage at Carnegie Hall to giving a recital at a department store. And where was that recital to be held? In the radio department, of course, ninth floor (December 5, 1932, 9). Rather than destroying the primacy of the radio, well before Adorno discovered him, Theremin was helping, by selling receivers at Gimbels, to guarantee its ubiquity.

Hence, the theremin, Adorno's hoped-for answer to radio authoritarianism ultimately proved to be a dead end, almost before Adorno had thought to examine its potential. After all, given Adorno's long-held reservations about technology's progress, it is unlikely he would have upheld the idea that a purely technological solution could lead to an aesthetic redemption. Is any technological innovation, after all, ever free of its imminent subsumption by the market? But was it therefore the case then that there was no way out for the members of the radio body? In Adorno's published writings from the period, there is a decided pessimism about the answer to that question. Indeed, in the "Fetish Character" essay, Adorno entertains the notion that in the face of the overwhelming totality of the radio voice, one could productively hear in the musical detail a spark of individuality under siege. But he quickly squelches that hope: "The diversion of interest from the whole, perhaps indeed from the 'melody,' to the charm of color and to the individual trick, could be optimistically interpreted as a new rupture of the disciplining function. But this interpretation would be erroneous" (306). The individual detail, Adorno claimed, like the familiar movements of a symphony or the hook of a hit song, were fetishes, sonic "possessions" that held listeners in their thrall, ultimately binding them ever closer to the radio body.

Later in his career, however, Adorno would retreat somewhat from this position, suggesting that in hearing the individual detail being dissolved into the totality of the work and by understanding how the singular moved through and against the social whole, one could likewise "hear" and moreover feel how human individuality itself faced dissolution in the social whole. For Adorno, in a typical dialectical move, it was in hearing this subjective demolition that the particular details—and by extension the listening individuals—were able to preserve some sense of identity, even as that identity was lost in the process. The collapse of particular into whole was never, Adorno claimed, absolute, just as the human was never fully machine. Thus, in 1965, Adorno writes in "Little Heresy" that "because the two do not merge fully into each other, the individual detail also acquires its own rights, which go beyond the whole" (322).

In this analysis, the "charms" afforded by the radio body were precisely what promised to save the individual. The idea that the individual could linger over and savor the detail before inevitably being sucked back into the whole nonetheless offered the promise of nonidentity with the physiognomics of the radio broadcast, even if only provisionally. This ability to be "charmed" by the detail, the solo, the color, or the melody was not, it should be stressed, an utter refusal of the new type of humanity the radio spawned. That, for Adorno, would either simply be a reactionary position or a purely romantic one (one need not read too far into his jazz writings to understand how he feels about the sham individuality of the solo, for example). Instead, within the technological and economic parameters set out by Modernist aesthetic practices, Adorno believed that one could carve out a space in which the listener hears the mechanism at work while at the same time experiencing the nonidentity of the mechanism's gears with the whole machine.[8]

As Adorno beautifully explains in *Minima Moralia*, the charm of listening in the age of the radio body derives from seeing behind the artifice of those charms, allowing oneself to be simultaneously taken in by their dazzling display with pleasure—and even with joy—and yet understanding that those "colors" are deceits, all for show. "The bliss of contemplation consists in disenchanted charm," he insists. "Radiance is the appeasement of myth" (225). Rather than outright resistance to technology, however, Adorno proposes a delicate oscillation. The listener can hear the cupboards talking, but he can't believe what they say—or to return to Sheeler's "Self Portrait," the subject can revel in experiencing the self in the technological translocations of the telephone, but he can also hang it up and gaze at his hazy reflection.

Adorno's solutions, such as they are, will perhaps rightly raise the objection of being themselves utopian, but unlike Brecht's solution to the radio body, or Theremin's, Adorno's solutions place the task of and the hope for resistance to the radio squarely in the court of the individual. In this, as it is elsewhere, Adorno's humanism is radical both in its stubborn desire to retain the human coupled with its willingness to concede the end of the fable of humanity. The key to our salvation is knowledge, both of history and of this new "self." Thus, Adorno writes in *Current of Music* that education is a crucial component of the subject's ability to take a stand against the expectations and demands of the broadcasters. "Right listening means above all the overcoming of the current false listening" (qtd. in Hullot-Kentor, "Right Listening" 196.) What is required, therefore, is that the individual take the task of education to heart, to hear what broadcast technologies of all sorts threaten to do to notions of free will and self- determination, and to understand how now a century of recorded sound and images has utterly transformed what it means to be human. It is a task that is alluring in its simplicity and its possibility of success while at the same time daunting in forcing subjects to countenance the idea that the myth of human exceptionalism has passed. Adorno's challenge to listen differently is ultimately just as terrifying as the idea of a radio voice that transforms every molecule of our existence, for if we fail in this task, we have no one to blame but ourselves.

Notes

1. I am greatly indebted to Robert Hullot-Kentor for allowing me to see the advance page proofs of his manuscript while I was writing this chapter.

2. Sheeler's painting was exhibited under the name "Still Life" until around 1931, when Abby Aldrich Rockefeller bought the painting and the title was changed. It now belongs to the collection of the Museum of Modern Art (Troyen and Hirschler, 96).

3. Overrun them quite literally, if one follows the logic of Ben Singer's essay "Modernity, Hyperstimulus, and the Rise of Popular Sensationalism" in which he links the jarring, sensational shocks of early cinema with the frequent newspaper depictions of trolley deaths and traffic accidents.

4. See, for example, Lazarsfeld, Adorno, "Scientific Experiences of a European Scholar in America"; Morrison, "Kultur and Culture" and *The Search for a Method*; Hullot-Kentor, "Right Listening" and "Second Salvage."

5. I examine many of these network publications in my *Adorno in America*. Portions of this essay expand and elaborate on themes and ideas that I address in the book.

6. One place to possibly begin such a survey would no doubt be the Italian Futurists, and Marinetti and Masnata's "La Radia" (1933), which claimed that through the radio, Futurism would "overcome the machine, 'with an identification of man with the very machine destined to free him from muscular labor and immensify his spirit.'" At the same time, the radio, much like Edison's phonograph, would enable the Futurist to "overcome death 'with a metallization of the human body and the purification of the life spirit as a machine force" (255). The problems presented by the Futurist manifesto were manifold, not least of which was the question of how such a mechanization of the human body was to be effected and implemented. But technological considerations aside, the utopian gesture of "La Radia" presented its own difficulties, at least for listeners opposed to radio as a tool of authoritarianism. Although Marinetti and Masnata claim that the "pure organism of radio sensations" will be inextricably tied to "the immensification of space," that expansion of space resonates uncomfortably with German fascism's insistence on *Lebensraum*, particularly in light of the essay's exhortation to "overcome patriotism 'with a more fervent patriotism thus transformed into authentic religion of the Fatherland warning to Semites that they should identify with their various fatherlands if they do not wish to disappear" (256–57). In the case of the Futurists, radio is no tool to resist authoritarianism impulses; instead, the union of humanity and technology is imagined as an increasingly efficient means to guarantee political subjugation and racial oppression.

7. Brecht ultimately changed the title of the play to *Ocean Flight* in response to Lindbergh's admitted sympathies with National Socialism.

8. I am grateful to members of a roundtable discussion group on Adorno at the 2005 Harvard English Institute for helping me refine this idea.

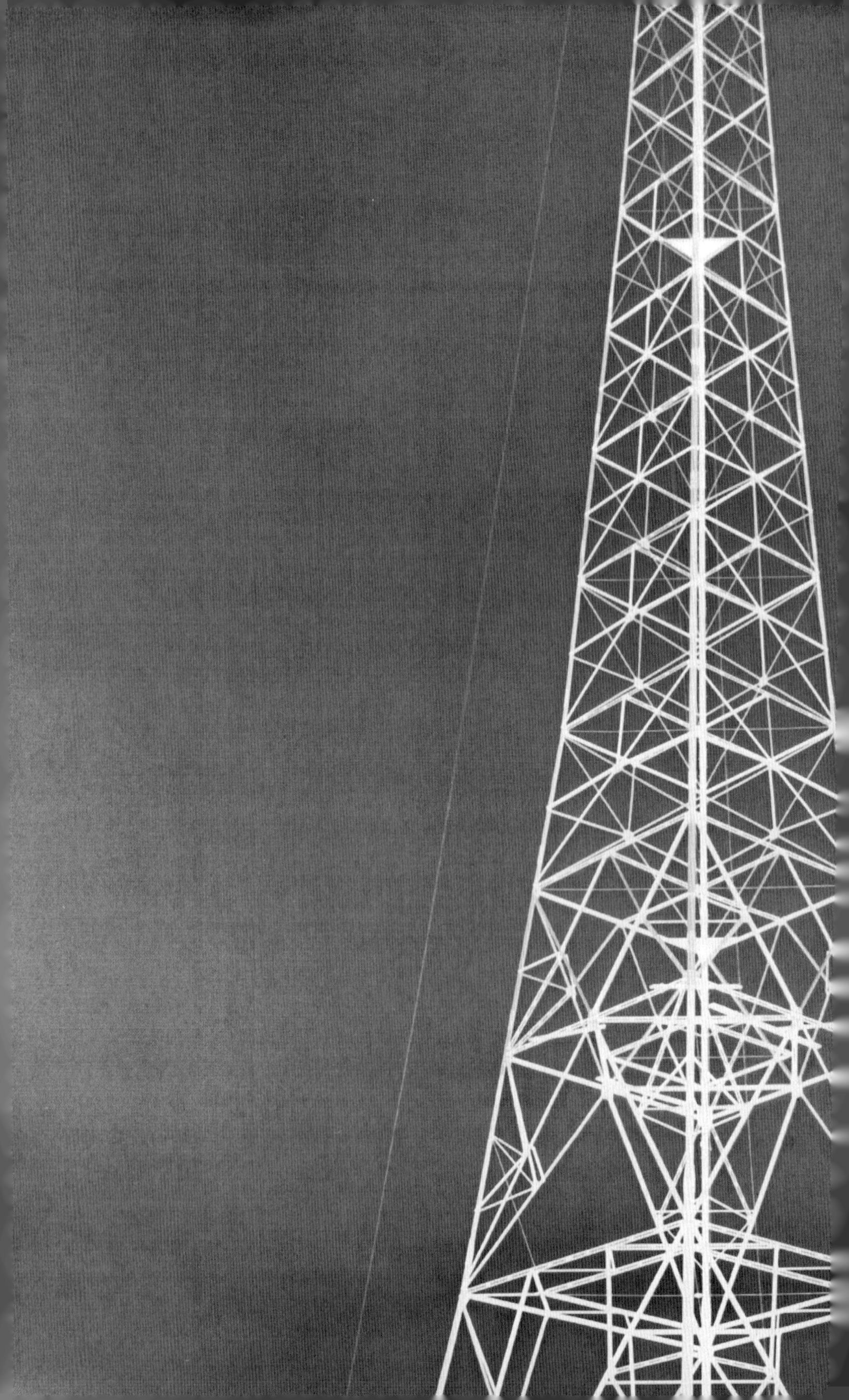

PART II PRESSURES & INTRUSIONS

CHAPTER 6

Gertrude Stein and the Radio

SARAH WILSON

Gertrude Stein returned to the United States in 1934, a year of fierce debate over the Federal Communications Act and the regulation of American radio. As she traveled the country, she could not have missed the fact that radio broadcasting had captured the imaginations of Americans. Stein had long been an avid reader and critic of popular culture and the media—her relationship with American newspapers predated her late romance with the radio. However, the radio in particular acted as a powerful formal model for Stein's late writing.[1]

Radio's influence can be traced in Stein's political and aesthetic strategies during her American tour, and it emerges as a dominant note in her World War II texts. Broadcasting provides a suggestive means of connecting Stein's early aural experimentalism (as in the multiple, echoing voices of "Bon Marche Weather") with her later, more popular, idiom. Resolutely oral, dialogic, and changeable, Stein's artistic project finally finds its formal corollary in mid-century radio. Tracing the influence of the radio in Stein's late writing also makes it possible to extend our analysis of Stein's use of indeterminacy in language to her more audience-focused texts, with the effect of complicating our readings of her investment in communication and communal meaning-making. Through the 1930s and 1940s, Stein wrestles with the idea of radio as a kind of public sphere—a forum in which self, other, and community can be constituted through talk. Her aurality must thus be understood as being as profoundly public in its orientations as it is private.[2] Finally, hearing the radio in Stein's late writing advances our understanding of the cross-fertilizations of "high" and "low" Modernist cultures while beginning to acknowledge radio's own distinct thematic and stylistic contributions to mid-century Modernism.

In "I Came and Here I Am," published in *Cosmopolitan* in February 1936, Stein describes the exhilaration of making a radio broadcast:

> it was, it really was, as if you were saying what you were saying and you knew, you really knew, not by what you knew but by what you felt, that everybody was listening. It is a very wonderful thing to do, I almost stopped and said it, I was so filled with it ("I Came" 72).

Broadcasting fills Stein with the feeling of everybody—of everybody listening. Just as Stein hoped to do in *Everybody's Autobiography* (1937), the radio creates "everybody" by creating the audience, a kind of community that understands itself as existing in (varying) relation to a mass medium.[3] This audience is not passive, and the broadcast is not unidirectional; as Stein's voice fills the airwaves, she in turn is filled by listening. The radio broadcast conveys a sense of an immediate and concentrated present; it begins again and again, as Stein's characteristically insistent phrasings indicate to us. It applies itself to representational questions that Stein's writing had been addressing for the three preceding decades. As she proclaimed to the readership of *Cosmopolitan*, Stein was smitten with the distinct form of connection that the radio seemed capable of performing.

The *Cosmopolitan* article represents the enjoyment of broadcasting as constituted by a distinct kind of knowledge, knowing "by what you felt." That is, the appeal of the radio is not exclusively informational but extends intellectually, just as it does physically, into more intimate and emotional territory. Stein's experience of the America of radio evangelist Father Coughlin would have made this extension clear. The emotional appeals of the radio form would achieve dominance in the United States by the late 1930s and early 1940s, when the threat of war made strongly felt connection and communication across the geographic and cultural divides of the United States seem even more imperative. As the American war machine engaged, pundits assigned the radio a central role in the creation and maintenance of "national morale." Radio assumed this central role by dint of its distinctive form of address, according to James Rowland Angell of NBC; he attributed the medium's influence to

> (1) the immediacy of its conveyance of news; (2) the vast mass of persons thus reached, many of them having only delayed access, if any, to the newspapers,

and not a few being unused to reading, or incapable of it; (3) the psychological appeal of the living human voice as contrasted with cold type—even when accompanied with the barrage of photographs now so universally employed by the press (355).

Stein's writing of this period also explores radio's distinctive formal command over the emotions. In *Ida* (1941), after having drifted without affect through a series of spaces, occupations, and husbands, Ida hears the national anthem on the radio and cries (674). In this scene, the radio's appeal is so immediate that it results in a disproportionate response. Ironically, the "living voice" reproduced by the radio has greater access to and effect upon Ida than do most of the truly living voices around her. Ida is a guarded public figure, but this medium penetrates her reserve. While the content conveyed by the radio in this case is clearly public and nationalistic, its form grants it access of unparalleled intimacy. Accordingly, this medium generates private feeling and directs it into public channels. It recouples the emotional and intellectual responses to truth and in the process, redefines truth.

When it operates in this way, the radio formalizes a response to expression that Stein considered essential to the understanding of her work. In a 1937 radio interview, Stein explains that the reader accesses what her writing is about when he or she responds to it with enjoyment: "The reader does know [what Stein is thinking about] because he enjoys it. If you enjoy you understand if you understand you enjoy. What you mean by understanding is being able to turn it into other words but that is not necessary" ("Radio Interview" 95).[4] Stein here distinguishes the interviewer's translation-as-understanding from her own response-as-understanding. Her response is not a re-transcription, but a creative act. Stein's version of understanding extends beyond intellectual engagement with the linguistic. It puts the reader in a less passive position by requiring his or her emotional participation in a communal creation of the meaning of the material.[5]

Participation of this sort was increasingly expected from radio audiences in the 1930s. One of Stein's longtime correspondents, the "Kiddie" (William G. Rogers, a doughboy from World War I), described in a letter to her the natural impulse to respond that he experienced while listening, in a lunchroom, to one of her radio broadcasts: "we heard you very plainly for a couple of minutes and I wanted to interrupt and say hello," he confided.[6] Much of the correspondence that President Franklin D. Roosevelt (FDR) received from Depression-era Americans was in response to the intimate "conversations" started in his *Fireside Chats*. Quiz shows such as *Vox Pop* demanded the participation of the audience in answering questions on the broadcast and in suggesting questions by correspondence. Another booming segment of the radio market was devoted to discussion shows, including the extremely popular *America's Town Meeting of the Air*, which aired weekly on NBC from mid-1935. Stein left the United States before *America's Town Meeting of the Air* began broadcasting, but she would sample its cultural effects on the GIs whom she encountered at the end of World War II. Her extended relationship with the University of Chicago academic community (chronicled in *Everybody's Autobiography* and represented by the lectures collected in *Narration*) makes it likely that she was also familiar with another successful radio discussion program that ran weekly on NBC from 1933, the *University of Chicago Round Table*. Indeed, the discussions that Stein describes (in *Everybody's Autobiography*) having at the University of Chicago suggest that she was casting her very own University of Chicago round table.

The discussion programs of the 1930s (both networks ran several) were particularly provocative in their approach to audience participation. Not unlike Stein's writing, these programs attempted to reorient audience enjoyment away from the certainty of conventional knowing. Surprisingly, the marketing strategies of the major discussion programs trumpeted their cultivation of intellectual complication, something that we most often associate with Stein's avant-gardism.

America's Town Meeting of the Air

George Denny, the founder of the popular *America's Town Meeting of the Air*, claimed to have conceived the show out of dissatisfaction with a neighbor who "would rather be shot than caught listening to Roosevelt on the radio," who "just won't listen. Even with the radio right there in his room and a chance to hear what the other side has to say for itself, he deliberately closes his mind" (Overstreet 3). According to Denny, *America's Town Meeting of the Air* was meant to access the energy the neighbor put into seeking out familiar perspectives and shift it outward. The program was intended to market difference of opinion to the nation, and it employed the unique access of radio to do so. It traveled around the country recording its broadcasts to ensure diverse representation. An episode consisted of a series of advocates addressing a central topic from their different perspectives (the first broadcast, May 30, 1935, heard from proponents of fascism, communism, socialism, and democracy in response to the question "Which Way America?"), followed by questions and responses from the audience.

The incorporation of the audience into the discussion form was particularly effective at troubling the division between performance and audience and at undermining the notion that the masses passively consumed mediated content. Harry and Bonaro Overstreet's book-length study of the program, *Town Meeting Comes to Town* (1938), celebrates Denny's radio program as the ultimate exploration of the radio's capacity in this endeavor. According to the Overstreets, *America's Town Meeting of the Air* was designed to put the emotional immediacy and intimate access of the radio to the service of public discussion; it would circumvent audience leanings toward the familiar and comfortable and insist upon multiple, irresolvable perspectives. That is, according to the Overstreets, *America's Town Meeting of the Air* represented a kind of participatory radio that recouples emotional and intellectual engagement, just as Stein's writing does.

Indeed, most of those involved with the program seemed to consider the volume of mail generated by *America's Town Meeting of the Air* a critical indicator of its success. George Denny proudly asserted that the very first broadcast "brought in a flood of three thousand letters" (Denny 373). Franklin Dunham of NBC cited with pride the 100,000 letters that NBC received for *America's Town Meeting of the Air* in 1937 (Dunham 78). Jeanette Sayre, research assistant to the Princeton Radio Research Project and the *Town Meeting of the Air*, published one of the first academic studies of radio fan-mail analysis. The Overstreets' study goes further and cites extensively from the correspondence received by the program. Responses from schoolteachers, ex-soldiers, city dwellers, and residents of remote rural areas stretch over numerous pages of their book. The use of quotation in *Town Meeting Comes to Town* extends beyond the presentation of evidence. Instead, the Overstreets seem to imply that the program's inclusiveness of a diversity of voices is a formal approach that breeds such inclusiveness in those who come into contact with it. They are no longer satisfied with referencing other voices; instead, they must hear them and allow them to be heard.

According to these writers, radio was negotiating a new kind of public sphere, one constantly spinning off unpredictable micro-versions. The idea of a public sphere was important to Stein, especially in the 1930s and 1940s; it figures in her depiction of salon culture in *The Autobiography of Alice B. Toklas* and her discussions of "publicity" in her post-American-tour writings. During the 1930s, radio seemed to promise to serve as an aural version of the "face-to-face communities" that John Dewey looked to in *The Public and Its Problems* (1927) for the reinvigoration of twentieth-century participatory democracy.

According to Nancy Fraser, some version of Habermas's public sphere and the public constituted through it remains critical to ideas of democracy. However, as Fraser makes clear, the public sphere as traditionally conceptualized is inadequately attuned to social inequality; her theorization of "subaltern counterpublics" suggests that "participatory parity" is more likely to be achieved in the context of a plurality of publics (14, 9).[7] Radio, especially as it became dominated by networks in the 1930s, has understandably been seen as presupposing the inadequately flexible, homogeneous public sphere that Fraser, among others, critiques. What remains underexplored is the degree to which radio of the 1930s was aware of these deficiencies and attempted to address them.[8] All of the marketing noise generated by *America's Town Meeting of the Air* does suggest that at least an appearance of mobility among the diverse and heterogeneous publics making up the United States of the 1930s was in the program's commercial interests.

In a radio broadcast made at Lyon in 1945, based on her experience of wartime Europe, Stein asserted the importance of the radio in bringing different voices together: "Ecoutez le radio. On ne pouvez [sic] pas imaginer d'entendre parler au radio l'esperanto. Non c'est ce qu'il nous interesse au radio c'est la multiplicite des langues. que chacqu'un cree d'une facon vibrante en son propre langue."[9] Broadcasters of the 1930s and 1940s were also insistent that American radio was fundamentally democratic in its aims and its techniques. In a *Public Opinion Quarterly* special supplement on "Public Opinion in a Democracy," published in 1938, spokesmen for both major American networks underlined their networks' commitment to the representation of a diversity of opinion. NBC's Franklin Dunham wrote, "Radio honestly strives to present not only two points of view on any subject brought to its forums, but as many points of view as there are, or at least as can be made articulate" (77), while his equivalent at CBS, Sterling Fisher, similarly insisted that in general, "it is the policy of the radio to present as many important and varied views as possible" (79). The networks were anxious to present the radio as adaptable to an unlimited range of audiences, modernistically adopting and discarding forms and discourses from hour to hour.

Of course, as many thinkers of the period pointed out, the pronouncements of network representatives are an inadequate basis for a judgment of the medium's performance in the 1930s. Thomas H. Reed, a prominent scholar of government and member of the National Municipal League, believed that the commercial motives of major networks precluded effective education, civic or otherwise, on their parts. As radio scholars have recently shown, ethnic and racial diversity was increasingly squeezed off the airwaves with the expansion of network control in the 1930s (Hilmes 1–33, 75–96).[10] And yet the insistence of contemporary rhetoric upon the diversity represented on the radio remains an important and intriguing key to understanding the role of American radio in the 1930s and 1940s. Regardless of the accuracy of the networks' claims for diversity, the idea of diversity clearly remained of great value to them.

Even Stein may have recognized the split between the theory of diversity on the American airwaves and its reality. In fact, by the 1940s she was listening to American propaganda in occupied France, and diversity was clearly only one of many of radio's claims whose correspondence with reality was questionable. Stein probably appreciated the radio's failure to restrict its claims to demonstrable realities. The strain of aurality in her work had always been that which most resisted realistic reading. (Indeed, the very degree to which aurality seems to resist theorization even today would, for Stein, seem immensely exciting.) For her, the formal and representational possibilities of radio arose from the fact that the medium was less tethered to straightforward realism (and thus possibly more open to alternate "realities") than were other popular media.

Radio and the Postwar United States

The influence of the form of radio on Stein's work is felt nowhere more powerfully than in her last major work, *Brewsie and Willie* (1946). *Brewsie and Willie* is constructed as a series of conversations between GIs. However, it is not one of Stein's plays—that is, it is a vocal performance that is not meant to be embodied. *Brewsie and Willie* takes up Stein's preoccupation with the capacity of voice to mediate social connection. In *The Autobiography of Alice B. Toklas,* Stein assumed a down-home, intimate voice that would have broad appeal and thus engineer far-reaching social connection. *Brewsie and Willie* goes beyond the salon setting of *Alice B. Toklas* to represent a rootless public *performance* of connection. The performance of connection in *Brewsie and Willie* is multiple, in multiple senses: it involves many voices; it involves conflicting interpretations; it involves multiple occurrences (a late version of

Stein's "beginning again and again"). That is, *Brewsie and Willie* resembles a form popularized by *America's Town Meeting of the Air*.

Brewsie and Willie is itself a cultural study, taking its form from the differences that Stein observed between the GIs of 1944 and the doughboys of 1918. In *Wars I Have Seen* (1945), Stein explains the difference between the two American armies as one verbal performance. The doughboys would drink silently or tell stories. The American army of 1944 "conversed, it talked it listened, and each one of them had something to say" (248). The American turn to talk that Stein celebrates in *Brewsie and Willie* cannot be exclusively attributed to the influence of radio. However, the radio is suggested by the GIs as a possible source of their new talkativeness: "Some of them said the radio had a lot to do with it, they got the habit of listening to information, and then the quizzes that the radio used to give kind of made them feel that it was no use just being ignorant" (*Wars* 256). The GIs present the radio as both a source of information and (through the quiz show) a site of questioning. Stein's interlocutors explain their own capacity for conversation at least in part by recourse to their radio listening skills—in this they follow Franklin Dunham of NBC who described the role of the audience as to "'respond' or listen," which equates the two acts (77). Brewsie, the main GI conversationalist of *Brewsie and Willie*, makes this same equation: "Listen, said Brewsie, listen to me. I want to know why do you fellows feel the way you do" (716). Their listening will necessarily entail their response to him. Conversation is not all voice—in fact, radio seems to suggest, talking and listening are inextricable, parts of the same role. Of course, to assign full responsibility for this style of reasoning to the radio would be to diminish dialogue's ongoing fostering of the ethos of response, balance, and discussion in which no position is static or explicable but all positions require constant re-exploration. However, it was clear to Stein in the forties that radio listening had had surprisingly positive intellectual effects on the GIs.

What *Brewsie and Willie* suggests is that the formal implications of the radio discussion format extend far beyond the implications of its content. The rhetoric of diversity marshaled by the networks in the thirties and even more ferociously during the war years shows its effects in the particular conversational style that Stein finds at work in the GIs:

> The last American army used to ask questions, why do the French people put walls around their houses what are they afraid of what do they want to hide. . . . This army does not ask questions like that, they consider that people have their

habits and their ways of living, some you can get along with and others you can't, but they are all perfectly reasonable for the people who use them. That is the great change in the Americans, they are interested, they are observant, they are accustomed to various types of people and ways of being, they have plenty of curiosity, but not any criticism, that is the new army. (*Wars* 252)

In other words, the point is not simply that the GIs talk but that they assign a certain performative value to talk. No longer can conversation gain them answers or explain away the peculiarities of a different culture. In this new conversational format, talk continually constitutes and reconstitutes differences; it multiplies ways of being, extending diversity rather than controlling it. This public sphere is not one of consensus but rather one of constant interaction between positions of difference.

Brewsie and Willie takes the form of a broadcast of this exciting GI talk. The talk's centrality to the text is conveyed through the lack of quotation marks, which indicates Stein's unwillingness to appear to be formally bounding this talk. The novel consists of a series of conversations among American GIs and nurses. Brewsie, a thoughtful GI, and Willie, his gruffer sidekick, are heard in most of the scenes but not in all of them. The conversations do circle uneasily around a central topic (the nature of a postwar United States), but they approach this topic from a myriad of different perspectives and never succeed in resolving anything. If anything, the talk confuses the participants further; as Willie reminds Brewsie, "you just keep on thinking and talking the more foggy you feel" (719).[11] As far as Brewsie is concerned, all of this talking is "how to get going away from what everybody has gotten the habit of thinking is the only way to do, kind of swinging a big truck around, said Jo, and making it come around a corner. No, said Brewsie, not that, but to find the way that looks the same and is different or find the way that looks different and is the same" (753). Brewsie's conversational agenda is difficult to distinguish from Stein's Modernist one. However, the radio-popularized discussion format enables the detachment of this agenda from solitary "genius" figures. The end of chapter 12 finds all of the conversation participants suddenly looking around for the missing Brewsie, which suggests their capacity to detach the form from the agent from whom they first learned it.

The conversations of *Brewsie and Willie* figure as moments of community-forming discussion and contemplation, scheduled "Not every day, said Jo. Mostly every day, said Willie," or with just enough regularity to be dependable without being predictable (726). Two nurses who discover the sessions in the third chapter return in most subsequent chapters; by the end, they are important contributors to the conversation and have introduced many of their friends to the forum. Like the radio parties that broadcasters were encouraging in the contemporary United States, these GI conversations powerfully enact the discursive construction of community. And yet they do not require agreement for the construction of community. Indeed, as Brewsie suggests, the conversations offer a way out of a dissatisfying community predicated on agreement: "I think we are sad because we have different feelings but we articulate all the same" (772). The relationships instantiated by the discussion format both arise from and further enable different articulations.

As the conversations of *Brewsie and Willie* begin again and again, the GIs and nurses together seem to move toward "not an answer but a way to go on" in a culture of jobs and job-mindedness, consumption and the installment plan (749). The way to go on, of course, is not to be found in Brewsie's social or economic theories, his evocation of the American pioneer spirit, or any of the other answers he fumbles toward. However, Brewsie's insistence on the possibility of an answer is precisely the energy that keeps the conversations going and keeps the participants interested and interesting. It is not simply the process of discussion that Stein values in this text[12] but also the naiveté that keeps conversation vital. It is this "innocence" that Stein elsewhere labeled the "new hope" of the World War II generation ("New Hope" 143). Brewsie's engagement, his creative willingness to produce interpretation and misinterpretation, keeps him and his peers from becoming the kinds of passive consumers that Adorno and the Frankfurt School theorists feared they would be. Much as we may agree with Willie that "there aint any answer," we also see that simply accepting that knowledge would rule out all but passive consumption (730). The conversational project must be sustained—it is a value in and of itself—and Willie's knowingness cannot sustain it.

Brewsie and Willie's series of conversations ends on the uncertain note of redeployment. A discussion suggests that this radio-mediated conversational ethos has yet to take root in American culture, where, according to Janet, "nobody talks like you boys were always talking" (776). The body of the text ends on a note of insecurity; Jo hopes for a newly conversational nation while the conversational stalwart Willie gruffly disbelieves that "those on the job" will ever talk (777). Yet even the cynic Willie does not entirely abandon the fantasy of a discursively constructed community—he simply locates it in the spaces of leisure, away from the job. Not job-mindedness but entertainment will preserve this form and keep Americans talking to each other. Radio did seem optimally positioned to facilitate the new leisure culture, and in leisure Stein finds a space for endangered talk.

Stein's epilogue to *Brewsie and Willie*, addressed "To Americans" and written in the first person, takes up the anxieties expressed by the GIs about their return home. According to her, the postwar era is critical to the definition of the nation; if the United States is not to "go poor," it must stop pursuing conventional solutions to its problems and devise something truly new. To achieve this, according to Stein, "you have to really learn to express complication. . . . Remember the depression, don't be afraid to look it in the face and find out the reason why. . . . Look facts in the face, not just what they all say, the leaders, but every darn one of you" (778). Stein's epilogue itself enters into a kind of conversation, speaking back to both her text and her readers while remaining formally distinct from both. If *Brewsie and Willie* adopts the form of the radio, broadcasting conversation, then Stein's epilogue reminds us that listening cannot be passive. The self, even for the participant "outside" the boundaries of the form, must understand herself as implicated and involved in the negotiations of the form.

Broadcasting Race

It is all very well to note Stein speaking from outside the formal boundaries of an established conversation, but we must keep in mind the license granted by her status as a cultural icon in the thirties and forties. Her epilogue to *Brewsie and Willie* has the distinct flavor of the Rooseveltian fireside chat. Other figures remain more fully outside the formal boundaries of *Brewsie and Willie*, the radio, and the nation as imagined community, and their participation helps to construct the limits of the radio-mediated public sphere. Most obvious among these outsider figures is the African American. African Americans do not have speaking parts in the conversations that make up *Brewsie and Willie*; their words, when they appear, are quoted by white participants in the conversations. Although they figure repeatedly in *Brewsie and Willie*, African American soldiers are noticeably excluded from the expressive form being explored by the text.

The position of African Americans in both *Brewsie and Willie* and American wartime radio reinforces the importance of attending to the *form* of expressive programs. As content, African American culture and questions of race were not considered outside the purview of radio. Indeed, a large part of radio's success could be attributed to its popular jazz programming throughout the 1920s and 1930s. The first triumphantly popular radio serial was *Amos 'n' Andy*, a blackface comedy that planted race squarely at the center of the topics engaged by radio programming.[13] By the 1940s, the American "race problem" had finally begun to figure in public debate, by virtue of the wartime equation of racism and Nazism.[14] The conversations of the white GIs and nurses in *Brewsie and Willie* reflect this new turn: they include tales that reflect the inadvertent relaxing of prejudice in the unfamiliarity of wartime surroundings and tentatively suggest that this relaxation may translate back into the postwar United States. As content, African Americans figure in these forums.

Formally, the story is quite different. *Brewsie and Willie*'s resistance to the *formal* integration of actual black voices—as opposed to white "racial ventriloquism" in the style of *Amos 'n' Andy* (Watkins 21, Barlow) or white paternalism in the style of earnest liberals on many of the discussion shows—follows that of mid-century radio. Indeed, even on the deliberately provocative *America's Town Meeting of the Air*, black voices were represented in this period by only three men: Langston Hughes, Richard Wright, and Walter White of the National Association for the Advancement of Colored People (NAACP) (Savage 241). Ironically, African Americans were cast as ill-suited to participation in the discussion of the "racial problem" by virtue of their "bias" on the topic. Here the free and diverse discussion reveals a culturally constructed formal limitation.

Stein seems quite aware of this formal failure of the radio. *Brewsie and Willie* attempts to critique this limitation by enacting it. In an unusually speechless moment in *Brewsie and Willie*, the following scene unfolds:

> It was late afternoon and the streets were narrow and three Negro soldiers came along, there was a very little girl and her mother, one of the Negroes fell on his knee like a cavalier before the little girl and took her hand, the mother went on and then stood slightly flushed looking at her little girl, the little girl a little flushed shook the hand of the kneeling soldier, he said a word in French, she answered him, she was a very little girl, only five years old, the other two had gone on, he rose from his knee and he went on, the little girl went along with her mother. (728)

This interaction is not conveyed via conversation, as is virtually everything else in the text, but by narration. Its incongruity immediately calls attention to the absence of voice—we do not hear the African American soldier, any more than the average American heard African American voices on the radio. This compelling figure both demands our attention and resists resolution. He particularly seems to resist representing anything other than himself, as if defying the kind of cultural duty that blackness was often compelled to perform in popular entertainment.[15] This soldier registers as content; he is not a participant in the form. However, his very inscrutability registers his resistance to this casting.

The French that the African American soldier is described as speaking connotes a cosmopolitanism lacking in most of the white GIs. This flexibility extends even beyond the aural. Playful, theatrical, the soldier performs a connection between himself and the young girl, a connection whose eloquence somehow achieves representation in a text otherwise fixated on the representation of voice. Indeed, the scene suggests in several ways that the African American soldier is conversant in multiple languages, employing different forms of voice to express himself in a formally limited field. However, to suggest this flexibility on the part of the African American GI, *Brewsie and Willie* must deviate from its discussion-dominated format. Suddenly the text seems to express insecurity about the ability of contemporary radio and radio-inspired forms to register other voices and unusual performances of voice.

This insecurity is well founded. Wartime radio programming ineffectively attempted to balance the need for greater engagement with questions important to African Americans and the fear of broadcasting "inflammatory" material and voices into an increasingly unstable nation. Even before the racial tensions of the war, African American "voice" was insistently cast as musical and theatrical production. During the war, the Armed Forces Radio Service responded to demands for African American representation in radio programming for the troops by transforming *Freedom's People*, a series that discussed the contributions of African Americans to the nation, into *Jubilee*, a "fine Negro variety show" (Hilmes 263).[16] Reporting in 1944 on the role of the mass media in the improvement of race relations, L. D. Reddick confirms that "the usual rôle of the Negro in radio is singing spirituals and folk songs and singing and playing jazz music." However, the radio escapes the more scathing indictments that Reddick hands out to other mass media; according to him, "the Negro comes nearer to receiving the same treatment 'as everybody else' over the radio than with any of the other agencies of mass communication." Indeed, according to Reddick, African American voices may be more effectively broadcast through musical programming, which is usually widely disseminated, while discussion programs favorable to the African American are not carried by southern stations (384, 385).

Stein's text does not seem to know what to make of this culturally imposed limitation of the radio form. On the one hand, jazz programming does not seem equal to the discursive "facing of the facts" that Stein's epilogue to *Brewsie and Willie* calls for in the postwar civic conceptualization of the nation. And yet, while the conversation about race was significantly muted after the war victory, African American musical and theatrical voices retained a significant hold on the nation. Scholars of the form have long suggested that jazz (and, during World War II, bebop) constituted both formal and political programs of resistance for African Americans.[17] Stein's correspondent Richard Wright seemed to be of that opinion also, explaining to Stein in a letter of 1945 that "I'm told that one point of solidarity between Negroes and whites in this war was Negro hot music, that when black boys met white boys, they could talk about jazz and swing. It seems like a sort of pass word."[18] If network radio sought to evade the "facts" by substituting jazz for African American voices, then, African Americans used jazz to broadcast their own facing—and reshaping—of the facts.

Stein's radical formalism aligns with the radical formalism of jazz here; her resistance to reading radio as a realistic medium suggests that her words "facing the facts" should not be read as advocating reproduction of the facts. From its outset, radio had the capacity to problematize the idea of "actual black voices." It often did so inadvertently when producers refused to cast African American actors for black roles because they didn't "sound like a Negro" (Barlow 31). Walter White made the complexity and contradictions of race in the United States apparent in his day-to-day life and on the radio, but when *America's Town Meeting of the Air* broadcast on television, the makeup man "was instructed to darken down White" and "lighten up" one of the other "white" panelists (Savage 238). Radio suggested a realm of vocal performance in which alignment with visually verifiable (and visually monitored) "realities" became dangerously slippery. When Langston Hughes participated in "Let's Face the Race Question" on *America's Town Meeting of the Air* in 1944, correspondence from one viewer suggested that the form of the program in fact complicated the imperative to "face the race": "What percentage of the audience was colored and how many of those who asked questions were colored? We couldn't tell over the air" (Savage 212). Blackface programs like *Amos 'n' Andy* worked to stabilize this point of slippage by instating dialect as a marker of blackness,[19] but figures like White, Hughes, and Wright undermined this aural regime by self-identifying as black while not sounding like either Amos or Andy. Radio's gift to the mid-century formulation of race was aural confusion.

In the adamantly visual *Life* magazine, Stein proudly wrote of her own role in discursively promoting such confusion; she relates a sergeant's complaint that "I confused the minds of his men, but why shouldn't their minds be confused, gracious goodness, are we going to be like the Germans, only believe in the Aryans that is our own race, a mixed race if you like but all having the same point of view" ("Off We All Went" 140). In confusion, point of view becomes unstable, as does the relation between self and other. Confusion is mixture, slippage, the collapse of boundaries—and it is a strategy long employed in Stein's writing.[20] Confusion of voices and the identities supposedly signified by these voices; of seemingly stable racial positionings, communities, and alliances; of divisions between form and content, discussion and performance—all of these were enabled by the mass dispersal of the disembodiment staged by the radio. While, on the one hand, the African American soldier seems to represent the limit case for the discursive formation of community, he also subtly implies that radio has the formal capacity to be productively confused about its own limits.

Even in its most powerfully networked phase, radio tended formally toward such indeterminacy. After all, what Stein responds to in radio is not its far-reaching capacity as a vehicle for propaganda but its far-reaching ineptitude at this task. As United States Commissioner of Education J. W. Studebaker wrote in 1939, impermanence is foremost among the "natural limitations of radio . . . radio is an excellent medium for engaging the interest of the public at large; but in order that this attention be translated into lasting results, other activities of a much more far-reaching nature must be sponsored, to take advantage of the widespread interest which radio is able to arouse" (489). Stein's appreciation of the creative capacities of wandering attention is well known.[21] The very impermanence of the radio broadcast ensured that the discussions it promoted would soon wander in different directions. As far as Stein was concerned, the shape of the nation and the public spheres constituting it could no more be directed than could the radio talk through which it took form.

Talk, as performed by mid-century radio and Stein's mid-century texts, can provide and promote communal confusion; through the performance of this confusion, a flexible and improvisatory community of communities comes into being. In Stein's work of the 1930s and 1940s, radio is employed as a form that enables mêlées—confusions of voices, identities, races, and programs. While reaching a broad audience, it pursues the cacophonous experimentation that characterizes Stein's early writings. In this way, radio formally enacts the Modernist constitution of "contested public spheres," forums in which community is in perpetual discursive formation and deformation. Stein's pursuit of this utopian vision of radio marks her as a thinker of her time, to be numbered among the radio boosters, if in an altogether unusual way. It also suggests that she presciently sensed the pertinence of mass media forms to Modernist formal experimentation. Radio in particular was a powerful formal model for an intellectual and expressive moment that valued the broadcasting of multiple voices.

Notes

1. By treating radio as a "form" I mean something akin to what Ian Baucom does when he emphasizes Frantz Fanon's request that his readers "conceive of the radio not as an instrument but 'as a technique'" (25).

2. Radio's intimacy of address was often considered responsible for its broad public significance. This suturing of intimacy and public efficacy, the personal and the political, is particularly suggestive in the context of important feminist studies of Stein's intimate politics such as those of Marianne DeKoven, Catharine R. Stimpson, Lisa Ruddick, Ellen Berry, and Harriet Chessman.

3. The topic of audience and the kind of identities it enables bedeviled Stein in her post-tour writings. For more on this topic, see Curnutt and Bryce Conrad.

4. The testimony of another journalist, quoted by Meyer to preface this Stein interview, suggests that the aurality of the experience is constitutive of this brand of understanding: "To hear Miss Stein read her own work is to understand it—I speak for myself—for the first time.... you see why she writes as she does; you see how from sentence to sentence, which seem so much alike, she introduces differences of tone, or perhaps of accent" (86). Indeed, the journalist's unreflecting use of the word "see" to convey understanding shows just how much conventional concepts of understanding must be recalibrated to admit of Stein's aurality.

5. For more on Stein's radical approaches to the idea of participation and dialogue, see Chessman.

6. William G. Rogers to Gertrude Stein, ca. 15? Nov. 1934, YCAL MSS 76, Series II, Box 121, Folder 2611.

7. In Fraser's words, the Habermasian public sphere can be understood as "a theater in modern societies in which political participation is enacted through the medium of talk" (2).

8. In fact, the understanding of the cultural work done by *America's Town Meeting of the Air* put forward by the Overstreets is not unlike the understanding of the cultural work done by late-twentieth-century TV talk shows recently put forward by the Mass Media Group of the Committee for Cultural Studies at the City University of New York. According to this group, late-twentieth-century TV talk shows "constitute a 'contested space' in which new discursive practices are developed in contrast to the traditional modes of political and ideological representation" (Carpignano et al. 96). Recent TV talk shows, according to the Mass Media Group, are constructed around

the audience and its response to a central topic; they are radically inconclusive; their approach is therapeutic rather than cognitive. In their quest for a lively exchange, they become a site for the circulation of alternative discursive practices. While *Town Meeting of the Air* hewed more faithfully to traditional debate format, it was inconclusive and considered the audience the primary player in its dramas. As such, it must be understood as attempting an early version of a mass-media "contested space" public sphere.

9. Stein, "Broadcast at Lyon" 4. YCAL MSS 76 Series I, Box 9, folder 172. ("Listen to the radio. One can't imagine hearing esperanto spoken on the radio. No, what interests us about the radio is the multiplicity of languages, which each one vibrantly creates in its/his/her own language." My translation.)

10. See also Vaillant.

11. As Willie later adds, "there aint any answer, there aint going to be any answer, there never has been any answer, that's the answer. Listen to me, that's the answer" (730).

12. For an important and related reading of talk, thinking, and complexity in *Brewsie and Willie*, see Abraham.

13. For more on this, see Ely.

14. For an excellent and wide-ranging discussion of race and commercial and governmental public affairs programming, see Savage.

15. The cultural employments of blackness are particularly well explored in scholarship on blackface; see Lott, *Love and Theft* and Rogin.

16. On this see Sklaroff.

17. See Robert G. O'Meally, ed., especially Lott, "Double V, Double-Time."

18. Richard Wright to Gertrude Stein, May 27, 1945. YCAL MSS 76, Series II, Box 131, Folder 2876.

19. Despite her own experiment with a version of blackface in "Melanctha," Stein also deplored certain representations of African American voices: "Dialect in books was upsetting, even then and even now, then when there was no esperanto and now when there is no esperanto" (*Wars* 23). Book and radio versions of dialect were comparable in the ways in which they unsuccessfully systematized styles of speech that were essentially protean. Melanctha's speech is profoundly unlike these versions of dialect, and Richard Wright's famous response to the accuracy of Stein's depictions of black speech in "Melanctha" stands as testimony to the efficacy of her nonrealistic approach to the representation of voice. Stein's depiction, esperanto-like, crosses boundaries rather than policing them.

20. For an alternative approach to the role of indeterminacy in Stein's work, see Ashton.

21. For more on this, see Berry.

[CHAPTER 7]

The Voice of America in Richard Wright's *Lawd Today!*

JONAH WILLIHNGANZ

> He is seen, but he does not see; he is an object of information, and never a subject in communication.
> —Michel Foucault, *Discipline and Punish*

Radio, it has been said, conquered America. The metaphor seems apt, even if radio's reign was relatively short. Everything that makes up the experience of American radio—its technology, institutions, genres, and markets—formed in less than twenty years. No medium had saturated a culture faster. In 1920, there was not a single radio station or commercial radio set in America. By the late 1930s nearly everyone owned a radio, and its intimate, disembodied voices were experienced everywhere, often simultaneously.[1] The effects of radio's development were just as remarkable. It helped create mass-market culture and established a new medium of power, a medium of disembodied speech and sound that, for many, seemed godlike and capable of literally hypnotizing the country.[2]

As this volume of essays makes clear, writers found the formation and experience of radio powerfully suggestive. For many, radio became a sign of cultural transformation, a source of narrative or poetic devices, or a new vehicle for the literary enterprise. In America, where tensions between high and low culture were not as strongly felt as they were in Europe, a number of writers and artists embraced radio, especially before its heavy commercialization. Some wrote for and performed on radio—we might think of Gertrude Stein or Archibald MacLeish. Some inflected their work with the kind of disembodied voices radio produced—we might think of poets such as H. D., Ezra Pound, and T. S. Eliot, or novelists such as Henry Roth. Others, such as John Dos Passos, Sinclair Lewis, and Richard Wright were wary of radio from the start, and for them the experience of radio was even more suggestive. For these writers, radio was not a sign of the times, a source of aesthetic strategies, or a means to democratize literature; it was a way to describe how mass-market media were helping to formulate and install a new way of exercising power. For these writers, radio helped reveal the way the subject was becoming, in Foucault's phrase, "an object of information, and never a subject in communication" (199). Radio helped them imagine the modern subject as a kind of dead medium, a relay losing its capacity to generate its own signal, a disappearing voice.

One reason this literary engagement with radio is important is that it strongly challenges traditional and even revisionist theories of Modernism and mass culture. It reveals that, at least in America, writers responded as much to the mass-market media's organization of power as to its products. Traditional theories of Modernism, from New Critical to Frankfurt School, saw Modernism as aesthetic heroism, autonomous art standing against the degraded, formulaic genres of industrial capitalism. Revisionist theories have complicated this picture by challenging the line drawn by this "Great Divide" and by demonstrating that the relation between Modernism and mass culture is more dialogic than dialectic.[3] But like traditional theories, they also tend to see Modernist works engaging the content of mass culture rather than its institutions. When we examine how American literature engaged radio, we find these approaches to Modernism and mass culture have limited value. This is especially true when we look at American novels at the end of the Modernist period, novels such as John Dos Passos's *The Big Money* (1936) and *Number One* (1943), Sinclair Lewis's *It Can't Happen Here* (1935), Kenneth Fearing's *Clark Gifford's Body* (1942), and Richard Wright's unpublished *Lawd Today!* (completed 1937). These novels are more interested in the effects of mass communication than the effects of mass culture. For them, radio is not its content—not programs, not representations, not end product. It is instead a structuring of experience and of power, a process of social relation that crystallizes where and how power operates in modern culture. When we look at how American literature engaged radio we find not the familiar critique of mass culture but a critique of how discursive power was becoming paramount yet invisibly organized. The literary engagement with radio described here asks us to rethink the theories of Modernism and mass culture.

Another reason American literature's engagement with radio is important is that it records what many sensed was happening to the human voice. American novels in the 1930s use radio to help describe a dual movement in modernity toward the reification of the human voice (the voice becomes a thing) and toward the endowment of objects with speech (things come to have voices).[4] In these novels, subjects increasingly speak clichéd, nongenerative, dead speech, or lose the power of speech altogether; objects, on the other hand, begin to produce the speech that matters, the speech that acts. The radio, in its production of seemingly ubiquitous, omniscient, invisible voices hailing disconnected, silenced subjects in their private spaces, becomes the speaking object par excellence. It becomes a sign of how power is increasingly discursive and how that power is moving from subjects into objects.

In this essay I focus on how one novel in particular, Richard Wright's *Lawd Today!*, figures radio in this way. Radio proves a powerful emblem for Wright, giving him a way to express the particular kinds of disempowerment experienced by blacks living in the urban North of the United States.[5] It is a novel that finds radio's disembodied voices terrifically disturbing, and not just because its voices produce demagoguery on a new scale. Like other American novels of the period, *Lawd Today!* understands radio as a kind of aural version of Jeremy Bentham's panopticon, a way of breaking the dyad of speaking and being spoken to. For Wright, it is this break that most accurately expresses the way white power is exercised over blacks. Radio is not so much the purveyor of stereotypes and false consciousness as it is the vehicle by which the subject is transformed from Kenneth Burke's creative "symbol-using animal" into a dead medium—a simple circuit or relay for information and ideologies.[6] The protagonist of this novel, as we will see, is hailed constantly and his labor maintains the nation's oldest communication network; but he himself has no power to engage the voices that hail him or that he serves. The experience of radio in the novel comes to signal this condition and demonstrate the reification of the human voice.

My chief claim here is that *Lawd Today!* makes the experience of radio emblematic of the patterning of cultural power by aligning it with the experiences of fascism and racism in the 1930s. Each experience—that of radio, fascism, and the racism of the period—is figured as losing one's voice to disembodied voices. Each experience is figured as a dispossession of voice, a loss of a natural capacity to communicate, to enter into the speech situation of one's culture. Each experience is of mystified voices and hypnotic power (control through forms of speech). Each experience is of the calculated and programmed masquerading as the authentic and unmediated. In *Lawd Today!*, the radio is to the listener as fascism and racism is to the subject. All operate as inanimate, magical, silencing voices.

By equating radio with the disempowerment of fascism and racism, Wright wages a critique of the mass media very different from the critique traditionally associated with texts of the Modernist period. For Wright, the problem the mass media pose is not mass culture but mass communication, not *things* but the *process* of social interrelationship produced by mass-market media—especially radio. For Wright, as for other 1930s American novelists, mass-market media are destroying authentic, dialogic communication—and they are doing so at the very moment communication seems to become the prerequisite for a subject's self-sovereignty and historical agency.

☉ ☉ ☉

The existence of ideology and the hailing or interpellation of individuals as subjects are one and the same thing.
—Louis Althusser (175)

Now what was I dreaming? It seemed very, very important that he should remember. He screwed up his eyes, but the dream steps were drowned in a vast blackness, like a slow movie fadeout. He had been going somewhere in a great big hurry; he had been thirsting, longing for something. But each time he had almost got to it, each time it was almost his, somebody had called.
—Richard Wright, *Lawd Today!*

Written in the mid-1930s, but published posthumously, *Lawd Today!* narrates in detail one bleak but typical day in the life of Jake Jackson, a young black postal worker in Chicago.[7] Jake is not a sympathetic character: he's given to drinking, loafing, beating his wife, and he is quick to blame his unhappiness on anyone but himself—and he is unhappy about nearly everything. The novel makes clear that Jake creates much of his own misery, and when he comments ruefully that his life seems no different from a slave's, this smacks more of ignorance and self-pity than perceptiveness. But the novel also makes clear, in the way naturalist novels do, that its characters and their choices are strongly conditioned by their social context. In the novel's descriptions of Jake's morning routine, his visit to a barber and local gambling house, his swing shift at the post office, and the evening carousing with friends, we find Jake's life belongs to him only a little—that he is powerfully and unconsciously shaped by the forces around him. What is unusual about the novel's brand of naturalism is that these forces are almost always expressed as unseen voices.

The day that *Lawd Today!* narrates is special in one respect: it is February 12, Lincoln's birthday. This is announced by the radio address that opens the first section of the novel, a broadcast honoring Lincoln that both wakes Jake and surfaces throughout the novel. Jake hears the Lincoln broadcast at home, at the barber, in a diner, at a parade, at work, and even at the nightclub he visits with his friends at the end of the novel. Passages from the broadcast also introduce each of the novel's other two sections, describing a decisive moment during the Civil War and then Lincoln's assassination. Throughout, these broadcasts serve as ironic counterpoint, the great liberator's life set against lives that seem anything but liberated. Jake greets them with almost no interest, as though Lincoln's victories have no real meaning for him, especially compared to his immediate needs and appetites. For Jake and other black characters who hear the program, Lincoln's legacy is almost incomprehensible. Even so, the radio's voice leaves an impression on Jake. It is an uncanny voice that invades, silences, and commands, and it is a voice that he associates with the world of whites.

Critics of *Lawd Today!* have generally lumped the broadcasts in with the other forms of mass-market media Jake experiences throughout his day—newspapers, magazines, mail circulars, and even movie posters. They have seen the broadcasts, along with other media that fill Jake's day, as suggesting how much mass-market discourses condition modern consciousness. This has led to somewhat predictable readings of the novel, where the mass media interpellate subjects who, to one extent or another, attempt to negotiate or contest that interpellation. These readings focus on the novel's liberal incorporation of mass culture, in the form of newspaper stories, flyers, posters, and the radio addresses, and typically pit these discourses against stretches of vernacular-loaded dialogue between Jake and his friends to produce a rather familiar, Modernist contest between mass culture and authentic experience (here African American idiom and folk tradition). Vincent Perez argues, for example, that *Lawd Today!* describes mass media's attempt to colonize consciousness and "the capacity of a subcultural group to disrupt the ideological sway of media culture." The novel stresses "Jake's interpolation by 'mass culture' and estrangement from an implied 'authentic' folk culture" but the vernacular exchanges between Jake and his friends "illustrate the critical capacity as well as vitality of Black Urban culture" (161). For Perez, mass culture's messages are always open to refashioning, available for negotiation, so Jake and his friends can resist the terms of the culture and "refuse to internalize their own objectification" (163). Similarly, Brannon Costello suggests that the mass media's messages—such as myths of success—are countered by the characters' traditions and culture. Radio and other mass culture outlets alienate the characters from their own authentic culture but can be countered as long as the characters hold on to African American forms of communicating among themselves—playing the dozens, for example (Costello 39–50). For Perez, Costello, and other critics, the radio broadcasts stand with other forms of mass culture against the characters' authentic cultural heritage.

In my view, the incorporation of radio in *Lawd Today!* serves a different purpose and suggests a different attitude toward mass-market media. To be sure, the juxtaposition of the Lincoln broadcasts and Jake's day creates dramatic irony. And some of the ad-pitches in the initial broadcast might be linked to Jake's many recycled platitudes to suggest mass media's ideological conditioning. But the regularity of the broadcasts, their similarity to the representation of white speech, and Jake's struggle to engage the speech of either all suggest another reason for radio's presence. It is not the content of the radio addresses so much as the experience of their voice that is striking here, and the way that experience is so closely aligned with racial subordination and fascism. Each is represented almost identically to the others: as losing one's voice to disembodied voices, to absent presence. Each experience is figured as the dispossession of the human voice, accompanied by the rise of ubiquitous, coercive, unseen voices. Radio here does not stand for mass culture but for the way Jake experiences his world, a world dominated by racism, capitalism, and their complex effects. Radio helps specify how these forces operate in Jake's life and, most important, makes the capacity to speak and have that speech matter the key to engaging these forces. The experience of radio in the novel reveals how Jake and his friends may be able to resist the myths of the mass media, but any "negotiation" of them depends on their capacity to enter the conversation—to be a subject in communication, not an object of information.

As I've indicated, radio broadcasts both introduce the novel's three sections and appear regularly within the narrative. As a result, the addresses function in two different ways. First, standing outside the narrative, the broadcasts frame and comment on the narrative, surrounding the narrative with disembodied voices. Second, as part of the narrative, the broadcasts introduce action, set agendas, and occupy the minds of the characters. In the opening pages, the radio's voice operates in both ways. First, the disembodied voice is represented as framing or even constructing all existence. The voice of the announcer initiates the novel, dictates the time and place, and begins its hails:

> LADIES AND GENTELMEN, JACK BASSETT SPEAKING! AT THE NEXT TONEBEAT THE TIME WILL BE EXACTLY EIGHT O'CLOCK . . . LOOK OUT YOUR WINDOW! . . . DOESN'T IT MAKE YOUR HEART SKIP A BEAT TO SEE OLD GLORY FLOATING THERE SO BEAUTIFULLY IN THE MORNING BREEZE? (4)

The radio's voice, then, establishes the setting of the novel, and in some sense the setting is a world in which one is constantly spoken to and directed by voices. Next, the disembodied voice acts as a force within the narrative. To start, the voice literally raises to consciousness the protagonist Jake. The narrative begins with the distant voice of a kitchen radio insinuating itself into Jake's dream world. In his dream, Jake is commanded to mount a flight of stairs by a voice that he cannot see:

> No matter how hard he squinted his eyes and craned his neck, he could not see the top of the steps. But somebody was hollering and he had to go up. He hollered, *Yeah, I'm coming right up, in just a minute!*(5)

Jake struggles to comply with the voice, which grows louder and louder, but the steps recede before him as he climbs. The voice of radio takes over Jake's dream, colonizing even his unconsciousness with a hailing that is incomprehensible and unanswerable but which coerces his body nonetheless. Finally, the voice becomes so loud that it wakes Jake—literally calling him to consciousness and putting his day into motion. As we will see, the radio voice will continue to operate within the narrative, though less dramatically, to prompt the novel's action.

In these opening pages, we also find the first association between the voice of radio and the voices of the novel's white characters. Both the radio voice and the whites' voices are ideology in action—unseen, unanswerable forces that supply the terms through which one relates to the world—operating very much according to the metaphor Althusser has used to describe the operation of ideology: vocal hailing. What Jake hears as he drifts from dream-state to waking-state is the announcer's voice coming from a radio in the next room, but what he thinks he hears is his boss calling him: "*that old sonofabitch up there sounds just like my boss, too!*" (5). This voice sounds familiar to Jake and it will feel familiar to us later as well. It strongly resembles the voices of his white employers: disembodied, seemingly able to reach him anywhere, and obliging obedience. And, as we shall see, there are other similarities. When Jake begins finally to make out "the voice that boomed so loud in his ears," it describes (white) historical figures who demanded to be heard: "GARRISON . . . DECLARED HIMSELF OUTSPOKENLY AGAINST SLAVERY AND OPPRESSION . . . I WILL NOT RETREAT A SINGLE INCH—I WILL BE HEARD"(6). When Jake attempts to respond to the voice describing these figures, nothing happens. Later, white characters will dictate in no uncertain terms the situation of communication—that they will be heard, and that Jake will not. Here the radio's voice also compels Jake's body into seemingly endless labor, and at work the white foremen, whom we hear but never see, will do the same. And perhaps most obviously, the typographic representation of the radio voice—always in all capitals—is duplicated when representing the speech of many whites in the novel, particularly his supervisors at work. Right from the start, then, the experience of radio becomes associated with Jake's subject position as a lower-middle-class black man in a white-run world.

One of the most important consequences of aligning radio and the black experience of white power is to make communication central to a subject's consciousness and agency. The alignment forges a strict identity between power and the capacity to speak, to be heard, and to have one's speech matter. As the opening scene develops, we find that Jake at some level understands his struggle for self-sovereignty and agency as a struggle to silence the disembodied voices that seem to control him, and to make his own speech count. That is, Jake's experience of the radio voice and its association with his white boss immediately suggest to both Jake and the reader that power hinges here on speech. First, Jake yells at Lil, his wife, to turn off the radio in the kitchen and makes clear that the milkman, whom he has overheard talking with Lil on the porch, must leave. He spends most of his morning trying to assert himself by demanding that Lil occupy the position he did in his dream—silent and compliant. He continuously demands that Lil shut up, listen, and show him that his voice has an effect on her—all of which she resists, even when Jake physically threatens her. When she claims to be listening, Jake tells her repeatedly to "act like it" and speak only when spoken to (10). When Lil cracks under a string of insults and talks back to Jake, he becomes incensed, screams "you can't talk to me this way!" and finally does beat her (17). Later, after Jake bathes and shaves, Lil continues to defy Jake's obsessive demand that she respond to his voice. When he calls to her out on the porch, she doesn't acknowledge him until his "voice swell[s] throughout the flat like the roar of a lion" and even then she comes "leisurely to the door." What enrages Jake here is not only her resistance but also that Lil has been speaking to someone else: "Running your old fat mouth like always, hunh?!" (25).

Jake's attempt to control the situation of communication, at least in his own home, continues when he sits down to breakfast and the newspaper. He reads portions of the paper aloud and then responds at length to them, partly preaching to Lil and partly just talking to himself. He begins with the paper's lead headline:

ROOSEVELT STRIKES AT MONEY CHANGERS
WILL DRIVE THEM FROM THE TEMPLE, HE SAYS

"Hunh," Jake grunted as he laid the paper aside and took up a slice of toast. "That's what he says! And what he says is just so much hot air. Nobody'll ever tell these rich American men what to do. Naw, siree!" (32)

Jake frequently poses his encounter with the newspaper as a conversation, characterizing the headlines or their subjects as speaking and then giving those voices a piece of his mind. His responses are generally ignorant, xenophobic, sexist, and racist, and they are frequently ironic, as is the response here. Jake, who can pronounce on very little and cannot gain the attention even of his wife, declares the president's voice to be "hot air." But Jake's long, loud, convoluted replies to the newspaper indicate again his awareness (and the novel's conviction) that to be without voice is to be without power. His effort with the newspaper is no more successful than his effort with the radio or with Lil. He strains increasingly to make his responses forceful, repeating some version of "that's what I say!" and trying to discover something to make at least Lil recognize him, "something to say, something that would rouse her out of her smug complacency... that would rouse her to a sharp sense of his presence"(28, 31). But nothing works. Nothing he says gives him presence.

Jake's obsession with silencing Lil and his compulsion to respond verbally to every newspaper story seem idiosyncratic and strange until Jake moves out into the world of the street, his friends, and especially his job. We find that the speech situation that Jake tries to establish at home with Lil and his newspaper is the situation he himself experiences everywhere else. We discover that Jake is talked down to and drowned out by nearly everyone and that his life is guided by voices beyond not only his control but also his comprehension. For example, after a stop at his mailbox (where he talks back out loud to the mail circulars in the same way he did the newspaper), Jake visits a local gambling parlor to play "policy," a complex form of lottery. He recalls his dream and its voice and feels strongly that they will guide him to play the right numbers. In this scene, both a book that explains what numbers to attach to his dream and the numbers themselves "call" to Jake, compelling him to throw away almost all his hard-earned money. Jake is represented as both silent and blind. When he approaches the tables a woman asks him "What you saying, Jake?" and he responds, "I ain't saying nothing" (45). When Jake spins the wheel to play the lottery's numbers, he is blindfolded, left to listen to unseen voices calling out his fate. Later, when Jake's job at the post office is on the line (for beating Lil), he finds himself again at the mercy of an unseen voice. A telephone call from the postmaster's office (for which he has paid handsomely) decides again his fortune. These scenes replay the opening moments of the novel, describing Jake's powerlessness again as subjection to unseen voices, voices like the radio's voice.

That radio voice, describing Lincoln's inaugural address, the siege of Washington, and other Civil War events, is heard throughout the first section of the novel—at the barber, at a lunch counter, even on the street. Jake responds to the voice very little, and when he does it is with clichés and empty platitudes. But Jake does begin to recognize that its power must be met with likeness—that the voice must be met with a voice. On the way to work with his friends Al, Bob, and Slim, Jake witnesses a parade. It is in this scene that an organized form of black power first appears and that Jake first connects black power to producing a voice or sound. The parade is a large, colorful, military-style procession of the fictive "International Negro Uplift Association," and its description strongly resembles accounts of the parades put on by Marcus Garvey's Universal Negro Improvement Association. Jake and his friends are mesmerized. Two things make Jake balk, though: the group's call for a repatriation of blacks to Africa and the elaborate trumped-up costumes and military ranks. But the aural sensations of the parade stay with Jake and his friends: first, the group's declaration that to Jake "sounds like the Constitutootion!" and then, especially, the music: "They did not talk; they were feeling the surges of memory the music had roused in their minds. They did not agree with the parade but they agreed with the music" (110).

It's clear that this scene and the description of the music's effect are intended to emphasize how Jake and his friends are much more interested in their sensual appetites than any political consciousness. But they also begin to lead Jake to imagine that the response to white power, to the disembodied voice, must be, literally, a voice. As we shall see in a moment, when Jake fantasizes about defying the whites at work, he fantasizes about a black leader who commands, compels, and even destroys with the power of his voice.

Before this, though, the novel makes clear that the power of Jake's voice relies not on the form of its speech but on its context. After the parade, Jake, Al, Slim, and Bob board the elevated light rail uptown to work. In this scene we find an example of the traditional, authentic form of dialogue that many critics see as a response to the mass culture Jake encounters in the novel. The friends spy a beautiful woman in the car and begin whispering and whistling softly together. Jake then sings in an undertone and he is answered in turn by each of his friends:

"Oh, Lawd, can I ever, can I ever? . . ."
Bob screwed up his eyes, shook his head, and answered ruefully:
"Naw, nigger, you can never, you can never. . . ."
Slim sat bolt upright, smiled, and countered hopefully:
"But wherever there's life there's hope. . . ."
Al dropped his head, frowned, and finished mournfully:
"And wherever there's trees there's rope." (111)

This segment reminds us of an earlier call-and-response dialogue, when the friends play the dozens, concocting insult after insult to one another's mothers. Both dialogues forge a connection among the four men, as does a later, long segment of dialogue among them at the post office in which the identity of the four speakers becomes indistinct. The dialogue in each case recalls the blues, the linguistic improvisation of black vernacular speech, and a strong sense of shared experience. These dialogues do indeed stand in sharp contrast to the mass-mediated speech Jake encounters, but they are also presented to us as a kind of closed circuit, a form of communication that has no bearing on the discourses that matter to the men's position in the culture. In the later segment at the post office, for example, their dialogue is observed almost anthropologically by the whites, as a curiosity, but in no way does their dialogue challenge the whites. After the sequence above, Jake, Slim, and Bob all burst into raucous laughter and the scene closes with an image that underscores just how removed this authentic speech is: "[the] passengers turned and stared, wondering what on earth was the matter with those four black men" (111).

Jake's experience of working in the mailroom of Chicago's main post office makes up the second section of the novel, and it is this section that most strongly aligns the radio with the black experience of white power and equates power with the capacity to communicate. It is this section that also aligns the exercise of the unseen, coercive voice with fascism. These alignments begin with the description of the workplace itself and continue to be formulated throughout the action and dialogue. The first indication we get that the disempowerment experienced at the post office is related to speech comes as Jake arrives: "As he mounted the steps he wondered if he would have to go on this way year after year 'til he died. Was this *all*? Deep in him was a dumb yearning for something else . . ." (116). A moment later Jake is asked for the second time in the novel "What you saying, Jake?" and again he responds, "Ain't saying"(117). As he enters the post office Jake finds himself internally and externally speechless.

The post office is portrayed from the start as a dusty, gloomy, but almost living organism that watches and sonically commands Jake and his friends. It is figured as a vaguely panoptic space, teeming with "dingy lights partly hidden by green shades" that resemble "dull, glowering eyes." More important, it is a space whose sounds govern Jake's and his friends' bodies. Its "penetrating drone," for example, "fill[s] their bodies with a faint, nervous tremor"(117). The space reverberates with "the clatter of machines" and "the constant sound of rusty steel grating against rusty steel." The canceling machines stamp so loudly that they shake the floor and make Jake's body vibrate (137, 147). This attention to the sound of the workplace leads to an unusual description of the dehumanizing effects of standardized, deskilled labor. Jake and his friends are certainly alienated from their labor because they have no connection to the communication they are facilitating (during a break one says "I wouldn't get so damn tired if I knowed where some of this mail is going" [150]). But they are also represented as being silenced by their labor. The sorting and stamping machines make conversation impossible and induce a rhythm that lulls them all into sleepy, docile, inarticulateness, unable to say anything or have anything to say. Jake and his friends merge with the drone of the post office, and their work produces an internal drone that "weigh[s] their tongues into silence" (150).

The most significant sound at the post office, though, is the sound of white voices. In fact, the post office is most of all a space of white voices and, like the radio voice, these are represented as ubiquitous, invisible, and unanswerable. Whites here are ever present and dictating but almost never seen. Be they Jake's bosses, the shift supervisors, the foremen, or even the secretaries, whites are represented nearly solely by their speech. Almost no descriptions of physical appearance are given, and frequently the presence of white characters is indicated only by the sudden appearance of their speech in the text. Even at Jake's hearing, which occurs at the start of the shift, his boss Swanson and the supervisors are represented almost entirely through their dialogue. Out on the mailroom floor, whites' voices become almost totally disembodied, and the typography of their voices frequently matches the representation of the radio speech. Throughout, these disembodied voices command bodies. The first voice is the detail clerk:

> They got their timecards from the racks and punched in. A voice was bawling:
> "LINE UP FOR DETAIL!"
> As they fell into line and moved toward the Detail Station, they could hear the detail clerk barking out numbers. (128)

This clerk and others are heard continuously during the mailroom scenes, issuing commands such as "CLEAN OUT," "FILL IN," and "INSPECTION" (128–44). In one hushed exchange, Jake and his friends sum up a bit wryly the way they experience white power in terms of speech:

> "The white man's Gawd in this land."
> "If he says you live, you live."
> "And if he says you die, you die." (133)

Al, Bob, Slim, and Jake are resigned for the most part to their situation, but Jake's cockiness and quickness to anger draw him into a confrontation with an inspector. This confrontation, much like the one between Jake and Lil, casts speech as power. But this one also figures the white voice as insuperable. The encounter begins by the inspector interrupting a dialogue between Jake and Bob:

> "That reminds me," began Jake. "I . . . "
> "INSPECTION!"
> A sudden voice boomed into Jake's ear and made him start. (140)

The inspector demands to know why Jake is making so many mistakes sorting the mail, but the confrontation quickly becomes an argument about who is allowed to speak. Jake is reported, essentially, for talking, and we see once again how power is figured as the right or capacity to speak, or even make any sound. Both sound and speech belong to the white man:

> "You've been running your mouth like a blue streak for half an hour! Why don't you quit playing around and do your work!"
> Jake's neck grew hot. The inspector had spoken in a loud, harsh voice.
> "I'm going to give you a writeup!"
> "Do it and quit yelling at me!" Jake snapped.
> "Don't give me none of your lip!"
> "Don't give me none of *yours*!"
> "Who do you think you're talking to!"
> "You didn't have to yell at me!"
> "I'll talk to you like I damn please!" (141)

The exchange is similar in many respects to Jake and Lil's at the start of the novel, though here Jake is on the other side. We understand better now why Jake was so desperate in that earlier exchange and why he so quickly resorted to physical violence. At the end of this altercation, the inspector tells Jake he'll get 200 demerits and, referring to the write-up, says ominously: "You're going to hear from this" (142). This last remark to Jake stresses once again that the power whites exercise, their power over blacks, is expressed and felt as a voice from a thing, a disembodied voice.

For the rest of this scene two feelings build in Jake: that he is being watched and that he is patrolled by disembodied voices with whom he has no right or capacity to engage. The sense of being observed, and the power of that observation, comes up at the start of this fight with the inspector: "He looked at Jake for a whole minute before he spoke" (140). Just after the fight, Jake's boss Swanson appears with a tour group of whites. Once again there is no description of Swanson and his voice has the effect of just "appearing" or floating in and out. And then, attached to the disembodied voice, comes again the sensation of being watched:

> ". . . from here the mail is sent to state sections, where . . ."
> The voice was moving on. He heard murmurs of laughter, light, silvery . . . *They're looking at us like we was monkeys in a zoo!* (143)

As Swanson's voice passes by, Jake is plagued by a feeling of powerlessness and this leads him into an infantile fantasy of destroying the America he has defended for much of the novel. He dreams of millions of black soldiers attacking the United States, himself on the deck of a battleship surrounded by black generals, and then:

> a voice commanding: "FIRE!" *Booooooooooom!* A black shell screamed through black smoke and he saw the white head of the Statue of Liberty topple, explode, and tumble into the Atlantic Ocean . . . *Gawddamn right!* (143–44)
>
> Jake continues "building dreams of a black empire" and it is just when "black troops were about to conquer the whole world" that "a metallic gong boomed throughout the Mailing Division" and a voice yells out "TWELVETHIRTY CLERKS CHECKOUT FOR LUNCH!" The machines give a dying moan, Jake sighs, and turns on his heel "with almost a prayer in his heart" and thinks "*thank Gawd for that* . . . "(144).

We find in Jake's fantasy, and even in its interruption, several more associations of sound, speech, and power. We also find the suggestion of what it will take to combat white power: a single, disembodied voice that can unify all blacks and literally dictate destruction. The imaginary figure that Jake concocts to answer his real experience recalls the military commander of the parade, and the quality of his power suggests fascism. The figure's voice, in all capital letters, also recalls the novel's other voices, the voices of the radio, and the white characters, and so here we experience an alignment of the radio voice, the experience of white power, and fascism. This alignment emerges again later in this section of the novel, when Jake, Al, Slim, and Bob have a chance to talk with one another toward the end of their shift. In their dialogue they express a desire for a strong-man who "knowed how to lead and who could lead . . . who would know how to speak" (182). They then decide that this figure must also be able to bring all blacks "under one command," a requirement they remember was propounded by a "colored guy who use' t' preach over the radio." They cast about for examples and arrive at "Hitler . . . and Mussellinni" (183–84). In Jake's fantasy and in this dialogue the yearned-for response to white power is a figure who can act on whites the same way Jake and his friends feel they are acted upon: a fascist whose power flows from a disembodied voice. The fantasy and the dialogue capture the way oppression tends to breed the desire to oppress, and oppress in kind. They also capture the way the disempowered tend to project the solution to their disempowerment onto a figure outside themselves. And, most important for us here, they tie together the experiences of white power, fascism, and the radio voice.

In the third, final section of the novel Jake gets drunk at a nightclub with his friends and several prostitutes, is robbed, and returns home in an alcoholic rage to revenge himself on Lil for reporting him to the post office. The radio broadcasts are heard once again, with similar effects, and the association between speech and power reaches its height. The most striking development of the section is Jake's speech, which in the final chapter seems to almost break open in desperation. As he wanders home, still drinking, he begins yelling into nothingness. When a limousine and then a streetcar shoot past, he shouts, "WHEN YOU GET TO WHERE YOU GOING TELL 'EM ABOUT ME!" When he later begins shouting at Lil and she pleads for him to stop, he yells, "GAWDDAMMIT, I WANT 'EM TO HEAR!" When she pleads again, he screams repeatedly: "LET 'EM HEAR! LET 'EM HEAR!"(215–18). Here at the end, for the first time, Jake's voice is represented in the form that has been reserved for the voices of radio and of whites. Both this typographic representation of his speech and the speech itself signal the relation between sound and power developed in the novel. The form and content of his speech also demonstrate dramatically that Jake experiences his struggle for self-sovereignty and agency as a struggle to make his voice matter. He understands at some level that he is at the mercy of voices he cannot engage, voices like the radio voice. Wright adds to this dialogue an image that probably best captures Jake's condition. Before Jake makes his way up to his apartment, "he found himself hugging tightly at a steel telephone pole, opposite his home. A dim light burned in his window"(215–16). Jake stands outside communication in two ways here. He embraces part of a communication network but is not a participant. And he looks on a space that he has, partly out of the experience of disembodied voices, transformed into dumb violence.

Jake's day and the novel end dismally. Jake once again assaults Lil, and she is forced to defend her life by stabbing him with a shard of glass from the window Jake has smashed. Recalling but reversing the final moments of James Joyce's *Ulysses*, much of Lil's final dialogue is a repeated "Naw ... Naw ..." Jake's dialogue finishes with "I'm going to kill you!" and then "a plaintive whimper" as he slumps unconscious from the blow Lil must deliver. And the novel closes with a sound that stands in contrast to the closing of that other landmark of Modernism, T. S. Eliot's *The Waste Land*: "Outside an icy wind swept around the corner of the building, whining and moaning like an idiot in a deep black pit" (219). Instead of Molly Bloom's affirmative "yes I said yes I will Yes" or Eliot's cautiously optimistic invocation of "Shantih shantih shantih," both produced by a human voice, we are left with the sound of a natural force—a blind sound of misery. The suffering subjects upstairs have no voice, or, more properly, have voices that have become static things in relation to the culture—objects of observation, perhaps, but never engaged in communication. Their world is a world of disembodied voices that dictate the conditions of their lives, and their disempowerment is figured as the incapacity to respond to these voices. They are silent and their silence is death. Though radio does not close the novel, their experience of its voice remains the most powerful evocation of their condition.

Lawd Today! does not set out to formulate a critique of radio. But, as I have shown here, it formulates that critique nonetheless. In linking the disempowerment experienced by blacks in the urban North so closely to the experience of radio, the novel asks us to consider the power relations that inhere in the way radio came to be configured in the period, power relations closely resembling those championed by fascism. Such power relations "break" communication, transform subjects into dead relays of information, and abandon the world to implacable, inanimate voices.

Notes

1. Radio emerged in the 1920s but became a pervasive force only in the 1930s. The first radio broadcast in the United States took place in 1920, but until the late 1920s the medium remained experimental, confined to urban areas and still open to configuration. That is, radio did not become a mass medium in the way we experience it today until the 1930s. Audiences were very small, sets were expensive, and programming was very limited. After the first regulation of the airwaves in 1927 and the sudden and rapid commercialization of programming, radio exploded. Between 1930 and 1940 the number of radios in the United States grew by more than 100 percent. In 1925 fewer than 20 percent of households had a radio; by 1939 almost 90 percent had at least one. See Brown 2–3. Good accounts of radio's development in this period and similar statistics can also be found in Barnouw, McChesney, and Smulyan.

2. E. B. White, in a 1933 essay, "Sabbath Morn," called radio "one of the chief pretenders to the throne of God" and remarked that when people in his community spoke of radio they didn't mean "a cabinet, an electrical phenomenon, or a man in a studio" but rather "a pervading and somewhat godlike presence which has come into their lives and homes"(*One Man's Meat* 97). William Carlos Williams, in a poem dedicated to Franklin Roosevelt called "Death by Radio," captured the way radio's voice had become a means and sign of almost supernatural power: "We felt the force of his mind / On all fronts, penetrant / To the core of our beings / Our ears struck us speechless. . ." (54).

3. The "Great Divide" is Andreas Huyssen's term for the dialectical relationship between Modernism and mass media theorized by Theodor Adorno. Whether traditional or revisionist, most accounts of literary Modernism still formulate it as a reaction to modernity and its cultural products. Some challenges to the traditional

story of Modernism that I have in mind here are those posed by Andreas Huyssen, Paul Gilroy, Thomas Strychacz, Rita Felski, Walter Benn Michaels, Ann Douglas, and Michael North. One significant challenge that sees Modernism in relation to the structures (as opposed to content) of mass-market media is Raymond Williams's *The Politics of Modernism*.

4. The human voice had, of course, come unhooked from the body and begun to lose its status as the sign of presence and authenticity since at least the 1880s, with the invention of sound recording and transmission, and inanimate things had been chattering away since Karl Marx and Emile Zola. But not until the 1930s had the disembodied voice been experienced as ubiquitous, untraceable, and shared in real time with untold others; and never before had the construction and delivery of the voice been so thoroughly effaced.

5. A moment's reflection on the experience of the telephone, phonograph, and radio suggests why radio's voice seemed so magical and momentous. The telephone's voice was usually experienced in private space, in real time, as dialogic (answerable), and as ephemeral (unrecorded, so unrepeatable). The phonograph's voice was also usually experienced in private space, but as monologic (one-way), asynchronous (never in the present), and permanent (repeatable). The radio's voice shared some qualities of each of these—its voice was usually experienced in real time, as monologic, and as ephemeral. But unlike the voices of telephone or phonograph, the voice of radio was experienced as ubiquitous, simultaneously experienced with uncounted, anonymous others, and without traceable, material origin (such as a telephone line or record) or recognizable mediation (operators, machinery). It is also worth noting that in the 1930s the experience of the radio voice was more pervasive than the other two, even though radio had been introduced some thirty years later. The schema here is my own, but phenomenologies of these different media can be found in Peters 205–25, Kittler, *Gramophone* 78–114, and Danius 1–23 and 147–88.

6. "Symbol-using animal" is the first phrase Burke uses to define the subject in his 1963 article "Definition of Man." The whole definition, which he casts as a short poem, runs: "Man is a symbol-using animal / Inventor of the Negative / Separated from his natural condition by instruments of his own making / Goaded by the spirit of hierarchy (or moved by the sense of order) / And rotten with perfection." See Burke 5.

7. Originally titled *Cesspool*, an early version of *Lawd Today!* was completed as early as 1935. Various versions were submitted to and rejected by publishers between 1935 and 1937. The present version of the novel appears to have been completed in 1937. The novel was first published by Walker and Company, in 1963. I refer here to the 1991 Library of America edition of the novel, which restores punctuation, formatting, colloquialisms, that were emended in the Walker and Company edition. For more on the novel's publishing history, see Arnold Rampersad's note in this edition (909).

CHAPTER 8

Annexing the Oracular Voice

Form, Ideology, and the BBC

DEBRA RAE COHEN

In 1934, as part of a report on the potentialities of broadcasting in South Africa, John Reith, the director-general of the BBC, summoned up the following vision: "As the assegai to the naked hand, as the rifle to the assegai, so and much more is broadcasting, rightly institutionalised, rightly inspired, rightly controlled, to any other instrument or power, in the service of wisdom and beauty and peace" (*Into the Wind* 205). To unpack this statement, with its implicit assumption of the timeless "wisdom" of an imperialist and symbolically male-gendered modernity, its simultaneous evocations of violence and peace, of beauty and discipline, of bureaucracy and the individual heroism of the divinely inspired, is to recognize the contradictions that by the 1930s had come to define the BBC and thus inform British perceptions about the nature of radio itself. But these contradictions did more than that: the tension between earlier, idealized conceptions of the medium and their autocratic actualization in the BBC helped shape not only 1930s literary responses to radio but also 1930s literary form.

Although literary thematizing of the mass media in Britain during this decade has itself been exhaustively chronicled, those critics who take note of the formal influence of broadcasting tend either to conflate its textual traces with those of the cinema or to single out as "radiogenic" only those elements, like montage, that can be construed as subversive of radio's perceived homogenizing and totalizing effects.[1] Such formulations tend to efface not only the distinct effects on textual production of the proliferation of sound both programmed and ambient but also the way those particulars changed over time in the distinctive monopolistic British context. This chapter thus argues for a historicized model of the "radiogenic," positing that the very contradictions and cultural tensions that surrounded the developing image of wireless under the aegis of the BBC had formal literary impact and helped to shape the period's distinctive generic experiments.

If the BBC was, as Reith claimed, immune by nature of its peculiar monopoly status from the imputation of commercially "debasing the currency" of broadcasting (*Into the Wind* 144), it was all the more vulnerable to being judged by the face on its coinage. From early on it was widely understood that despite the bland, impersonal façade of the BBC—what Churchill called its "pontifical anonymous mugwumpery" (qtd. in Blythe 47)—its product bore the impress of Reith's own emphatic prejudices.

True, Reith's early public pronouncements, especially his 1924 apologia, *Broadcast over Britain*, had stressed radio's democratizing potential, echoing what Head of Talks Hilda Matheson recalled as "the dizzy height of prophecy" unleashed by the liberatory connotations of "wireless"—in Gillian Beer's terms, "a conception of the universe newly magical" (Matheson, "Record" 507; Beer 154). Reith's book ends with a rush of religious mysticism, paying homage to the mysteries of the ether—with which "wireless," says Reith, "is in particular league" (*Broadcast* 223)—and conceiving broadcasting metaphorically as but a feeble simulacrum of the "word of power" (224) of an infinite god. This discourse of humility in the face of the divine, though, is both consonant with and designed to legitimate Reith's self-positioning as Arnoldian apostle and arbiter of culture, "called"—a word he uses repeatedly throughout the book—to give the people not what they want but what they need. Reith's benign assurance that the power of broadcasting will produce "a more intelligent and enlightened electorate" (113) gives way late in the book to a grander vision:

> Wireless. . . . ignores the puny and often artificial barriers which have estranged men from their fellows. It will soon take continents in its stride, outstripping the winds; the divisions of oceans, mountain ranges, and deserts will be passed unheeded. It will cast a girdle round the earth with bands that are all the stronger because invisible. (219)

Leaving aside the geographic peculiarities of Reith's purply sententious prose, what's evident here is the degree to which the democratizing mission has already become, rhetorically, a totalizing one, his promise to make "the nation as one man" already (at least retrospectively) shadowed by the question of just which "one man" he means (qtd. in Scannell and Cardiff 7).

In the politically charged context of the early 1930s, Reith's sweepingly imperial rhetoric (as in the quotation with which I began), his Olympian refusal to answer criticism, even his immortalization in bad Latin on the façade of the grandiose new Broadcasting House, led perhaps inevitably to comparisons with Mussolini—comparisons whose trenchancy may be measured by the fact that he was both denigrated and (in those days before the invasion of Abyssinia) praised in the same terms. Even as Reith's 1930s diaries chronicled his own increasing doubts about "whether democratic principle and purpose could best and quickest be served by democratic means" (*Into the Wind* 169), he was termed—with varying degrees of irony—a Medici-like patron, "the Judge of What We Ought to Want," "the Napoleon of Broadcasting," "a very excellent Hitler for this country," and a possible "Dictator of England" (Sieveking 5; qtd in Blythe 48, 50; Reith, *Into the Wind* 254; *Reith Diaries* 213). These characterizations of Reith both stemmed from and in turn fueled perceptions of the BBC, especially on the Left, as monolithic, nonresponsive, impervious, and thus increasingly dangerous; in 1935 William Beveridge called it (though in a "not-too-serious" debate in the pages of the *Listener* itself)—"the most devoted believer in one-way conversation that the world has ever seen ("Does the B.B.C." 1). Such perceptions underscored the degree to which Reith's missionary zeal actually heightened social division as it emphasized the construction of a unified citizenry.

Leftist commentators like Charles Madge of the social research organization Mass Observation recognized even BBC blandness as strategic, necessary in order to simulate "a heavenly benevolence which is as incapable of self-interest as of indiscretion" (157). It was thus as much a deceptive construction as the artificial gentility of the distinctive BBC accent, itself a focus of suspicion and contempt; Keith Williams cites the contemporary parody of the BBC's motto, "Nation Shall Speak Posh unto Nation" (153). Ironically, the very uniformity of the BBC accent precluded the appearance of the identifiably Scots Reith behind the microphone; D. G. Bridson tells the story of the single occasion when Reith announced some English election results and "listeners had rung up to complain.... The Radio audience had been taught to expect the BBC to speak BBC" (53).[2]

Yet Reith's individual nonappearance (he was by-lined in the *Listener* only ex officio, as "The Director-General") allowed the organization itself to become his "voice": as the dictum of the announcements editor put it, "The BBC is one Corporation and can only be thought of by the listener as individual. It has many voices but one mouth." This memo of November 13, 1936, goes on, significantly, to elaborate the metaphor in military terms that imply the presence of both ordered bureaucracy and commander-in-chief: "It is a commonplace that 'announcers sound all alike.' That is a tribute to their training. . . . Captain X of the Regiment giving an order *should* and *does* appear to sound like Captain Y giving the same order" (qtd. in Briggs 123). "Though its voice be the voice of a tailor's dummy," warned Raymond Postgate in the 1935 pamphlet *What to Do with the BBC*, "its hand is the hand of Sir John Reith" (54).

In light of the tensions revealed in these often hyperbolic characterizations, much of the distinctive self-conscious mythologizing of the 1930s—a process Patrick Deane sees as muting what he calls, in Orwell's terms, the decade's "confused uproar of voices" (9)—must be read in the context of the BBC's own perceived effective univocality. Robert Giddings has condemned what he calls "the fashionable tendency to dismiss the BBC with an obligatory flourish of the postmodernist hand" ("Radio" 144) as coercive and univocal; my interest here is not in essaying the truth of these characterizations—let alone in postmodern terms—but in gauging the effects of their contemporary currency. My focus therefore differs from that of critics like D. L. LeMahieu, who, following David Cardiff, concludes that the 1930s were actually for the BBC a time of "quiet accommodation" to popular tastes (285), and Todd Avery, who, following Paddy Scannell, quite correctly stresses the extent to which radio *actually* and over time proved more egalitarian than Reith could have wished (26–28). Though this may be clear in retrospect, it was not often the judgment of contemporaries.

Indeed, the "pluralistic soundscape[s]" (Cuddy-Keane 92) of early literary Modernism shaped in part by the new exposure to disembodied voices give way, in this second generation, to a thematizing of voice in which exactly those aspects of wireless that had seemed most potentially liberatory manifest themselves metaphorically as their dark opposites. The freedom of "voices in the air" becomes an unsettling separation of sound from visual referent; accessibility becomes inescapability; education, indoctrination; radio's phatic power an almost Marinettian destructive force; and its peculiar intimacy, intrusion, seduction, violation.

The editorials in the *Listener* in the first several years after its establishment in 1929, in their peculiar mixture of defensiveness, arrogance, pedagogical condescension, and self-congratulation, make clear the desire of the BBC to discourage such impressions even as they underscore the extent to which the monopolistic institution had become associated with the medium itself. From the outset a self-referential enterprise designed to regulate listening, the *Listener* found itself in the paradoxical position of stressing the limitless democratic potential of wireless ("Prejudice and Education," "Points of View") while issuing dicta for proper modes of receptivity;[3] in its first issues, for example, the paper included articles on how to set up wireless discussion groups as a means of minimizing "the danger of mechanising thoughts through broadcasting" ("Discussion Groups" 60)—even as it stressed that all groups should be headed by trained leaders in "direct touch with the B.B.C." ("The Speaker on the Hearth" 355). Criticism of the dictatorial potential of the monopoly was met with similar rhetorical contradiction; peevish denunciations of the "crude, nose-counting idea of pseudo-democracy" ("What the Public Wants" 232) alternated with sophistic attempts to disarm: wireless is "transient and intimate," a mere correction to the former tyranny of the written word ("A Place in the Sun" 748); it serves as an equivalent of the medieval jongleur, bringing joy to the distant hearth ("The Minstrel and the Microphone" 436). The need to assert expertise in the service of Reith's Arnoldian mission competed with the desire to portray the process of wireless communication as transparent and domestic—as, in effect, unmediated.

The 1929 editorial "The Oracle from the Microphone," representing the initial "awe" at the workings of wireless as now almost passé, attempts to vest the coercive power of the medium entirely in the consciousness of the untrained listener; now, it argues, such awe has been obscured by the "sense of intimacy" among listeners encouraged by the "sympathetic manner" of announcers who "have attained so close a contact with their listeners that the effect of the medium by which they have achieved it is almost annihilated" (48). The editorial goes on, as if despite itself, to reassert the "prestige" of wireless, casting the relationship between listener and broadcaster, however, as one of "discipleship" derived from the medium itself—a sleight of hand that anoints wireless itself as a kind of authoritative voice[4] while disguising the agency of the institution. As a gesture, this is reminiscent of Reith's desire to have radio sets redesigned so as to eliminate the "philistine obtrusion of the apparatus"; radio is to be overtly domesticated in order to expedite the "real purpose for which it is there" (Foreword 5; *Broadcast* 89).

This very ubiquity of broadcasting, and its observed efficiency in creating what Arthur Calder-Marshall termed a population of "radio-bibbers" (85), created an especial ironic tension for left-wing writers, who saw in the BBC both the tremendous potential of the "mass-wish" and its Reithian betrayal. Economic pressures, as Keith Williams has noted (15), forced many of them into active participation in a BBC that, as one of them put it, they "mentally bracketed . . . with Parliament, the Monarchy, the Church and the Holy Ghost" (Bridson 19)[5] and that they found equally impervious to change. The institution's blanding mechanisms of internal surveillance and control (memorably compared by Malcolm Muggeridge in 1940 to the operations of a sausage machine)[6] stifled hopes for revolutionary demystification from within. The disturbing monoglossic power of the apparatus, seemingly impossible to ignore, rival, or subvert, thus became for leftist writers the ironic target of formal appropriation, and radio—its physicality, impact, and ideological structure—*the* key metaphor by which to render the problems of the contemporary situation.

Thus even sound itself, in the leftist fiction of the period, is generally presented as a suspect construction, denatured, desensitizing, debased. In his 1938 Marxist bildungsroman, *Starting Point*, for example, C. Day Lewis renders England as a nexus of noise, abrasive and mind-numbing, that vitiates the political will. From the opening scene, set in 1926, in which "the crackle of conversation" (12) at a cocktail party throws up disconnected phrases like a poorly tuned receiver,[7] to the repetitive looping of formulaic commonroom gossip, to the hollow falseness of the rituals of sexual exchange, to the "remote and meaningless" intellectualism of the "well informed . . . discussion circle" (269), Day Lewis symbolically recapitulates the characteristic broadcast modes of the Reith years as a kind of social symptomology. Each of his four protagonists suffers from a distinctive form of what one might call aural pathology attributable to the "broadcast" climate, making up an array of personifications that reflect BBC-induced social ills. Theo, an unscrupulous, Wilde-ish figure addicted to the poison thrust of wit, scripts events in his head like a radio play and goes murderously mad when his sallies lose their effect and he is reduced to the status of audience. Henry, deferring in his "intermittent deafness" to those he identifies as "more clever and interesting than himself," plays the passive listener, a version of Adorno and Horkheimer's helpless victim of mass culture, "his head . . . a tunnel" into which "voices [are] thunder entering, passing through, receding" (33). John, ashamed of his class origins, so accommodates himself to the sloganeering "banter" he feels necessary for success—as if mimicking a BBC accent—that he can no longer recognize the authentic voice of working-class misery but hears it as "falsely bright," "a conjurer's patter" (217).

Day Lewis's hero, Anthony, though conscious from the outset of how the very banalities of sound can serve as a mechanism of ideological control (as when he identifies the "bright, professional coquettishness" with which another man speaks about religion), nevertheless must struggle against the strength of those mechanisms, the allure of "sonorous certainties" and his own desire to surrender to an authoritative voice (78, 151). His attempts, as a teacher, to pluralize discourse—although he knows he can be fired for "broadcasting [revolutionary] opinions" (292)—can be read as setting up, in a sense, a pirate station that fails due to "monopoly" control of access to students' minds. In keeping with the trajectory of the political conversion narrative, it is, of course, only the Communist Party, at novel's end, that frees Anthony from aural false ideologies. Not only does it free his voice—speaking in the workers' cause "he found his feet and the words came easily" (308)—but also reclaims sound itself from predigested artificiality: the last pages of the novel are full of evocations of the unfettered, natural female voice, singing maternally, as if in a counterpoint to masculine political action.

But while it may seem as though what I've detailed here simply represents a metaphorization of the whole panoply of Frankfurt School arguments against mass culture, it's clear that Day Lewis isn't demonizing broadcasting per se but only its contemporary, Reithian, manifestation. Like many leftist writers of the period, Day Lewis recognizes "the dream turned nightmare" of radio but still needs the power of the dream—as demonstrated by his own long involvement as a BBC broadcaster, despite being routinely censored.[8] The end of the novel articulates this tension by representing the forces of history as an alternative, progressive, "speaking" power whose instructions Anthony ventriloquizes; "history had called them out of the ranks," he muses, "and given them her secret orders" (317). His liberation is, in a sense, his surrender to a different broadcast, a different voice of command, equally imbued with the oracular "hyper-presence" that radio affords (Coyle, "This rather elusory" 35), its uncomfortably intimate, even erotic power (here bizarrely represented as impregnating Anthony with the future). And Day Lewis himself, of course, speaking through Anthony in a last visionary flight worthy of Reith himself—though politically antithetical—partakes of that power, annexes its univocality.[9]

This annexation becomes clearer still when the novelist's voice *becomes* the oracular voice, in what Samuel Hynes, borrowing from Auden's 1935 essay "Psychology and Art To-day," terms "parable-art." As Hynes applies the term, it refers to the peculiar form of political allegory practiced by Auden and his "circle"—*The Orators*, Auden and Isherwood's plays, the early novels of Rex Warner. Hynes distinguishes between propaganda (by which he seems to mean all 1930s art inflected with the ideals of Socialist Realism) and that art, parable-art, that teaches "love, not ideology" (15). In emphasizing this opposition, however, and particularly in his claim that parable-art is "non-realistic, because it takes its form from its content and not from an idea of fidelity to the observed world," he overlooks the importance of the aural. On the level of both content and form, parable-art enacts what novels like Day Lewis's only thematize: a fidelity to the *heard* world that recapitulates the tensions implicit in 1930s perceptions of broadcasting. Parable-art plays out the process by which authority is invested in the radio voice by a deliberate retreat from conventional modes of declamation: as with a radio talk, the "natural" voice of the parableist must become artificial in order to sound natural again (Briggs, *Golden Age* 126).[10]

Rex Warner's 1938 *The Professor* foregrounds this process from the outset. A grim and spare anti-fascist fable, the book chronicles the last days in the life of a distinguished and humane scholar of classics who is elevated to the chancellorship of an unnamed European country at a time of crisis,[11] when division plagues the nation and fascist armies loom at the border. The Professor himself, wedded to "the fatal belief that somehow things were bound to get better and better" (Curry 409), embodies both the fatal flaws of liberalism and those elements of it worth preserving. As introduced by the authorizing and judgmental voice of history, his tale is framed and rendered exemplary: "easy though it is to name the man a pedant and dismiss him as misguided, his contribution to a civilization that may one day be organized or given room to flower will be found, perhaps, to have been not altogether nil" (4). The lack of specificity in the opening denunciation of the Professor, who is declared to be "for his own time . . . through a pure kind of blindness, most inapt" (3)—a judgment that could come from the Right as well as the Left—allows the impersonal voice, like the broadcast voice, to partake of the oracular, to create a readerly "discipleship," even as it draws attention to the process of doing so. The positioning of this voice as the posterity of an as-yet-unrealized future both evokes the oracular hyperpresence of destiny—as with the voice of history at the end of Day Lewis's novel—and simultaneously reminds us of the contingency of any historical judgment. The book, then, becomes a vehicle for retelling, an artificial staging of language under the sign of the parableist, with the parable itself one in which the thematics of voice are paramount.

The very "bareness and cramping" of Warner's novel (Reeve 51)[12] attests to its emphasis on the aural, on the mechanisms and ethics of speech and listenership: the Professor's trials are presented as a series of tortures-by-voice in which liberal models of discourse are gradually dismembered. The classicist's belief in rational debate renders him oblivious to the fact that real-world material conditions produce language that is performative or coercive; he is unconscious of the irony that it's only his authorizing classroom presence that mandates equal time for all views. His naiveté extends even to the way the exigencies of capitalism encourage mendacious speech; thus, encountering a gas-mask salesman hawking his wares, he is perturbed by the man's "expression of semi-idiocy, an overweening confidence that no sane person could possibly feel" (28). Warner parodies the Professor's idealism by juxtaposing it to the "open discussion" (32) represented by orators in the park, who urge on vapid and apathetic crowds various ludicrous forms of pacifism in language that echoes early idealized images of wireless: insubstantial ether is to serve as the negation of force. Leaving the park, the Professor, too, orates to no one, waving his arms "in an appealing gesture to nothing in particular" (42).

This image of the absent audience recurs and gains tragic resonance over the course of the novel, leading up to its central scene, in which the Professor prepares to broadcast to the nation to explain his economic program. The Professor's image of radio, as of speech itself, is that it is transparent, democratizing, and benign; indeed, he thinks of "reason" in terms like those Reith uses of wireless, dwelling on "the attractive power of a reason that permeated frontiers and dominated the interests of classes" (172). Like the *Listener*, which, in one of its self-justifying editorials, described the microphone as "a curious touchstone of sincerity" ("Voices from the Past" 634), he attributes to radio a purifying influence: "for, as he would often say, when the person of the speaker was invisible all inessentials and vulgarities were removed and the path of communication from mind to mind was clear" (181–82).

Yet a proleptic dream, in which he is giving to an invisible audience a speech "of which the purport was so urgent that the actual words he was using made no impression at all upon his mind" (126)—in which, in other words, the force of the medium overrides its content—hints at the coercive power of the medium itself, a mystification that the narrative, to point up the Professor's naiveté, is at pains to underscore:

> From the windows one might have seen the whole street packed with faces, still eagerly upturned in expectation, although now their attention was directed not so much to the windows themselves as to the black protuberances of loud speakers which had been placed at regular intervals on balconies along the front of the building. In other streets, too, the sight would have been the same, while in hundreds of thousands of homes families were gathering around radio sets in large or small rooms, staring at the instruments, whether home-made or expensively manufactured, as though those arrangements of wood, glass and wire were oracles, gods, or idols. (180)

The Professor's dream foreshadows the outcome of the broadcast: he is left unknowingly speaking, literally, to no one, as fascist sympathizers seize control of the apparatus and preemptively denounce him. His willful ignorance of the mediatory mechanism, here a synecdoche for any structure that corrupts or subverts the ideal liberal free-exchange model of the "polis," is illustrated in his irritated dismissal of the airplane noise that hovers at the edge of his consciousness throughout the book; such harbingers of political reality are brushed aside with the same annoyance the Professor feels when unable to retrieve "some rare Greek word, a word, perhaps, signifying a bathtub or a certain kind of fish" (118).[13] After the broadcast, the collapse of his illusions is tied to the inescapability of mechanical noise, culminating in the horrific din of the fascist invasion, in which "the outer world seemed to have become all one metallic roar and drone" (236). The earlier democratic tolerance for all words as valuable and equal is shown to have allowed, and is now horrifically equated with, the fascist expunging of all discourse: "Reason could hardly exist now where words had to be shouted" (237–38).

Even as the Professor belatedly comes to understand the words of his Marxist son, who described his submission to "the terrible and necessary dictatorship of an idea" (81), the narrative itself enacts that submission; just as the "dictatorship" of the Marxist idea can alone rescue the best parts of liberalism, so does the monologic voice of the parableist become, as the BBC claimed to be, the monopoly that guarantees eventual free speech.[14] The key word here is "necessary," as in Auden's "necessary murder"; while the word expresses the tension between the assured and oracular prefatory voice of "history"—a voice expressing a unity within which the Professor no longer exists—and the mind in the process of conversion, it also encapsulates the narrative's paradoxical discomfort with the annexation of oracular voice.

Edward Upward's *Journey to the Border*, a parable that presents itself as a dramatization of the movement away from what Hynes would call the tenets of parable-art to those of propaganda, illustrates a peculiarly complex version of this narrative discomfort. Like Day Lewis's *Starting Point*, it chronicles a conversion from introspection to Marxist action, here encapsulated into a single day in which an unnamed private tutor struggles to escape the implications of his political inertia, first by retreat into various forms of fantasy—which bring him dangerously close to "the border" of sanity—and finally by abjuring all fantasy for the "reality" of political commitment. The trajectory parallels Upward's own late-1930's rejection of his earlier experimental writing, which he came to find "impermissible" according to the tenets of Socialist Realism, in favor of an implacable dedication to "practical socialism."[15] In her book on writers of the 1930s, Janet Montefiore deftly skewers the ironies here—that "the obviously autobiographical 'tutor' obeys Marxist reason, rejects fantasy, chooses action and realism—and, after six dedicated years in the Communist Party, produces a grotesque, introspective novel about the temptations of fantasy" (31). Yet her explanation for this seeming contradiction falls back on Upward's individual artistic proclivities rather than locating the novel in the context of contemporary tensions surrounding aurality, ideology, and form.

For here, as in *The Professor*, the text both articulates and is shaped by these tensions. The tutor embodies at various points in the novel all the various wireless-related "aural pathologies" that marked Day Lewis's characters in *Starting Point*: artificial pre-scripting of conversations, passive listenership, exaggerated deference to upper-class discourse, the temptation to surrender to the voice of command. Yet because Upward renders all these pathologies through the consciousness of the tutor himself, each is invested with a level of presence that lends it a temporary legitimacy. The tutor, himself acting as a version of the parable-artist, appears over and over to be "speaking" a new reality into being—an illusion undercut by the insistent ringing in the tutor's left ear that, like broadcast static, reminds the audience of the operations of the governing apparatus.

At one point, while being passively borne along in his employer's car, listening to him rail against the inconvenience caused to prominent men by striking miners, whom he terms "damned spongers" (52), the tutor attempts to impose a new mode of perception, practice a kind of channel-switching;

he wants "to hear differently" (51). But he finds himself unable to control the process: "As he listened [the first conversation] grew fainter and fainter, became a mere ghost-gauze of sound. And beneath the ghost-gauze another conversation, briefer and more indifferent, grew louder and louder. It was about fishing and fox-hunting . . ." (53). Like a listener tuning from national to regional programming—and I'm reminded here particularly of Raymond Postgate's criticism of the patronizing "dullness and vulgarity" of the regional service (64)—the tutor succeeds only in substituting another conversation that, although nominally different, is structurally and ideologically the same, each grounded in the same privileged exercise of monopoly power.

Yet the tutor persists in his attempts at reinvention, ignoring the admonitory ringing in his ear, until—in a nightmare version of broadcasting's intimacy as invasion—he feels himself physically controlled, "slowly freezing," unable to combat "the forces of boundless horror" (198). At this moment of crisis the ringing bursts into "ghostly" audibility (199), reveals itself as representing the tutor's own thoughts, the previously repressed half of "a dialogue with [him]self" (201), and proceeds to harangue him into a recognition not only of his pathology but of its only possible cure—the rejection of his former habits of "thinking and feeling" (219) in favor of revolutionary action. This is the point where the novel, too, ostensibly changes form, sheds its taint of fantasy—since, says Upward, "a modern fantasy cannot tell the truth"—and emerges into engagement with what he calls "the fundamental realities of to-day" ("Marxist" 48, 47). Indeed, Upward later went to great pains to identify the novel's hybrid form as a kind of textual dementia reflective of the tutor's own false consciousness, rather than, as in the works of Kafka, "a primary fantasy in its own right" (qtd. in Croft 291).

Yet this very emergence from false consciousness into right-thinking—or, rather, left-thinking—is rendered problematic by its depiction as the surrender to a voice. That the voice represents itself, nominally, as the tutor's own enables Upward retroactively to suppress the fantasy in his text by literalizing it away, exorcising, as it were, the ghost in the machine. One might argue that he reverses the process of naturalization-by-design that Reith had called for in order to render domestic the radio apparatus. And yet Upward's "rational" voice itself seems to perpetuate mystification: it has none of the tutor's tentativeness, but reproduces, in its seductive reasonableness, its air of casual command, the very accent of the "British Mandarinate" (Cockburn 10)—or of the BBC. And the use of the term "ghostly" audibility—like the "ghost-gauze" of the earlier conversation—reminds us that this oracular voice, too, is the disembodied product of a parableist's "broadcast" mechanism. As at the end of Day Lewis's novel, the hyperpresence on which the concluding conversion depends, though overtly opposing the pathologies of the text, is structurally implicated in the very aspects of broadcast power that produce them.

In availing himself of the oracular power of parable, then, in order to argue its disavowal, Upward, like Warner, enacts the contradictions of 1930s perceptions of broadcasting; his profoundly self-loathing text demonstrates the degree to which those contradictions shaped even the terms on which the annexation of the broadcast "voice" could be negotiated. The desire of writers like Upward to "create new forms" ("Marxist" 54) responsive to populist concerns was crucially mediated, to an extent to which they were not always aware, by the Reithian BBC. In his essay "The Revolution in Literature," published in 1935, for example, Day Lewis predicts that under the pressures of communications technologies literature would be forced to change, "to decide," in his words, "what its real job is" (512). Ceding realism to the new technologies, he posits that what will survive will be on one hand "a form of writing somewhat akin to music, depending on highly elaborated sounds, intense verbal subtlety, and complex patterns of association," and on the other, "morality writing—conveyed through fairy-tales, allegory, satire, and perhaps a new kind of semi-religious drama" (537)—in other words, "parable-art." The irony here—beyond the fact that this defense of what "printed words [can] do that can't be done better" (512) by other media was itself actually first delivered as a BBC radio talk—is that both of the "streams" of new literatures he envisions are themselves radiogenic. The first, epitomized by Joyce's contemporaneous *Finnegans Wake*, focusing on sound, enacts the reception of voices in the air; the second, parable-art, harnesses what we might call the carrier wave, the oracular power of the medium.

The extent to which the unacknowledged radiogenic pervades the analysis of even so broadcast-savvy a commentator as Day Lewis suggests the continuing need to reevaluate the historiography of the entire Modernist period in light of what Frank Biocca calls the increasing "salience of all aural experience" (63). In particular, the analysis of 1930s genres—as in Hynes's strict contradistinction between "parable-art" and propaganda—has traditionally been grounded in a fundamentally visual model of realism that renders central the documentary focus of Storm Jameson, who called for the writer to present fact "as the photographer does" (15). Continued critical emphasis on the centrality of the "public eye" in the formation of 1930s genres is to a large extent the reinscription of visual bias derived from the fact that, as Douglas Kahn wryly puts it, "Narcissus possessed better technology than Echo" (*Noise* 7).[16] But it's also true that our theoretical models for the modern effects of technology on aesthetic form—from Benjamin to Kittler and beyond—tend to foreground technologies of reproduction, and have thus shaped an ever-more-nuanced history of Modernism in which radio nevertheless continues to be shortchanged. Despite what BBC producer Lance Sieveking called the "ghastly impermanence of the medium" (15), its ephemera shaped literary production in ways we are only now beginning to trace.

Notes

1. I'm thinking in particular here of Keith Williams, whose comprehensive and insightful *British Writers and the Media* reproduces both of these patterns.

2. Indeed, the organization presented itself as not merely reflecting but actively promulgating English pronunciation as "generally recognized and accepted among educated people," representing such standardization as a matter of national "reputation" ("Stabilising" 120).

3. These included haughty condemnation of the idea of car radios: "Broadcasting has its dignity or rather its propriety" ("Week by Week" 889).

4. "The medium seems to exercise some sort of absolute criticism upon the material it conveys. It improves what is intrinsically good and destroys what is bad with a finality not exercised by any theatre, cinema, lecture room or concert hall" ("The Oracle" 48).

5. By the early 1930s the BBC lauded itself as an institution in terms nearly as hyperbolic: see, for instance, "Farewell to Savoy Hill."

6. "Whatever was put into it must either take on its texture or be expelled, a waste product; though different meats were inserted, the resultant sausages were indistinguishable" (44).

7. It's worth noting in this connection that the "cocktail-party problem" was an official radio term for the inability to locate a specific sound (Cameron 92). I thank Jane Lewty for this reference.

8. The files on Day Lewis at the BBC Written Archives Centre at Caversham include a long and occasionally aggrieved exchange from 1934–1935 between the writer and Talks producer G. N. Pocock in reference to a planned talk in the series *Youth Looks Ahead*, in the course of which Day Lewis was cautioned repeatedly about toning down the political content of his literary talk. An internal memo from 1939

notes that Day Lewis's earlier work was relentlessly blue-penciled on policy grounds and cautions that his tendency to include political rhetoric had led to unbounded trouble. See Lambert for a snarky and cogent account of BBC modes of censorship: "long-term censorship of talks planning" was supplemented by the "short-term censorship of talks scripts," with the speaker, "at the mercy of the expert in broadcasting," induced to make changes "of substance as well as form, in the name of 'broadcasting technique.' . . . Has the BBC a 'black list' of persons who have offended it in some way, and are therefore forbidden access to the microphone? Not exactly; but it is remarkable how often those who have criticised the Corporation, or proved indiscreet or 'difficult' as talkers, are discovered to be deficient in some essential of the technique of broadcasting" (80–81).

9. In charting the tensions here it's worth noting that Day Lewis in his memoirs locates his de-conversion from communist political praxis—at just about the time *Starting Point* was issued—in his "revulsion" from his own enjoyment of the "exercise of power over an audience"(*Buried Day* 222, 223).

10. See also Scannell and Cardiff 161–67 and Matheson, *Broadcasting*, chapter 3.

11. Issued at the time of Hitler's takeover of Czechoslovakia, the novel is largely patterned on the annexation of Austria, with, as N. H. Reeve points out, elements of the Spanish Civil War mixed in (58).

12. Says Frank Kermode, "In Warner's novel, classrooms, parks, and streets are merely sets before which long serious debates are staged; though sometimes they are invested with a dreamlike terror" (71).

13. "Irritation" is the word used throughout as well to mark the Professor's reaction to modes of speech he finds uncongenial or irrational.

14. See, for instance, "Creating a Demand," "Points of View."

15. "Statement" 212, "Marxist" 53. Upward outlines his thinking in the essay "An Interpretation of Marxist Literature," which was published a year before *Journey to the Border*. In it, he posits that in the "classless future" a "higher . . . scientific" version of the "'fairy' story—celebrating the triumph of man over dangers and difficulties" might be possible, but that any depiction of "the emotional truth about present-day reality" requires a personal commitment by the writer "in his everyday life" to the workers' cause (54). Upward later substantially modified his position, referring in a 1978 interview with Alan Munton and Alan Young to "what without realising it I was trying to do earlier on, which is to turn imaginative writing into something that is just a political statement" (44); he explicitly distinguished the "deliberately antimodernist" cast of his late trilogy, or "dialectical triad," *The Spiral Ascent* (1962–77) from Socialist Realism ("Statement" 216; Kermode 57). This retrospective recasting has resulted in some disingenuous misreadings: Richard Johnstone, for example, as Andy Croft has pointed out, bizarrely reads Upward's struggle with generic form as a "failure" that he attributes to a failure of political commitment (qtd. in Croft 306); Stephen Tabachnik makes a similar argument in reference to Rex Warner's *The Wild Goose Chase*. But while Croft is right to mock Johnstone's blithe contention that "it is now a commonplace" that 1930s left-wing writers embraced traditional rather than

experimental literary modes, he himself understates the extent to which Upward's essay embraces at least the terminology of Socialist Realism (qtd. in Croft 305, 271). See Peter Marks on the relatively limited effects of Socialist Realism in England.

16. Often such analyses ironically undermine their own terms, as when Janine Utell argues that with the omission of Woolf's planned photographs for *Three Guineas*, "a radical and threatening point is silenced" ("The Loss of History").

CHAPTER 9

Desmond MacCarthy, Bloomsbury, and the Aestheticist Ethics of Broadcasting

TODD AVERY

Since the beginning of the Bloomsbury boom in the late 1960s and early 1970s—when biographies of Lytton Strachey and Virginia Woolf and the explosive interest in the latter sparked by second-wave feminist critics heralded the reemergence of Bloomsbury into both literary-critical and broader cultural consciousness—writers have typically located the group in the history of aestheticism, a late-Victorian cultural phenomenon that, until recently, was almost universally perceived as an aesthetic movement as elitist in its own way as was, supposedly, its Modernist legacy. As Michael Holroyd wrote long ago, the Bloomsbury Group "represents more truly than anything else the culmination and ultimate refinement of the aesthetic movement" (53). Aestheticist principles, inherited from art-for-art's-sake and decadent Victorian writers like Walter Pater and Oscar Wilde, inform a great deal of Bloomsbury's cultural productions and political writings. However, the Bloomsburyans were no mere Modernist reincarnations of George Du Maurier's notorious Jellaby Postlethwaite lunching on "an aesthetic midday meal" of a freshly cut lily in a glass of water (Small, Plate 3), or of the Oscar Wilde pilloried in Gilbert and Sullivan's *Patience*. Rather, as widely connected and politically very deeply engaged early twentieth-century intellectuals, the Bloomsburyans were seismographically sensitive to the effects of a rapidly changing technocultural landscape upon residual Victorian cultural and ethical ideals, aestheticist and otherwise. Indeed, the label "Bloomsbury" itself, as the radio historian Kate Whitehead argues, is perhaps a misleading moniker for a group of cultural figures who spent a great deal of time at the British Broadcasting Corporation (121).

The Bloomsbury Group's involvement in radio during the 1920s and

1930s is a key example of how an important group of Modernist intellectuals strove to preserve their deeply held ethical-aesthetic beliefs between the wars while adjusting them to fit the demands of an increasingly technologized mass culture—and more specifically, the demands of radio, a new and, in its capacity to connect with vast numbers of people, unprecedented medium of mass communication. Bloomsbury's involvement in radio is also an important example of how some Modernist intellectuals bridged the cultural Great Divide—"the categorical distinction between high art and mass culture" (Huyssen viii)—of the early twentieth century. As such, it demands a further reassessment of facile high-versus-mass cultural distinctions and illuminates the eagerness with which some "highbrows" challenged the ideological foundations of an emergent mass-communications medium while embracing the medium itself to help shape the mass culture of which radio was quickly becoming an integral part. Nearly all of the Bloomsburyans gave talks at the BBC between the wars: E. M. Forster was a regular and highly regarded "talker"; and one might discover nuances in talks by Clive Bell, Roger Fry, J. M. Keynes, Molly MacCarthy, and Leonard and Virginia Woolf that fail to find expression in those by the group's more prolific broadcasters. However, Bloomsbury's most deeply held opinions on the ideological underpinnings of what Robert Giddings has called "the Reithian imperial experience" ("John Reith" 153), and their most fully considered views on the utopian or, at least, politically progressive potential of mass culture, are to be found in broadcasts by Desmond MacCarthy, a core member of the Group and one of the early twentieth-century's most respected literary journalists.[1]

Desmond MacCarthy's Literary Values

The theoretical foundations of Bloomsbury's ethical engagement with radio lay in nineteenth-century ethical aestheticism and in G. E. Moore's book *Principia Ethica*. Bloomsbury's belief in the irreducible ethical value of conversation and their faith in the "capacity of the human spirit to overflow boundaries" (Woolf, *Three Guineas* 143) dovetailed with radio's unprecedented ability to perforate social borders, mix classes, and effect a general democratization of moral valuation. In these regards, Bloomsbury's ethics sharply contrasted with the idealist Christian ethics of the BBC's founders and early administrators. Following Matthew Arnold's prescription for national health, these self-described cultural and moral arbiters wanted to establish the BBC as a microcosm of "*the State*, or organ of our collective best self, of our national right reason" (58, italics in text). They did this by working to impose a moral agenda on British culture and society that would, they hoped, ensure the "entrenchment of the privatized interiorization of the public sphere" and interpellate radio listeners to moral conformity through radio talks and other broadcasts (Menser 300). As John Reith explained to the Crawford Committee on broadcasting in 1924, the BBC, as a public service monopoly, had a moral obligation to promote such conformity. On the practical level, he insisted that the BBC ought to uphold Arnoldian cultural "standards"—"the best that has been thought and said in the world"—in order to promote a unity of national opinion. For Reith, those standards were ultimately religious ones.

Reith's cultural and moral agenda collided with Bloomsbury's valorization of conversation as a supreme ethical good—a lesson that many of them learned from the philosophers Henry Sidgwick, G. E. Moore, and other colleagues at the turn of the century in meetings of the secret Cambridge Conversazione Society, commonly known as the "Apostles." Moore's *Principia Ethica*, a groundbreaking work in analytical ethics, is commonly referred to by Bloomsbury scholars as the "Bloomsbury Bible." In it, Moore celebrates as by far "the most valuable [i.e., good] things, which we know or can imagine . . . certain states of consciousness, which may be roughly described as the pleasures of human intercourse and the enjoyment of beautiful objects" (188). (Although some of his Bloomsbury friends appear to have understood the first of these terms rather more corporeally than Moore had intended, by "intercourse," Moore means, in the idiom of the day, conversation.) He goes on to describe "the ultimate and fundamental truth of Moral Philosophy"—namely, "That it is only for the sake of these things—in order that as much of them as possible may at some time exist—that any one can be justified in performing any public or private duty; that they are the *raison d'être* of virtue; that it is they . . . that form the rational ultimate end of human action and the sole criterion of social progress" (189). Conversation, as Kate Whitehead writes, constituted Bloomsbury's "most prolific output"; she also suggests that despite the pressures the BBC administration applied on its broadcasters to promote "the best that has been thought and said" and to conform to conventional moral standards, "radio was the ideal medium" for Bloomsbury's conversational ideal, which itself contested the reification of any absolute moral standard (121). To explore Bloomsbury's involvement with modern technoculture at the BBC is to show how, as what Michel de Certeau might have called cultural "poachers," the Bloomsbury talkers and advisors tactically deployed their conversational facility to preserve their integrity as aesthetic and ethical outsiders while struggling to fulfill the Forsterian injunction, "Only connect . . ." and to consecrate a mode of thinking which celebrated heterogeneity in the determination of social, cultural, and ethical value.

The May 14, 1930, *Listener* magazine editorial, "Literary Values," enlists Desmond MacCarthy in the ranks of cultural figures "assist[ing] to keep alive the spirit which animated men like . . . Matthew Arnold" who had theorized culture as a sort of secular evangelicalism (844). This is perhaps the first popular association of MacCarthy with the Arnoldian tradition of literary and cultural criticism. As such, "Literary Values" countered the growing and more ambivalent critical association of MacCarthy with Bloomsbury's "insolent" choice "to linger in the aesthetic vacuum of the 'nineties," as Q. D. Leavis would put it later in the decade (406–7). F. R. Leavis, with a fervor equal to his wife's, deplored Bloomsbury's literary, cultural, and ethical values. He nevertheless lends some support to the *Listener*'s assessment of MacCarthy's place in contemporary criticism. In a 1932 essay in *Scrutiny*, the journal he had founded the same year, Leavis diagnosed "What's Wrong with Criticism." In MacCarthy, Leavis wrote, "criticism undertakes its essential function of keeping an educated body of taste and opinion alive to the age, of testing, nourishing and refining the currency of contemporary culture" (133). According to Leavis, criticism at the present time was diffusing very little sweetness and light, and contributing increasingly fewer fresh currents of thought to the mainstream of national consciousness. MacCarthy thus seemed to be a welcome anodyne to this process of cultural decline. Leavis's favorable opinion of MacCarthy would be shaken as the decade progressed. As MacCarthy's reputation as a broadcaster solidified and his aestheticist sympathies grew more apparent, Leavis's suspicion of radio too became more pronounced.

The characterization of MacCarthy as an Arnoldian critic has persisted until recently. In 1986, for example, René Wellek called him "practically Arnoldian" (89). However, even as F. R. Leavis was praising MacCarthy for upholding the Arnoldian tradition, he was also beginning to suspect that the BBC, "the new organ of culture of which so much is expected" (143), where MacCarthy was working as principal literary critic and many of the other Bloomsbury intellectuals and their close associates were bringing their talents to the microphone, had begun to neglect its announced obligation to the national culture. In his comments on a series of talks on modern literature by Harold Nicolson, a close friend of several Bloomsbury Group members and the husband of Virginia Woolf's erstwhile lover Vita Sackville-West, Leavis indirectly indicts MacCarthy on charges of aiding and abetting this neglect and implies that Virginia Woolf's novels also were symptoms of a general cultural decline:

> It is . . . without extravagant hopes that we turn to the British Broadcasting Corporation. . . . It has been taking its function with admirable seriousness. . . . And good educational work the BBC has, in some ways, undoubtedly done. But how little it can be expected to reverse the process we have been contemplating . . . Mr. Harold Nicolson's notorious talks on *The New Spirit in Literature* should have been sufficient to establish. (143)

Nicolson's talks, on such writers as T. S. Eliot, James Joyce, D. H. Lawrence, and Virginia Woolf, were printed in the *Listener* in late 1931 and early 1932. Neither the BBC nor the *Listener*, Leavis complained, favored "'sensitiveness of intelligence,' which, as Arnold tells us, produces 'deference to a standard higher than one's own habitual standard'" (145).

The *Listener* also published, on September 23, 1931, a week before Nicolson delivered his first broadcast in the series, the transcript of a talk titled "The Magnifying Glass on Modern Literature." The purpose of "Magnifying Glass" was to introduce *The New Spirit in Literature*; its author was Desmond MacCarthy, who anticipated the underlying though unspoken impetus behind Leavis's critique of Nicolson in particular and of contemporary criticism in general. "All changes in art," MacCarthy says, "are caused by changes in beliefs and morals, and behind the new literature of the nineteen-twenties such changes lie" (479). Although MacCarthy takes "the new literature" to task for having "a narrow basis" of intense concentration on individuals' "idiosyncratic response to things," he also aligns himself with the "new spirit." For he resists appealing to reified standards of "the best" in terms of morals as well as craft and insists that the listening and reading public need "a readjustment of the point of view, which dismisses, as wilfully ugly or immoral, work which is really a caustic diagnosis of evils or an attempt 'to rid the bosom of perilous stuff'" (480). The BBC may have wished, as the *Listener*'s editorial on "Literary Values" maintained, to preserve its version of the Arnoldian spirit. But MacCarthy's introduction to Nicolson's talks, and those talks themselves, announced the arrival of a new spirit within the precincts of Broadcasting House. This new spirit was opposed to Reithianism. In spite of John Reith's best efforts, radio, by the early 1930s, was in fundamental ways beyond his control and was becoming eminently congruous with the spirit of Bloomsbury's ethical Modernism.

The relationship between the Bloomsbury broadcasters, preeminently MacCarthy, and the Reithian BBC may be figured as a contest between conceptions about the common good. For Reith and most of the other stewards of public service broadcasting, the public good was ineffaceably articulated with evangelical morality and nationalist, even imperialist, ideology. For the Bloomsbury Group, to the contrary, the good was linked to a politics that valorized both intimacy and internationalism in self-conscious resistance to evangelical, nationalist, and imperialist ideals. Just as G. E. Moore had wrested ethical philosophy from the centralizing forces of Victorian moral thinking by elevating intimate relations between individuals over obedience to religious or other traditional moral standards, so too the Bloomsbury broadcasters wielded their belief in conversation, friendship, and internationalism as a tactical weapon against the relentlessly centripetal strategies of the Reithian BBC.

The Art and Ethics of Reading

In the past two decades, some literary critics have begun paying close attention to how the act of reading, conceptualized as the effort to connect with others as they appear in print, may provide a model for ethics in general. In "Innovation, Literature, Ethics: Relating to the Other" (1999), Derek Attridge employs the methods of literary impressionism and stream-of-consciousness narrative to explore the ethics of reading through a critical lens cut by such poststructuralist ethical philosophers as Emmanuel Levinas and Jacques Derrida. For Attridge, "Ethics makes impossible demands" (30). Reading also makes impossible demands, in that the act of reading literary or other texts involves an inevitably futile attempt to understand the "singularity" of the "other." But however futile this effort may finally be, it must, Attridge insists, be made—for to put forth this effort is to understand how both the self (the other's other) and the other exist in a relation of continual, mutual self-fashioning. The Levinasian demand, "respond to the other as other," like Forster's injunction to "Only connect . . . " (the ellipsis of which suggests uncertainty in the sequel—after connecting, what then?) may appear morally commonsensical: by definition, being moral presupposes taking into account one's duties and obligations to others. Nevertheless, as Attridge explains, to think of ethical activity as the sincere, creative attempt "to respond fully to the singular otherness of the other person" (30) is to understand the ways in which selves emerge only through creative interactions with other, always-emerging selves, and hopefully "in turn [to] provoke inventive responses . . . to other persons and bring about a more widespread alteration in intersubjective behavior" (24). Ethics, in this formulation, precedes existence. That is, in fact, Levinas's fundamental point. Indeed, existence turns out to be a function of ethics: one exists in proportion as one engages in the strenuous creative effort to make sense of the other's own creative effort, vis-à-vis oneself, to exist; one's entry into existence is a function, therefore, of the responsibility one chooses to accept for another. This theory of ethics contrasts with conventional moral thinking, relying, as much of it does, on notions of respect, tolerance, difference, agency, and so forth, themselves embedded within a philosophical tradition that presumes the unique, self-contained individuality of the individual person—an enlightenment notion that has been under increasingly trenchant scrutiny since the advent of poststructuralism in the 1960s. Writes Attridge, "Only in accepting responsibility for the other do I bring it—or let it come—into existence; and there is a sense in which the responsibility precedes even the I that is said to accept it, since the act always remakes the actor" (27–28). In the same way, the act of reading always remakes the reader; and it always remakes that which is being read.

It would surely be claiming too much to say that when Desmond MacCarthy sat down in front of the BBC microphone, at 7:30 one Thursday evening in late 1932, to broadcast the first in a series of eighteen, twenty-minute talks on "The Art of Reading," he had been thinking of reading in terms of process metaphysics or of the ethics of intersubjective relations between perpetually emerging others. In effect, however, it was on those very relations, and on the cultural politics attending them, that MacCarthy, then one of the BBC's most popular broadcasters, spoke that evening and on subsequent Thursdays for the next five months. In his talks, MacCarthy offered the fullest broadcast expression of G. E. Moore's pervasive influence on Bloomsbury. "The Art of Reading" talks contain MacCarthy's most sustained treatment of a single critical and ethical problem—how one might read, and why reading is important. Moreover, as did Clive Bell's *Art*, Forster's *What I Believe*, Fry's "An Essay in Aesthetics," Keynes's "My Early Beliefs," Lytton Strachey's preface to *Eminent Victorians*, and Virginia Woolf's "Mr. Bennett and Mrs. Brown," MacCarthy's talks on reading constitute a Bloomsbury manifesto of ethics and aesthetics. MacCarthy was less overtly concerned with political problems than were Keynes, Forster, and the Woolfs. But his adherence to Moore's fundamental ethical-aesthetic principles enabled him to develop a quasi-anarchic theory of reading that, however politically disengaged it appears to be at first glance, yet champions, as insistently as do the aesthetics of MacCarthy's Bloomsbury friends, what Peter Stansky has called "the 'democracy' of art, of sensibility, the equality of the aesthetic reaction" (250).

By doing this, MacCarthy also subtly positions himself as an internal critic—a poacher—of the "democratic" ideals of British public service broadcasting as these ideals were theorized, implemented, and refined by Reith and his colleagues in the early days of British radio. Max Horkheimer and Theodor Adorno, in their analysis of the culture industry in the mid-1940s, write of the "democratic" character of radio. Focusing on two of the three major modes of broadcasting administration then in existence—or, to borrow Raymond Williams's phrase, two of the three existing "cultural formations" of broadcasting: namely, commercial broadcasting (as pioneered in the United States) and totalitarian mass communications (as in their native Germany under the Nazi regime)—Horkheimer and Adorno overlook the third model, that of public service broadcasting in the national interest, a model peculiar at that time to Britain. Radio, they write in their radically skeptical analysis of the uniform broadcasting practices of the former two models (that is to say, the practice of broadcasting uniformity that they embody), "democratically makes everyone into listeners, in order to expose them in authoritarian fashion to the same programs put out by different stations. No mechanism of reply has been developed.... Any trace of spontaneity in the audience of the official radio is steered and absorbed into... a selection of specializations... and sponsored events of every kind" (95–96).

Reith too considered radio broadcasting—and more particularly, public service broadcasting—a "democratic" medium. Like Horkheimer and Adorno later on, he was suspicious of the American commercial model, though unlike them he appears to have sympathized with Nazi methods of social control (*Reith Diaries* 56–57). Under his leadership, British radio as Reith imagined it was to be both a scourge to Philistia and a help to "democracy" by functioning as a hypostasis of the divine. Under the royal charter that established the British Broadcasting Corporation as of January 1, 1927 (and which permanently transformed the organization from a business venture into a semi-autonomous public service that operates under "regulat[ion of] a 'licence and agreement' which are conferred by the government"), the BBC, as Andrew Crisell writes, is bound by a specific set of obligations:

> It was, and is, obliged to inform, to educate and to entertain; to report the proceedings of Parliament; to provide a political balance; and in a national emergency to broadcast government messages. It may neither editorialize nor carry advertising. Its income is guaranteed from broadcast receiving licences and it strives to maintain a position of editorial independence. (28)

Reith exercised an extraordinary amount of direct personal control over the day-to-day workings of the organization—as evidenced by the large number of internal memos directed to him daily by administrators in all branches of the service and by the degree of personal responsibility he accepted or claimed in internal and external negotiations with lecturers, performers, and lobbyists for various artistic, intellectual, and moral agendas. Operating within the general guidelines articulated by Andrew Crisell, he forged a particular "democratic" agenda for radio that constituted a sort of third way between two broadly accepted notions of democracy. As Crisell writes:

> One notion, to which the BBC broadly subscribed, was that democracy consists of giving all the people what they want. But this is undemocratic in the sense that within a limited resource such as broadcasting then was, and because people have differing tastes, nobody gets *enough* of what they want. The second notion, to which many of the corporation's critics subscribed, was that democracy consists of giving the *majority* of the people what it wants—which is also undemocratic, positively despotic, in the sense that the minority gets nothing at all. The complaint against the BBC, then, was that the majority did not get enough of what it wanted—and a great deal of what it did *not* want. (33, italics in text)

As a believer in the fundamentally "democratic" nature and responsibility of the medium of radio itself and of the BBC as its guardian, Reith, Crisell explains, attempted a way out of this critical impasse. He

> posited . . . a third notion of democracy which was concerned neither with majority nor universal preferences but with what [he] perceived as universal needs: for the aim was to open up to all those who had been denied by a limited education, low social status and small income the great treasures of our culture. . . . Reith's policy offered a chance of spiritual if not material enrichment [and] was always ready to discriminate on the listeners' behalf between "the good" and "the inferior" in popular culture—often on moral rather than aesthetic or intellectual grounds. (35)

In the Reithian view of democracy, radio is, in a sense, a socially and technologically promiscuous public resource that respects no traditional demarcation of social or economic class in its ability to unite an entire population. It is able to do so, for example, through the sonic dissemination of imperial standards—by bringing "rural areas . . . into direct contact with . . . Empire institutions, the clock which beats the time over the Houses of Parliament, in the centre of the Empire, is heard echoing in the lowliest cottage in the land" (Reith, *Broadcast* 220). It exerts its "consolidating influence" also by making quickly and universally available such phenomena as "the momentous utterance of a statesman, the exposition of a scientist, the eloquence of a preacher, or a great ceremony of widespread interest" (219, 220), and by sending through the air debates of local, national, and international import; orchestral music; the sounds of nature; and even, paradoxically and most curiously, the no-sound of *silence* as a palliative for the increasingly noisy and frenetic modern world: "The song of the nightingale," Reith writes, "has been heard over all the country, on highland moors and in the tenements of great towns. Milton has said that when the nightingale sang, silence was pleased. So in the song of the nightingale we have broadcast something of the silence which all of us in this busy world unconsciously crave and urgently need" (221). Ultimately, however, the Reithian view of democracy, based as it was on his perception of universal needs, relies on a centripetal and quasi-imperial belief in the moral supremacy of his Arnoldian notion of "the best." "As we conceive it," Reith writes in one of his most famous pronouncements on the social obligation of broadcasting, "our responsibility is to carry into the greatest possible number of homes everything that is best in every department of human knowledge, endeavour and achievement, and to avoid the things which are, or may be, hurtful. It is occasionally indicated to us that we are apparently setting out to give the public what we think they need—and not what they want, but few know what they want, and very few what they need" (*Broadcast* 34).

Michele Hilmes writes of the ways American broadcasters during the 1930s developed reading styles that added semantic nuances to radio scripts in order "to subvert institutional and social control [by] undermining the power of the written word" (121). As "the most influential English newspaper critic of his time" (Rosenbaum 65–66) and "the leading literary journalist in England between the wars" (Levy 1–2), Desmond MacCarthy would hardly have wished to subvert the power of the written word; rather, as a devout adherent to his friend G. E. Moore's aestheticist ethics, he used not only the written word but also the spoken word to challenge, on air, the institutional and social authoritarianism inherent in the Reithian cultural project. Although in "The Art of Reading" MacCarthy repeatedly celebrates the powerful effects that literature may have on readers' lives, he does so not by appealing to a criterion of intrinsic meaning and value such as that contained in Reith's interpretation of "the best that has been thought and said in the world" but by destabilizing that criterion through a valorization of the relationship between reader and work in the determination of literary value. MacCarthy was a critic for "the people" and, by his own estimation, a "purveyor" of literature to the public ("Prophets" 117). He offers his listeners critical evaluations of many literary touchstones; he also encourages them to develop their own capacities for making meaning from literary texts and for determining those texts' worth in the context of listeners' individual lives.

The London *Times*, in its weekly schedule of BBC broadcasts on September 29, 1932, announced MacCarthy's "Art of Reading" series with the following advertisement: "Mr. Desmond MacCarthy will deliver a talk on 'The Art of Reading' at 7.30 on the National station. This is the introductory talk to a new series on literature. Mr. MacCarthy will take various widely read books and attempt to discover the qualities which have made them famous" ("The Art of Reading" 8). The announcement was three-quarters correct: MacCarthy delivered his talk at the scheduled time; it was the first in a new series; and he indeed devoted his allotted thirty minutes each Thursday evening to "various widely read" works of literature, including Defoe's *Robinson Crusoe*, Milton's *Il Penseroso* and *L'Allegro*, Boswell's *Life of Johnson*, Tolstoy's *Confessions*, Wordsworth's *Prelude*, Ibsen's *Hedda Gabler*, and Charlotte Brontë's *Jane Eyre*, among others. However, in the opening minutes of his first talk, MacCarthy made it clear that he would not explain the qualities that had made his chosen texts famous. Nor would he discuss these works' intrinsic excellence for his listeners' intellectual benefit and moral edification. He did not want, in short, to impose on his listeners a homily on a universal standard of literary taste, and he did not presume, notwithstanding his status as a well-regarded literary critic and noted broadcaster, to know what his audience wanted. Just as, for Moore, goodness was a function of individuals' empathic relationships to other individuals, and beauty, a particular state of mind arising out of an active relation between perceiver and perceived, so too for MacCarthy the value of literature lay in the intensity of the response it provoked in its reader. In *Principia Ethica*, Moore had argued that the "mere existence of what is beautiful has value, so small as to be negligible, in comparison with that which attaches to the *consciousness* of beauty" (189, italics in text). In his discussion of the locus of ethical goodness and aesthetic value, Moore had also foregrounded personal experience and aesthetic "feeling." In the very enjoyment of beauty, as in the pleasures to be had from conversation and intimate relationships, Moore had written, "there is included, not merely a bare cognition of what is beautiful in the object, but also some kind of feeling or emotion" (189). MacCarthy echoes these thoughts in his first "Art of Reading" talk, where he explains the purpose of the series:

> I do not want to lecture. . . . Nor do I want you to agree with the general judgment upon famous books. It is no doubt a sign of education to hold approved opinions about the comparative merit of authors, to know by hearsay that Milton is a greater poet than Byron or that *Don Quixote* is one of the greatest novels. But unless there is personal experience behind this knowledge, to know such facts is [to know] pieces of information. . . . [A]rt and literature stand in a different relation to man. The study of literature is as much a matter of feeling and perceiving as of knowing. (MacCarthy Papers, Lilly Library)[2]

Later in the decade, Virginia Woolf would criticize the vaunted, "paid-for" culture, education, and morality of men of the "educated class" (*Three Guineas* 4). Here, resisting the temptation to lecture over the microphone, MacCarthy anticipates Woolf's argument by criticizing a mode of literary valuation that requires the abdication of empathy in favor of conformity to traditional judgment.

Throughout "The Art of Reading" series, MacCarthy insists upon the non-utilitarian pleasure to be gained from reading. He maintains also that the critic's function is to encourage his or her readers or, in this case, listeners, to get "as much pleasure as possible" from books—and presumably from radio talks on books as well. Thus, he avoids the secular transcendentalism of J. S. Mill's greatest happiness principle, of T. H. Green's idealism, and of the morality that Arnold had linked with culture and that Thomas Huxley, Herbert Spencer, Leslie Stephen, and others had derived from evolutionary theory. In his second talk, "Matter-of-Fact Fiction—Defoe," MacCarthy invites his audience to be "fellow pleasure-seekers. . . . I enjoy the idea of sharing with you my delight in [*Robinson Crusoe*, which] has been enjoyed by millions and for over two hundred years . . . has given delight to young and old." A week later, in his talk "Romantic Adventure—Scott," MacCarthy tells his listeners that "from observing myself and other people I think that . . . the best approach to literature is that of one who reads for pleasure." MacCarthy was not the only Bloomsbury Group member who placed the pleasure of reading over its instrumental value. Nor was he the only one of them who broadcast this belief on air. Forster, in a BBC talk on the contents and pleasure-value of his library, aligns himself with MacCarthy; he calls himself a "lover" of books, and characterizes words as "the wine of life" ("Library" 294).

MacCarthy's series of talks is pointedly directed against those literary critics and cultural arbiters, such as the Leavises and T. S. Eliot, who in the early 1930s were assiduously fighting the good fight to preserve Victorian—more specifically, Arnoldian—cultural and moral values in the age of mass communications. Eliot gave the Charles Eliot Norton lectures at Harvard in late 1932 and early 1933—published in 1933 as *The Use of Poetry and the Use of Criticism*—at the very moment that MacCarthy was delivering his talks in London, and in these lectures Eliot acknowledges the relevance of personal pleasure to the aesthetic experience but refuses to make pleasure the marker of literary value. Associating pleasure with individualism, Eliot adamantly opposes "any ... theory which is erected from purely individual-psychological foundations" (7), such as those of Walter Pater, whose literary impressionism appealed to MacCarthy and Woolf, and especially of I. A. Richards, who had been a student of G. E. Moore. Eliot prefers the jurisprudential certainty of intrinsic and transhistorical value. Woolf and MacCarthy, to the contrary, wield the concept of "reading for pleasure" as, in Gilles Deleuze's sense of the terms, an "ethical" foil to canonical "law" and law's hypostasis, "morality." In a way that recalls the ethical thinking of such diverse writers as Walter Pater, Oscar Wilde, and Bernard Williams, Deleuze explains the ethics-morality distinction thus:

> [E]thics, which is to say, a typology of immanent modes of existence, replaces morality, which always refers existence to transcendent values. Morality is the judgment of God, the *system of judgment*. But ethics overthrows the system of judgment. The opposition of values (Good-Evil) is supplanted by the qualitative difference of modes of existence (good-bad). . . . Law is always the transcendent instance that determines the opposition of values . . . but knowledge is always the immanent power that determines the qualitative difference of modes of existence. (73–74)

For MacCarthy, the fundamental function of literature and literary journalism was not to reinscribe a preordained system or rules of judgment, nor to grant readers access to the material with which to "readjust" the literary canon (Eliot, *Use* 100). Rather, this function was, as Attridge puts it, to "provoke inventive responses" not only to the literary work but also "to other persons and bring about a more widespread alteration in intersubjective behavior" (24).

Pleasure was a mainstay of MacCarthy's literary criticism; it also informed his very way of life. He indulged this penchant for pleasure in the long, enchanting lunchtime conversations for which he earned a certain notoriety—as in A. G. Macdonell's fictional portrait of him as an inveterate luncher-out in *England, Their England* (23–25)—and in his newspaper articles and radio talks. He gives his quasi-anarchic hedonism full vent in "The Art of Reading." In his ninth talk, on "Old Ballads," he urges each of his listeners to "yield yourself" to the poetry—a comment that recalls his championing of the eccentric aesthetic theorist Vernon Lee, whom he had once praised both for upholding art-for-art's-sake values and for introducing the concept of "empathy" into British aesthetics. Throughout "The Art of Reading," MacCarthy links friendship, individual judgment, and pleasure to align himself with the aesthetic and ethical values of aestheticism, a movement of which he was perennially fond. In his fourth talk, on "Romantic Adventure" in the novels of Robert Louis Stevenson, he rhetorically befriends his listeners and lauds what he considers to be Stevenson's aestheticism:

> I often read Stevenson. One reason why I turn to him is that he writes to give me pleasure. How few modern authors do! They write to do us good, to expose us, to scold us, to teach us, to express their contempt for us . . . few write to entertain and delight us. . . . Stevenson is bent on giving us pleasure all the time, by his phrases, his characters, his stories. It is a much humbler aim, but more rarely attained. Each of his books is an independent effort to that end.

Each of MacCarthy's own talks is an independent effort to a similar end—namely, that of celebrating, in Deleuze's senses of the terms, an "ethical" as opposed to a "moral" way of life or style of living. In a later talk, he speaks of Dickens's "desire to move us" and locates the political force of Dickens's novels in their attempt to appeal to as wide a readership as possible. Dickens had, MacCarthy says, an infectious "love for his fellow men." As a result, "Dickens's art was not exclusive, that infection could reach all sorts and conditions of men."

When writing of Dickens, MacCarthy fails to mention Dickens's own thoughts on the liberatory potential of reading. MacCarthy's approach to reading, however, closely resembles the use to which the young David Copperfield puts it: it offers Dickens's young hero a vehicle of escape from the physical and psychological violence he suffered at the hand of his authoritarian stepfather, and it holds out to the young David the romantic hope of a better world existing somewhere outside the walls of his late father's attic room. MacCarthy's repeated appeal to pleasure as the purpose of reading is a basic element of his ethical aestheticism. Despite all his talk of pleasure, however, the individual pleasure to be gotten from reading represents for MacCarthy not simply an end in itself—that is, not the *only* end in itself—but, rather, one of several interlocking ethical ends. Shortly before beginning his "Art of Reading" series, MacCarthy wrote a brief portrait of Henry James, one of the aestheticist idols he had acquired at Cambridge. In this essay, MacCarthy recalls his and his Bloomsbury friends' early preoccupation with aesthetics and ethics. "Our generation," he writes:

> at least that part of it with which I was best acquainted and most at home, was interested in those parts of experience which could be regarded as ends in themselves. Morality was either a means to attaining these goods of the soul, or it was nothing. . . . These ends naturally fined themselves down to personal relations, aesthetic emotions and the pursuit of truth. ("Henry James" 164)

Thirty years after his Cambridge days had ended, MacCarthy still considered this vision of ethical and aesthetic relations the clearest and most perceptive he had ever encountered. Configuring pleasure (aesthetic emotions), personal relations, and the search for truth as the essential characteristics of a good life, MacCarthy adumbrated certain key points in poststructuralist ethical-aesthetic discussions of art, culture, literature, personhood, and moral systems as "complex and constantly changing fields of interrelated forces, possibilities, nodes, and tendencies" (Attridge 29)—and of ways in which recognition of this changing complexity may foster an acknowledgment of "the everydayness of creativity and inventiveness, their occurrence on a scale that reaches from the minute to the momentous" (29).

Reading was, for MacCarthy, a paradigmatic ethical activity on an intimate, everyday scale. In his view, readers' enjoyment of literary works precedes and encourages inventive responses to them and fosters a heightened sensitivity to others as well as a recognition of one's own implicatedness in others' (texts' and individuals') perpetual emerging into being. His approach to reading also represents, historically, his effort to distance himself from modes of literary valuation such as T. S. Eliot was propounding during the months MacCarthy was delivering his "Art of Reading" talks. His most emphatic affirmation of his central critical principles comes in his talk titled "Milton's Shorter Poems":

> It is best to enjoy any author before one understands him. Indeed, in my opinion, it is little use trying to understand him before one has enjoyed him. That is what often seems to me wrong with the teaching of literature. Students learn all about a famous book or a famous author except what they could have found out for themselves.... Take then ... from every book what belongs to you in it.... I'm sure that this is the right way to set about studying literature. True, this method won't necessarily help you to pass examinations or impress others by your cultured conversation, but it is the best way of making literature part of your life and that after all is the most important thing.

Is MacCarthy offering his readers a placebo? Is he simply promoting an art of reading whose underlying purpose is to mystify literature—"aestheticize" it, in Walter Benjamin's sense of the term—by removing it from its social context and from the material conditions of its production, and emptying it of political content? By claiming that one need not pass examinations to experience literature as richly as possible, is he discouraging listeners and the children of listeners, socially less fortunate than himself at a time of grave world political and economic crisis, from aspiring to formal education such as he himself had received and which held out the possibility of "cultivation" and of upward social and economic mobility? Is he employing the new communications technology of radio and the new cultural formation of public service broadcasting with the Arnoldian and Reithian aim of "making the will of God prevail" by exploiting a technocultural medium to which, in Horkheimer and Adorno's words, "no mechanism of reply has been developed" (96) and in relation to which the common listener literally had no voice? One might muster a "yes" to each of these questions. But to do so would require lifting these talks themselves out of the institutional and historical contexts of their production and out of the history of the variety of ways Bloomsbury's ethical-aesthetic beliefs buttressed their politically oppositional stances. It seems to me that Desmond MacCarthy levied the opportunities offered by public service broadcasting to his countercultural, counterethical, and counterhegemonic advantage precisely by working within this specific cultural formation to promote the aestheticist and ethical ideals that he shared with his Bloomsbury Group colleagues and which opposed the official ideological and moral agenda of the Reithian BBC. Raymond

Williams has argued that by virtue of their relentless adherence to a forward-looking belief in individual agency and liberation as the goal of cultural, economic, and political struggle, the Bloomsburyans

> lived and worked [their] position with a now embarrassing wholeheartedness: embarrassing, that is to say, to those many for whom "civilized individualism" is a mere flag to fly over a capitalist, imperialist and militarist social order; embarrassing, also, to those many for whom "civilized individualism" is a summary phrase for a process of privileged consumption. ("Significance" 60)

In his 1993 Reith lectures, published in the following year as *Representations of the Intellectual*, Edward Said remarks upon the hold the ideology of nationalism still exerts on intellectuals no less than on others around the world today. "All of us," Said says, reminding us of an obvious but, in terms of world history, significant fact, "live inside national borders, we use national languages, we address (most of the time) our national communities" (98). The spatial metaphor of the border is interesting here because it points to one of the two basic categories by which we make sense of lived experience. Given the technocultural context of the BBC studio in which Said uttered his observation, it is even more interesting because it foregrounds, seventy years after the BBC was founded, the ways radio and nationalism remain tightly bound at a time when media theorists are increasingly attuned to the complexities of global information flows. The ideology of national space operates no less powerfully now than it did when John Reith decided it was the BBC's duty to "make the nation as one man."

Michel de Certeau writes of ways that "things *extra* and *other* (details and excesses coming from elsewhere) insert themselves into the accepted framework, the imposed order. One thus has the very relationship between spatial practices and the constructed order. The surface of this order is everywhere punched and torn open by ellipses, drifts, and leaks of meaning" (160, italics in text). De Certeau's observation about how individual inhabitants of physical and ideological spaces negotiate them to serve their own purposes applies well to Bloomsbury's involvement with the BBC. Much like de Certeau's urban pedestrian, the Bloomsbury talkers, led by Desmond MacCarthy, inserted themselves into a space that had been built with the materials of a liberal nationalist ideology—and which was punctured and torn by internal and external stresses during its first quarter-century of existence—and employed trowels of detail and hammers of excess to make that given space habitable for themselves and for others. Like Oscar Wilde, their equally excessive predecessor in subcultural or countercultural politics, they believed that "a map of the world that does not include Utopia is not worth even glancing at, for it leaves out the one country at which Humanity is always landing" (Wilde 498). Bloomsburyans, too, wanted to construct a new place of their own design where their utopian ideals of intimacy, internationalism, and beauty could universally flourish, and their radio talks provide abundant evidence of the integrity of their effort to create this new world.

Notes

1. As part of its tenth anniversary special edition on January 19, 1939, the *Listener* published a "pictorial centerpiece" titled "Masters of the Microphone," which shows a collage of twenty-three noted broadcasters standing in the art deco main reception hall of Broadcasting House before an Eric Gill sculpture, "The Sower," with its subscription, "*Deus incrementum dat*" ("God giveth the increase," from *Corinthians* 3:7), and beneath a legend carved into the smooth stone lintel that, translated from the Latin, reads:

> This temple of the arts and muses is dedicated to Almighty God by the first Governors of Broadcasting in the year 1931, Sir John Reith being director general. It is their prayer that good seed sown may bring forth a good harvest, that all things hostile to peace and purity may be banished from this house, and that the people, inclining their ear to whatsoever things are beautiful and honest and of good report, may tread the path of wisdom and uprightness. (Glancey)

Some of the broadcasters assembled for this "group portrait" have been largely ignored if not wholly forgotten by media and cultural historians, few of whom could readily call up the faces of F. A. Voigt, Christopher Stone, Geoffrey Tandy, S. P. B. Mais, Sir Walford Davies, the oft-heard Vernon Bartlett, or the euphoniously named Raymond Gram Swing. Others, however, remain, though not (or not primarily) because of their impact on early British broadcasting, very much alive in historical memory today: their ranks include G. B. Shaw, Winston Churchill, Stanley Baldwin, H. G. Wells, Harold Nicolson, W. B. Yeats, and MacCarthy.

2. All quotations from "The Art of Reading" are taken from Desmond MacCarthy's manuscripts and/or typescripts of the series, in the Desmond and Mary MacCarthy Papers, Lilly Library, Bloomington, Indiana. These talks, some of them abridged, were also published in the *Listener*.

CHAPTER 10

"We Speak to India"

*T. S. Eliot's Wartime Broadcasts
and the Frontiers of Culture*

MICHAEL COYLE

On May 26, 1941, T. S. Eliot gave a reading of "East Coker" for the *We Speak to India* program of the BBC's Eastern Service; the reading was in fact the sixteenth installment in a series optimistically (in that desperate period for the Allied war effort) called *Turning Over a New Leaf*. This broadcast marked Eliot's first reading of his own poetry over the airwaves. That he chose to do for India what he had previously been unwilling to do for Britain is striking, all the more so because it was five years before he consented to a rebroadcast of the reading for the BBC Home Service West of England (March 17, 1946). For all that Eliot had grown friendly with Zulfiqar Bokhari, Indian Programme Organiser for the BBC, his motivation seems less personal than—in the broadest of senses—"political." While doing his bit to help defeat fascism, Eliot was deeply concerned that this global conflict not destroy culture itself. By war's end this concern had deepened, leading Eliot to take an ever more conservative view of "culture" as healthy only when removed from the business of civilization and increasingly to concern himself with the frontiers between them. Indeed, this view might more properly be regarded as reactionary, in that it returned to the convictions of Victorian sages like Matthew Arnold and John Henry Newman. But however easy it is to imagine how the pressures of war might produce this kind of reaction, it remains curious that Eliot turned to a distinctly modern technology to define his new role as cultural sage: that he took to his role of frontier warden using a medium indifferent to boundaries and that he undertook this mission not by direct addresses to the people of Britain but by speaking to overseas audiences.[1] In the account that follows, however, I suggest something more: that this development in Eliot's cultural-critical position could *only* have happened using the medium and genre of the radio talk. Eliot never considered that radio broadcasts represented a trivialization of his talents. As I have discussed elsewhere, he was keenly alive to the distinct characteristics of the radio talk as a genre, and like the intellectuals of the BBC Brains Trust (Julian Huxley et al.), he recognized the confidence that the average listener had in persons of authority and learned to speak accordingly. This recognition also separated him from cultural conservatives like Cyril Connolly, who wrote late in 1942 that "we are becoming a nation of culture-diffusionists. Culture diffusion is not art. We are not making a true art" (285).

Eliot began broadcasting to Europe and India to reaffirm what he saw as the profound bond among those peoples sharing in the Western tradition, and he seems to have regarded India as sharing in these bonds. Of course this project took for granted the subaltern condition of the subcontinent, subject to the British Empire. That it overlooks the extent to which literature and "culture" served the imperial powers as what Gauri Viswanathan has called "masks of conquest" is obvious, and my focus on Eliot's overseas wartime broadcasts to Europe as well as to India does not make such questions irrelevant. For now, however, it matters first to observe that it was only under the pressure of world war that Eliot began broadcasting to the world beyond the shores of Britain.

By 1941, Eliot had been broadcasting, mostly for the BBC, for thirteen years. What had begun as an experiment gradually developed into a commitment, Eliot taking care to develop the distinctions between a broadcast talk and a public lecture and working to create an audience whose presence he could not and did not take for granted.[2] But in those thirteen years he had broadcast almost exclusively to Britain; in 1931 one of his John Dryden talks had been rebroadcast in the United States, and five years later he had interviewed Irish writer Maura Laverty in Dublin—but otherwise he had broadcast exclusively for various BBC services, most often the London Regional service, and sometimes the Home or National services. The 1941 reading of "East Coker" thus marked a turning point in two ways: not only did Eliot read from his poetry for the first time but he also directed his reading beyond British shores and to the Empire. My aim in what follows is to demonstrate the connection between these two developments; the near necessity of

Eliot's having imagined his first broadcast reading for a foreign audience has much to tell us of the strains driving what Andreas Huyssen has called the "compulsive *pas-de-deux*" between Modernism and modernity (57).

However ephemeral sound waves in the air might be, by the early twenty-first century we have found many ways to document and preserve radio broadcasts. Such was not the case before the Second World War, and so it is perhaps not surprising that Eliot's long commitment to radio broadcasting has passed with little critical comment.[3] Only a few of his broadcasts were recorded in a publicly available form, and so much of what once was "broadcast" to multitudes has largely vanished. What traces remain are generally literary. Scripts for many of the talks survive in the BBC Written Archives Centre (there is also a script in the T. S. Eliot Papers, Houghton Library, Harvard College Library), and others may well be found among the papers held by the Eliot estate. Furthermore, many of Eliot's scripts were subsequently redacted and published in periodical form. On the basis of this evidence and the voluminous records of the BBC (records that ordinarily document titles and durations but not Eliot's actual language), we can reconstruct patterns of activity and sometimes even the substance of his radio talks.

Eliot began broadcasting in 1929 and, admitting one early hiatus of five years, continued virtually to the time of his death: a period of approximately thirty-five years. His broadcasts fall conveniently into four groups. In the first period, 1929–1931, Eliot delivered nineteen talks, all in multipart series and focused on literary topics like "Tudor Prose" or "Seventeenth-Century Poetry" (both in six parts). In the second period, 1936–1939, Eliot's interest in radio seemed to decline, and he made only seven talks on various literary and community topics. But the outbreak of war launched a new period of activity, and between 1940 and 1947 Eliot broadcast at least thirty-six times; eleven of these broadcasts were directed at European audiences, ten of them were made for the BBC Eastern Service, and between 1941 and 1943, six broadcasts were made for Bokhari's programme, *We Speak to India*. Taken together, these numbers tell us that Eliot conceived 75 percent of his broadcasts in this period for overseas audiences. That change should command our attention—not least because it wasn't permanent. After 1948 Eliot's broadcasting activities were increasingly involved with the BBC's new Third Programme, a species of minority programming concerned primarily with matters artistic and intellectual. His interest in and loyalty to the Third Programme redirected his broadcasting activity, and while between 1948 and 1963 Eliot spoke over the air another thirty-six times, only seven of those broadcasts were for one of the BBC's foreign services.[4]

The period of 1940–1947 is, thus, distinct in Eliot's career, and it coincides with a significant retrenchment in his critical career. The most important phase of his broadcasting activity, Eliot tended to speak about culture itself and especially about the ultimate unity of European culture. The history of Eliot's broadcast talks and readings consequently reflects the larger history of the BBC—a history that Eliot actively helped shape, eventually becoming not only one of its most celebrated speakers but also, after World War II, an outspoken champion of BBC radio, urging it to resist the temptations of both television and American-style broadcasting.[5] Eliot's broadcasts to European and Asian (particularly Indian) audiences comprise a special chapter in his life; in them we can see Eliot working to redefine his personal sense of mission as well as his preeminent role as what Americans might call today a "public intellectual."

The relation of these international broadcasts to the war effort was oblique at best. The German bombing of London (the Blitz) raged from September 7, 1940, through May 10, 1941; during this period Eliot made only one broadcast—"Towards a Christian Britain," Eliot's contribution to a series of talks put together by Dorothy L. Sayers, *The Church Looks Ahead*. The infrequency of his broadcasts during the Blitz owed both to the pressure and mayhem of the nightly bombings and also to his chronic ill health, including a two-month bout of influenza, soon followed by other illnesses (Ackroyd 259–64). But of Eliot's commitment to the war effort there is no doubt; he had enlisted as "an air-raid warden for his area of Kensington" as soon as war was declared, and these duties required him to sit up all night two nights a week (253–54, 258). Indeed, during this period he worked for the British Council, visited with American GIs stationed in London, and seems at the time to have regarded *Four Quartets* as "patriotic poems" (264, 266). In the same way, his very setting aside time for radio talks might be regarded as an exercise of civic or even patriotic responsibility. And yet, for all that, not once in any of his broadcasts did Eliot ever speak of the war effort or even sound an unmistakably "patriotic" note. The question therefore is twofold: why, at that desperate moment in history, did Eliot reposition himself as he did, and why and how did his radio broadcasts function in that repositioning?

Certainly patriotic considerations played a part, and there were good reasons for the BBC to redouble its efforts to reach out to India. At the outbreak of war, with Indian leaders increasingly frustrated by British recalcitrance over the question of Indian independence, India divided over the question of whether to support Britain or Japan. When the British governor general and viceroy of India, Victor Alexander John Hope, declared India's entry into the war he necessarily did so unilaterally—without consulting the leaders of the Indian National Congress. Britain needed the support of India and for the most part got it, despite Mohan Singh Deb's "Indian National Army" fighting for the Japanese. But the BBC's Eastern Service generally trod gently on political questions, ordinarily working to affirm the values of British culture without reference to the values of British government. "Masks of conquest" and propaganda work, to be sure, but work to be distinguished from the nakedly political.

The BBC currently presents its story this way:

> It has been said that the war made the BBC's reputation. It certainly made the BBC World Service, in terms of its scale as well as its reputation.... the biggest expansion came early in 1940 and 1941, ahead of American involvement in the war, when the outlook for Britain was bleakest. The Government asked the BBC to increase its overseas effort three-fold. A special service for North America was introduced, offering entertainment as well as news of the British struggle. There were services in every major European language, from Scandinavia to the Balkans, plus services for the Soviet Union, Persia, India, Japan and many more.[6]

Among the other important writers and poets involved in the shaping of these services was the young Eric Blair—George Orwell—fifteen years Eliot's junior and employed by the BBC only since August of 1941 but who was hired by Bokhari as a talks assistant for the Eastern Service. As Clive Fleay and M. L. Sanders explain, Orwell was engaged to help both with "cultural broadcasts" and with "the preparation of weekly news broadcasts, 'Through Eastern Eyes'" (503–18):

> The distinction between these two areas can be exaggerated, for it is misleading to describe the so-called "cultural" broadcasts as educational, if this is intended to contrast them with propaganda. All the programs to India and elsewhere in which Orwell took part or were scripted by him were contributions to an overall propaganda effort conceived before Orwell ever joined the BBC. Z. A. Bokhari, in welcoming Orwell to the Eastern Service, gave a detailed account of the work of his department, which involved a number of broadcasts which could

be termed "cultural" and which were aimed at a student audience in particular. Bokhari was arranging at the time with Herbert Read for a team of Dons to give talks on books that were on Indian University syllabuses. (505)

Eliot's ten wartime broadcasts for the BBC Eastern Service participated in and were representative of this expansion, although Eliot himself would have never recognized his radio work as propaganda. It is not possible at this time to quote from Eliot's letters to Orwell or to Bokhari, with whom he was already familiar and on good terms. Suffice it to say that after several approaches from Orwell, Eliot wrote to Bokhari asking just who was this Eric Blair; Bokhari explained that it was none other than George Orwell and successfully urged Eliot to contribute.

Despite the fact that Eliot's principal topic from 1937 to 1941 had been Church of England issues, it is thus no surprise that all of Eliot's broadcasts for the Eastern Service were literary in nature or that the first four (1941–1942) were for the *We Speak to India* program. That is, Eliot's subject matter owed not only to his own interests, and not only to Orwell's, but to broader BBC wartime policy. First came the reading of "East Coker" remarked above—Eliot's first broadcast ever of his own poetry. That reading was eventually succeeded in October of 1942 by readings of "Dry Salvages" and "Burnt Norton"—notice that although he read three of the *Four Quartets* he did not read them in order. Two months later (December 1942), Eliot gave a reading of "What the Thunder Said," for Orwell's poetry magazine, *Voice*. These readings of his own work were soon supplemented by, interspersed with, contributions to the series *Masterpieces of English Literature*, speaking first about "The Duchess of Malfi," and then about "'The Voice of His Time': on Tennyson's *In Memoriam*." Subsequent talks took up the work of Edgar Allan Poe (2/12/43), John Dryden (4/1/43), and even James Joyce (9/26/43) (it shows a certain sensitivity on Eliot's part that he saved his talk on Rudyard Kipling for the BBC Swedish Service).

To be sure, Eliot had broadcast to student audiences before the war; his "Poetic Drama and the Modern Poet" (11/20/36), for instance, was a broadcast for the National Service to sixth forms. And Eliot had begun his broadcasting career by speaking exclusively about poets and about literary matters, continuing to do so (though no longer exclusively) for the rest of his life. But in his wartime radio work a difference in emphasis emerges: a difference perhaps possible *only* in radio work and explainable neither by the historical pressure of wartime nor by the accidents of personal friendships and acquaintances, however much these factors shaped his development. This difference finds definitive expression in Eliot's final broadcast to India and is best understood in terms of his much-discussed postwar work on culture—and I will turn to these things shortly. But although all of Eliot's broadcasts between 1941 and 1946 (when he began his work for the Third Programme) were made for overseas audiences, only the ten above were framed for India; the rest were aimed at European audiences: to Sweden (mostly), to France, and—only after the fall of Hitler's Reich—to Germany.[7] Given that these European broadcasts cannot be said to be directed to a subaltern audience, they raise different (though related) issues.

Eliot recorded his first talk for Europe, entitled "Poetry and the War," on July 24, 1942. Even though the talk was later published in the New York journal *Common Sense* (October 1942), as "T. S. Eliot on Poetry in Wartime," it matters hugely that this broadcast was for the BBC program *Swedish News Talks*, and that Sweden remained politically neutral. This short talk suggests the direction of Eliot's subsequent broadcasts to Europe. Addressing the various and sometimes clamorous calls for "war poetry," Eliot explained why he thought such a question should not be asked. The issue, he felt, concerned not just the current war, "but all wars":

> While a poet, as a man, should be no less devoted to his country than other men, I distinguish between his duty as a man and his duty as a poet. His first duty as a poet is towards his native language, to preserve and to develop that language. As a man, he has the same duties as his fellow citizens; as a poet, his duty is to write the best poetry that he can, and thereby incidentally create something in which his people can take pride. And the artist who will do the most in this way for his own people, will be the artist great enough, like Shakespeare, to give something precious not only to his own country but to the whole of Europe.[8]

Here as elsewhere, Eliot struggled to rekindle or preserve the ability of his audience to imagine Europe as a "whole." He did not seize on Shakespeare, for example, as a national poet but as a *European* poet. His aim, even in the early days of the war, was to prepare the groundwork for a peace that could mean something more than the cessation of hostilities.

Within five weeks of that first talk, Eliot broadcast again to Sweden, this time offering a reading from his own poetry. It was only the second reading of his poetry he had ever made, and he chose works from the whole of his career up to that point: "Four Preludes," "Journey of the Magi," "Ash Wednesday" I and II, "Burial of the Dead," "Burnt Norton," and excerpts from "The Dry Salvages." Significantly, he did not read from "Little Gidding," and no part of what he read could be construed as "war poetry." The kind of broadcast-reading he declined to make to promote his career in peacetime he gave in war to exemplify the arguments he was making elsewhere about "culture."

No less interesting in terms of Eliot's choices is his next Swedish talk, of December 30, 1942, titled "Rudyard Kipling."[9] Not surprisingly, Eliot acknowledged Kipling as more versifier than poet but nevertheless recognized in his work the spark of something more: "while I speak of Kipling's work as verse and not as poetry, I am still able to speak of individual compositions as poems, and also to maintain that there is 'poetry' in the 'verse.'" A similar qualification marked Eliot's comments on Kipling's role as an apologist for empire, but as Eliot turned to this issue, his reflections took an unexpected turn, especially given the apparent obscurity of much of his own poetry. What Eliot said about Kipling's role as popular poet and writer reflects broadly on his own activities as a public commentator on "culture" and more particularly on his activities as a BBC broadcaster:

> Kipling certainly thought of verse as well as prose as a medium for a public purpose; if we are to pass judgment upon his purpose we must try to set ourselves in the historical situations in which his various work was written; and whether our prejudice be favorable or antagonistic, we must not look at his observations of one historical situation from the point of view of a later period. Also we must consider his work as a whole. ("In Praise" 154)

Eliot clearly thought of radio as "a medium for a public purpose" and approached his European broadcasts in terms best understood as a response to the crisis of global conflict. This position is essentially historicist: it matters infinitely less that the work of art should answer to its time than that later moments answer to the work. Here again we see the same discrimination between culture and conflict that is so evident in his talk "Poetry and the War," Eliot once again serving as warden of the frontier.

Nevertheless, it is not immediately clear why he should have imagined Kipling a subject attractive to a Swedish audience. In fact, the choice of topic is rather striking: Eliot began broadcasting to Europe at the same time he did India, and to speak of the sometimes bellicose and, until after the First World War, imperialist Kipling to Sweden almost suggests a categorical confusion. As it turns out, however, the topic of Kipling returns him to the questions he addressed in his previous Swedish talk on poetry in wartime: the artist who will "do the most for his own people will be the artist great enough, like Shakespeare, to give something precious not only to his own country but to the whole of Europe." Such an artist will not address the topical details of battle and war but the more profound question of his or her nation's collective spirit—of its cultural health or disease. What in Eliot's view readers of Kipling miss is his turn, in the last part of his career, to that kind of profound attention: "In [Kipling's] later phase England, and a particular corner of England, becomes the center of his vision. He is more concerned with the problem of the soundness of the *core* of empire; this core is something older, more natural, and more permanent" ("In Praise" 155). More permanent, that is, than shifting political frontiers.

In other words, Kipling, or at least the late Kipling, becomes for Eliot a cultural critic. His interest lay not in "civilization" in the abstract but in *a* civilization. It was for this reason that Eliot concluded that whereas "we expect to have to defend a poet against the charge of obscurity, we have to defend Kipling against the charge of excessive lucidity." This defense implicitly explained Eliot's own purpose, both in the largest terms and in regard to his speaking about Kipling to a Swedish audience.

In the next year and a half, Eliot made no further European broadcasts, although in that time he made three broadcasts for the Eastern Service. Then, on June 4, 1944, on the occasion of the Liberation of Rome by Allied troops, presented with a historically significant opportunity, Eliot recorded his last broadcast to India. The occasion and even the title of this talk promised to be the most topical he had ever made, but what Eliot delivered proved instead in keeping with his earlier talk, "Poetry and War." By June 1944, the tide of the war had unmistakably turned in the Allies' favor, and the liberation of Rome might justifiably have been taken as cause for jubilation. The BBC producers who planned the broadcast certainly thought so, and their announcer spoke the following introduction: "We present this evening two talks in honour of the liberation of Rome. For twenty years the Eternal City has lain under the Fascist or the Nazi yoke. Today it is free." The announcer then introduced Eliot, whom he presented as "one of the foremost English poets and critics of today, President of the Virgil Society and ex-President of the Classical Association, who will speak of the European debt to Roman literature."[10] Eliot did just that: his four-minute talk betrays not the slightest note of jubilation, nor the most evanescent trace of victorious pride. On the contrary, he insisted on the spiritual kinship of all Europeans, and submitted, meditatively and with an eye to the future, that the bonds among Europeans had been forgotten in peace before they were broken in war. To reaffirm those bonds it would behoove the victors of war not only to shoulder their debt but to do so with sorrow for the breach, and humility and piety toward the legacy of all left to us by the writers and poets of Rome.

Eliot's effacing of the distinction between Latin and Italian literary tradition was not simply a political convenience but anticipated the arguments he would begin making to Germany in 1946. But however noble and philosophical the gesture to insist on the cultural unity of Europe, it is less certain why Eliot thought such a broadcast suited for a South Asian audience. Indian support for the British Empire, against the German or even the Japanese Empire, was not always enthusiastic, but it is hard to see how Eliot's meditations on European unity could have impressed the anti-British resistance led by Mohandas Gandhi and the Indian National Congress. Particularly in view of Gandhi's rejection of European civilization, Eliot's commitment to India remains one of the unstudied puzzles of Modernist history. But when Eliot resumed making such appeals and such arguments to Europe, they became striking in another way. With one significant exception, he did not broadcast to Europe again until the broadcasts to Germany after the war's end. That one exception involved an unusual broadcast to France. In November of 1944, with the Wehrmacht retreating rapidly to the Rhine (and the temporary Allied setback of the Battle of the Bulge still three weeks away), Eliot spoke in French about "Intellectual Cooperation," for the BBC's French Service.[11] It was a harbinger of the important broadcasts to come.

After one further Swedish broadcast (February 15, 1945), introducing a series of literary talks, Eliot launched what amounts to the last great critical project of his career: a project that would culminate, though not end, with his book *Notes towards the Definition of Culture* (1948). In March of 1946, Eliot made a three-part broadcast entitled "Reflections of an English Poet on European Culture."[12] He recorded the talks in German, for the BBC program *Famous Contemporaries* and used his time at the microphone to press his vision of European unity—precisely the vision he had begun articulating in such broadcasts as "Poetry and the War," "Rudyard Kipling," and "The Liberation of Rome."

The plan for Eliot's series was simple: each talk would examine a different basis for the unity of European culture. In the first, he would discuss art; in the second, ideas; and in the third talk he would speak to that old oxymoron, the nature of culture. Eliot began informally, striving for the kind of intimacy between speaker and listener that had always attracted him to radio.[13] He acknowledged that this talk was the first time that he had ever "addressed a German-speaking audience," whether in the form of a public lecture or of a radio broadcast, and proceeded to offer his credentials for taking on so vast a topic. Not least, he observed that English is a "composite" language, drawing on many sources and enjoying "constant possibilities of refreshment from its several centres: apart from the vocabulary, poems by Englishmen, Welshmen, Scots and Irishmen, all written in English, continue to show differences in their music" (*Christianity and Culture* 188). From this local beginning, he went on to argue that for Europe in general as for Britain in particular, "the frontiers of culture are not, and should not be, closed" (191).

The second talk focused on his years as editor of the *Criterion* and offered his experience as an illustration of the failure of Europe in general. Eliot attributed the eventual failure of the *Criterion* to "the gradual closing of the mental frontiers of Europe" (194), and drew a distinct lesson: "a universal concern with politics does not unite, it divides. It unites those politically minded folk who agree, across the frontiers of nations, against some other international group who hold opposed views. But it tends to destroy the cultural unity of Europe" (195). Recognizing that such a judgment might seem naïve, Eliot allowed that politics affects culture, and in turn is affected by that culture. Nevertheless, speaking at last to the postwar moment, he charged that "nowadays we take too much interest in each other's domestic politics, and at the same time have very little contact with each other's culture" (196). This tendency, Eliot warned, could lead in either of two destructive directions. The first, the mistake of Hitler's Germany, regards all other cultures as inferior; the second, the mistake of Stalinist Russia (though Eliot did not name it), would "lead towards the ideal of a world state in which there will, in the end, be only one uniform world culture" (196).[14] Regarding either direction as a terrible error, Eliot presented what is in essence an Arnoldian compromise: he distinguished between "uniformity" and "unity," and between "organisation" and "organism." Politics pursues the first, poetry—or "culture"—the second. The health of Europe requires, he counseled, both that "the culture of each country be unique" and also that "the different cultures should recognize their relationship to each other, so that each should be susceptible of influence from the others" (197).

This counsel led Eliot to the heart of his topic: "the distinction between the material organisation of Europe, and the spiritual organism of Europe" (197). The very distinction submits Europe's profound cultural unity and gestures both to establish the irrelevant profanity of political concerns and to push aside the "material devastation" (202) of the previous fifteen years. It is unfortunate that we have no evidence of how Eliot's talks played to German audiences. Eliot's broadcasts were, by any accounting, made in virtually surreal circumstances: Eliot spoke to a Germany under the military occupation of four nations, affirming all the while the fundamental unity of victors and vanquished. And yet Eliot would not have considered his talk as propaganda, not even "cultural propaganda" against potential Soviet aggression; in fact, Eliot would almost certainly have maintained his broadcasts fought against the propaganda of *any* political cause.

In this regard, it is useful to distinguish Eliot's radio broadcasts from those made by his sometime friend and often testy rival, Ezra Pound. To begin with, Pound and Eliot regarded radio in very different terms. Eliot believed always that radio could serve the cause of the angels; but—as Jane Lewty notes later in this volume—Pound regarded radio as "the devil box," writing that it is a "God damn destructive and dispersive devil of an invention" (*Letters* 442, 441). And while Eliot purported to speak without reference to national or political identity, Pound seized the microphone as an opportunity to speak politically where his political and national identity would have precluded any such opportunity.

Consequently, their broadcasting activities took very different shapes. Pound broadcast for Minculpop—the Italian (Fascist) Ministry of Popular Culture. After one talk in January 1935, he began recording talks regularly in early 1941. For the next two-and-a-half years he held onto the microphone as though it were a lifeline, with three or four of his broadcasts often airing in a single week. But by July of 1943, Pound's unfortunate involvement in the mass media was effectively over and the regime for which he had been speaking destroyed.[15] Eliot's broadcasting activity, by contrast, was sustained over a period of thirty-five years, and he rarely broadcast twice in the same month. Pound's and Eliot's approaches to radio differed no less dramatically. Pound delivered his talks in a cracker-barrel yankee accent; he purported to speak as one average man to the masses of average men. Eliot, however, never spoke down to his audience but rather invited them to look up with him. And whereas Pound explicitly intended his broadcasts as a form of propaganda, Eliot explicitly eschewed propaganda in any immediate form. Pound, although he did not speak directly to allied troops, directly challenged the purpose and even legitimacy of the Roosevelt administration. Eliot by contrast never spoke directly to political questions. And if Pound shared Eliot's concern with the preservation of Western culture, he rarely restrained himself to literary discussions or to claims about the unity of European literature; Pound's charge to his audience in April 1943 that "the supreme betrayal of Western civilization is manifest in the [Allied] alliance with Russia" (Doob 268) exemplifies the extent to which for him cultural issues immediately led to political or economic questions.

These distinctions do not demonstrate that Eliot's talks were perfectly "disinterested" (to return to Arnold's shibboleth) or apolitical, but they do suggest that the politics of Eliot's broadcasts were complexly mediated. Eliot's radio persona was judicious and gentle, conciliatory at a time when partisans on all sides were suspicious of conciliation in any form. Before the end of 1949, Eliot would speak to Europe on four additional occasions, one of which was a broadcast for the BBC's German Service: an introduction to a reading of his own "Journey of the Magi."[16] Thereafter, between 1950 and his death, he spoke over one of the BBC's European services only twice more, a staying away that was not parallel to a general falling off of Eliot's radio activities. For in that same period, Eliot remained a stalwart supporter of the BBC in both word and deed and became a particular champion of the BBC's Third Programme. In other words, Eliot's turn to Europe can be identified with the particular project we have been discussing, a project that he continued to develop through late 1949.

The last broadcast that Eliot recorded for an audience specifically beyond the shores of Britain would also prove among the most important of his European broadcasts. Airing on October 13, 1953, the eleven-minute talk was called simply "Literature" and figured as the sixth part of a series by different speakers called *The Unity of European Culture*.[17] The series of talks was sponsored by "the Central and Eastern European Commission," an "unofficial body composed of statesmen and public figures from the countries of Europe—the whole of Europe" (*Law* 3). Whatever the composition of the whole body, it has to be said that the speakers in this series of broadcasts were exclusively English (including that naturalized Englishman, Eliot). The commission's overt aim was "to bridge the gap between East and West, and to assert, even across the Iron Curtain, the essential unity of Europe, its civilisation and its culture" (3). Although this commission advocated "no war of liberation," it asserted that "the present boundaries of Europe are not permanent" (4). Ultimately, it hoped "to create a platform for the discussion of [Eastern Europe's] problems" so that "when the time of liberation comes, there will be a responsible and informed body of opinion able to help in the material, political and cultural reconstruction of [the] countries" behind the Iron Curtain (5).

In one sense, this commission provided an unlikely context for Eliot's talk, since he himself rejected political solutions to cultural problems and generally eschewed speaking on political questions. He was not to depart from such resolutions in this talk, and he established very quickly that his position on "culture" remained profoundly Arnoldian: "To me, the unity of European literature has always seemed a self-evident *necessity*; to me, the rapid circulation throughout Europe of the best that was being thought and written in each country of Europe has seemed as essential for the continued life of literature as is the function of breathing for the life of a human being" ("Literature" 19). If anything, Eliot's tendency to represent culture by analogies with the human body was growing more pronounced, not less. He still emphasized the difference between unity and uniformity (the first a matter of spirit and culture, and the second of politics and civilization) and averred that such unity depended on differences among the several literatures of Europe. And all the while, his implicit cautions against Soviet-style ideas of culture continued to drive his discussion. European unity "today" is, he maintained, threatened by "modern and erroneous conceptions of the Nature of Man—what we call ideologies" (21).

Eliot's wartime radio talks would almost certainly have differed both in form and content had they been written by the author of *The Use of Poetry and the Use of Criticism* (1933) or *After Strange Gods* (1934). In "The Problem of Education" (1934), for instance, he had avowed that "at the present time . . . I am not very interested in literature, except dramatic literature; and I am largely interested in subjects which I do not yet know very much about: theology, politics, economics, and education" (11–12). Even at the threshold of war, in 1939, Eliot could write that "the state of arts and letters is a symptom of decline" ("Last Words" 274), and "the specifically literary symptoms of decline . . . cannot be treated by themselves; the demoralization of society goes much deeper" (273)—suggesting in the process that such decline might be more interesting, more urgent, than the Arts being studied. But by 1943, in the serial essay "Notes towards a Definition of Culture" (January–February 1943), a profound change was evident in his thinking wherein the pressure of civilization on the arts—on culture—was itself the problem. When Eliot redacted these essays into *Notes towards the Definition of Culture* (first published in November 1948; note the new specificity of the article, *the*), he provided as epigraph the *Oxford English Dictionary's (OED's)* primary definition of "definition": "the setting of bounds." During the war Eliot grew increasingly concerned with definition and with the monitoring and even policing of such bounds, particularly that between culture (the idealist realm of the arts) and civilization (the realm of politics and technology).[18] The former he saw as unifying and spiritual, the latter as divisive and merely material. This is the position he maintains not only in the two definitive talks of summer 1944, "The Liberation of Rome" and "The Responsibility of the European Man of Letters," and the two principal talks of that fall, "Intellectual Cooperation" (in French) and "Bridgebuilders." This preoccupation with frontiers would relax somewhat in Eliot's final years,[19] but it does in any case characterize his cultural-critical thinking during and after the war and presents us with one final paradox. Or perhaps two.

It was in his radio work, in those wartime talks targeted at foreign audiences, that Eliot's preoccupation with frontiers was first manifest. The paradox is that the medium by which he pursued this concern itself was and is no observer of boundaries. Eliot's position depends on his ability to put technology to use. But the idea of "use" takes us to the second, already evident paradox. Eliot's talks about culture were themselves subject to use—offered themselves to be used—by ideological state apparatuses. Introducing *The Use of Poetry and the Use of Criticism*, Eliot finds Matthew Arnold's doctrine of "culture," which he condenses into the conviction that "poetry is not religion, but it is a capital substitute for religion" as "a hopeless admission of irresponsibility" (24). Nevertheless, in affirming "the spiritual kinship of all Europeans," as he did in his talk on the Liberation of Rome, or in deliberating "the distinction between the material organisation of Europe, and the spiritual organism of Europe," as he did in the first of his broadcasts to Germany, and doing so in terms of a common poetry, Eliot returns to an essentially Arnoldian ideal of culture. But however much his talks of 1944–1946 conform to the general ecumenicity of his previous broadcasts, in addressing Indian or German audiences on the unity of European culture, these talks test severely ecumenical limits in severe ways.

He would, of course, have seen this conception of culture as marking a spiritual rather than an ideological failing, and in that regard he was more or less in keeping with contemporaneous conservative thinkers. But the phenomenon of the leading poet of the day, a poet who represented the "Modernist" impulse in unmistakable form, using mass media to promulgate and popularize an essentially Victorian discourse is as striking a conjuncture of heterogeneous historical forces as might be imagined. He was, to put the matter in slightly different terms, using technology to warn his audience of the importance of preserving culture from the malign influence of technology—and the politics that deploy it. In this respect Eliot is not so very different from other broadcasters of the day such as Gerald Heard and James Jeans who spoke about radical scientific advancement—often in radio communications—over a still-uncanny medium.

This contradiction in Eliot's radio work emerges only with his overseas wartime broadcasts, both to India and to Europe. The forces that prompted this change are manifold, the causes overdetermined, but we can today see this much. First, twelve years of broadcasting, along with the growing prestige of the BBC, seem to have impressed on Eliot the power of the new medium. Like Pound, he could regret the consequences—radio was, he averred in 1950, in no small part responsible for what he saw as "a new illiteracy, and a much more difficult illiteracy to overcome [than that faced by earlier eras]—namely, the illiteracy of that part of the population which has had its elementary schooling but has become illiterate through lack of occasion to use what it has been taught. This secondary illiteracy is a new phenomenon. It is aggravated by the effect of radio and cinema, and by the replacement, in popular periodicals, of words by pictures" ("Notes" 11). Notice that Eliot says "aggravated" rather than "caused": unlike Pound, Eliot did not dismiss radio as "the devil's box" but imagined that only radio could reach the areas of cultural life damaged by the sources of this secondary illiteracy. He sought to appropriate the chief instrument of the new mass culture to speak against its most characteristic impulses. This hope doubtless relied on the singular BBC model of noncommercial radio, but it was not necessarily a foolish hope. Indeed, after the war, in its creation of the "Third Programme" to counteract the influence of American Armed Forces radio, the BBC demonstrated a very similar hope.

A second force, perhaps inevitably, was BBC Director General John Reith's conviction that radio could have the effect of "making the nation as one man" (qtd. in Scannell and Cardiff 7). Reith's conviction demonstrates a still common conflation of the principal sense of the word "culture," which could refer on the one hand to the common life of an entire people, and on the other to the quasi-spiritual, inner development of individuals. That Eliot, too, respected both senses of the term was evident even as early as his celebrated essay of 1919, "Tradition and the Individual Talent," where (invoking "tradition" rather than "culture") he argued both tradition "cannot be inherited" but only obtained "by great labour" and also that "the mind of

Europe—the mind of his own country—[is] a mind ... much more important than his own" (*Selected Essays* 4, 6). And so, striving as he generally did for a conversational, sometimes even intimate tone, Eliot was in certain ways striving to make analogues of the solitary reader and the listener at home beside his or her radio; in neither case is the effect of the language influenced by the dynamics of crowd response. Having, over twelve years of work, approached at last something like a Reithian conception, Eliot at last ventured in 1941 to fuse the two parts of the analogy and read his own work over the air.

Why make such a broadcast to India rather than to Britain? The primary force must have been, and "must have been" is all we can say until Eliot's correspondence possibly reveals his thoughts, the pressure of the war itself. Bokhari's instructions to Orwell are incisively pertinent in this regard. But it matters that Eliot read only three of the *Four Quartets* and that he did not read them in order. We know that, at least at the time, he regarded them as "patriotic poems" (which is not at all the same thing as "war poems"). I believe that in reading the poems out of sequence and delivering only fragments of a whole, Eliot was responding to convictions about the integrity of cultural life. The fusing of the parts requires active, energetic engagement from listeners; the fusing of the parts implicitly invites the audience to participate in a wholeness of which individual listeners might have not previously been aware.

After the war, Eliot came to distinguish among different kinds of technology, chiefly between radio, which he continued to love—perpetuating an idealistic model of wireless that had largely faded by the 1940s—and television, which he abhorred.[20] In Eliot's view, where radio might serve to transmit language, television exacerbates the post-seventeenth-century separation of art from life, replacing the liminality of frontier with absolute disassociation. Before the war he was more ready to conceive of art, or culture, in terms of its use to civilization. During the war, in a way that essentially contradicted post-Reithian BBC strategy, Eliot virtually reversed his position and, witnessing the destruction of Europe's great cities, came more fervently than ever to value the idealist realm of culture.

Historians often use the outbreak of war to mark breaks in historical development, but Eliot's radio work suggests the extent to which even the cataclysm of war should be understood in terms of longer historical duration. At precisely the same time Horkheimer and Adorno, responding to the ways that National Socialism had seized German radio, were developing a hermeneutics of suspicion, Eliot continued to understand both radio and the culture to which he saw it as servant in idealist terms. Horkheimer and Adorno published their attack, "The Culture Industry," in 1947 and almost immediately critical theorists embraced it as politically correct. But that materialist analysis made little impression on Eliot, and his thinking continued to develop in antithetical ways.

Eliot's understanding of radio owed much to the example of BBC Director-General John Reith, whose own idealistic (but not pluralistic) notion was that radio could serve as the nation's one voice. As Debra Rae Cohen and Todd Avery observe earlier in this volume, Reith tirelessly quested after an essentially Arnoldian vision of culture:

> As we conceive it, our responsibility is to carry into the greatest possible number of homes everything that is best in every department of human knowledge, endeavour and achievement, and to avoid the things which are, or may be, hurtful. It is occasionally indicated to us that we are apparently setting out to give the public what we think they need—and not what they want, but few know what they want, and very few what they need." (Reith, *Broadcast* 34)

It is today difficult not to be alarmed by Reith's, and perhaps by Eliot's, confidence. But for all the differences between Reith and Eliot, they shared the conviction that the ideals of "culture" could and must remain untainted by politics. Adorno and Horkheimer regard such a distinction as not only impossible but undesirable. We live today in the world they described rather than the one Eliot did, and we are still counting our losses.

Notes

1. In observing that Eliot targeted these broadcasts at foreign audiences, it is nevertheless important to remember that the BBC, then as now, was in the habit of rebroadcasting talks, and not just for the service where they originally aired but on other services as well.

2. See "'This rather elusory broadcast technique.'"

3. I have discussed these broadcasts in three previous publications: "'This rather elusory broadcast technique'"; "Eliot on the Air" and "The Radio Broadcasts of T. S. Eliot"; and "The European Radio Broadcasts of T. S. Eliot." Archie Henderson is currently at work on a revised edition of *The Bibliography of T. S. Eliot*, and he has already uncovered additional broadcasts to those I enumerate below, though not in any large number.

4. This number does not include his broadcast for Radiodiffusion Française in 1949 or the two he made in the United States in 1947 and 1950. There may be additional

broadcasts made for the national services of the various nations of western Europe; apart from one broadcast for Irish radio, my research thus far has not encompassed more than the sound and paper archives of the BBC.

5. I discuss this aspect of Eliot's relations with the BBC in "Eliot on the Air."

6. See the BBC home page, special section on wartime broadcasting overseas: http://www.bbc.co.uk/heritage/story/ww2/overseas.shtml, accessed August 12, 2007.

7. There were also two broadcasts for the BBC North American Service: "Bridgebuilders" (11/15/44) and another titled "The Significance of Charles Williams" (10/5/46)—both made well after the entry of the United States into the war.

8. I quote from the published version of this talk; the Eliot estate currently withholds the right to quote from those of Eliot's scripts that survive in the paper archive of the BBC.

9. Probably a version of "In Praise of Kipling's Verse," an essay that Eliot published in *Harper's* in July 1942. The quotations that follow are from the *Harper's* essay.

10. Typescript located in the BBC Written Archives Centre, Caversham. Allied troops had entered Rome on June 4, 1944; Eliot prerecorded his talk that very day, and it aired at midday on the next, June 5 (on the Purple Network of the BBC Eastern Service). Eliot returned to some of the concerns of this broadcast, though reproducing next to nothing of its form, in a broadcast for the Third Programme of September 9, 1951, entitled "Vergil and the Christian World." That talk was slightly redacted and published in both the *Listener* (September 13, 1951) and in *Sewanee Review*, 61.1 (January/March 1953); it was later collected in Eliot's *On Poetry and Poets* (London: Faber and Faber, 1957).

11. Eliot recorded this broadcast for the BBC series "Demi Heure du Soir," and it was broadcast on November 8, 1944.

12. All three of these talks were later published, with English and German on facing pages, as *Die Einheit der Europäischen Kultur* (Berlin: Carl Habel Verlagsbuckhandlung, 1946). The second was first published in English in *Adelphi* 23.3 (April/June 1947) and was later republished along with the first and the third talks as an appendix to *Notes towards the Definition of Culture*, which first appeared in November 1948.

13. The nature of Eliot's attraction to radio and the peculiar strengths he regarded as belonging to a radio talk as opposed to a public lecture or a published essay are the topics of my essay "'This rather elusory broadcast technique.'"

14. Eliot continued to advocate the importance of decentralizing culture in the years ahead. Of particular interest is a broadcast he made in June 1947 for WBIB, in New Haven, Connecticut. See Gallup C524a.

15. For a fuller account of Pound's broadcasts, see Carpenter 541–42 and 583–84; see also Heyman 149–51. Heyman notes that Pound made one broadcast for the so-called Salò Republic on December 10, 1943; thereafter Pound continued to produce radio scripts for Minculpop until April 1945, but there is no evidence that any of these scripts were ever aired. Thanks to Jonathan Gill for reminding me of this dénouement to Pound's broadcasting "career." Most of Pound's radio talks have been collected; see Doob.

16. Prerecorded on December 9, 1948, that broadcast aired on Christmas day. The poem itself was read in German by actor Mathias Wieman.

17. Eliot prerecorded the talk on the previous day. The talk initially aired over the BBC's European Service but was rebroadcast February 2, 1954, for the BBC's Third Programme. A recording of this talk is available for audition in the British Library National Sound Archive. The entire series of broadcasts, including Eliot's, was published as a pamphlet in December 1953 by William Clowes & Sons, Ltd. My quotations come from the pamphlet. The series comprised an introductory talk by the Rt. Hon. Richard Law, P.C., M.P., who spoke to represent the purposes of the Central and Eastern European Commission; Christopher Dawson on religion; Denis Healey, M.P., on Socialism; Julian Amery, M.P., on political unity; Richard O'Sullivan, Q.C., on the legal tradition; T. S. Eliot on literature; and Sir David Kelly, G.C., M.G., on diplomacy.

18. See Eliot's *Notes towards the Definition of Culture*; reprinted in *Christianity and Culture* 85–88.

19. I have described this preoccupation at length in *Ezra Pound, Popular Genres, and the Discourse of Culture* (18–26).

20. See Eliot's "The Television Habit" and "Television Is Not Friendly Enough."

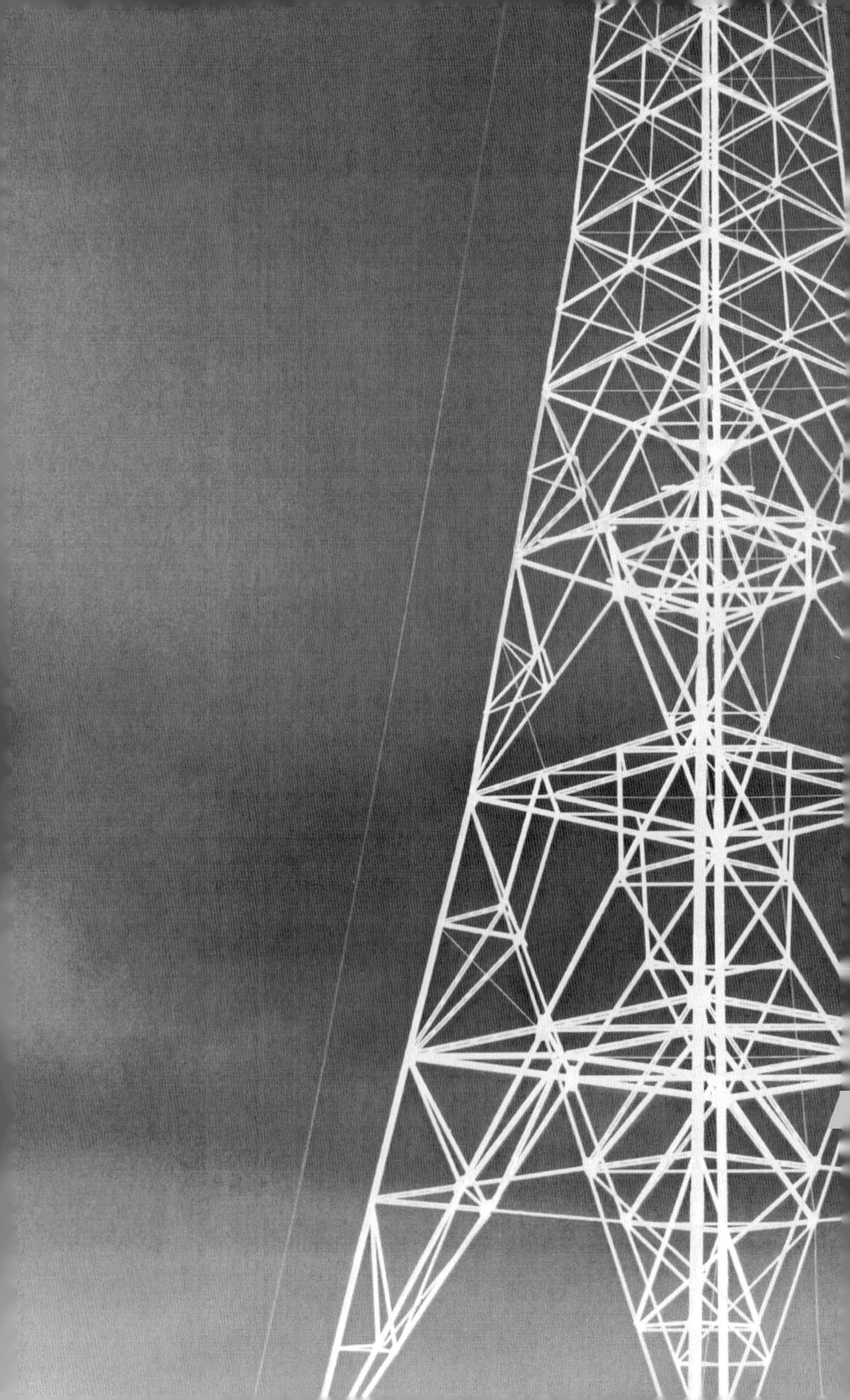

PART III NEGOTIATIONS, TRANSACTIONS, TRANSLATIONS

CHAPTER 11

"What They Had Heard Said Written"

Joyce, Pound, and the Cross-Correspondence of Radio

JANE LEWTY

> If I can't upset this pound of pressed ollaves
> I can sit up zounds of sounds upon him
> —James Joyce, *Finnegans Wake* (499)

A critic is easily susceptible, as Michael Whitworth notes, to the idea that "everyone" writing during the early twentieth century was utilizing a new science in some way, whether through metaphor, key image, subject matter, or adaptation (211). However, the topic of *Broadcasting Modernism* is more than a simple historical conjunction; it implies the recasting of texts and writers in order to locate a particular mind-set, that which hears a disembodied voice emanating from a corner of a room, "as queer as any transaction with a ghost in Shakespeare" (Kenner, *Mechanic Muse* 36) or, as in the searing conclusion to Tillie Olson's *Yonnondio* (1934), "the veering transparent meshes of sound, far sound, human and stellar, pulsing, pulsing" (191). Whitworth adds that "the full machine is never apparent" (211), meaning that no author is likely to leave a comprehensive report of, in this case, the growth of wireless and its network[s]; instead, we have the recognition of its uncanniness, a stray broadcast word finding its way into a poem. It becomes necessary to categorize the different "reverberations" of radio: for example, its effect on the structure of written words as seen in Guillaume Apollinaire's calligram "Ocean Letter" (1914), which imprints a view of the modern world in a frieze of undulating lines suggestive of wireless waves. Or the idea proposed by Rudolph Arnheim in 1936 that "no external action has to be directly represented" (178) in a radio "monologue," thus suggesting a correlation to the stream-of-consciousness technique of Modernist fiction, perhaps best explained by Virginia Woolf, who, in her novel *The Waves* (1931) sought to "do away with exact place and time" (*Writer's Diary* 143). Indeed, the textual incorporation of wireless in Modernist literature may have inspired the very illogicality of Modernist process—this being a topic of vast enquiry, despite the fact that (to adapt Whitworth's remark) the use of wireless "might have [had] no coherent purpose other than to assert topicality [and] modernity" (211).

Conversely, Adelaide Morris's view that certain inventions "decisively altered the nature of poetry and literature" ("Sound Technologies" 37) is most seductive when approaching the huge compendia of Modernism, *Finnegans Wake*, *The Cantos*, *The Waste Land*, and enquiring as to whether radio is either a leading principle of the text or a vital undercurrent, ebbing and flowing throughout. It is arguable that the condition of Modernism (that which diminishes, recycles, erases, disinters) in some way shadows radio, which contains all of those characteristics. Whenever any "gap" is surmounted, as achieved by the dawning of radio-communications, the girdle around the world, a void is opened up due to the acknowledgment of that void. As John Durham Peters recognizes, it is a constant "fear of inescapable solipsism" which informs the "microdramas" of Modernist literature (16); for instance, one possible reading of *The Waste Land* is that it functions as a vast "telephone poem," wherein stray voices emerge from the text as pure utterance and return misunderstood. Figures in Modernist literature are frequently suspended in stasis and unable to communicate; they act as silent broadcasters fruitlessly emitting signals, as shown at the close of Woolf's *Between the Acts*, where the characters address one another in thought but dare not literally vocalize their feelings. "I often think," wrote musician Carlos Chavez in 1927, "that at present the radio is frequently, at best, a voice speaking well, but not understood, or imperfectly understood, or heard inopportunely" (133)—a remark that serves to be both cryptic and exacting. Its premise will resonate in the following discussion of James Joyce and Ezra Pound, who not only wrote in "electrickery with attendance" (Joyce, *FW* 579)—meaning that they freely incorporated their immediate exposure to the medium—but also that each, in his own differing way, recognized the indeterminate quality of radio, how the vast expanse opened up between transmitter and receiver could affect the smallest of words, spoken or written.

"Joyce had never quite known what to make of Pound," writes Forrest Read (262). Was he Wyndham Lewis's "revolutionary simpleton" (39) or a more complex blend of "world prophet and technologist" (Read 262) who constantly upheld his own dictum of "direct action" (Joyce, *FW* 167), resulting in his fall from the impresario of the 1920s to a "lonely commander-in-chief-elect" of Mussolini's fascist regime? (Read 262). This confusion was echoed by not only Pound's contemporaries but also his future readers, who also grapple with the fact of beautiful poetry juxtaposed with destructive and harmful impulses.

Pound's broadcast talks for Rome Radio between 1941 and 1943 intrude themselves insistently into any discussion of his achievements. They preclude any praise of Pound or dampen existing arguments for his genius, his generosity, and his status in twentieth-century poetics. How Pound first took the microphone has been eulogized and also dissected, not least by himself. In 1940, he wrote to Ronald Duncan that one of the visitors to his home in Rapallo, Natalie Barney, deposited a radio set and "fled the village" forthwith (Pound, *Letters* 441; Doob 236). At the time, Pound considered that despite being a vile incursion into everyday life, "the loathing of [radio] may stop diffuse writing": the performative aspects of "drammer [and] teeyater" could be harnessed into a medium that could disseminate the word. Additionally, "the histrionic developments in announcing" suggested the possibility of finer audition on the part of the listener, or "at least to a faculty for picking up the fake in the voices" (441–42). By "voices," Pound was referring to the debatable quality of certain radio transmissions; however, this statement was accompanied by a trenchant observation that writing was subject to the same scrutiny. The dramatist or playwright, Pound added, must measure his output "against the personae now poked into every bleedin' home and smearing the mind of the peapull" (442). Consequently, to maintain his artistic standards, he "*may* clarify his style in *resistance* to the devil box" (442). This statement can be interpreted as a mournful acceptance of the new medium and its status in the arts, or the beginning of Pound's paradoxical relationship with radio, which saw him recognizing its capacities for creative experiment but also utilizing it as a site of invective—and thus gradually becoming one of the "personae" to which he had so fiercely objected.

Pound's broadcasts were fueled by a desire to meld these two sides of his response. When taking steps to speak on Axis propaganda radio, to aid and abet Mussolini's war effort by letting his American listeners know that they were "MISinformed" by the Roosevelt administration, which was supposedly overrun by "a kike gang" (Doob 135) and operating a "false accounting system" (214), Pound still believed himself to be autonomous. "No-one

ASKS me to be political," he explained (375), repeatedly asserting that "the use of THIS radio, of me on this radio" (281) was to speak "a true record" (246) owing to superior insight on "the questions that are NOT discussed in certain circles" (281). In helping America to "oil up the machine and change a few gadgets" (205) by applying fascist ideology, Pound fell into the role of an investigative journalist who functions as both receiver and diffuser, as it were, publicizing his findings for the greater good. Notably, in one speech, Pound castigated the "rotten" press for clogging the public's perceptions of political events, adding, "you can't expect me to stenograph all your noises" (135), clearly envisioning himself as the translator, one who may clarify the garbled message. Moreover, he sought to volunteer his own wisdom, as an archive of data worthy of being shared, a service that connected areas of relevance. The dutiful, ideal, listener would "TRY to get the main threads and cables" of an information overload" (191) that blended history, literature, the cult of money and bigotry, with a specific reading list of Aristotle, John Adams, and Enrico Pea's *Moscardino* among many others in order to support and illustrate his principles. One can see that Pound's foray into a radio space accentuated his role as solitary reformer, his belief that his talks accorded with his duty as an American citizen.

In "not speakin' officially," and with nothing "to go by save my own intuition" (Doob 148), Pound had suspicions that his stance would be misunderstood. In March 1943, shortly before his indictment for treason, he predicted: "My talks on the radio will have to be judged by their content. Neither the medium of diffusion or the merits of my exposition can be the final basis of judgement" (261). Unskilled in propagandist technique—unlike members of the Buro Concordia in Berlin, Joseph Goebbels's unit of professional broadcasters with real knowledge of military tactics and strategy—he nevertheless championed Mussolini and was unrepentant in his anti-Semitic stance, being of the opinion that "Jerusalem synagogue radios from London and York" (290) were a far more malevolent influence than "ole Ezry speaking" (178). Shortly after his indictment on July 27, 1943, Pound wrote a letter to Attorney General Sir Francis Biddle that reiterated his objective: to "protest against a system which creates one war after another, in series and system" rather than the events taking place at the time (qtd. in Carpenter 624). True, the war rarely took center stage in the radio speeches, one of the few exceptions being April 27, 1943, when Pound suggested that U.S. troops in North Africa should withdraw immediately. Pound's racial intolerance further complicates the idea that while he purported to be merely a conduit for external affairs, he considered his radio broadcasting a tool of enlightenment and a marker, or extension, of his public self with all its bombast and performance.

Ironically, Pound learned of his treason charge via the BBC—the whining bastion of "crass imbecilities" (Doob 145) full of "brain monopolisers" (154) with voices like "an advertisement for Bird's custard" (270). The BBC's attitude may have confirmed Pound's earlier notion of the "histrionic" nature of broadcasting, against which he had certainly developed his own style. In the letter to Ronald Duncan he had said that only those who were a "purrfekk HERRRRkules" (Pound, *Letters* 442) would "survive" the noxious presence of wireless. By climbing inside the devil box, Pound was performing his own act of resistance, a freedom fighter sifting truth from "the fake in the voices" (441–42): an apt project, given that he had so far dedicated his life to the premise that obfuscation and obscurity were the destroyers of language and its communicative power. Crucially, Pound's radio speeches often expressed the worry that he was "once more to be accused of 'speakin' in a ramblin' manner" (Doob 177).

It is therefore unsurprising that in 1934, after an oft-strained decade of castigating Joyce over the "circumambient peripherization" (Read 228) of *Work in Progress* (which would become *Finnegans Wake*), Pound concluded that Joyce "has mumbled things to himself; he has heard his voice on the phonograph and thought of sound, mumble, murmur" (Pound, "e. e. cummings" 210). In Pound's opinion, the linguistic vitality that was so present in *Ulysses* had been diffused by contact with a medium that turns speech into something unfamiliar and thus subject to more than one interpretation.

This concern that Joyce's work was being somehow clotted by sound may be placed within a dialogue between the writers about communication and its breakdown, whether through the impenetrability of a text or misfires of the spoken word. Although not explicit or virulent, Joyce's depiction of Pound in *Finnegans Wake* is comparable to Pound's own attack on Joyce's inaccessibility and his tendency to portray the seductive effect of words and their slippages. Pound is a facet of the speechifying figure in Book I (56) who speaks a "mauderin tongue in a pounderin jowl" (89). "My unchanging Word is sacred," proclaims "Professor Jones" in Book I, vi; "The word is my Wife, to exponse and expound, to vend and to velnerate" (167). As the tireless advertiser of Joyce's work, Pound is heard through the "ritual rhythmics" (36) of the tribal drum, the "plangerpound" (56) of thunder, and most significantly, the radio, "bawling the whole hamshack and wobble down in an eliminium sounds pound" (309) across "seven seas crowdblast" (219)—a chilling prediction as Joyce did not live to see "race pounds race . . . all roads to ruin" (566). By means of these intermittently sharp associations, Joyce inserts a nod to his promoter, suspecting he had "pillaged the pound of the extramurals" (579). As Forrest Read adds, Joyce conceives Pound as "a fully developed opposite" (264). Joyce is thus the first "biographer" to attempt such a characterization, asserting his license to do so in Book III, iii, when depicting the Shaun/Yawn figure who disperses under examination. Amid what is described as a "static babel" (*FW* 499) the interrogators tell of warmongering and betrayal, as Shaun is inhabited by a "dramaparapolylogic" (474), which renders him "somewhit murky" (34–35). Notably, Shaun the ventriloquist is markedly different from wild Shem the Penman, his brother/alternative half. He is a "derevatov" of his father (505), and, by that token, a desired projection of the future. Joyce is venturing the idea that he has usurped his mentor in surpassing Pound's oracular and verbal abilities; he himself is becoming the "new Rabalais" who exemplifies Pound's discourse of action, history, allegory, ideology. It is arguable that Joyce represents one half of the self-other dichotomy raised by the fact of Pound's radio broadcasts and that Pound was indeed "th'author . . . picking up airs from th'other over th'ether" (Joyce, *FW* 452). As this essay argues, although Pound had found the ideal medium for his multitude of voices, it was Joyce who upheld the schism between "elegy and evangelism, poetry and polemics" (Read 269) that led to Pound's subsequent, oversensitized reaction to his own theories of language and his demise into the "parsonifier propounde" (Joyce, *FW* 378) of his own words.

In Book III, i of the *Wake*, Shaun floats to the upper levels of the dream, props himself up, and begins to speak, "a voice from afar" (407), after he has been summoned by the "echoating" (404) washerwomen along the banks of the Liffey. Immediately prior to his first word, he cups his hand to his ears and hearkens "to scented nightlife as softly as the loftly marconimasts from Clifden sough open tireless secrets . . . to Novia Scotia's listing sisterwands" (407). The speakers of the *Wake* interact in this complex and unique way, often successfully connecting but also colliding, superimposing on one another, and hovering at the periphery of understanding. Radio is arguably the "key" to *Finnegans Wake*; certainly, Harry Levin asserted that the "loudspeaker element" of radio would be a "medium" for its interpretation (67). What Levin implies, however, is a resoundingly modern replacement for the "archangel's trumpet," a call to order. The *Wake* in its entirety announces itself as the last word in soundplay, but radio is also surreptitiously embedded in the text. James A. Connor, without elaboration, offers the compelling suggestion that the *Wake*'s characters "communicate across space like dream radios" (21). Therefore, it follows that the reader must be constantly alert to fluctuation, amalgamation, and fissure.

Joyce's direct reference to the pioneer of wireless is a touchstone in the *Wake*, whereby the failures of the night, its missed understandings, may result from the speakers' "blarneying Marcantonio" (483), a diverse radio script that ebbs and flows through the text. The *Cantos*, envisaged by Pound in 1910 as a "bombastic rhetorical epic," placed Marconi as a significant influence, alongside "Pierpont, Bleriot, Levavasour . . . etc., clothed in the heroic manner of greek imitation" (*qtd. in Carpenter 147*). Pound's claim that he "anticipated" radio in the "first third of Cantos" (*Letters* 442) would be developed in the Rome broadcasts, when he implied that electricity literally coursed through his veins, referring to how a "certain Loomis [Pound] succeeded in sending wireless signals, he invented wireless technology." Regrettably, "nothin' practical came of it, til Sig. Marconi got it into a system" (Doob 322, 177). Both *Finnegans Wake* and the *Cantos* deploy radio within the macromass of the text; certainly, Pound's conscious tribute to radio in the semi-explanation of Canto 18–19 enhances his dictum in *Guide to Kulchur* (1938) that the substance of an age is "what you can pick up and/or get in touch with" (217).

Indeed, the loud, argumentative voices of Canto 18 are a strange melee of order and fragmentation; the repetition of "And/And/And/And" hammers the ear, yet there is a fluid exchange of personages melding into a narrative that carries over into Canto 19:

> War, one war after another
> Men start 'em who couldn't put up a good hen-roost
> Also sabotage . . .
> XIX
> Sabotage? Yes, he took it up to Manhattan
> To the big company, and they said: Impossible (*Cantos* 83–84)

The montage effect continues in the jargon of Canto 20, snatching at themes, epochs, and images; the opening lines resonate with five languages, beginning, "Sound slender, quasi tinnula" (Lat: "little bell"; *Cantos* 89). Hugh Kenner remarks how the deployment of the word "'Sound' bounds that quality by adducing Homeric, Catullian, Propertian detail," allowing words to become "inblends" of other words spoken/written (*Pound Era* 112–13). Pound, ever convinced that language is not fixed but fluctuating, is, in these early cantos, experimenting with a method by which to construct, or reaudit, his epic; he advances the idea of a radio cosmos where voices exist in perpetuity. This allows for the juxtaposition of opposing elements, figures, economics, cultures, civilizations creating a single entity which, Pound would write in Canto 116, "coheres alright/even if my notes do not cohere" (811). Within this arena, a series of fragmentary units can repeat, repulse one another, conjoin, and fade away. Pound's suspicion as to his own effectiveness in "cohering" this structureless chaos (which nevertheless needed structure to function as a poem) suggests his need for a stable, unifying center—or even a kind of lightning rod to dissipate what might be likened to an electrostatic field wherein particles are "charged" with varying degrees of density and acceleration. This automatically places responsibility upon himself, the poet, who must recognize the disparate elements and arrange/rearrange accordingly. Joyce's pleasure in listening to his own voice on the phonograph and reveling in its distortion must have appeared, to Pound, as not simply resembling "a little crowd" (Wyndham Lewis 39) but succumbing to a tidal cacophony.

Joyce furthered this creation of a radio-imbued text. Indeed, *Finnegans Wake* may be read as the only true representation of "radiospace," a void simultaneously vacant and populous that calls attention to the fact that while sound exists at either end of any telecommunications exchange, there is free-flowing cacophony in the middle, a "sonorous silence" (*FW* 230) that hovers until someone, or something, provides ingress. The sleeper of *Finnegans Wake* is, in the words of Donald Theall (151), a "machinic assemblage of machinic assemblage" who functions as the channel to, and from, this negative space. The much-dissected opening of Book II, iii, locates HCE—the central figure of the Wake, Humphrey Chimpden Earwicker, in his many linguistic, and literal, permutations—as the auditory vigilance of the *Wake*, who takes readings on the noises that emanate from the non-sensed dark, and whose legendary ear, a "meatous conch" (*FW* 310), translates cryptic signs and renders them haphazardly interpretable. In his house "of the hundred bottles with the radio beamer tower (380), the sleeper is primed for "distancegetting" and "tuned-up by twintriodic singalvalvus pipelines" (309). This implies that the "enginium" (310) is the sleeper himself. Not only is "the ear of Fionn Earwicker aforetime . . . the trademark ear of a broadcaster," but he is also the "radiooscillating epiepistle to which . . . we much ceaselessly return" (108), "capable of amplifying "one thousand and one stories, (15) through his "ears, eyes of the darkness" (14).

Certainly, one can trace any technology through the Joycean maze. As Theall notes, machines of communication operate simultaneously on three levels. First, "traditional sign systems (hieroglyphics, alphabets, icons, drawings)"; second, "technologically mediated modes of reproduction (books, telephone, film)"; and last, "crafted modes of popular expression dependent on either the traditional or the technologically mediated (sermons, pantomimes, riddles, comics)" (139). It could be argued that radio encompasses all three insofar as it affects the power of inscription—by causing sounds to be fixed in one place—and provides a platform for every type of oral expression. Recent critical works such as Louis Armand's *Techne: James Joyce, Hypertext and Technology* (2003) have mapped Joyce's work alongside communications technologies of the early twentieth century, as they not only affect the structural logic of his work but also, as Armand contends, reveal Joyce's awareness of these developments. Not all Joyceans find this theoretical approach convincing; as Michael Begnal points out, though radio may indeed be a "central symbol" in the *Wake*, uncertainty arises from a "lack of recognition on the part of the reader" as to who is speaking (26). Note that this conflicts with Pound's need to facilitate intellectual commerce between speaker and reader/receiver by locating voices in the flux. Laurent Milesi observes that Joyce's portmanteau idiom in the *Wake* is so pliable that it allows language to exist in a "cosmopolitics" (151). Joyce's desire to let any fragment of the *Wake* speak to any citizen of the world is that of "the imaginative forces of poetry . . . bridging the post-babelian linguistic gap, if only in a dream" (151). For instance, Book II, iii, is retold several times in wireless variants; the Mime of Mick, Nick, and the Maggies is "wordlosed over seven seas crowdblast in celtelleneteutoslavendlatinsoundscript" (*FW* 219). Latin was once the *lingua franca* of the Western world, its syntax conveyed through a series of affixes attached to a word stem. Here, Joyce is implying that in radio-space, morphemes and even phonemes (the smallest linguistic unit) are randomly discharged and then recombined with intent. Therefore when considering the *Wake*'s rejection of a single communicative framework, it follows that Joyce's presentation of "radio-space" serves as an homage to the medium of radio itself, that which permits the state of subversive encoding yet also embodies the notion of an all-encompassing mode of speech.

The "thunderwords" of *Finnegans Wake* often replicate this dichotomy. Their presence in the text resembles what Eric McLuhan describes as a "divine "fiat!"" (McLuhan, *Role* 38) occurring at junctures of change; they comprise the sound of the change and the significant wording(s) of the change.

Mainly, "the displaced former situation—or at least some of its components—is absorbed by the new situation" (39), thus creating a multiplicity of aural/oral sensations. McLuhan's exegesis of each thunderclap begins with an inventory of the syllables and phrases contained in it, noting, in the case of the third thunderword in Book I, ii, that "articulate speech is [actually] a form of stuttering; consonants interrupt the songs of vowels" (82). The consonant-laden thunderword itself, with its "klikkaklakka" opening, may point to the defective ear of the sleeper himself, "pinnitrated" (*FW* 309) by the sound of onomatopoetic stammering that constitutes a stream of interference. McLuhan considers that the inclusion of a "vollapluck" (34) within this chapter (from Volapück, an *ersatz* language), is significant, demonstrating Joyce's opinion that "technological language is also an artificial language, and is therefore of grammatical interest" (82). It is not always clear what "technological language" may be, although the third thunderword in particular replicates the "the clip, the clop! . . . Glass crash" (*FW* 44) of early radio broadcasts, whose special effects in drama productions were primitive to say the least, and invariably beset with static, or "white noise"—exquisitely and dramatically rendered in Book II, iii by the sound of oil on flames, "Scaald!" (324). If Joyce's radio listening was a contributing factor to his thunderwords, then "technological language" may be a lay-phrase to depict the act of molding words from torn vibrations, otherworldly noise turned into a grammatical experiment. Moreover, given that the thunderwords amalgamate and condense certain "set-pieces" of the text, they amplify the *Wake*'s themes of reinvention and digression, "resnored . . . alcoherently" (*FW* 40) through the haze of a dream, a drunken stupor, or, most conceivably, a blanket of sound. Joyce plays with the inevitable collapse of words dispatched by various means, technological or otherwise. Any utterance picked up by a single listener is a sound reproduced and mutated along its journey. His willingness to engage with radio in the role of a "practitioner," rather than a theorist, marks Joyce in contradistinction to Pound. By this I mean his intention to pursue gleefully what Morris terms the "shifting, speeding, slurring, sliding and slowing" ("Sound Technologies" 34) of delimited space, the sonic abeyance where transfiguration of words is inevitable.

Pound's more direct attempt to resolve art and science is widely documented,[1] the prevailing critical opinion being that Pound was willing to master technical vocabulary in order to bolster his poet's role as social agent, or "new-mint the speech" (*Selected Prose* 361). A discourse of action would naturally derive from physics, as the advent of radioactive waves, in particular, would inspire "a language of energetics" (Kayman 526), as shown in "I Gather the Limbs of Osiris," where fact-finding is described as akin to negotiating an electric switchboard. Daniel Tiffany proposes a "schism in Pound's attitudes about technology," pointing to the "supernatural aspect of. . . . technological media," which prompted comparisons to more occultist procedures (248). In his opinion, Pound sees how the artist-as-medium, passive to impulse, might "[register] movements in invisible ether" (Pound, *Gaudier-Brzeska 106)* and thus be jolted out of lassitude. Believing he had ingress into "the circle absolute . . . loosed from the accidents of time and place" (*Selected Prose* 362), Pound had hoped to obtain the best knowledge "in the air" (23), arguing that words are alive with "a force like electricity" (34). In order that "the juxtaposition of their vertices . . . be exact," they require the idea coherer/writer to transpose the message accurately.

The *Wake*'s sleeping hero, the "man-made static" (*FW* 309) who is "mediumistically gifted" (380) and "highly charged with electrons as hophazards can effective it" (309), exemplifies the process Pound described. He becomes "someone imparticular who will somewherise for the whole anyhow" (602), the "cluekey to a world room beyond the roomwhorld" (100), which gives the impression of a supine figure being plugged into a network and fed in metered doses of information. In some ways, Joyce's formulation here echoes Pound's notion in his early writings on chivalric love: "The senses at first seem to project for a few yards from the body. Effect of a decent climate where a man leaves his nerve-set open, or allows it to tune into its ambience" (Pound, Literary Essays *152*).

Such analogies linked Pound's sensibility with ideas of wireless transmission and reception long before he took the microphone. In portraying the donative artist at work, Pound was aware that "he draws latent forces, or things present but unnoticed" from his environment (*Selected Prose* 25). Theoretically, the writer could dictate the arena of influence, able to "not only record but create," by emitting "order-given vibrations" which attracted certain signals (376). In the resulting selection process, he must "departmentalise such part of the life-force as flows though him." Pound added in 1915 that, "the best artist is the man whose machinery can stand the highest voltage. The better the machinery, the more precise, the stronger, the more exact will be the record of the voltage and of the various currents which have passed through it." The issue here is that for Pound, wireless justified his early artistic conjectures. First, his efforts to create a poetics informed by the disciplines of electric science would color the Rome broadcasts with personal philosophy; namely, that in acting out his famous dictum of the "antennae," thinking, as Kenner writes, "not only of the mantis, but Marconi" (*Pound Era* 156), Pound fell victim to an apparatus he initially regarded with suspicion but that eventually proved to be, as Read notes, "the apt medium for expressing the kind of modern language he had created" (269). Timothy Campbell writes elegantly on the "syntax" of fascism, how it might be conceived as a radio relay, whereby static is twisted into a formative address heard by listeners who cannot reply. In essence, "fascism, like Pound's poetry, might be profitably viewed as a subsystem of a wireless network, with its own information processing and human interfaces" (169).

The correlation of the three is compelling, particularly in regard to the loops, permeations, ideogrammic forms, and voicings of Pound's work; and indeed, many Modernist epics in which, as Adelaide Morris recognizes, "sounds cut in, rise, then fade away" ("Sound Technologies" 32) are irrefutably, in Joseph Frank's terms, "based on a space logic that demands a complete reorientation in the reader's attitude towards language" (qtd. in Morris 34). Campbell is referring to institutions, but I wish to utilize his argument to register the interactions, failed or otherwise, within and without texts such as the *Cantos* and *Finnegans Wake*. Evidently, their textual denseness occludes an instantaneous connection; the comment by Laurence Rainey quoted by Campbell in regard to fascism and the body politic may also apply in this case: "Only the master aviator, he who has dictated the script, is able to decipher it from high above" (Campbell 169). The Modernist text itself is a site of uncertainty that, instead, promotes a "blindness" and urges us to "lift we our ears, eyes of the darkness" (Joyce, *FW* 14).

Therefore, it is useful to address the link between Pound's broadcasts from the studio at Rome Radio—a silent, tomblike space—and his active role as a translator. Tiffany points out that the verb "to translate" means to extract something from one sphere into another; the original "[arriving] from a distant realm of secrecy and silence" (179). Translation connotes an interaction devoid of logic, explained by Jacques Derrida as "the trance of the trans," wherein "transferential magneticization" (172, 178) occurs between textual bodies far removed, an inconceivable cross-border conversation. Hugh Kenner opines that "[Pound] does not translate words. The words have led him into the thing he expresses" (Pound, *Translations* 11), that is, into atavistic shades of his own diction; Kenner's stance implies that Pound is personally involved, in no way "transparent" in the sense of Walter Benjamin, who thought a genuine translator should disappear after arranging the "afterlife" of a text (*One Way* 17, 82). Pound would argue that he achieved the latter, a controlled "bringing over" as in *The Spirit of Romance*, where he cites Dante's *Purgatorio*, Canto 24, line 52: "I am, within myself, one who, when love breathes into me, take note, and go making manifest after what manner he speaketh" (35). Such self-effacement occurs in the poem "Histrion" (1912), where the poet is subject to visitation by a stronger force and is duly extinguished. It might be said that Pound's resurrecting of a dead author—Cavalcanti, Arnaud Daniel, or Remy de Gourmont—is an explicit attempt to fuse with a previous plane of existence. Aware of, for example, "Marlowe's unbridled personality moving behind the words" (*Spirit of Romance* 194), Pound cannot refrain from involvement. As all ages are "contemporaneous," his role is not passive but accumulative; the voices may speak through him, but, as Kenner remarks, "we are dealing not with inflow but homeomorphism" (*Pound Era* 169), a formulation that underscores Pound's idea that translation, while illuminating facets of the original, also functions as an "instrument" to probe the original text, thus becoming a method of extracting items for future use. Here too, the discourse of electricity is present; a text transmits signs from a bygone era, and the translator officially deciphers the code, often ventriloquizing in the effort. Maud Ellmann shows how Pound resorts to "impersonation, forgery, pastiche . . . as it [encourages] the commerce of the living and the dead" (147). This observation reminds us that translation is an insane hypothesis by its very condition: two spheres united by a general equivalent, the poet, whose "art lies in the silences that canalize the text, suturing one era from another" (170). Existing between those spheres is what radio commentators would term "transmissional space" (Kahn, "Histories" 20), a vacuum only given representation by the exchange of a signal. As aforementioned, Pound creates a similar kind of cosmos for timeless interchange and reanimation where words exist at either end. They "converse," but the channel himself is merely functional, like Hugh Selwyn Mauberley, a "consciousness disjunct / Being but this overblotted / Series/ Of intermittances" (*Personae* 201). This practice would inexorably lead to radio broadcasting, which, notes Ellmann, "attracted [Pound] because it kept language in the air" (181). Pound had written of art as "a fluid moving above or over the minds of men" (*Spirit of Romance* 5) containing facts, impressions, and voices to imitate, although Ellmann questions Pound's urge to condense his own writing, to resist the "diffuse" by subsuming himself in radio. Years prior to the Rome broadcasts, Pound explained how the "child who has listened to ghost stories goes into a dark room" (*Spirit of Romance* 17), just as he, in a similar fashion, settled in isolation to conduct, and prolong, his commitment to the idea of a "spiritual" current. On air, Pound inadvertently crafted a state wherein his words were infected, stylistically, by countless others, all of which are logically manifest in the disfiguring garble of radio static: "Transmission. I RECognized my own voice, and COULD with effort identify the matter . . . but no one not knowing the text could have understood the meaning" (Doob 221).

Though assured in his role as a broadcaster—as the connective element, speaking sense and clarifying his style to fit the medium—Pound demonstrated an anxiety over his dissolution within the ether comparable to the acknowledgment of dangers inherent to translation: that his voice might buckle under the weight of ages. In "name" only could he appear on the radio: Ezra Pound always talking as a result of the poet's efforts. A letter to Joyce laments his own tendency to dig up "corpses of let us say Li Po" rather than "preserving the bitched mess of modernity" (Read 148). In the radio scripts, Pound outlines methods of translation over the air, namely, "sortin' out what is ascertainable" (Doob 373), such as "HELARXE more or less twisted from a line of Aeschylus" (35), and suggests that any student of literature should "incorporate" his or her own knowledge into classic writers, in an osmotic exchange. In one broadcast, after debating Aristotle's influence on Cavalcanti, Santayana's "manuscripts or proofs of something," and his own preference for Italian, Pound suddenly breaks off: "But other voices are silent. You say I am also losing something. I don't deny it. I don't hear from Mr Eliot or Mr Cummings . . . the best writers in England and America do NOT get to the microphone, which is the only way of communication left open" (375).

Uncertainty pervades this statement; Pound knew himself to be revivifying abstract bodies rather than imparting contemporary knowledge on a busy circuit. Christine Froula points to the "prophecy of loneliness" in Canto I, not merely because there is no one to "share a joke with" (129) in the absence of his old friends Yeats, Ford, Eliot and Joyce, but that "the old poet ends wrecked in a sea of words that have broken apart from their meanings" (130). In Pound's broadcasts, every connection was derived from a bygone, half-imagined realm, and the process seemed antithetical to its intent: "[d]on't know which, what to put down, can't write two scripts at once. Necessary facts, ideas come in pell mell" (Doob 192). The only definite audience was, as e.e. cummings retorted, the "Oppressed Minority of One . . . Mr Lonelyheart himself" (316), reverberating in a deathly space. By extension, Allen Tate viewed the *Cantos*, in their entirety, as "talk talk talk, not by anyone in particular to anyone else in particular, they are just rambling talk" (67). Any verbal exchange is shrouded, akin to speaking over the wireless, where Pound is aware he "might as well be . . . talking Chinese with a foreign accent, so far as making this statement clear" (Doob 262); he is "OUT OF DATE" (130) and undefinable.

In his work with Ernest Fenollosa's Chinese transcriptions—published in 1915 as *Cathay*—Pound sacrificed accuracy for acoustic impact, alleging that "Chinese sound is no use at all. We don't hear parts of it, and much of the rest is a hiss or mumble" (qtd. in Carpenter 267). He adhered to Fenollosa's Japanese reading, and therefore retained the essence of the original. Indeed, the poems are layered soundscapes wherein "wing-flapping storks" are glazed across larger spaces, "ten thousand valleys full of voices and pine winds" (*Translations* 196). In "The River Song," musicians retrieve, and adapt, fleeting aural perceptions in "this flute . . . the twelve pipes here" (191). Similarly, in his version of the Japanese *Noh* plays (1916), Pound is preoccupied with poetic impact and how entities exert their presence through voice. In "Tsunemasa," the spirit looks back upon the world; he is charged with "universal unstillness," flickering wayward until only "the thin sound" (265) remains, "a voice without form." Many *Noh* figures become constituents of an echo or fragment of speech, easily extinguished "like a fire-fly's flash in the dark" ("Awoi No Uye," *Translations* 328), but able to read the thoughts of others with a telepathic consistency. Such a device asks the reader to decipher "who is talking by the noise they make" (qtd. in Carpenter 446), given that communication occurs within an interiorized space. The effort is as though listening to music, which, in Pound's opinion, is "a composition of frequencies, microphonic and macrophonic" ("Antheil" 304). The transposition of a *Noh* play is a process in which every cadence should be observed; it creates a polyphonic effect, akin to hidden loudspeakers sporadically placed in a room. Furthermore, Pound stresses the way in which a *Noh* text seems to "go off into nothing" at the end in a fluttering motion. The final words have a certain ethereality; they drop into silence, no longer heeded ("Suma Genji," *Translations* 237). Here, Pound anticipates the style of "Hugh Selwyn Mauberley," a poem where Pound sought to "cut a shape in time" from speech, mainly "durations, either of syllables, or implied between them" (*qtd. in Carpenter 371*). Passages are at once truncated and fused by ellipses which create a juddering of speech: "Drifted . . . drifted precipitate/Asking time to be rid of . . . /of his bewilderment" (*Personae* 198).

Pound's translating abilities were tested by "Awoi No Uye," a play of multiple personalities and hauntings. The ghost manifests Court Lady Awoi's jealousy, which, in turn, splits into a "hannya," or devilish force. Both come "aimlessly hither" from the world of "split-moving lightning," attracted by distant music and the corpse of Lady Awoi herself (*Translations* 323). In modeling "Awoi No Uye," Pound endeavors to differentiate between the abstracted forms, rendering a supernatural sphere wherein spatial distinctions are irrelevant. As Pound's translations often suggest, the impermanent beings of *Noh* are affiliated to sound; they are fluid yet evasive, often flocking to a conductor in the same way that the sleeper in *Finnegans Wake*, "perpetrified . . . by soundwaves" (23, 29, 26), turns "a widermost ear" (448) into the night and receives an auditory "melegoturny" (309, 230): "Hear more to those voices. Always I am hearing them" (571). During Pound's radio broadcasts, as his spot on the dial at 29.6 KW was harried by "Orful KRRumpzzz! of static or atmosphere or whatever" (qtd. in Carpenter 592), he may have recalled Lady Awoi, lying immobile while her demons are envoiced. From the studio space, he could easily imagine "Jewish substance thinly veiled" (Doob 149) on the air. Whenever Pound dropped to a murmur, the engineers would "turn on more current" (387), pumping him into a boundless ether. Tellingly, he defined one broadcast as "this spasm" (100), which implies a transient figure capable of being intercepted and depleted.

As Froula notes, the "four-dimensional language" of the early *Cantos* consists of words whose meaning "belong[s] to history, and . . . half-obscured by time's passing; yet their style records the past" (129), evinced by the opening lines which serve, in the words of Wyndham Lewis, as "the removal of old worlds into new quarters" (116). They are a translation of Homer's *Odyssey* Book XI, wherein Odysseus descends to the underworld to find that words are no longer self-explanatory or familiar. Leon Surette considers that the initial descent is not repeated, comparing the *Cantos*—in keeping with much of his commentary—to a "séance [where] dead souls pass before us, speak to us, and are overheard by us" (124–25) awaiting to be caught and bestowed with speech. This is an ideal description of one of Pound's readings at St. Elizabeths in 1951, remembered by David Gordon as reminiscent of Chinese ceremonies "in which a ghost would speak through the voice of a living man," adding, "it made your hair rise to hear him bring back the dead" (117). Snatching, and recycling, of "patched . . . histories" (*Cantos* 460) is, of course, the mainstay of the *Cantos*, wherein Pound mediates between many different orientations; for instance, a moment when Joyce, "Jim the comedian," rises eerily in Canto 74, singing "Blarrney castle me darling" (as Read notes, "as he might best like to have been remembered" [275]) among a profusion of other "companions," all of whom deliver shards of semi-remembered words: "'forloyn' said Mr Bridges (Robert)" . . . "a friend' s/d mr cummings" (*Cantos* 521–22).

In Rilke's "Sonnets to Orpheus," the poet-singer forges a state where "aeons communicate with aeons" (*aeonen reden mit aeonen*) (26) across an expanse in which time is undifferentiated, resembling the ethereality of radio-space. Such disembodiment and dissemination implies that sound may be situated in two places at once, yet both, as Kahn writes, "[bear] sonic content" ("Histories" 20). Quite possibly, this was how Pound appeared to David Gordon on the lawn at St. Elizabeths, spanning realms in the effort of retrieval. Indeed, Humphrey Carpenter attests that Pound's voice "sounded ten years younger" as he taped a number of cantos in 1962, but only when using the microphone (895). At intervals throughout the Caedmon recordings, made in June 1958, it is as though Pound moulds phrasing, or "bodies," from "fluttering" words, like the collage of a *Noh* play. His delivery of Canto 92 lingers on the trembling sounds of the sea, "chh . . . chh," which eases into "ch'u," finally becoming, "fiu chiamat/e qui refulgo" ("I was called and here I glow"), a phrase by Cunizza da Romano, from Dante's *Paradiso* IX. The line is cued by a rattling of pebbles, turning "with the wave" (634). I see a correlation with Stephen Dedalus's generative thought-pattern in the "Proteus" chapter of *Ulysses*, where the "crackling wrack and shells . . . (45) and "loose drift of rubble" (50) herald the "fourworded wavespeech: seesoo, hrss, rsseeis, oos" (63). The nature of "Proteus," indeterminate and fluctuating, ensures that the slightest emphasis upon a word can often affect our reception of Stephen's perambulating. As ever, hovering behind the scriptal spiral is another word, effected by a simple verb change—for example, in lines 453–63, where "lipped" becomes "mouthed" with its safer connotations of drinking, absorbing, and gradually subsiding into an airy nothingness. The phrase beginning, "His mouth moulded issuing breath, unspeeched: ooeeehah: roar of cataractic planets, globed, blazing, roaring wayawayawayawayawayaway" (60) engages every facet of speech: tongue, lips, larynx. It demands accuracy by the very fact of its evocation and therefore heightens the precision contained in the movement. Yet, if delivered too rapidly, the consonants collide, and we hear imprecision, a (perhaps deliberate) blurring of purpose.

The visualization of this, on the page, is deceptive. After all, as Kenner remarks, "a sentence is a sound in itself on which other sounds called words may be strung" ("Sound of Sense" 10). We read the words, "Oomb, all wombing tomb" (*FW* 60) and also see what it signifies; the "allconsuming" spatial expanse in which Stephen is affixed, yet free-floating. To engage thoroughly in Stephen's experiment is to hear the repeating voice inside poetry, and to hear specifically *his* poetry, as he is only a successful poet subconsciously. Here, we see the amalgamation of words publicly uttered, eddying from the portals of memory and reanimated in a different form. Words become pliable once again, cross-fading to a different register. Similarly, Pound's reading of Canto 16, as featured in the Caedmon sequence, is a montage of war anecdotes, full of sliding, eliding language. A slangy French monologue is beset with interruptions, gradually mutating into harsh mimicry of a Russian accent. Later, the speaker claims, "I can still hear the old admiral," and duly imitates a speech trait, "'with the face of a A y n . . . . ' he pulled it out long like that: 'the face of a y n . . . . gel'" (*Cantos* 71).

Disintegration also occurs in the blundering words of Canto 4, which contains fragments of fallen Troy, a "thin film of images" (16), and the procession of Artemis and her attendants to the Spring at Gargathia, where Aecton would shortly thereafter find her. George Kearns remarks that that "since the revival of gods in the Renaissance, there has been no poet who brings us so intimately into their presence" (27). On the recording, Pound barely chants; he is literally the "old man seated/Speaking in a low drone," buffeted by voices that fleetingly gather and disperse. For example, the chirp of swallows, "Tis, Tis," lapses into the name of "Itys," which imperfectly echoes Soremondo's question: "It is . . . ?" (*Cantos* 13). Lines spoken by "muttering Ovid" imply the panic of delirium: "Pergusa . . . pool . . . pool . . . Garagaphia" (15). They seem to encapsulate the "personality shot to atoms" (635) so meticulously drawn in Canto 92. Carpenter considers Canto 4, drafted in 1919, to be a decisive moment in Pound's methodology for his "endless poem," wherein history is set "'ply over ply' . . . without any emphasis on Ezra the observer" (347). Shortly before recording the Canto, Pound wrote to Archibald Macleish, "I don't merememeber [sic] a damn thing about it" (qtd. in Carpenter 814), an observation replete with meaning. Pound's reflections upon work completed prior to the radio broadcasts were tainted by his knowledge of their communicative failure, their futile relay of impressions, and the attendant erasure of the self.

In the aforementioned passage from "Proteus," Stephen Dedalus hears—or imagines he hears—a celestial clamor of unfathomable proportions, the "roar of cataractic planets" (60) being the only explicit noise in focus.

Legendarily, the ear of the somnambulist and the schizophrenic share the same capacity as that of the seer: messages are heard, but regardless of their definitive presence, there is no certainty that they originate from a source outside the psychology of the subject himself. Classic texts operate in this way; in fact, Julian Jaynes remarks of the *Iliad* that "the Trojan war was directed by hallucinations" (176), insofar as mortals freely converse with gods. In the last century, with the burgeoning of psychiatry, the inner voice has become a symptom of mental breakdown. Murray Schafer asks if the voices and sounds heard with such potency in ancient times "have they really disappeared or were they merely suppressed because they are too frightening or irrational for the modern mind?" (34). Ordinarily Stephen Dedalus would be dismissed for having such audacity, for seemingly hearing the music of the spheres, which speak to him and him only, looped on an interior circuit. Yet, Stephen philosophizes, he *is* a philosopher in transit, and he should deduce that every aspect of humanity exists in a silent vacuum before it actually happens, as does—most terrifyingly and unquantifiably—the universe itself.

Similarly, upon being repatriated in 1946, Pound suspected he'd lost his "grip." Subject to court orders, he underwent psychiatric evaluation by Drs. Winfred Overholser and others at Gallinger hospital, Washington, who consistently probed him into speech. During his trial for treason Pound stood mute as four specialists produced similar reports on how his words were often delivered with telegraphic urgency and easily distracted from their course. Overholser's judgment that Pound's "production" was often in "bunches of ideas" (qtd. in Cornell 81) recalls his broadcasting methods. As mentioned earlier, Pound's talks would deviate from their advertised title, "Superstition," or "Communist Millionaires," yet he would confidently bind the disparate elements. Years later, at St. Elizabeths, Marcella Spann noticed that Pound would talk in entire "raps . . . paragraph and blocks of paragraphs . . . continually practicing his poetry, [the] sort of way Homer must have practiced on his after-dinner audiences in Ionia" (159). Another recurring trait during Pound's interrogation was his complaint of head pain, attributed to his ordeal at the Disciplinary Training Center (DTC) in Pisa, May–November 1945, where he was held for a week in an outdoor cell. On June 14, a camp psychiatrist had reported some disturbance in the prisoner, who worried that he might forget certain important messages to relay and claiming connections in half-a-dozen countries, which would jibe with his self-employment as Dr. Ezra Pound in "the academy of the air" (Doob 377).

During his diagnosis, he generally preferred being "within talking distance" of a potential respondent; seemingly, Pound was aware that the microphone had been wrested from his "grip" mid-monologue and that he was therefore de-activated. Later, Pound admitted that his "main spring had gone haywire at Pisa . . . as though the upper third of the brain were missing and a fluid level existed at the top of what remained" (Cornell 180). In accounting for Pound's previous depiction of the brain, in *The Natural Philosophy of Love* (de Gourmont 1922), as a "great clot of genital fluid held in suspense or reserve" (172), one might infer that Pound felt like a faulty battery, the accumulator of words unable to function. As he had suspected in *The Spirit of Romance* (1910), "Man is—the sensitive physical part of him—a mechanism . . . rather like an electric appliance, switches, wires, etc" (92)—not so dissimilar to the *Wake*'s "radiooscillating epipistle" (108) "tuned up by singalvalvalus pipelines" (309). The point is that while supposedly engaged in a contest of wits with many opponents, Pound was no longer able to filter his flow of rhetoric or be comprehended by others. This position was equivalent to the difficulties of broadcasting: "Transmission so BAD for last three nights that I am on the point of telegraphing . . . effect is either whisper or rattle/a bump bump bump, the minute one turns on enough current to hear (qtd. in Redman 222).

Pound took issue with the staff at Rome Radio, who omitted to advertise his broadcasts and, conceivably, omitted to "switch him on." It appears that Pound's condition at his interrogation almost mimicked these conditions; he stated, "I broke—my head . . . when I am not rested it goes beat beat beat in the back of my head" (Torrey 202), as though he were a malfunctioning microphone or even dismembered in some way. By identifying himself with facets of radio, Pound demonstrated that the act of "giving" his broadcasts was experienced in a sharp, visceral manner and was thus conceivably a contributing factor to the feeling that his entire cranium might burst open while he was under scrutiny. Pound's psychological state—though notoriously unclassifiable, the subject of political and ideological debate—was surely the result of being sapped by a number of factors, in particular the *Pisan Cantos*, most of which were written in the DTC directly following his period of intense radio activity. Pound was forced to interconnect early affinities with the present crisis, as indicated in Canto 77, which restages a topic aired on Rome Radio in July 1942: "30,000, they thought they were clever, / Why Hell/ they cd/ have had it for 6000 dollars / and after Landon they picked Wendell Wilkie" (487).

Here, Pound is alluding to scurrility in the U.S. presidential campaigns of

1940. Wilkie was the Republican nominee, vilified by Pound over the radio for complying with the international monetary conspiracy. The earlier radio script is virtually identical to the Canto; it outlines the same information, which was given to Pound by an unidentified source (Doob 208). Though a minor detail of the *Pisan Cantos*, this suggests that Pound could visualize his script, implicitly mouthing its delivery. The lines are segmented to denote a pregnant pause: "Why hell . . . they could . . . have had it for 6000." I see this as the terrestrial anchoring of words within a site of constant motion. Anthony Woodward describes the Pisan "voice" as "gently, insistently, intoning against the turbulence . . . he is passive in the flux" (64). The process, he continues, is beyond the poet's control, such as "when he dwindles into mutter" or when other voices arrive in "hints and guesses" (66–67), such as the wind "as hamadryas" (*Cantos* 445) to signify the "dryad," otherwise known as the poet H. D. Wendy Flory argues, for a casual precision and artful nostalgia in the *Pisan Cantos*, freed from "evasions, distortions [and] obsessions" (200). I would argue, however, that distortion is elemental to Pound's poetic project and can never be evaded, given that he is the channel, the series of intermittances, ever, as Kenner writes, invaded by "the great dead" who speak through him and "receive his signature on their cadences" (*Pound Era* 486). Pound's re-staging of the radio talk is an attempt to trap his own voice, the inner voice that the caustic, defaming tongue had held back, and thus transform diatribe into poetry. However, to repeat verbatim what has been uttered is easy; what is almost impossible to express is the unheard. In "Proteus," Stephen Dedalus turns his back to the sun—turns his back on the visual—and writes a poem. He imagines pinning it down, as the act of inscription fixes the "unspeeched" (*Ulysses* 60) and pulls it toward earth. Consequently, the script is apperceptual, able to be seen and read, solidified into stasis and autonomy. Stephen asks, "Who ever anywhere will read these written words?" They are simply "somewhere to someone in your flutiest voice" (60), that is, the literary impulse responding to the unconscious or to the vibrancy of space, wherein there is no guarantee of a reply. This episode recalls Pound's plea to his old friends who cannot catch his wavelength or revolve on the never-ending orbit of intellectual commerce. In 1918, in his response to "Proteus," Pound told Joyce that the chapter was "much easier to see . . . in print" (Read 143), as if, even then, Pound wished to know "who was talking" in the sounds he heard. Such a comment might be seen to clash with his homage to Francis Picabia a year earlier, in the *Literary Review*, where he claimed that "the New Man . . . orients his inner ear towards things to come" and that any serious artist was comparable to hidden geniuses "who worked out the determinants that Marconi made use of in his computations for the wireless telegraph" (Pound, *Literary Essays* 47). It is this paradoxical stance that marks Pound's thinking about radio from the Rome broadcasts forward, his lauding of radio as "the ONLY medium still open" (Doob 283), while recognizing the prescience of his own writings. Pound's original conception of a "nerve-set" (*Literary Essays* 152) and the body as a mediumistic tool was generative; the artist could "departmentalize such part of the life force that flows through him" (346) and create accordingly. The eerie prescience of his conviction in "As for Imagism" (1915)—that "where the voltage is so high that it fuses the machinery" one merely has the "emotional man, not the artist" (346)—was replayed in his experience of radio, with its literal atmospherics, interference, and his communicative breakdown on more than one level.

Despite Pound's claims that his talks on the radio must be "judged by their content" and not "the medium of diffusion" (Doob 261), his lashing critique of Joyce's sound-sense in 1934 betrays a more complex reaction to the ways in which technology may intercept the pure, untainted voice of poetry before it is emitted and therefore subject to interpretation, much of which is erratic. Although in Pound's view Joyce may have sat within "the grove of his thought" ("e. e. cummings" 210–11) and listened to himself repeated endlessly, it was the "ventriloquent Agitator" (Joyce, *FW* 56) himself who became a discarnate voice, returning as an oral hallucination in his own writing, eventually concluding that "what he speaks for all in debt; he owes/ For every word" (*Drafts and Fragments* 32)

Notes

1. For example, Ian F. A. Bell sets out to "locate the scientific provenance of Pound's major items of vocabulary" by studying Pound's usage of electromagnetism to explain concepts of the "vortex" and, indeed, "tradition." Bell successfully reaffirms "the issues of science that Pound's modernism incorporates [by extending] their contexts in which discussions of his poetics have tended to reside" (3). Here he refers to Hugh Kenner's classic *The Pound Era* (1972), which tracks Pound's referencing of many scientific developments rather than focusing on the reiteration of electrical analogies that were so important to his artistic stance.

CHAPTER 12

"Speech without Practical Locale"

Radio and Lorine Niedecker's Aurality

BROOK HOUGLUM

On February 14, 1952, American poet Lorine Niedecker sent a copy of her newly completed radio script "Taste and Tenderness" to poet Louis Zukofsky. She included a letter with the script that discussed specific scenes and meditated on the aptness of radio for poetry:

> Radio *should* be a good medium for poetry—speech without practical locale. Stage with all its costumes and place and humans tripping about too distracting sometimes. Poetry and poetic drama—suggestion—the private printed page plus sound and silence. I remember when MacLeish and [radio dramatist] Norman Corwin were so excited about radio. It doesn't pay, that's all! (Penberthy, *Niedecker* 191)

When Niedecker invokes radio as "a good medium for poetry," she indexes the aural components of poetic writing and reception. Niedecker's reasons for considering radio a suitable medium for poetry are telling. The electronic medium engages aural rather than visual perception; unlike stage performances whose visuality might distract an audience from the crafted language of a script or make a subtlety obvious, radio pieces rely on verbal and sonic evocation. Radio, in foregrounding sound, also relies on and isolates speech for broadcast apart from sensory data that might accompany a jointly visual-verbal performance. For Niedecker, it is the circulation of sounds and silence along with the "private printed page" and a listening unfixed by visual perception that create poetic drama.

Niedecker's interest in rendering rhythms and phrases of speech, coupled with her sustained attention to aspects of sound in language, drew her to radio throughout her career. She regularly listened to and annotated radio programs in letters, worked as a scriptwriter for programs that aired on Madison, Wisconsin, radio station WHA in 1942, and wrote two radio scripts in the early 1950s. Niedecker's writing participates in an early and mid-twentieth-century climate in which changing concepts of sound and voice in poetic texts resonate with and against modern media and technological shifts. Modernist attention to "the musical phrase" (Pound, "A Few Don'ts"), the portrayal of particulars directed "along a line of melody" (Zukofsky 273), or "struggles of noises and of various distances" (Marinetti, "La Radia" 268) rather than metronomic or traditionally rhymed structures emphasize sound as a key feature in attempts to render poetics "anew." George Orwell's essay *Poetry and the Microphone* (1945) articulates a potential effect of exchanges of poetry and radio when he writes that poetry reading on the air may generate a sense of texts "as *sound* rather than as a pattern on paper" (167). Modernist poets, as writers, readers, and listeners of radio programs, engaged electronic sound through a medium that was also developing new codes and models for conveying and receiving information through sounds and speech. Characterized by assemblage and the rendering of distinct and multiple speakers, radio programming beginning in the 1920s shares attributes with Modernist poets' texts that employed fragmented, quoted, collaged, and stream-of-consciousness voices. This paper contends that the radio was a sustained subtending component of Niedecker's composition practices, at times providing a context for her reflections on orality and aurality in poetry and at other times offering a venue for which to write, a subject to write about, and a means to experiment with genre and method. By considering Niedecker's practices of writing script-poems and radio scripts, listening to radio, and incorporating speech in poems, we might understand more closely her attunement to precise qualities, durations, rhythms, and materials of sound that generates a poetics of aural collage, speech reportage, and voice experiment.

"I Heard on Radio": Aural Perception and Reception

Throughout Niedecker's poetic career,[1] she demonstrated an abiding attention to rendering sound and assembling particulars of speech in poetry. Literary critics have emphasized Niedecker's careful structuring of sound as characteristic of her work: Peter Quartermain asserts that sound is the "chiefest" distinction of Niedecker's poetry, signaling her "amazing management of *sound*, and the ways in which she uses sound to manage sense" (226, 221); Peter Middleton notes an "extraordinary precision in [Niedecker's] use of sound in poetry" throughout her career ("Folk Poetry" 204); Jenny Penberthy cites her "ready ear for charged speech" in composing poems based on overheard or read language (*Niedecker* 44). The relationship between the poet's attention to sound and aurality and her interest in radio, however, has been little investigated.[2]

Aural perception was central to Niedecker's poetics. She describes objects and events in terms of their sounds and employs devices such as assonance, alliteration, and spatial organization to elicit and encourage aural reception. She quotes and writes distinctive speech patterns and phrases as a way to situate the meaning of particular material within its heard rhythms and tones, with *how* it was communicated. Beginning in the 1930s, her work foregrounds such concerns. In her early pieces, Niedecker tests features and patterns of sound and speech as she experiments with genre, form, voice, and surrealist technique. In "Progression," an eight-part poem from 1933 that moves between lexicons of seasons, socialism, and landscapes, Niedecker writes: "the emotion of fall has its seat in the acoustic gland; wind: strong distance in closest places" (*Collected* 32). The "acoustic gland," or aural perception, guides this piece as it carefully notates environmental sound and employs neologism to create echoes between sections. In Section III of the poem, for example, she writes: "what can you do that yellowing season of earth / with more than nine hundred ninety / recombinations of yellows / since rain crossed the modes / of your brooding?" (Niedecker 27). Section VIII answers with its own verbal "recombinations" in the line: "jesticulate in the rainacular or novembrood / in the sunconscious" (32). Sounds are used here to (humorously) promote paradox, as in the contrast between brooding *in* a "sunconscious," which suggests a private, but bright, psychological mode, and then contrasting the "sunconcious" with the "rainacular," or popular, public experience of weather as shared language. The sequence employs sound to suggest sense, recall previous lines, and produce a vernacular particular to the poem.

For Niedecker, aural perception was central to epistemology, likely partially due to her poor eyesight.[3] She had an ear for the sounds of her surroundings, notably of the precise qualities of regional birdsong, and her letters evidence the precision with which she isolated and characterized specific birdcalls. For example, in 1937 she writes to Zukofksy of hearing the "vigorous echo" of a whippoorwill (Penberthy, *Niedecker* 124), in 1952 of a Baltimore Oriole whose "sound seems tunneled in" (195), and in 1962 of being "tuned" to a night of "frog trills and barred owl's scary noise" (310). For Niedecker, listening produces the knowledge that enables identification of birds: she writes in a letter May 19, 1946, about bird-watching with the granddaughter of naturalist Thure Kumlien, that her guide "always had to *see* the birds to appreciate 'em whereas I knew by their sound what they were and knowing what their colors were in my mind, was happy enough" (140). Listening also produces an interior mode of mental perception as sound conjures color, or as sound invokes characteristics that are often attributed to visual perception alone. Niedecker's attention to the sounds of birds produces lines such as two stanzas of the semiautobiographical poem "Paean to Place" (1968) where the speaker mourns the mother's "not hearing canvasbacks / their blast-off rise / from the water / Not hearing sora / rails's sweet // spoon-tapped waterglass- / descending scale- / tear-drop-tittle" (*Collected* 263). Her lines evoke and perform the sounds they describe: the "blast-off" of canvasbacks conjures a sound of a splash through its repeated "a" sounds, and the line breaks and alliteration of the s, r, and t evoke the sora rails's descending, ringing call. Throughout her career, her knowledge of sounds in her local environment generates material for her experiments with rendering sound, and speech, in writing.

Along with environmental sounds and human speech, radio was a component of Niedecker's soundscape. Her frequent correspondence with Zukofsky from the 1930s until her death, and with poet Cid Corman in the 1960s, register her sustained practice of radio listening, which we might think of as the reception of sound and speech assembled and transmitted from a variety of "locales." Reports of radio listening are part of the fabric of her oft-incorporated material in letters that includes fragments of conversations, books, letters, musical listening, and the tones of birdsong. In the published letters to Zukofsky there are twelve references to radio programs. Several instances paraphrase or index radio speech: April 29, 1945, she writes, "Did you hear [Soviet Foreign Commissar] Molotov's voice on radio? If only the translator's voice had been as strong and convincing as M's" (Penberthy, *Niedecker* 134); December 15, 1952, she "caught it fast over the radio with one ear—it seems this horse in one of the southern states writes with his foot . . ." (202); June 26, 1957, she writes, "Philadelphia had 100 heat and New York's pretty bad, I heard on radio" (237); November 6, 1961, she reports:

"Heard Nehru on radio on Meet the Press. The Leader of the Neutrals! I've always thought the world of him" (295). Listening to the Third Party political speeches on July 25, 1948, she writes that she "joined the crowd (by my radio) in laughing and crying at the same time when the climax of [Glen] Taylor's appearance came—his ballad singing with his wife and mother and son" (154), indicating a participatory mode of interaction with the medium. These accounts of listening isolate particular fragments of broadcasts for written report, demonstrating how radio is subject to Niedecker's habit of notating live and written speech (or song) that she finds compelling, humorous, or distinctive.

Radio is particularly germane to considerations of Niedecker's poetic practice, I would argue, because it transmits an eclectic mix of spoken voices and programs that appeal to Niedecker's valuation of unique speech patterns and acts of listening. Radio news, music, weather reports, and literary programs were a source of interest to Niedecker, a way to listen to and engage with multiple national and international locations and events while situated in one place. Roland Barthes, focusing on the telephone as an instrument typifying a new modern mode of intersubjective listening, proposes that due to the advent of modern sound media, "roles implied by the act of listening no longer have the same fixity as in the past" (258). He writes of a mobile, circulating listening that disperses signifiers, disrupts fixed networks or roles of speech, and externalizes listening (259). When Niedecker writes that "radio should be a good medium for poetry" as it enables "speech without practical locale" without the encumbrances of a live stage, she engages Barthes's sense that the concept and practice of radio shifts "fixed networks," roles, and modes of perception that accompany conventional forms of listening and spoken performance. The lack of a programmed visual register is central to Niedecker's valuation of radio for poetry, but in her work, she also unfixes conventions of dialogue through assembling spoken fragments alongside other material and by drawing attention to atypical acts and exchanges of speech.

Speech Experiments and Vocal Assemblage

The poems "The President of the Holding Company," "Fancy Another Day Gone," and play script "Domestic and Unavoidable," written in the 1930s, pay particular attention to voices through organizing poetic, succinct, and idiomatic speech in script form. As Penberthy has noted, these scripts are not intended as radio plays; Niedecker published "The President" and "Fancy" under the heading "Two Poems" in *New Democracy* (May 1936) and *New Directions* (1936), and envisioned "Domestic and Unavoidable" as a "series of 'print stills' projected on a screen" (Penberthy, "Life and Writing" 5). I would also suggest that this early work participates in Modernist and avant-garde projects of assemblage that can be aligned with early twentieth-century experimentation with the recording, broadcast, and arrangement of voices over new sound technologies. In her cross-genre compositions, Niedecker merges the form of the play script with the form of the dramatic monologue to construct sites of multiple and juxtaposed voices, forming distinct pieces that are also aligned with her later work's attention to voice and speech.

Published in *Bozart-Westminster* (Spring/Summer 1935), the nine-voiced poetic play script "Domestic and Unavoidable," in particular, constructs distinct but unnamed speakers who converse by linguistic association and appear only as shadowy projections in contrast to the visually described presence of a young man working at a desk in his study. Production cues in "Domestic and Unavoidable" emphasize the offstage or off-page sound of the voices located off of the study. Before dialogue occurs, the text cues a sonic shift:

> *A confused murmur of voices of men and women from dining room soon becomes merely a suspicion of sound as of air in a tunnel or as a loud speaker of a radio turned on but not speaking—movement in stillness out of which the action of the words comes clear.* (Niedecker, *Collected* 68)

This "fade-out," replacing murmuring voices with the static or vacuum hum of a "suspicion of sound," enables attention to the proceeding individual fragments of speech. The radio speaker operates as analogous to an opened circuit, an electric silence, a circulating stillness that facilitates the hearing of dislocated voices. In her essay considering Niedecker in the context of sound technologies, Lisa Robertson writes that the "turned-on but still" radio in this passage "gives meaning to the drifting, delocalized voice" (12). The radio in "Domestic and Unavoidable" can be likened to Niedecker's later sense of radio as facilitating "speech without practical locale." Offstage, shifting voices in the play operate in dialogues characterized by their collective completion and disconnection:

> Woman low—Have you been . . . .
> Woman high— . . . . to the bread eaters lately? (69)

Conversations also proceed through echo and elliptical form, as in the following exchange.

> Old man—They don't have a minister; they have a doctor.
> Woman husky—Oh, do you think we should indoctrinate at certain points?
> Gentleman loud—Well, one thing . . . .
> Woman low— . . . . announces a fabricoid . . . .
> Woman high— . . . . and another . . . .
> Gentleman gentle— . . . . assembles a divinity. (68–69)

While narrative strains can be constructed in the script, frequent semantic and subject shifts draw attention to the acts of speaking, interactions and associative resonance between lines ("doctor," "indoctrinate"), and spatial organization of the script.

In considering Niedecker's construction of voice in the "Domestic" script, we must investigate the (juxta)positions and positioning of speech that typify the piece. As a play, or a script projected onto a series of screens, "Domestic and Unavoidable" creates a disconnect between the spotlit center of action and the space where the majority of speech takes place. Niedecker's use of offstage voices draws attention to a decentered and distant vocal space. The dashes following each speaker's designated voice tag and the space and ellipses surrounding much of the language provide a visual analogue to the distal quality of the voices. This draws attention to the qualities and loudness of the unseen and unnamed speakers, as indicated by the tags "gentle," "husky," "high," "low," "loud," "old," "plain," "illumined" (*Collected* 68–70). It is significant that the visible "young man in study" is the only character whose voice is not described, as he is "seen." By subverting the normative visual center of theater, Niedecker's construction foregrounds the tones and rhythms of fragmentary speech and a sense of the overheard and anonymous.

Niedecker's use of the radio in the opening section signals to a reader or viewer how to locate the murmur of voices, as static, as proximate *and* distant; at the end of the play, the "confused murmur" returns "offstage" and finally "becomes sound" (70). Sound here marks the end of an exchange between the young studying man and a young girl whose voice, because "she is never seen, is intimate" and inaugurates a final four-voiced elliptical series. Two gentlemen and two women state: "Minockua . . . . / . . . . the day is fattening . . . . / . . . . Brimble . . . . / . . . . the Brand . . . ." (70). As in many exchanges in the play, words such as "Minockua . . . ." and ". . . . Brimble . . . ." seem to be drawn from slippages between multiple conversations rather than a cohesive narrative statement and invite enjoyment in the sounds of the fragments themselves. As speech is dislocated from any determinate context, it participates in the unfixing and rearrangement of models of communication that Barthes associates with modern telephonic modes. Niedecker draws attention to the breakages that promote new aural and semantic relationships to verbal exchange more radically in "Domestic and Unavoidable" than in some of her later work, but signals an approach to voice, sound, and language that later constructions also engage.

(Dis)located Speech in Folk and Radio Work

Niedecker's sustained attention to speech and sound found practical and theoretical grounding in the medium of radio at several points in her career. Her radio work for Madison station WHA in 1942 provided her with an opportunity to write scripts that contributed to wartime radio programming jointly sponsored by WHA and the Wisconsin Council of Defense, and to hone her skills in writing for aural reception. The radio script work grew out of her employment as a writer and research editor between 1938 and 1942 at the Federal Writers' Project, a branch of the Works Progress Administration, and at the Wisconsin Writers' Project.[4] Niedecker's attention to speech patterns and sound in poems is evident early in her career, but she cultivated her process of importing spoken language and written text into her poetry throughout this period. Her Writers' Project work complimented and contributed to her folk project, which generated poems based on local speech; in leading to radio script-writing employment, it also contributed to her later radio script "Taste and Tenderness," about the Jameses, and her radio adaptation of Faulkner's *As I Lay Dying*.

Niedecker's work for federal and state Writers' Projects afforded opportunities to research and write about Wisconsin history and culture. She participated in an effort that produced *Wisconsin: A Guide to the Badger State (1941)*, entries for a proposed Encyclopedia of Wisconsin Biography, guidebooks of major cities in the state, and radio scripts that dramatized nineteenth-century life in Wisconsin and figures of interest such as naturalists Increase Lapham[5] and John Muir and suffragist and author Zona Gale. Her research enabled her to sift through accounts of lives and quoted speech that she could also incorporate into her own writing, including her folk poetry that borrowed from both living and quoted speech.

Penberthy notes that most of the folk poems published in *New Goose* (1946) are constructed "almost entirely out of overheard local speech," evidencing a method dependent on "an opportunistic ear, ready for the irregular sounds of living speech, for any undiluted linguistic possibility" (*Niedecker* 43). An example of such overheard and transcribed speech is the untitled poem "Here it gives the laws for fishing thru the ice—" which reads:

> Here it gives the laws for fishing thru the ice—
> only one hook to a line,
> stay at the hole, can't go in to warm up,
> well, we never go fishing, so they can't catch us. (Niedecker, *Collected* 98)

This selection enters a situation as a speaker paraphrases the rules for ice-fishing at an unnamed body of water. Because the circumstantial details—the location, the relation of the speaker to the listener—are not given, the emphasis turns to the rhythms and diction of spoken language, the pauses and colloquial "well," the imbedded anti-authoritarian critique of the "laws" that refuse a fisher a chance to "warm up," and the humor of the final admission that "we never go fishing" anyway. Literary critics of Niedecker's *oeuvre* produced during this period have noted how the poems decontextualize speech and deemphasize the position of the speaker (Quartermain 220, Willis 101). Elizabeth Willis asserts that found "folk" material was ideal for Niedecker in particular because it allowed her to engage in anonymous[6] and multiple-author composition (99). The speech quoted in Niedecker's folk poetry is often unidentified and seamlessly combined with other found language. These aspects of the folk poetry, which set speech on the page little marked by authorial comment or conventions of quotation, suggest the "off-stage" operation of radiophonic speech and sound that the script of "Domestic and Unavoidable" makes literal.

A letter dated October 26, 1949, exemplifies Niedecker's practice of notating heard speech; it details the literary content of a weekly CBS radio show, and I quote it at length as it demonstrates Niedecker's regular attention to the program, her transcription of dialogue as for a script, and her response to the discussion.

> This morning it was Don Quixote (Quixot, [Mark] Van Doren said, and Qeehoty, Howe said) with the two regulars, Van Doren and Howe and there's always a visiting third, this time, Samuel Putnam. . . . Last week they had Hill who had

just written "To Meet Will Shakespeare". . . . Today Samuel Putnam said (or Putnum?—the one who used to write for the Daily Worker?) said he supposed the greatest adventure of man is to find God. Van Doren: Yes, Don Quixote is going with all haste where he knows he'll find God, I suppose, but remember what Sancho said: "You can't make a worse mistake than dying while you're still alive." Perfect? I wish when they use God they'd take just three minutes to define—maybe then they'd forget the word. (Penberthy, *Niedecker* 162–63)

In this selection, Niedecker transcribes, paraphrases, and comments on the radio discussion. At the heart of Niedecker quoting Van Doren quoting Cervantes on radio is her delight in Sancho's line. Her attention to Sancho's aphorism indexes her attention to concise exchanges and unique phrases of speech. Niedecker's critique of the unqualified or undefined term "God" situates her as a participant in the discussion, demonstrating an engaged listening practice. Her notation of differing pronunciations ("Quixot," "Qeehoty") actively registers the interaction, and occasional dissonance, of multiple voices. This passage reads as a precursor to Niedecker's own radio scripts, which also employ multiple voices as they "script" speech in a dramatic fashion that experiments with individual and collective utterance.

Niedecker's work in the early 1950s on a script version of *As I Lay Dying* and a play about Henry, William, and Alice James, "Taste and Tenderness," demonstrates two different methods of radio drama writing: adaptation and original composition.[7] The radio plays are sites wherein Niedecker practices techniques of importing, adapting, and condensing speech, and of scripting sound effects; these methods also contribute to her composition of poetry, as she continues to write poems in the early 1950s alongside the radio plays. The writing processes coincide on occasion; source material gathered in preparation for the James play finds its way into poems, and overheard speech that might have been made into poetry she positions in the script.

Niedecker adapted and incorporated language from local speech and letters into her radio drama. She writes of a piece of overheard speech that inspires a line for the James play. She heard her father's friend Walter Ladwig tell of seeing someone who was "weak physically and financially—as though financially were another category of the human body and spelled probably *phy*nancially! I'm putting it in the play" (Penberthy, *Niedecker* 195). Accented with a homophonic prefix the line produces a double-entendre. She also includes in "Taste and Tenderness" a line of Zukofsky's that he writes of forgetting he spoke: "It's tough to be forced to the wall by the so-called idealistic—to be forced to admit one's a genius and an outcast" (14).[8] These unattributed fragments of adapted speech, while not in the extant scene and hence decontextualized from dramatic progression, point to Niedecker's abiding attention to collecting and rendering spoken words in text.

Her extensive reading on the Jameses also produced material for poems that she placed in the "For Paul and Other Poems" manuscript she worked on in this period. Niedecker laments to Zukofsky that she is not able to include a sympathetic letter from Henry James to Alice Norton in the radio script, but as Penberthy has noted, this material becomes the poem "Sorrow moves in wide waves" (*Niedecker* 70; Niedecker, *Collected* 148). Two other poems involving the Jameses, "Jesse James and his brother Frank" and "May you have lumps in your mashed potatoes,"[9] *were* included in the manuscript "For Paul and Other Poems." The wide reading and working through material that she engages in through radio script composition enable both read and spoken particulars to circulate in new contexts and take on alternate meanings.

The dislocation and transcribing of speech and text that Niedecker engaged in while composing folk poetry and writing radio scripts established methods that became crucial to her poetics. Throughout her career, she utilized "anonymous" speech as found material, and gathered pieces from letters, reading, and conversation to construct poems. I would like to suggest that radio programs also offered a source of material for Niedecker but that the speech she recorded from them is often incorporated in poems that aren't earmarked, and the papers that might have indicated such are lost.[10] Niedecker's radio listening, attentive to vibrant and eclectic language, contributed material that resulted in at least two poems written in the 1960s: "The obliteration" and "*So he said / on radio.*"

An early draft of "The obliteration" reads "The radio talk this morning / was of obliterating / the world / I notice fruit flies rise / from the rind / of the recommended / melon" (*Collected* 429), locating the source of the speech in a radio program, while the version she published in *Lines* (May 1965) resituates the source of the talk in dinner conversation:

The obliteration
of the world
his dinner speech
tonight I beseech
you

>   eat
> the recommended melon
> before the fruit flies
> >   rise
> from it (*Collected* 211)

An example of one of Niedecker's haiku-influenced five-line stanza pieces, "The obliteration" combines intimate conversation with a personal entreaty to eat the melon spontaneously and immediately in response to the threat of imminent obliteration. The intimate setting and response balance the large topic of nuclear disaster; the two stanzas hang in the balance of one another's five lines, meeting in the single-word lines "you" and "eat." The particularly consonantal end-rhyme of "speech" and "beseech," separated by a word and caesura, emphasizes the spoken-ness of the speech heard and plea imparted; the hard "e"s echo again in the following "eat." In the final sequence, the letters "f" and "r" resonate against one another in the words fruit, flies, rise, from. The space between "flies" and "rise" further accents the sense of import and weighted anticipation that the lines evoke. The published poem shifts the voice of the radio talk to a more proximate, private, dinner speaker and thereby buries the source of the material to establish the poem's specific effect.

Penberthy writes that books and letters were particularly fruitful sources for Niedecker's poetry, and that the "letter-poems do not allude to their origin—we are seldom or only subtly reminded that they are condensed fragments of letters" (*Niedecker* 85); as an example of one of the few poems that cite a letter, Penberthy notes Niedecker's "*Letter from Ian*," which indicates through its title that the poem employs material received in a letter from poet Ian Hamilton Finley.[11] The poem "*So he said / on radio*" indicates a radio program as source material through employing a similar offset title as that in "*Letter from Ian*":

> *So he said*
> >   *on radio*
> I have to fly
> wit Venus arms
> I found fishing
> to Greece
> then back to Univers of Wis

> where they got stront. 90
> to determ if same marble
> as my arms (Niedecker, *Collected* 209)

Location is key to this poem that traffics in extensive flight, and locating the speaker on the air facilitates a reader's reception of the poem as overheard speech in a way that grounds the initial strangeness of the images. The unidentified speaker states that he will fly to Greece with "Venus arms" then back to the University of Wisconsin, which holds "stront. 90," or strontium-90, a radioactive isotope and product of nuclear fallout.[12] Arms function in the poem as the missing marble arms of Venus de Milo (finally found by the speaker?) and also invoke weapons in the sense of the arms Venus delivers to Aeneas as depicted by Virgil and represented by painters such as Nicolas Poussin and Anthony van Dyck.[13] The poem does not provide a context for the speech, though it does suggest a connection between the radioactive element that produced popular anxiety in the 1950s and 1960s, spawning comic book superheroes such as Spiderman and the X-Men, and the flight of the speaker, situating the lines in terms of the discourse of nuclear bombing that Niedecker registers in several poems and letters of the period. "*So he said / on radio*" decontextualizes speech in the manner of much of Niedecker's "unmarked"[14] folk speech but marks its source in a way that many of her poems, based on speech, letters, and perhaps radio programs, do not. I believe that Niedecker employed the title here to accent the particular kind of radio-announced speech that the poem records so as to design a space for the poem to inhabit in a reader's mind.

Reading Aloud, Silently

In Niedecker's 1960s correspondence and conversation, she engaged in dialogue with Corman,[15] Basil Bunting, Kenneth Cox, and Bob Nero about reading poems aloud to an audience or for recording.[16] To Nero, Niedecker writes: "A tape of, by, me? Nice of you to ask but I'm not sure my reading would be the best. (Altho actually I say my verse to myself a million times, sometimes whisper it 'aloud' for moosic)" and "Reading poetry aloud—well, I might not be too good at it, altho sound means a great deal . . . " (qtd. in Faranda 120). Niedecker values the aural components of poetry, the listening to speech and sound over the public oration of them. She writes to Cox in 1970 that she doesn't approve of reading aloud, as poetry for her

> is a matter of planting it in deep, a filled silence, each person reading it a silence to be filled—he'll have to come to the poems—both writer and reader—with an ear for all the poems can give and he'll hear that as Beethoven heard tho deaf. (Niedecker, "Extracts" 42).

Niedecker's attention to sound and aurality is complicated by her predilection for an interior, silent mode of reception.

Radio offers a middle space between the public stage and the private page, but importantly, Niedecker also finds such a space available in the private reading of poems. Writing to Corman in 1967, Niedecker states that poetry performed aloud can produce greater (presumably unnecessary) drama due to the presence of a "somewhat inattentive audience." She asserts that a poet's knowledge of such an audience during composition can also generate more prosaic lines; the visual or "staged" reading produces different effects than a reading conducted through nonvisible oration or privately. She writes:

> Poems are for one person to another, spoken thus, or read silently. How would the bug on the branch, walking to the end of it, or the raindrop there—your poems—be read to a hall filled with people? If I close my eyes I look for the words on the page. If the silence could be governed among the people, if your voice came from somewhere not seen, i.e. radio, or out of suffused light—perhaps [performing aloud would be] OK. If your ear is acute you sound your poem in silence. (Faranda 121)

The speech that Niedecker collects, transcribes, and condenses in poems constitutes voices coming from "somewhere not seen," the sound that radio or one's own acute ear renders. Here the offstage, unseen sound of the "private page" suggests a specific kind of listening, to sound in silence.

Invoking qualities of radio transmission, along with those of "suffused light," offers Niedecker a set of conditions that limit the visual reception that some might find optimal. Thinking about how poetry might operate like radio enables Niedecker to articulate the conditions under which writing should be transmitted and received, and to theorize the movement from aural perception and composition to reception. Niedecker's earlier assertion of "poetry and poetic drama" as the "printed page plus sound and silence" speaks to an understanding of text as dynamic and as grounded in sounded components of language. Conceiving of a text, then, as "sounded in silence" convokes a particular kind of aural experience for the reader. We might approach Niedecker's concept of silent, aural reception by recalling her letter to Zukofsky, quoted earlier, that details how birdsong produces knowledge of the colors of birds in her mind, without recourse to sight. Niedecker calls upon radio, in the context of her critique of poetry performed aloud, to help situate a kind of listening that she understands as also taking place interiorly, "without practical locale."

Notes

I would like to thank Jenny Penberthy and Mary Chapman for their generous and productive criticism of this essay. I am also appreciative of Bernard Schermetzler's assistance at the University of Wisconsin-Madison archives and Scott Feiner's assistance at the Wisconsin Historical Society Archives.

1. Niedecker's induction into the late Modernist scene, finding *Poetry*'s "Objectivist" issue in 1931 exciting and resonant with her poetics, writing to Louis Zukofsky, and experiencing avant-garde artistic culture on visits to New York between 1933 and 1939, has been well documented. For a useful introduction to Niedecker's early years and poetic practice, see Jenny Penberthy's introduction to *Niedecker and the Correspondence with Zukofsky, 1931–1970*. See also Breslin. Niedecker's choice to reside in rural Wisconsin most of her life afforded a wealth of local poetic material, and wide reading and correspondences with other poets fed her cross-genre writing and experiments with form. She exhibited an early interest in surrealist technique, also writing "script" poems and prose in the 1930s, wrote "folk" poetry in the late 1930s and 1940s, constructed two radio plays in 1952, developed a "reflective" haiku-influenced poetics in the 1950s, and wrote research-based historical poems in the 1960s. In her lifetime, she published five books of poetry, including two that collect a span of works: *New Goose* (1946), *My Friend Tree* (1961), *North Central* (1968), *T&G: The Collected Poems* (1969), and *My Life by Water: Collected Poems, 1936–1968*. All citations to Niedecker's work in this article refer to Niedecker's *Collected Works* (2002), edited by Jenny Penberthy. All information regarding publication of Niedecker's work is drawn from Penberthy's notes in this volume.

2. The exception is Robertson's "'In Phonographic Deep Song,'" in which Robertson situates Niedecker's poetics of listening within the cultural milieu of sound technology. See *The Poetry Project Newsletter* 198 (February / March 2004): 11–12.

3. In a letter to friend Ronald Ellis in the 1960s, Niedecker comments on the difficulty caused throughout her life by a "noticeable failure in eyesight" ("Local Letters" 97); this progressive issue forced her to stop working as a proofreader for local paper *Hoard's Dairyman* in 1950 (Niedecker, *Collected* 6).

4. In September 1939, the Federal Writers' Project funding ended, but the Wisconsin Writers' Project reopened as an independent state program a few months later and was operational between 1939 and 1942 (WHS Archives, Series 1762, Wis Mss MM).

5. Some of Niedecker's folk poems from the 1940s draw material from texts and letters, such as the short poem: "Asa Gray wrote Increase Lapham: / pay particular attention / to my pets, the grasses" (105). Some work also drew from her WPA and

Wisconsin Writers' Project research (Penberthy, *Niedecker* 40). It is unlikely that Niedecker worked on the Lapham or other radio scripts, as the extant scripts that are signed do not note her name, but Niedecker was probably familiar with the radio script project. The Writers' Project's "Pioneer Recollection Series" aired from January through March 1939 on radio stations WHA (Madison) and WLBL (Stevens Point). The "Wisconsin Men and Women" series aired weekly between May 15, 1940, and May 28, 1941, on station WIBA (Madison). The earlier "Pioneer Recollection Series" scripts, with titles such as "Reminiscences of My Childhood, by Dr. J. E. Engsted" and "Life Story of Myself: By Joshua Wild" rely on monologues adapted from historical autobiographies of figures such as Engsted and Wild. In these scripts, an announcer introduces the figure, and then the script proceeds with a first-person account quoted from published material. The "Wisconsin Men and Women" scripts are more complex, constructing dialogue, multiple voices, and sound cues. The script "Wisconsin: Her Men and Women: Increase Allan Lapham" aired September 4, 1940 (WHS Archives, Series 1762, Wis Mss MM, 6:3–8:7).

6. Niedecker's decision to keep her status as a poet "anonymous" from many in her local community, partly so as to glean material and partly due to her tendency toward a quiet, unobtrusive lifestyle, has led to critical discussions about her position as a rural, "anonymous" woman writer. Penberthy discusses Niedecker's "anonymity" in her introduction to *Niedecker and the Correspondence with Zukofsky, 1931–1970*. DuPlessis situates Niedecker's "anonymous" position within class, gender, and literary contexts, arguing that such a position was chosen as it offered Niedecker a "non-elite, non-hegemonic literary career" (118).

7. The only extant fragment of Niedecker's original radio script on the Jameses, "Taste and Tenderness," is Act I, Scene 3, sent to novelist and essayist Edward Dahlberg in 1955 in response to his request for material for a proposed but never published anthology (Penberthy, *Niedecker* 191). Her adaptation of Faulkner's book retains much of the original language of the novel but drastically condenses and assembles the material for radio format while inserting sound cues and experimenting with character dialogue.

8. Penberthy notes that this line is a part of a portion of Niedecker's James script included in the Zukofsky letters. She writes, "Zukofsky evidently liked the comment and in the margin asked for its source. Below his query Niedecker wrote: 'LZ forgetting he was the one who said it!'" (*Niedecker* 14).

9. "May you have lumps . . ." was also later published in *Origin* 2.2 (July 1961): 28.

10. At Niedecker's request, her journals and papers were destroyed after her death.

11. The poem reads:

> *Letter from Ian*
> Aye sure
> a castle on a rock
> in the middle of Edinburgh

> They floodlight it—
> big show up there
> with pipe bands
> and all
>
> Down here along the road
> open your door
> to a posse of poets (207)

12. A large amount of strontium-90 was released into the environment in the 1950s and 60s during atmospheric nuclear weapons testing.

13. "Marble Arms" is also a company in Gladstone, Michigan, that has produced axes, guns, sporting knives, and other outdoor and hunting products since its incorporation in 1898.

14. The term "unmarked speech" is used by Holley to describe Marianne Moore's practice of not citing quoted material in her poems. Thanks to Mary Chapman for directing me to Holley's use of this term.

15. Corman was a proponent of reading aloud and recorded the only tape recording of Niedecker reading poems aloud in 1970, which is held in the Contemporary Poetry Collection at the W. A. C. Bennett Library of Simon Fraser University, Burnaby, B.C., Canada.

16. See Niedecker's letters about reading aloud to Bob Nero in Truck 16 (1975): 138–39, and to Cid Corman in Faranda 121–23. She reports discussing poetry reading aloud with Basil Bunting to Corman after Bunting visited in July 1967 (127).

CHAPTER 13

Materializing Millay

The 1930s Radio Broadcasts

LESLEY WHEELER

The startling newness of early radio, the speed at which it transformed American life, resonates with modern literature's parallel investment in change, originality, even revolution. Edna St. Vincent Millay, however, while involved in both enterprises, was hardly an avatar of the new. Although she promoted and embodied women's increasing social and sexual freedoms, she also performed the stereotypes of bohemian, femme fatale, and poetess with zeal; she was, in many ways, a conventional figure, and not only because she often wrote in forms and imagery that any Victorian would recognize as poetic. Nevertheless, Millay was, in a small way, a broadcast pioneer. In 1932 and 1933, Millay became one of the first poets to read her own work over American airwaves. In doing so, she responded to a call issued by many parties to "save" poetry by taking advantage of this innovative technology, this original way of transmitting poetry to a national audience. She also became an important example of how poets in the modern era used, and were used by, a developing medium.

Millay's broadcasts succeeded in reaching appreciative listeners, yet the surviving evidence indicates that she did not, in fact, treat radio as fundamentally new. For Millay, radio's effects closely parallel the advantages conferred by a much older technology: print. Both broadcast and printed poetry, that is, deliver an illusion of intimacy and presence despite distance (geographical, and in the case of books and recordings, temporal). Even public recitation by the author constitutes a materialization: the poet may be physically present in the lecture hall, yet the poetic self remains a performance managed much more convincingly by some writers than others. Millay regarded this illusion of presence and intimacy as the battery, the indispensable power source, for the twentieth-century lyric in any medium. Radio delighted her; she even wrote occasional verse, discussed in this essay's conclusion, in appreciation of popular radio performer Edgar Bergen and his wooden alter ego Charlie McCarthy. Nevertheless, Millay's broadcasts question the artistic value of novelty and register skepticism of radio's supposedly radical, utopian possibilities. For Millay, radio is a means, like print, to overcome distance, and a forum, like public recitation, in which poetry's tropes of sound may become briefly literal.

I begin with an account of Millay's on-air reading series, placing it in two contexts: the early history of broadcasting, and her own performance practices during enormously popular reading tours. Millay's broadcasts occur at an important juncture in radio history in the United States; their timing strongly inflects their meaning. Her radio work also harmonizes with recent scholarship on poetry readings and recordings, in particular the relation between performed and printed poems.[1] The second and third parts of the essay discuss the relationship between the audiotexts and printed versions of the poems Millay selected for one recorded broadcast. My analysis focuses on two concerns shared by these pieces and magnified by her style of delivery: tropes of sound and presence; and, more briefly, Millay's engagement with the idea of "naturalness."

Suzanne Clark argues, "The reader of Millay is not likely to find writerly pleasures in her text, called so frequently from play back to the spectacle of personality" (*Sentimental* 95). In fact, Millay's poems constantly question their own identity as writerly as well as aural texts. Further, Millay's broadcasts magnify the potential tension between print and performance remarked by so many poetry critics: does the real poem exist on the page, the stage, or the airwaves?[2] At stake are Millay's ambivalence toward distancing technologies (including writing itself); her conception of poetry as a dialogic art; and her persistent interest in the nature of sound and poetic voice. Her implicit answer to this question is that no version, no medium, possesses ultimate priority over another. Millay also reveals intimacy as an illusion in any medium. Unlike many Modernists and postmodernists, however, she regards this fragile illusion of presence as poetry's (and radio's) sine qua non.

Susan Smulyan writes persuasively in *Selling Radio* that "treating radio programs as literature ... misses the point of broadcasting; the material sent over the airwaves exists primarily to gather and retain an audience for advertising" (6). Millay's broadcasts were, arguably, radio programs in Smulyan's sense: they served her financial interest in self-promotion and served early radio's desperate need for material as well as cultural legitimacy. As many literary scholars have observed, literature is never pure of context, never entirely separate from commercial concerns, although it can secure prestige through a fantasy of autonomy from market forces. This essay demonstrates that broadcasting is one of many economically inflected contexts shaping the meanings of modern poetry. This is particularly true because network radio helped invent a national culture for the United States. Millay, already one of the nation's best-known artists, manipulated and was manipulated by radio to shape that culture. Her work deserves attention on its own account, but it also speaks to the limits and advantages of broadcasting for poetry generally.

The popular poetry of the modern era, including Millay's work, does not correspond well with the stories scholars have told about Modernism. The current moment in literary scholarship, however—characterized by a decline in "phonophobia," as Garrett Stewart calls it, and a renewed interest in acoustical technologies—offers an opportunity to revise the poetic history of the twentieth century. Millay's broadcasts suggest a different take on what is interesting, important, and provocative about this period. Her radio experiments suggest that the best insights about modernity do not necessarily emanate from the avant-garde, and that poetry can use new media to deliver on old promises.[3]

Broadcasts and Readings: Materializing the Author

In 1932 and 1933, American radio was undergoing a major transition. As Eric Barnouw and others document, the lively chaos of amateur radio in the teens and early twenties yielded, by the end of the latter decade, to the ascendancy of networks and the advent of commercial radio. During the 1930s, radio became a "pervasive influence in American life" (Brown 2). Instead of offering haphazard programming of local talent in the evening hours, as small transmitters associated with newspapers and department stores had done previously, the networks invented a national mass culture, bringing advice programs, dramas, and famous performers into homes across the country, all in the service of advertisement (Smulyan 6). Shortly after Millay's reading series ended, in fact, in March 1933, Franklin Delano Roosevelt began his "fireside chats," capitalizing politically on this technology of intimacy and sincerity.[4] During national crisis, with millions out of work and Hitler rising to power in Germany, radio seemed to possess utopian potential as "a unifying and culturally uplifting medium" (Hilmes xviii).

Radio's power to build community over geographical distances coexisted uneasily, however, with its increasingly commercial function. As Michele Hilmes argues, this tension sometimes manifested in contests between highbrow and lowbrow culture: "Broadcasting . . . became a key element in the ordering of the American cultural hierarchy. Early regulatory decisions attempted to mark radio out as a controlled and sanctioned space in which the 'vulgar,' such as black jazz performers or race records, could find only a tenuous and sanitized foothold" (186). Poetry readings, on the other hand, along with symphony, opera, lectures, and some drama, could offer cultural improvement that mitigated radio's infiltration of private spaces by hucksters.[5] Millay's one experience with radio prior to her 1932 reading is a good example: an opera called *The King's Henchmen*, for which Millay had written the libretto, was broadcast live in 1927 by the brand-new Columbia Phonograph Broadcasting System (Barnouw 222). This performance with Metropolitan Opera artists was marred by technical difficulties, but it augured the high-culture ambitions of young American radio networks.

American poetry's relationship to the radio commenced early in the history of broadcasting. News and talk radio began in the 1920s, with poetry readings by the announcers occasionally filling the gaps between programs (Barnouw 134, Kaplan 3). These recitations became popular in the late 1920s, and in 1930 WJZ, New York, broadcast several poetry readings by the authors themselves (Kaplan 4). Harriet Monroe devoted an editorial in *Poetry* magazine to this program, deploring the quality of the verse WJZ aired but insisting, "Poetry is a vocal art; the radio will bring back its audience" (35). Later the same year, César Saerchinger, the first U.S. "foreign radio representative," persuaded Britain's poet laureate John Masefield to broadcast to American audiences (ix): Masefield, who was an advocate for poetry recitation in many contexts, expressed hope that radio in particular could highlight the role of sound in poetry and widen its audience (34–35).[6] These calls continued well after Millay's first radio venture. Archibald MacLeish, for instance, published a verse radio play called *The Fall of the City* in 1937, prefaced by a passionate argument for this new genre, in which visual elements cannot compete with the "word-excited imagination" (x): radio's provision of large audiences "should deeply move the American poet whose present tragedy is his isolation from any audience vigorous enough to demand his strongest work" (xiii).[7] Likewise, in his 1949 book about poetry on the radio, Milton Kaplan expresses optimism about the future of poetry on the radio, arguing, however, that verse drama is better suited to the medium than lyric poetry.[8]

Millay, then, enters broadcasting at a moment of consolidation, reciting her poetry over one of the relatively new national networks. On Christmas Day in 1932, a Sunday night, Edna St. Vincent Millay read her poems over a nationwide hook-up on the WJZ Blue Network.[9] Audiences responded warmly to her work and she continued the broadcasts over a total of eight Sunday evenings through the winter of 1933. One of these sessions survives in recordings, enabling me to compare the sound of the broadcasts with printed remarks about them.

Millay would make famous and effective use of verse drama over the radio during the Second World War (Kaplan 14), but in the early thirties she was new to the medium. In fact, she may have been the first major American writer to broadcast her own work to the nation; her series represented an innovation for both poetry and radio. The full scope and effect of her early transmissions are hard to measure now. Poetic radio broadcasts, like poetry readings generally, are ephemeral events, surviving chiefly through contemporary accounts; recordings were relatively rare in the Modernist era. In this case, however, one of the sessions was preserved on two discs now archived in the Brander Matthews Collection at Columbia University with copies at the Library of Congress. In 2001, some of the poems from this recording, minus most of the introductory patter, were issued by Random House as part of an audio anthology.[10]

The archived recording is about twelve minutes long and seems to represent all or most of the program, not including any advertising that may have preceded or succeeded it.[11] This particular session clearly occurred during the middle of the series. She begins by explaining that she will not read her famous long poem, "Renascence," remarking that "so many of you have requested that" and promising to read it the following Sunday. Instead, she delivers eight shorter poems with brief intervening commentary. She identifies the collection in which each poem appears as well as its title but makes very few additional observations. In particular contrast to contemporary poetry readings, she never comments on the content of any of the poems, much less describes their sources in personal, social, or intellectual contexts. Millay presents these poems not as documents of personal experience or cultural history but as performance pieces.

Acting as a representative of high culture and deploying her considerable popularity over the airwaves, Millay serves corporate interests, both gathering an audience for advertising and easing fears over radio's bad influence. Further, she manipulates and advances radio's reputation as a "sincere medium" (Smulyan 78), a reputation that also serves the interests of advertisers. Millay's life and poetry were marked by radical social and political dissent, especially through her celebrations of female sexual freedom and resistance to censorship and discrimination, the latter exercised most famously through her protests against the Sacco and Vanzetti decision. The available information concerning her broadcasts, nevertheless, suggests that she did not select her most subversive poems for the airwaves, nor did she present herself in such a way as to challenge middle-class prejudices.

Her reading manner corresponds closely to contemporary accounts of her public style. Millay was trained to recite verse in an educational system strongly influenced by nineteenth-century theories of elocution.[12] Edmund Wilson, in fact, speculates that her transatlantic accent originated in this instruction: "I suppose it was partly the product of the English tradition in New England, and no doubt—since she had acted from childhood—of her having been taught to read Shakespeare by a college or school elocutionist" (749). Hilmes observes that "linguistic unity" was one of the utopian projects of early radio: "not only English, but proper, uninflected English, would become the national standard and norm—not a goal to be taken lightly amid the educational and regional diversity of the 1920s" (18). Millay's broadcasts, shaped by her mastery of the elocutionary arts, served an educational purpose even at the level of pronunciation.

Millay's performance skills were instrumental in her early success. They attracted the attention of the patron who funded her Vassar education: at the urging of her sister Norma, then working as a waitress at the Whitehall Inn in Camden, Maine, Vincent Millay played piano and sang for the summer guests, then recited "Renascence." According to Nancy Milford, one member of the audience, Caroline B. Dow, "was stunned by Millay's poem, but even more by this provincial girl's assured performance" (69). Dow arranged scholarships for Millay to attend Vassar after a year of preparatory coursework at Barnard.

Millay acted at Vassar and, after graduating in 1917, moved to New York

City and performed with the Provincetown Players. She soon became truly famous and successful as a performer of her own poetry.[13] Starting in the teens she recited her poems in a variety of venues, including bohemian parties, clubs, colleges, and large lecture halls. By 1933 she was not only a best-selling poet and a celebrity but also a veteran of protracted reading tours, which she claimed to dislike but which offered a significant source of income. In her letters, for example, she describes feeling like a prostitute during these events (181).

Descriptions of her performances typically emphasize the paradoxes of her physical presence: a powerful voice issuing from a slim figure in a long, formal gown. (Virtually everyone who reports on Millay's performances in articles, letters, and memoirs describes the fabric, cut, and color of her dresses.) They also indicate that she performed a series of roles as she read, altering her posture, gestures, and inflections to present a series of characters. Rosemary Sprague, for instance, describes how "the poet's face and figure change in interpretation from princess to slut at a lift of an eyebrow or twist of the lips, the movement of a hand or turn of the head" (137–38).[14]

Charles Bernstein writes that the poetry reading "materializes the text not the author," but the contrary seems true for Millay (13). Despite her delivery of each poem in the formal tones of her elocutionary training, even given her theatrical adoption of a series of characters, Millay clearly tried to materialize the author as well as the text. Further, although a few felt notably "unmoved" by her performances (Eastman 80), many experienced a connection across large halls with what they perceived to be the author's true self. Some audience members, despite the theatrics, found her poems to be "unobscured by posing and affectation" (Milford 260). As many of Millay's best readers have rightly observed, her persona was intrinsic to her work and its public success.[15]

Millay's colorful presence informed her live performances, but, like other modern era recitals, these were truly ephemeral; even contemporary poetry readings cannot be fully captured by video, and Millay's, of course, are only accessible now through print accounts. The poetic selves she presented were entirely vocal, and her presence more illusory, in her broadcasts.[16] The look of broadcasting studios, as well as Millay's appearance, were familiar to her listeners, so that they could visualize her speaking to them from a microphone somewhere in New York City.[17] Her listeners on those Sunday evenings were geographically but not temporally distant from the performance. In recordings, however, an illusion of presence is further attenuated. Millay hoped to reach posterity as well as paying contemporaries with her work, but sustaining the sorcery over generations is a tricky proposition; the recordings can no longer convey the qualities her contemporaries recognized as intimacy and naturalness.[18]

The recordings from the Brander Matthews collection indicate how intelligently Millay managed radio's relative limits and opportunities. As in her reading tours, she creates different voices for various poems by varying her pitch and timing significantly. Millay reads her sonnets from *Fatal Interview* in relatively deep, melancholy tones while other lyrics, especially "City Trees," elicit a high-pitched sweetness. Her slow, formal reading style also contrasts sharply with the intimate lightness of her commentary: in between poems, she speaks rapidly and casually. She successfully manipulates two media, the broadcast and print lyric, by understanding their point of intersection: all depend on the illusion of presence created by voice. The third medium under discussion—audio recording—was more difficult for Millay to manage because she did not anticipate how speaking and reading conventions would change in the second half of the twentieth century. Below, therefore, I treat the recordings primarily as documents of her radio practices. However, I do acknowledge that they also represent a foray into recording as a medium, and briefly analyze its outcome.

"To See You Speak": Print and Audiotext

Millay's selections for the recorded radio broadcast help define her on-air persona; they also reveal her understanding of radio's distinctiveness. Her comments about reader requests and plans for future evenings confirm that Millay chose a different set of pieces for each broadcast. In this particular performance, she reads short pieces from four volumes: *Renascence* (1917), *Second April* (1921), *The Harp Weaver* (1923), and *Fatal Interview* (1931). She skips the racier, urban poetry of *First Figs from Thistles* (1928) and the overtly political work collected in *The Buck in the Snow* (1928) in favor of poems concerning romantic love and the nature of beauty. Her playlist exhibits a variety of moods and ignores chronological order, proceeding as follows:

1. "God's World" (CP 32)[19]
2. "[Not in a silver casket cool with pearls]" (CP 640)
3. "[Moon, that against the lintel of the west]" (CP 656)
4. "[You say: 'Since life is cruel enough at best']" (CP 667)

5. "[Oh, sleep forever in the Latmian cave]" (CP 681)
6. "City Trees" (CP 54)
7. "[Euclid alone has looked on Beauty bare]" (CP 605)
8. "Elaine" (CP 96)

Although these choices surely represent a bid to please radio's heterogeneous audiences, they also reflect a particular concern with presence versus absence and the role of sound in poetry. While these themes intersect in many poems, in the following pages I will treat them separately, as far as possible.

In and beyond this broadcast, Millay's poetry urges the importance of sound not only through formal characteristics, such as rhythm and rhyme, but recurrent imagery of music and voice, especially birdsong. Millay chose poems for this program that invoke human voices and/or natural sounds, then turn away from them toward silence. Certainly it would have been difficult not to include these subjects, since such references dominate her work.[20] The context of radio, however, lends new resonance to these allusions. While printed poems engage silence visually through the existence of white space, and a performer standing before a crowd can use pauses strategically, silence over the radio becomes simply dead air. When the voice stops, the illusion of presence dissolves and the thread of connection between broadcaster and listener breaks. Although Millay was new to radio as a performance medium in 1933, her patter between readings demonstrates her desire to avoid aural white space. Before she reads "[You say: 'Since life is cruel enough at best']," for instance, Millay fills the air by remarking, "The next sonnet I'm going to read I'll have to hunt for because I've lost the page in the book. . . . I hope these pages aren't making an awful crackling noise. I know this is creating a pause for you." While Millay's comments create intimacy between listener and poet, they also throw into sharp relief the difference between unscripted speech and poetry reading. Between her firmly delineated performances of individual lyrics, Millay uses relatively casual language full of contractions, speaking more rapidly and in a higher pitch than she does while reciting verse.[21]

The content of the poems further highlights the interdependence of sound and silence. Millay begins the broadcast with an early poem, "God's World," apostrophizing creation with orgasmic passion that cannot be satisfied: "World, I cannot get thee close enough!" Radio affords simultaneous intimacy and distance, so Millay's poem exploits its new medium through that central metaphor. However, the final plea of "God's World" lays emphasis instead on the power of voice. Lest she be overwhelmed by loveliness, the speaker begs, "let no bird call," and Millay delivers these last words with particular slowness, elongating the final syllables of poetic ecstasy. This technique of stretching a poem's last phrase in performance and following that phrase with a pregnant pause in fact characterizes Millay's delivery of many of these pieces. The strategy both forestalls silence and invites it into the poem.

Millay also extends the final sounds of "[You say: 'Since life is cruel enough at best']." In this case, however, her strategy destabilizes rather than reinforces the printed poem's meaning. This piece appears in *Fatal Interview*, a book-length sequence of fifty-two Shakespearean sonnets chronicling a failing affair. Sonnet 38 is the only poem in the sequence to stage a dialogue between the pair, and it chiefly offers the male lover's excuses for ending the relationship. The first twelve and a half lines consist entirely of one convoluted sentence from the lover, failing to state a plain case for the relationship's dissolution. His wordy rationalization ends, appropriately enough, with an equivocal dash when the apparently impatient speaker intervenes: "Oh, tortured voice, be still! / Spare me your premise: leave me when you will." Her command to silence in short, direct phrases combines on the page with full rhyme and end-stopped lines to emphasize not only finality but also a tone of scathing disgust. At least in the 1933 broadcast, however, Millay's reading runs counter to impatience of the printed poem. Interpreting the last lines, Millay slows and deepens her voice, enacting a *reluctance* to part instead of a will to closure.[22]

Millay delivers "[You say: 'Since life is cruel enough at best']" and the other sonnets from *Fatal Interview* in a relatively low pitch, emphasizing their serious tone as well as the maturity of the speaker, whom the book characterizes as older than her gutless lover. When she performs the earlier "City Trees," however, she adopts a higher and lighter tone. Further, while she lends "City Trees" extra significance by remarking that "I thought of naming the book [*Second April*] for this poem," she also characterizes it with diminutive adjectives, referring to it as a "short poem" and a "little poem." While these comments trivialize the piece, littleness is also central to its point. Millay clearly identifies with the misplaced trees, and this contradictory language resembles the paradoxes of the petite, charismatic poet's physical presence. It also suggests the dialectic between sound and silence that characterizes not only this piece but also Millay's overall approach to the lyric in print and performance.

Speaking over WJZ, Millay raises her voice to evoke the "thin and sweet" music her speaker attributes to trees. This piece compares the voices of country trees with their urban sisters, who are "dumb / against the shrieking city air," to suggest the young poetess from Maine struggling to be heard against the clamor of Manhattan. The strong iambic rhythm, regular rhyme, and alliteration (especially sibilance) in both versions emphasize the music of poetry itself. The ending of the "City Trees," however, also calls attention to poetry's visual dimensions. It refers to sound as something she can see rather than actually hear: "I watch you when the wind has come,—" she apostrophizes the displaced trees, "I know what sound is there." If poems strive to make music, an art of sound, and yet on the page they can only offer inaudible signs of the will to music, this suggests that print cannot be poetry's primary medium. Reading poems, then, resembles reading sheet music: a skilled person can imagine what the notes would sound like, but the composition cannot achieve full existence until an instrument sounds the script.

"God's World," "[You say: 'Since life is cruel enough at best']," and "City Trees" invite Millay's radio audience to consider the centrality of sound and voice to poetry as well as highlighting the threat of dead air, the cessation of voice and connection. In so doing, they also emphasize the disembodied voices and illusion of presence that animate both printed poetry and radio as media. The issue of presence also haunts the other three poems Millay chooses to read from *Fatal Interview*. "[Moon, that against the lintel of the west"], for instance, beseeches that celestial body not to set so that the speaker may prolong her night with her beloved. In performance, Millay emphasizes syntax over line breaks, dramatizing her speaker's refusal of interruption. Future absence haunts the sound of the present.

Millay concludes the program with another piece in this mode, "Elaine," a dramatic monologue addressed to Lancelot by his abandoned lover. Elaine asks Lancelot to return to Astolat, then hypothetically discusses the questions she would not ask him and insists that he would not notice her presence—in fact, he would imagine that she had died and the gardens were empty. "I will not say how dear you are," she promises, and offers her own silence and even the landscape's quietness to please him: "So still the orchard, Lancelot, / So very still the lake shall be." The poem concludes with Elaine's own desire "To see you speak" from a distance, a reference to watching unheard sound that echoes the ending of "City Trees." Millay highlights the oddness of this poem's closure by reading against the iambic meter: instead of stressing the second and fourth syllables in the final phrase, "if you should smile," she places an unlikely accent on "if" and "should." The lilting surprise of Millay's performance focuses on Elaine's desperate self-prostration, on the conditional nature of her plea, and on the very small chance that she could woo Lancelot by effacing herself.

This seduction, premised on absence, strongly evokes the paradoxical nature of these radio broadcasts. Audiences listened to Millay's voice on wireless sets in rural living rooms, and like many announcers in that time, Millay cultivated the potential intimacy of this situation. She seems to have understood the irony of a disembodied voice: a reading shorn of theatrical spectacle seems to bring the poet closer to her audience than when she recites work in the same crowded hall. This is even more true in a live broadcast than it would be in a recording: no temporal distance exists between speaker and audience, although geography divides them.[23] By linking her position with Elaine's, Millay characterizes herself as an invisible seductress, seeking her audience's attention with exquisitely self-effacing modesty.

The Natural

Millay's constant troping on sound—hearing rather than seeing Beauty—in, for instance, "[Euclid alone has looked on Beauty bare]"—demonstrates her fascination with the relationship between poetry and performance. Her lyrics both depend on voice and call attention to its illusory nature, at least in poetry's textual incarnations. Further, Millay's first foray into radio demonstrates her grasp of that medium's similar magic: it manufactures intimate proximity despite distance and intervening machinery. Millay performs the same sleight-of-hand with the idea of naturalness. Just as her formal verse strives to convey impulsiveness and lack of artifice, Millay's mannered performance style, in fact, translated to authenticity for her contemporary audiences. Broadcast technology amplifies these effects. Millay's "naturalness" reveals important differences between Modernist and recent performance practices: the signifiers of authenticity have radically changed.

Some of the poems Millay chose to perform focus on resistance to natural processes: the speaker wishes to still the passage of time, for instance, in "[Moon, that against the lintel of the west]" and "[Oh, sleep forever in the Latmian cave]."[24] However, Sonnet 11 from *Fatal Interview* instead celebrates naturalness and derogates artifice. "[Not in a silver casket cool with pearls]" devotes its octave to descriptions of ornate, ingenious love-gifts. Both the casket and the poison ring are beautiful, valuable receptacles for well-concealed secrets, and therefore apt metaphors for the compact, cleverly wrought form of the sonnet. The sestet, however, compares the speaker's love to a series of unpretentious gifts offered openly: "cowslips in a hat," "apples in her skirt." The flowers and fruit are "natural" in that they arise from nature, unlike the casket and the ring, but they are also presented in a casual way as if unpremeditated by an uncalculating giver. Millay ends the poem by attributing a child's innocence to her speaker's closing remark: "'Look what I have!—And these are all for you.'"

Several contextual details draw my attention to these images. First, Millay may have been particularly mindful of the boundaries of the natural as she delivered her poetry through the relatively new technology of radio. Generally Millay resisted technological interventions between poet and audience—for example, there is a wonderful anecdote from one audience member, quoted in the recent biography, *Savage Beauty*, about Millay's refusal of amplification in the Los Angeles Philharmonic:

> She was to give a reading at the Los Angeles Philharmonic—a big place, packed to the top gallery. Bare stage, except for a standing mike. She came out, alone, wearing the usual loose something, green, I think. Standing well away from the mike, she began. Almost at once came cries of "Louder!" "Can't hear!," &, insistently,—"Use the mike!" A crescendo that drowned her out. She stood there, waited til it sank to grumbling, then gestured at the mike & said something like—"I will not tell my poems through this mechanical contraption. They come from me to you, direct. Please be entirely silent & I will make you hear me." Oh no! It started up again, and she resumed. Twice. My seat was very near the front, & I never felt such tension. Growing, too. There was resentment in it, then anger, finally real antagonism. I suppose it took 5 minutes, while she stood still & fought them. Scary minutes, for there was a sort of peak when she almost lost them. But she didn't. Somehow they did settle & listen. She said every poem she'd chosen, just with her voice, an hour or so of speaking. Then she turned to go off—& then the house came down. Cheers. People stood up. Some cried. It was a show of guts & stubbornness & pride. And foolishness, I suppose. (Milford 422–23)

Millay's training in theater enabled her to project her voice and communicate character in a large hall without amplification; this tale from the late 1930s reflects her confidence and experience. However, her quoted remarks also imply an aesthetic of intimacy and immediacy with which visible technology could interfere. Radio's difference, for Millay, may have resided in its resemblance to nineteenth-century reading practices: a voice delivering words at a normal volume in the family parlor, to a small group. As Barnouw observes, performers began to approach radio differently in the mid-twenties, when crystal sets in garages became cabinet-housed wireless sets in living rooms: "In 1922 performers still imagined themselves in a vast auditorium . . . but by 1925 a cozier image was established. Many artists liked to imagine the audience as 'a single person.' Letters encouraged this; no other medium had ever afforded an audience this illusion of intimacy shielded by privacy" (164).

A second reason for thinking about naturalness lies in the very sound of Millay's performance. To current listeners her pronunciation sounds comically artificial. When I play recordings of Millay to my undergraduates at Washington and Lee University, they invariably exclaim, "She sounds like Glinda the Good Witch!" However, this elocutionary manner seemed like the height of naturalness to many of Millay's own contemporaries. Perhaps responding to this very broadcast, one audience member wrote: "Don't ever change, and become stiff or formal or eloquent. . . . You sound so real, so natural, so—so very much alive" (qtd. in Milford 368).[25] This quotation—and it's not an isolated remark—illustrates how profoundly conventions of naturalness have changed in just eighty years. It also helps to ground the American poetry reading in history, demonstrating some of the profound changes that have occurred in an underexamined poetic institution.

Throughout the latter part of the twentieth century, the sound of poetic authenticity has been free verse presented in the manner Peter Middleton describes: "A person stands alone in front of an audience, holding a text and speaking in an odd voice, too regular to be conversation, too intimate and too lacking in orotundity to be a speech or a lecture, too rough and personal to be theater" (*Distant Reading* 262). Other performance aesthetics have coexisted with this one, from Beat-era chanting to hip-hop–influenced poetry jams, and perhaps the sound of authenticity in American poetry has shifted again—my current students are suddenly claiming a preference for formal verse, perhaps influenced by rap's accentual rhythms and intricate rhymes. However, in the 1930s, what sounded artificial were the deliberate jolts and disharmonies of Modernist *vers libre*. Millay, on the other hand, transmitted the sounds her audience had grown up with: formal poetry read aloud in parlors, recitation clubs, school auditoriums.

Millay's aims, in this respect, again resonate with the network interests, and not only because she pitches her performance to please a wide audience. As Smulyan argues, advertisers promoting radio sales in the 1920s pitched broadcasting as a "sincere" medium, as "incorruptible" as photography was understood to be: "the imposition of a machine was perceived to give the information an additional veracity. Radio, in the argument of the promoters, could protect the listener/consumer by automatically exposing lies" (78). The more radio is perceived as a trustworthy medium, the more advertisers are attracted to it, and the more profits networks stand to realize. Millay's poetic broadcasts capitalize on the increasing association of radio voices with sincerity but also help to bolster that association.

Millay's investment in "naturalness," on forging connections with her middlebrow audience, has contributed to her exclusion from the canon of Modernism, as Clark argues so convincingly. However, her manipulation of poetry's many media also signals how aware she was that authenticity constitutes a pose, conditioned by context. Millay's work may evidence more delight in art's illusions than some of her contemporaries. However, whether the definition of Modernism requires expansion or whether Modernism's very curricular and scholarly dominance needs to be challenged, Millay should not be relegated to that movement's margins. Her radio broadcasts, other performances, and the published texts all demonstrate a radically open approach to the lyric. For this reason, as well as for the challenges her poems and performance pose about gender roles, Millay's complex and entertaining work still merits the prominence it earned in her own time.

Conclusion

> Last Night I heard upon the Air
> A little man who wasn't there.
> He wasn't there again today
> I hope he'll never go away.
> —Edna St. Vincent Millay

Edgar Bergen, the famous ventriloquist, and his dummy, Charlie McCarthy, made their radio debut in 1936, a few years after Millay began performing in that medium. From a twenty-first-century perspective, ventriloquism meeting popular success over the radio is profoundly strange (Steven Connor 22, 402). However, the fragment of occasional verse above is evidence of Millay's attitude toward radio as a technology. Most important, it manifests her delight in radio's illusions. According to Margaret Cuthbert, the poet was "a Charlie McCarthy fan [and] once expressed her appreciation to Edgar Bergen" in the quatrain quoted above (62).

Millay's jingle echoes a well-known verse by writer and progressive educator Hughes Mearns, "Antigonish":

> As I was going up the stair
> I met a man who wasn't there!
> He wasn't there again to-day!
> I wish, I *wish* he'd stay away! (Baker 326)

As in Mearns's spooky rhyme, radio presents a paradox of presence in absence. The "Air" constitutes a medium for uncanny meetings; the broadcast voice enables an unlikely intimacy despite physical distance. For Millay and others, however, such hauntings were entirely welcome. In fact, Millay recognized that in these qualities, radio possesses an inherent likeness to the printed lyric poem—a medium similarly haunted by impossible presence.

Millay's broadcasts offer important insights into the intersections between performed and printed poetry, and how acoustical technologies (voice transmission in radio, particularly) complicate the dynamic. She anticipates Ong and McLuhan by understanding print itself as a mediating technology, different from but also resembling the estranging contraptions of broadcasting in the 1930s. Millay experiments with the "acoustical technologies that grew up with modernism," as Adalaide Morris puts it (Introduction 8), but for her it does not inspire Joycean cacophonies (as James A. Connor argues) or a renewed interest in national poetic forms such as epic (as Morris finds in "Sound Technologies").

Michael Davidson, writing persuasively about postmodern poets Allen Ginsberg, David Antin, and others, finds that some artists use the newly cheap and available technology of tape recording to produce a "poetics of presence" (117): tape recording, he writes, "transformed the notion of voice from something heard to something overheard" (99). Davidson's implicit allusion to John Stuart Mill's definition of lyric as "overheard utterance," however, actually undermines his point. The paradox of disembodied presence was, in fact, a central trope and strategy of the printed lyric long before recording technology became available or radio pioneer Reginald Fessenden managed to transmit the human voice. Print itself is a distancing technology; Millay's poetry proves this point. Radio's heterogeneous voices changed the sound of the world and infiltrated modern literature in the ways Connor and

Morris suggest, but broadcasting poetry does not necessarily transform it, or dismantle the lyric I, or force modern alienation upon texts or their audiences. Advances in acoustical technologies may, however, have fostered or inspired some kinds of poetry that are intensely sound-saturated.

Millay's poetry is more closely attuned to aural elements than to visual elements. However, it does demonstrate a persistent self-consciousness about both aspects of poetry. By encoding performance so insistently within printed poetry, and by dramatically performing poems that represent sound in visual terms, Millay interrogates the status of the lyric poem. Her testing of lyric boundaries, however, has been less visible because she mounts this challenge from a different direction than many of her contemporaries. Millay explores the limits and advantages of the modern lyric in various media. Her experimentation may not be recognizably Modernist, and yet it plays a significant role in the technological and cultural changes that transformed American life in this period. She was not only a fan of radio magic but also an important participant in it. Her broadcasts represent an important example of how twentieth-century technology shapes poetic practice, and of how poetry can interpret modernity.

Notes

1. Bernstein, for example, argues that audiotexts destabilize a poem's meaning by highlighting its multiform existence (10); although he is concerned chiefly with contemporary innovative poetries, his remark holds true for Millay's performances as well. Also see Middleton on the performance of authorship (*Distant Reading* 33–35).

2. This fundamental tension between poetry's visual and aural dimensions has been described by different theorists in different terms. See Frye on "babble" versus "doodle" (which he also calls "melos" and "opsis") (274), for instance, or, more recently, Stewart on "the phonic and the graphic" (24).

3. This essay benefits enormously from essay collections that focus on poetry variously called avant-garde, innovative, or experimental (edited by Bernstein, Morris, Kahn, and Whitehead); the scholars featured in them are responsible for much of the best work on poetry and radio. Nevertheless, I resist the idea that studying works aimed at relatively small audiences is the best way to measure the impact of acoustical technologies on literature.

4. See Barnouw 284 on Roosevelt's fireside chats. Smulyan argues for radio's illusion of sincerity and naturalness (77–78).

5. Hilmes's *Radio Voices* focuses on radio as a social practice with particular attention to its culture-building potential and its participation in shaping gender roles; see 14–17 especially.

6. Saerchinger's memoir describes his efforts to persuade the literary lights of Britain to broadcast to American audiences. His success was limited. The conditions of British radio during this period are somewhat different from those in the United States, but across the Atlantic some writers were issuing their own rousing calls to poets: for instance, George Orwell, in *Poetry and the Microphone*, investigates "the possibilities of the radio as a means of popularising poetry" (76).

7. As Barnouw observes, Kreymborg, Benet, Auden, and Millay did subsequently produce verse plays for radio (2.69). Also see Barnouw on the laws regulating copyright permissions on broadcast poetry performances (2.100).

8. McLuhan also writes about the radio "[giving] us back the poet's voice as an important dimension of poetic experience" (*Understanding Media* 53). For contemporary comments on the real and possible intersections between radio and poetry, see Breiner and Spinelli, "Not Hearing."

9. See Barnouw 191 on the history of the "red" and "blue" networks.

10. I listened to these recordings at the Library of Congress during the summer of 2004. Excerpts are available commercially through the *Voice of the Poet* series.

11. The Library of Congress bibliographic entry describes the originals as "1930s instantaneous discs"—this probably means 78rpm shellac discs. The original recording exists on two discs, each containing a maximum of 4 1/2 minutes per side; sometimes comments or the beginning of a poem are cut off.

12. See Middleton (*Distant Reading* 85–92) on the importance of elocution to modern era poetry recitation and Rasula on "the unique soundscape of Victorian poetics" (247).

13. For accounts of Millay's performance style, see Milford, especially 259–61, 270–74, 307, 419–23; Jean Gould, 73–74, 231–34; Eastman 80; Wilson 749–50; Sprague 137–38; Thesing 12–13.

14. Millay's highly gendered performances are especially interesting in light of public anxieties about women's disembodied voices on the radio, although these prohibitions applied to women announcers more often than to women performers; see Hilmes 136–41.

15. See Clark, "Uncanny" 3–26; Gilbert, "Female" and "Directions"; Miller 16–40; Walker.

16. Orwell posits that this separation of poet from audience in fact benefits broadcasting, praising "the special advantage of the radio, its power to select the right audience, and to do away with stage fright and embarrassment" (76). Broadcasting cannot offer immediate connection, which means for the poet that "the audience *has no power over you*" (77).

17. As Steven Connor writes, "the radio studio or theatre was often enough portrayed in photographs to be immanent in the listening eye of the audience" (402).

18. Milford quotes a friend of Margaret Cuthbert's: "'You know, Edna did not want to record her voice, Margaret persuaded her to do it in the name of posterity. I can still hear her talking to Edna, telling her what it would mean someday, in the future'" (368).

19. I abbreviate Millay's *Collected Poems* throughout as CP.

20. Allusions to sound and silence are particularly interesting in Millay's elegies. I discuss this in my book *Voicing American Poetry*.

21. Millay's remarks evoke the casual intimacy of many professional announcers. For instance, Kaplan quotes an opening ramble by Ted Malone, who started reading poetry on the air in 1928: "I see you are alone. . . . Now I'll just take this rocker here by the radio and chat awhile."(208).

22. Both printed and audio versions of the poem also manifest Millay's complex understanding of poetic voice. While Millay has so often been called a songbird, as if her lyrics are natural and instinctive, this sonnet mimics two "tortured voice[s]," distinct in tone both on the page and on the air. The only bird present is a seagull's chick, metaphorically representing the "love" or relationship rather than the poet. This creature is "hushed" because his life depends on silence and surrounded by the "hiss" of a dangerous ocean. Millay thereby emphasizes the conditions framing poetic sounds. An uneasy gap exists between the performed and printed sonnet, resembling the parallel divide between the sonnet and the voices it may conjure.

23. See Hayles, who describes the additional distance recording creates between presence and voice—temporal as well as spatial ("Voices" 76). Radio itself creates only spatial distance.

24. Some poems also occur in a hypothetical future; time is of particular concern in how Millay refers to nature.

25. See Furr, whose essay includes other telling examples from the Millay archives at Vassar.

CHAPTER 14

Updating Baudelaire for the Radio Age

The Refractive Poetics of "The Pleasures of Merely Circulating"

J. STAN BARRETT

Anxiety about audience preoccupied Wallace Stevens during the composition of *Ideas of Order* and affected his use of abstraction in his poetry throughout the 1930s. The flood of cultural production for which the 1930s is well known made Stevens defensive about poetry's place amid America's vast array of cultural offerings. In a letter Stevens wrote to Ronald Latimer in 1935 about reprinting *Ideas of Order* in a popular edition, Stevens agrees to Latimer's proposal without enthusiasm, stating flatly that "selling poetry now-a-days must be very much like selling lemonade to a crowd of drunks" (*Letters* 284). His concerns about poetry's diminished audience, somewhat tempered by his firm belief that poetry is properly intended for the social elite, were further complicated by his sustained interest in settling for himself the nature of the poet's social function. Pursuing this line of inquiry, almost obligatory for American poets writing during the Great Depression, Stevens composed several poems—"Farewell to Florida," "Sailing after Lunch," "The American Sublime," "Sad Strains of a Gay Waltz," and "Mozart, 1935"—whose images of crowds focus Stevens's thinking about a poetry uncompromised by pressures he imagined as the public's demands upon the artist. These poems inevitably failed to assuage Stevens's anxiety or resolve his complex and contradictory aspirations for poetry, and instead of any remedy, what emerges from them is a clear picture of the increasingly powerful compulsion Stevens felt to hold his audiences at bay.[1]

In *Ideas of Order* abstraction becomes Stevens's mechanism for coping with his desire to be socially engaged while satisfying a much stronger desire to distance his own thinking from the public's thoughts, which Stevens strongly associated with radio. Deliberately emptying his language of content, Stevens arranges poems like "The Pleasure of Merely Circulating" as screens to block or diffuse the associations of his poetic language with the ideas and discourses continuously broadcast over America's airwaves. His poems take up the work of restoring the intersubjective distance between writer and reader that he believed radio had helped to collapse.

"A Spirit Storming in Blank Walls": Updating Baudelaire

By the mid-1930s Stevens felt that one no longer needed to leave the house in order to jostle against the crowd, though by that time he had had at least a decade to grow accustomed to radio. Explaining to Louis Untermeyer in January 1925 why he had recently been too preoccupied to correspond, he remarks, "There are a great many things cutting in nowadays. There is a baby and a radio, and I am expecting to go to Florida in a week or so" (*Letters* 244). Stevens bought his first radio, which entered his home with a disruptive force commensurate with the arrival of his daughter, at the beginning of America's radio craze, even before the first nationwide broadcasting system had become operational. Nevertheless, in both "The Irrational Elements of Poetry" and "The Noble Rider and the Sound of Words," Stevens's remarks show that he still experienced radio as alien and intrusive, and he describes feeling besieged by radio's continuous talk about world events.

In "The Irrational Element of Poetry," a speech he delivered at Harvard in December 1936, Stevens calls the ceaseless reporting and discussion of world events "the pressure of the contemporaneous," which "from the time of the beginning of the World War to the present time has been constant and extreme":

> We are preoccupied with events, even when we do not observe them closely. We have a sense of upheaval. We feel threatened. We look from an uncertain present toward a more uncertain future. One feels the desire to collect oneself against all this in poetry as well as in politics. (*Opus* 229)

By the time he delivered his "Noble Rider" speech at Harvard in the spring of 1941, the sense of claustrophobia permeating his 1937 speech had become more intense still:

For more than ten years now, there has been an extraordinary pressure of news—let us say, news incomparably more pretentious than any description of it, news, at first, of the collapse of our system, or, call it, of life; then of news of a new world, but of a new world so uncertain that one did not know anything whatever of its nature . . . ; and finally news of a war, which was a renewal of what, if it was not the greatest war, became such by this continuation. And for more than ten years, the consciousness of the world has concentrated on events which have made the ordinary movement of life seem to be the movement of people in the intervals of a storm. (*Necessary* 20)

Even for so turbulent a period as the early 1940s, the level of anxiety about world events conveyed by this passage's crescendo would seem unaccountable were it not for the way the passage begins to reveal Stevens's profound discomfort with radio's properties as a medium. When Stevens characterizes the news as "incomparably more pretentious than any description of it," his use of the word "news" waivers tellingly, referring at once to the events that make legitimate but overwhelming claims on one's attention and to the news broadcasts themselves, which melodramatically proclaim "the collapse of our system" and the advent of "a new world." Radio stories *were* written to project "a much sharper sense of urgency and immediacy" than newspaper versions of the same stories (Czitrom 87);[2] but radio's overheated treatment of the day's news was only a symptom of those properties of radio that dramatically intensified the "pressure of the contemporaneous" for Stevens.

If the shocks Baudelaire received walking through crowded Parisian streets were an exemplary experience of nineteenth-century modernity, encountering a discursive crowdedness in one's living room each night was similarly emblematic of modern experience in the 1920s and 1930s. Radio's early observers intuitively compared these experiences. In their 1935 study *Psychology of Radio*, Hadley Cantril and Gordon Allport enthusiastically write, "Heretofore 'crowds' meant chiefly congregate clusters of people sharing and giving expression to a common emotion. But now, as never before, crowd mentality may be created and sustained without the contagion of personal contact" (21). Being rid of the "contagion of personal contact" is sanitizing and self-evidently salutary in Cantril and Allport's account. For Stevens, though, radio achieved this "crowd mentality" through a power to collapse interpersonal space more threatening than the "contagion" of physical contact. Early broadcasters cultivated ways of addressing the public that would erode interpersonal boundaries. They quickly discovered that effective radio technique involved using colloquial language and homely allusions, "[reminding the] audience that millions are listening," and "[painting] a picture of a vast, unified, national audience" (Douglas, *Listening In* 133). These techniques accentuated a power to overcome such boundaries still more fundamental to radio. Cantril and Allport write:

> When a million or more people hear the same subject matter, the same arguments and appeals, the same music and humor, when their attention is held in the same way and at the same time to the same stimuli, it is psychologically inevitable that they should acquire in some degree common interests, common tastes, and common attitudes. (20)

While the language of "psychological inevitability" now seems far too rigid to describe the range of responses listeners have to any given broadcast, Cantril and Allport accurately capture initial reactions to the novelty of hearing so many people discussing a single program or news report. Certainly for Stevens, the "extraordinary pressure of news" is related to its wide dissemination. "According to a *Fortune* survey made in 1939," David Czitrom writes in his history of radio, "70 percent of Americans relied on the radio as their prime source of news" (86). As never before, radio made commonplace the experience of hearing in others' conversations the substance of one's own preoccupations.

Radio then confronted Stevens as a set of unpleasant contradictions that upset the relations between distance and intimacy his poetry depends upon. Radio's audience was a collective, simultaneous attention, large and anonymous, an abstract and imagined energy spread out over vast distances; but at the same time, radio in the 1930s was still the startlingly intimate experience of a voice making its way across these spaces to address one familiarly in one's own living room. The intimate touch of an unfamiliar voice, the simultaneous feeling of isolation and of dissolving into an unimaginably vast community—for Stevens, these contradictions made the experience of listening to the radio uncanny. "Noble Rider and the Sound of Words" shows us how strongly attuned he was to the recurrence of this uncanny feeling when, in casual conversation with others, one hears the echoes of familiar ideas and suddenly finds oneself in an alienated relation to one's own thoughts. In the essay "Surety and Fidelity Claims" that Stevens wrote for The Hartford's in-house publication the *Eastern Underwriter*, he says,

A man in the home office tends to conduct his business on the basis of the papers that come before him. After twenty-five years or more of that sort of thing, he finds it difficult sometimes to distinguish himself from the papers he handles and comes almost to believe that he and his papers constitute a single creature, consisting principally of hands and eyes: lots of hands and lots of eyes. (*Opus* 239)

Similarly, in "Noble Rider," though he does not formulate the matter with such concision, Stevens expresses the fear that after fifteen years of listening to the radio, he has become a tissue of voices. When Stevens speaks of "the desire to collect [himself in his poems] against" the present's threats, he not only has in mind his exasperation at feeling an uncertainty about the future that grows the more he listens to news bulletins but also the threats to identity and self inextricably linked to the way radio mediates his experience of the war. In "A Postcard from the Volcano," Stevens imagines that future generations will perceive him as "a spirit storming in blank walls," haunting a mansion he describes as surrounded by a "windy sky" that "cries out a literate despair" (*Collected* 159, 21, 12, 13). In the 1930s the blank walls of his poetry's abstraction were erected as a measure of defense against the discourses of world events that were eroding the imaginative distance between individuals that Stevens saw as a prerequisite for poetry.

Like many writers in the twentieth century, Stevens intuitively understands media's effects through the metaphor of prosthesis, imagining the radio as an extension of the nervous system.[3] In *Civilizations and Its Discontents*, Sigmund Freud describes "man" as "perfecting his own organs, whether motor or sensory, or . . . removing the limits to their functioning" in order to become a "kind of prosthetic god" (43). Freud cautions, though, that humanity's "fairy-tale wish" of becoming a god was coming true "in the fashion in which ideals are usually attained. . . . Not completely; in some respects not at all, in others only half way" (44). In his popular and influential *Public Opinion* (1922), written before radio had become a prominent feature of American life, Walter Lippmann had already used this metaphor of prosthesis to consider how, in its partial realization, the fulfillment of humanity's fairy-tale wish affected American democracy. Lippmann's concerns arise from his recognition that Americans were increasingly called upon to make political choices about situations remote from their daily lives:

The world that we have to deal with politically is out of reach, out of sight, out of mind. It has to be explored, reported, and imagined. . . . [Man] has invented ways of seeing what no naked eye could see, of hearing what no ear could hear, of weighing immense masses and infinitesimal ones, of counting and separating more items than he can individually remember.... Gradually he makes for himself a trustworthy picture inside his head of the world beyond his reach. (18)

Despite his conviction that, however conscientiously assembled, newspapers can never transmit a worldview comprehensive and thorough enough to engender truly sound political judgments, Lippmann is optimistic about new technologies' potential for producing complete representations of the world. He simply wishes to discover methods of integrating the fragmented information technology that helps generate into linear, discursive forms. In effect, he calls for a benevolent government bureaucracy so perfectly organized that it renders the interrelation of information gathered throughout the globe transparent.

Stevens's response to radio, on the other hand, anticipates that the individual's capacity for representing and thinking about the world will never master the increasingly rapid dissemination of fragmentary and piecemeal information. Surprisingly, Stevens's understanding of radio follows premises most forcefully (and glibly) articulated by Marshall McLuhan in his *Understanding Media* (1964), which amounts to a dogged pursuit of precisely this metaphor of prosthesis. Though Stevens shares nothing of McLuhan's blithe satisfaction, like McLuhan, he assumes that "the effects of technology do not occur at the level of opinions or concepts, but alter sense ratios or patterns of perception steadily and without resistance" (18). For this reason, "the 'message' of any medium or technology" as McLuhan writes, glossing his most famous and oft-repeated dictum, "is the change of scale or pace or pattern that it introduces into human affairs" (8). In the third section of his "Noble Rider" speech, building to his remarks on radio, Stevens enumerates changes in the "normal conditions" of everyday life that impact the imagination: "The enormous influence of education in giving everyone a little learning," "the penetration of the masses of people by the ideas of liberal thinkers," the fact that people "no longer live in homes but in housing projects," and the way workers "become, at their work, in the face of the machines, something approximating an abstraction, an energy" (*Necessary* 18, 19). Stevens's list of concerns is a chain of metonymies for "change[s] of scale or pace or pattern" that enforce a distressing proximity of thought between people.

That changes of scale, pace, or pattern are decisive for Stevens becomes clear when he explains why, precisely, the pressures exerted on the imagination in 1941 are so much more substantial than those felt by "Coleridge and Wordsworth and Sir Walter Scott and Jane Austen":

> It seems possible to say that they [Coleridge et al.] knew of the events of their day much as we know of the bombings in the interior of China and not at all as we know of the bombings of London, or, rather, as we should know of the bombings of Toronto or Montreal. (*Necessary* 21)

Stevens's concerns are at once more urgent and less focused than, for example, those Virginia Woolf presents in a speech entitled "The Leaning Tower," which she delivered to Brighton's Workers' Educational Association in May 1940. Woolf's remarks, which benefit from her more incisive and more patient critical acumen, proceed from a startlingly similar set of observations. She is drawn to consider how the poet's imagination is impacted by disparate modern phenomena—war news heard over the "wireless" and an acute class consciousness, for example. Woolf suggests that such preoccupations of modern life have eroded the security and leisure requisite for the nineteenth-century artist's imagination and productivity. Because the consciousness of poets who began writing after the Great War (like W. H. Auden and Louis MacNeice) obliges them to critique a society whose injustices make their careers possible, Woolf argues, their work is necessarily compromised. Yet Woolf also sees these poets' highly developed capacity for self-criticism as pointing the way to a more promising art precisely because their ability to tell the truth will enable them to know themselves and others more intimately—"If you do not tell the truth about yourself you cannot tell it about other people," she writes (177). For Stevens, on the contrary, the radio's undesirable intimacy and its penchant for expanding one's conscious concerns do not offer any compensatory possibilities for poetry. This intimacy is simply a form of shock that threatens to reorganize daily experience as decisively as shock, according to Walter Benjamin, reorganized nineteenth-century urban experience for Baudelaire.

Borrowing from Freud's *Beyond the Pleasure Principle*, Benjamin argues that consciousness is an energy directed toward preserving the human psyche from the incessant shock of sensory perception. The more energy the mind devotes to consciousness to parry these shocks, the less receptive it is to sensory perceptions that escape consciousness but, registered by the mind nonetheless, survive as "deep memory traces" to become the bedrock of experience. Consciousness, on the other hand, "sterilizes memory for experience" (162). Individuals' exposure to endless sensory shock and the consequent expansion of their conscious life, according to Benjamin, pose a fundamental problem for modern life because they heighten individuals' craving for sensation while destroying the communal character of experience proper. In Benjamin's formulation, experience proper only comes about when individual memory traces mix with communal memory, especially in ritualized, communal activity. Something of elegy, then, clings to the poems Baudelaire writes for "readers to whom the reading of lyric poetry would present difficulties.... Will power and the ability to concentrate are not their strong points; what they prefer is sensual pleasures; they are familiar with the 'spleen' which kills interest and receptiveness" (*Illuminations* 155). Baudelaire marks the passing of a communal experience from which he himself was excluded by re-creating in the reader the shock that usurped it.

Whereas Baudelaire recognized himself in the "least rewarding type of audience" that he famously addressed as "*Hypocrite lecteur,—mon sembleble,—mon frère*," Stevens's empathy for his audience was limited by his conception of imagination as contingent on interpersonal space between poet and audience. When he considers the worker as reader, for example, his attitude verges on scornful: "The time must be coming when, as they leave the factories, they will be passed through an air-chamber or a bar to revive them for riot or reading" (*Necessary* 19). Stevens is primarily concerned with preserving those boundaries guaranteeing the solidity of his identity that allow him to imagine the world. At the heart of the third section of "Noble Rider," Stevens expresses his fear that radio is collapsing them:

> It is not only that there are more of us and that we are actually close together. We are close together in every way. We lie in bed and listen to a broadcast from Cairo, and so on. There is no distance. We are intimate with people we have never seen, and unhappily, they are intimate with us. Democritus plucked his eye out because he could not look at a woman without thinking of her as a woman. If he had read a few of our novels, he would have torn himself to pieces. Dr. [I. A.] Richards has noted "the wide-spread increase in the aptitude of the average mind for self-dissolving introspection, the generally heightened awareness of the goings-on of our own minds, *merely as goings-on.*" This is nothing to the generally heightened awareness of the goings-on of other people's minds, *merely as goings-on.* (*Necessary* 18–19, Stevens's emphasis)

Radio's power to erode even imaginative distance brings Stevens to a fevered level of anxiety that shows itself in the rhythm of this passage, in the aside "unhappily," in the extremity of the image he borrows from the life of Democritus, and most especially, in the phrase "*merely as goings-on,*" which he twice marks for emphasis to stress just how unsettling is familiarity with the detritus of others' minds. Having daily to hear in radio broadcasts evidence that the goings-on in a person's head could be regarded as the mere circulation or gratuitous movement of ready-made thought threatened the imagination for Stevens in a uniquely powerful way. His fears of mental proximity with others undoubtedly reflect his race, class, and gender anxieties. It is the unlooked-for confidence from Cairo, or the chaos of the worker's need for riot, or the unsettling eroticism of encounters with the thoughts of women that Stevens expressly wishes to avoid. But telling as these anxieties are, they are not simply the truth of Stevens's fear of the changes in patterns of perception that the modern world has introduced. They are preliminary expressions of the uncertainty that follows the discovery that the old criteria for identity, however problematic, do not hold. "We live in the mind," Stevens writes in the "Adagia" (*Opus* 190), but Stevens's mental life here is embattled, awash in the fragments of others' speech, and unable to integrate exposure to this debris into any conception of identity or experience.

"Poetry is a cure of the mind" (*Opus* 201), Stevens says in the "Adagia," and his poetic practice in the 1930s defends against the mental claustrophobia that threatens him. Stevens's defense is not conceptual. He does not, for example, evolve an idea of identity or experience that answers the threats he perceives. Nor does he give us an image that synthesizes his impressions of radio's crowd of voices, as Baudelaire's gambler synthesizes Baudelaire's impressions of the Parisian crowd.[4] Instead, Stevens evolves a use of language, a poetics that depends for its effects on undecidability and abstraction. His poems empty the words that compose them of connotative value, and thus his poems, though they exist in a space of heightened discursive struggle, are themselves emptied of explanation, of opinion, and of personal appeal. Stevens writes in "Noble Rider" that "a variation between the sound of words in one age and the sound of words in another age is an instance of the pressure of reality" (*Necessary* 13). Conflicts between the denotative and connotative values of words, Stevens continues, in which words' meanings (or their sound, as he puts it) change from one age to the next, "are nothing more than changes in the relation between the imagination and reality" (13). Over the course of the 1930s, Stevens responds to modernity's assault on the imagination by developing a refractive poetics. His poems parry the discursive connotations that accrue to words through public debate, and in this way, Stevens aims to restore the imaginative space that he saw the medium of radio as collapsing.

The Refractive Poetics of "The Pleasures of Merely Circulating"

Stevens's strange short poem "The Pleasures of Merely Circulating" illustrates the complex relation between Stevens's language use and his politics. In spite of its being "a gorgeous bit of nonsense,"[5] this poem exerts a fascination for critics proportional to the challenge of explaining why, precisely, its ideas and images exist in so uneasy a relation to its tone. It is a gorgeous bit of nonsense in spite of the fact that it touches on the most menacing social and political problems facing the Western World in the early and mid-1930s.

The poem comprises three four-line stanzas, the first of which is disarmingly airy and repetitive:

> The garden flew round with the angel,
> The angel flew round with the clouds,
> And the clouds flew round and the clouds flew
>   round
> And the clouds flew round with the clouds. (*Collected* 149, 1–4)

The second stanza sounds a far more ominous note, asking in a more abrupt and direct language whether there is any secret in the "cattle skulls in the woods" (*Collected* 150, 6), and whether "the drummers in black hoods" (7) mean anything by the rumbling of their drums. The third stanza recaptures the first's whimsical tone but begins with an observation whose specificity contrasts sharply with what comes before. The third stanza asserts enigmatically, "Mrs. Anderson's Swedish baby / Might well have been German or Spanish" (9–10), before concluding with the thoroughly unsatisfactory summation that everything going round "Has rather a classical sound" (12).

James Longenbach's concise description of the poem serves as a useful first approach. "'The Pleasures of Merely Circulating,'" he writes, "presents a vista of order so vast that it seems anything but orderly" and teaches "that orderly music should not lull us into complacency or blind us to a world where things are not so orderly" (152). His reading, which orients us toward the questions of order that clearly preoccupy Stevens in the 1930s, readily accounts for the grim irony that obtains between the poem's contexts and its cavalier spirit; but it does not contend with the frustration Stevens lays in store for the reader who aims to understand the poem in terms of the political and social problems it brushes against.

Such an understanding proves elusive. An excavation of the poem's historical contexts supports, to an unusual degree, an indeterminate number of readings that undermine any attempt to discover a coherent political argument in the poem. For example, Joseph Harrington writes of the third stanza:

> Swedes, Germans, Spaniards: we are all equivalent and abstract individuals in both liberal theory and in Stevens's poetic. Moreover, that things are interchangeable and go round and round has rather the sound of classical political economy: money can circulate due to its alienable and abstract character. (108)

These remarks advance Harrington's thesis that "a liberal political economy must be maintained for Stevens's poetic economy to remain healthy" (109), but Harrington's assumption of equivalence between Swedish, German, and Spanish is ill-founded. These nationalities cannot have been chosen arbitrarily by Stevens in 1934. Sweden was the envy of the world's capitalist nations then, its economy running prosperously in a time of global depression, as was well known to regular readers of the morning paper. In a letter dated May 12, 1933, Stevens writes: "Economically things are so low down there [in Key West] that a depression is an impossibility. If things go from bad to worse [here in Hartford], I am either going to move to a farm in Sweden or a houseboat in Key West Harbor" (*Letters* 267). Key West, because of its poverty, and Sweden, because of its prosperity, both seemed to Stevens impervious to the effects of the Depression. Spain, on the other hand, was sinking into its bloody civil war and Germany was organizing itself into a fascist state. Both national crises were accelerated and intensified by economic crises. The choice of nationalities in the poem highlights extreme differences in socioeconomic and political circumstances. Though the world would certainly go on turning if Mrs. Anderson's Swedish baby were born into a less stable political situation, this does not make those circumstances insignificant.

Stevens chooses nationalities that give his poem a measure of political gravitas, but there is no argument in the poem, no acceleration that would translate this weight into force. And though the poem's title suggests the futility of looking for such an argument, the ominous rumbling in the second stanza and the specific, political contrast in the third warn us that the title may be misleading. The word "circulating" is itself so volatile a word in the 1930s that it butts up awkwardly against the idea of pleasure. It conjures associations with a number of foreign and domestic crises that might be described as problems of circulation. Consider the following three examples:

War debts: In an arrangement that has aptly been described as a "surreal financial merry-go-round," the United States loaned money to Germany so that Germany could pay war reparations to England and France. England and France, in turn, used this money to repay its large war debts to the United States. This arrangement predictably led to disaster. This "inherently unstable" system, David Kennedy writes, was "rudely shoved out of balance when the stock market crash of late 1929 dried up the well of American credit, knocking a crucial link out of the circuit of international cash flows" (73).

Tariffs: To varying degrees Congress, Hoover, and Roosevelt all imagined economic isolation as an effective strategy for combating the Depression. Forbidding barriers hindering international trade were established, including the notoriously ill-considered Smoot-Hawley Tariff (1930), "the effect of which," Piers Brendon writes, "was to provoke massive retaliation abroad and to tighten the garrote on world trade" (72).

Inflation: The world had also recently seen the effects of money's fevered circulation. In 1923, Germany's efforts to "hold the mark at a rate of about 2,000 to the dollar" failed. The value of the mark diminished with meteoric speed, "[transforming life] into a bizarre paperchase." "In July 23 there were 353,412 marks to the dollar; in August, 4,620,455; in September, 98,860,000; in October, 25,260,208,000; in November, 4,200,000,000,000," Brendon writes. The pace of inflation was such that "patrons of restaurants found their meals becoming more expensive as they ate," and "factory workers saw their wages shrinking in value as they queued to collect them" (28).

Most conspicuously, the poem's airy feel sharply contrasts with the grim reality of money's failure to circulate in America in the 1930s. But once one begins to ask what "circulating" might have to do with the ominous drumbeating in the middle of the poem, it is difficult to know where to bring one's search to an end. Should one consider, for example, the grotesque correlation between the windstorms in the Dust Bowl, which began on Armistice Day, 1933, and the first stanza's image of gardens going round with angels and clouds? With a little imagining these gardens could be taken for the crop fields that disappeared into Oklahoma's skies.

This last correspondence illustrates how forced readings of this poem become when one tries to correlate specific events with the images in Stevens's poem. Stevens's poetics continuously court this problem, presenting the reader with a series of related difficulties. First, the words or images in the poem suggest a surfeit of political and social content. Second, the abstraction in the poem requires one to import a context in order to decipher this content. And third, the abstractions Stevens uses vaguely support an indeterminate number of contexts but clearly support none. The tension characteristic of this poem and others in *Ideas of Order* is therefore between an implicit invitation to the reader to understand words or phrases in terms of specifiable contexts and the poem's refusal to circumscribe any of the poem's assignable meanings.

This frustration intensifies the more closely one looks at the poem. The first stanza is thirty-two words long but makes use of only eight different words, three of which are function words. Those that remain—garden, angel, clouds, flew, and round—are set in a pattern as airy, centrifugal, and ungrounded as the movement the first stanza describes. The rhythm of the second stanza is more abrupt and threatening than the crisp repetition of the first, and the second stanza endeavors to enlist the reader's curiosity with the ominous question, "Is there any secret in skulls?" (4). The reader is back on the ground now, in the woods, with human agents (the drummers in black hoods) and with specific harbingers of a nameless threat (the cattle skulls). The contrast between these stanzas' tones is the poem's most vexing problem. Does the airiness of the first stanza ask the poem's readers to understand the cultish feel of the drummers in black and the unsubtle insistence of their rumbling drums as satirical? Does it ask that we accept the undifferentiated and unspecifiable pleasures of merely circulating? Or do the historical circumstances of the poem's composition give weight to the ominous rumbling, asking the reader to look skeptically upon whimsical pleasures, to countenance the warnings issuing from the woods in spite of the overdone and gothic character of the warnings' messengers? Perhaps because he views the poem with historical hindsight, Longenbach guesses that the airy order of the first stanza is falsely reassuring, that the problem of false reassurance is the poem's theme. But without the destruction of the Second World War in his or her mind, a reader in 1934 might well have taken the second stanza to be more overdrawn than the first, as a satire aimed at Chicken Little types.

The third stanza does nothing to resolve or explain the odd juxtaposition of the first two. Its first two lines, which ask the reader to evaluate whether being Swedish, Spanish, or German is a difference that matters in 1934, are the most specific lines in the poem even though Mrs. Anderson is not an identifiable figure. But just here the poem returns to its airiest language and deploys its most vacant terms: "Yet that things go round and again go round / Has rather a classical sound" (11–12). The syntax of this final clause is strange given the progress of the poem to this point. The adversative "yet" is the first rhetorical cue that the poem concerns itself at all with making arguments. It is tempting to conclude that this is simply the kind of thing we say if we happen to ask ourselves an unanswerable question like, "What if Mrs. Anderson's baby had been born in Germany or Spain?" The word "classical," though, the only qualifying term in the last stanza, gives a suddenly peculiar feel to an otherwise insouciant ending. The reader cannot begin to know how the word is used here. Is "classical" a reference to classical economy, as Harrington suggests? Does it connote a remoteness and painlessness utterly different from many Americans' daily experience of a disastrously stagnant economy? Or should we look only for the most common associations? The melodies of Mozart? The culture of ancient Greece? Answers to these questions are required to determine the significance of "yet" and to determine in turn the tone and import of the hypothetical meditation on Mrs. Anderson's baby. The rhetorical structure of the last stanza heightens the reader's desire to clarify the relations between the preceding stanzas, but Stevens then frustrates this desire and dissolves the dilemmas he creates in sound. This is what I mean by the phrase "refractive poetics." Stevens invites the reader to correlate his abstract phrases with specific contexts but deflects the reader from evaluating those contexts against any discursive position offered in the poem.

Stevens intuited something V. N. Vološinov argues is central to understanding language as an ideological medium. In *Marxism and Language*, Vološinov concludes that the sign and its uses are sites of cultural conflict. Each use of a word, according to Vološinov, is imbued with the value judgments of the word's user: "all referential contents produced in living speech are said or written in conjunction with a specific *evaluative accent*. There is no such thing as word without evaluative accent" (103). For Vološinov, of course, the evaluative accents that govern a word's use are largely determined by the speaker's class. Stevens was more concerned with the accents words gather through repetition. He saw in them shadows of the arguments and discourses he could not escape. As he says in "Noble Rider," these shadows affect how words "sound" from one age to another. Stevens sought to purge the language in his poems of such shadows by doing what Vološinov argues is impossible, by ridding them of evaluative accents. His technique was to plug words into contexts where their referential content makes no clear sense. In "The Pleasures of Merely Circulating," it may be that the word "classical" cannot be separated from all connotations, but because it has no content (what is a "classical sound"?), it is unavailing to attempt to paraphrase the word as it is deployed in the poem.

"The Pleasures of Merely Circulating" allegorizes Stevens's response to radio. It articulates his complaint against the circulation of discourse that Stevens could not tune out in the 1930s, and in the final stanza, it gives Stevens's poetic solution to his complaint. In his chapter on the radio in *Understanding Media*, McLuhan repeatedly demonstrates his interest in two characteristics of radio that correspond neatly with the first and second stanzas of Stevens's poem. The first is radio's ubiquity:

> News bulletins, time signals, traffic data, and, above all, weather reports now serve to enhance the native power of radio to involve people in one another. Weather is that medium that involves all people equally. It is the top item on radio. (298)

The first stanza corresponds to this sense of radio. Drawing on a lengthy literary tradition, Stevens deploys the garden as an easily recognizable figure for order. This stanza presents different gardens, or different patterns of order in the world, being lifted up into the air and circulated round and round, just as radio circulates the speech discussing and seeking to comprehend world events. The second idea McLuhan emphasizes is radio's power to foster a communal feeling deep within the individual's psyche:

> The subliminal depths of radio are charged with the resonating echoes of tribal horns and antique drums. This is inherent in the very nature of this medium, with its power to turn the psyche and society into a single echo chamber. (299)

McLuhan's style is imprecise and metaphorical, and one cannot help but be put off by a phrase like "subliminal depths," but the feeling McLuhan describes likewise concerned Stevens. The drums rumbling in his second stanza image radio's power in the 1930s to haunt the mind. Stevens blends in this stanza the ominously intrusive power of radio with the ominous import of news in the 1930s ("news more pretentious than any description of it") to give the obverse side of the first stanza's neatly circulating world of timely weather updates and news bulletins.

The word in this poem that most clearly retains its evaluative accent is "merely" from the title, and recalls the way this word figures in "Noble

Riders" when Stevens confesses his horror at seeing the goings-on in others' heads "*merely* as goings-on." The pleasures in this poem are, like the word "classical," hollow and emptied out, and the destitution of this pleasure is a pointed response to the conditions of modernity. In the emptiness and indifference of its resolution, the third stanza conjures what T. J. Clark calls "the true terror" of modernity,

> its being ruled—and obscurely felt to be ruled—by sheer concatenation of profit and loss, bids and bargains: that is, by a system without any focusing purpose to it, or any compelling image or ritualization of that purpose. It is the blindness of modernity that seems to me fundamental, and to which modernism is a response: the great fact, to go back to Adam Smith's insight, is the hiddenness of the "hidden hand"; or rather, the visibility of that hiddenness—the availability to individual consciousness of more and more "information" (a ludicrous, lobotomizing barrage of same) pointing to the purposelessness of social action. (8)

Like Stevens's poem, Clark's observations here bring us to a place where one feels the confession of impotence to be political at the same time one feels the absence of efficacy or consolation in the act. What is surprising in Stevens is his effort to make this emptiness the support of his poems. When he writes in "The Man with the Blue Guitar," "Poetry is the subject of the poem, / From this the poem issues and // To this returns" (*Collected* 176, 1–3), he describes the poem's trajectory across a space he has hollowed out and to which he gives a startlingly personal character. Perhaps understanding the futility of any effort to preserve imaginative space as such, Stevens recreates what replaces it, not the shock that Baudelaire sought to give his readers but something like the effect of radio's uncannily seductive voice: blind, vast modernity's intimate touch.

Notes

1. Stevens's craving for distance from the public is far more powerful in his work than his flirtations with social commitment. This chapter seeks to expand debates in Stevens scholarship that have too narrowly focused on whether or not his poetics may be described as political. The idea of a progressive-leaning Stevens has by now largely carried the day in Stevens scholarship. Milton Bates notes, "The politically engaged Stevens has become as much a critical cliché as the deconstructionist Stevens of the 1970s" (203). This argument, made most persuasively by Jacqueline Brogan, Alan Filreis, and James Longenbach, tends to claim that Stevens's poetics deliberately resist assimilation to any political program and that they offer conceptual distinc-

tions whose nuance, especially in the context of the 1930s, has an inherent ethical and political value. My essay presents an alternative historical explanation for Stevens's elusiveness in part because I think that the idea of a primarily progressive Stevens is more inaccurate than the still misleading notion of a politically indifferent Stevens.

2. To illustrate this difference, Czitrom compares two leads from stories "concerning the European political situation," both of which were "prepared by the UP [United Press news service] in April of 1939." The first paragraph of the lead written for newspapers reads: "Prime Minister Neville Chamberlain announced today that Great Britain had decided to conscript all men between the ages of 20 and 21 for six months of military training." The lead for radio begins: "Great Britain cast off centuries of tradition today in a desperate move to preserve the delicately balanced peace of Europe" (87). Czitrom excerpts these leads from Dowling Leatherwood's *Journalism On the Air* (Minneapolis: Burgess, 1939).

3. Czitrom traces this metaphor back as far as 1838, when Samuel Morse wrote of electromagnetic telegraphy "that it would not be long ere the whole surface of this country would be channeled for those *nerves* which are to diffuse, with the speed of thought, a knowledge of all that is occurring throughout the land" (177).

4. For Baudelaire, according to Benjamin, the gambler's mechanical gestures resemble the jerky and repetitive motions of the factory worker, and his continuous, compulsive self-submission to the workings of chance aim at a wish-fulfillment devoid of any relation to experience.

5. Patricia Yaeger describes the poem with this phrase in her essay "Consuming Trauma" (225).

CHAPTER 15

I Switch Off

Beckett and the Ordeals of Radio

STEVEN CONNOR

Listening In

The question that a radio aesthetics can never for long set aside is that of location. Where is radio? Where does radio take place and what place does it occupy when it does?

There are two standard answers to this question, both in their way amounting to the answer "noplace" and thus utopian. The first is given by Marinetti and Masnata in the futurist manifesto "La Radia" of 1933. According to this manifesto, the proper habitation of radio is everywhere. Its power is that of delocalization, such that radio itself names a greater power of radiation, diffusion, dispersal—"La Radia," which it both instantiates and to which it is itself subject. La Radia, Marinetti says, abolishes "the space and stage necessary to theater" such that "no longer visible and framable the stage becomes universal and cosmic." It promises "a pure organism of radio sensation . . . An art without time or space without yesterday or tomorrow" (267). Radio means the dispersal of all punctualities and particularities, of space and of time.

The second answer is that radio space is mind-space: that radio is always in fact enacted in the mind of the listener and that the signified or assumed locations of radio are in fact surrogates for this mind-space. The cosmic space of Marinetti's radiations shrinks to the buzzing, booming round O of the skull.

The strangeness of radio comes from the fact that contingency is of its essence. Where the telephone establishes a connection between two determinate interlocutors, traveling through space but moored securely at both ends of the line, and the phonograph fossilizes the act of listening and communication in a specific material form (the record and the apparatus needed to play it), radio occurs at the coincidence of two asymmetric actions—a broadcast that sends a signal out, with no clear idea of where it will be received, and a reception that always has the sense of an overhearing of an address that is not specifically directed at oneself. Hence, perhaps the long survival of the phrase—well beyond the 1940s—of the expression "listening in to the radio." Listening in, as opposed simply to listening to, implies that the program has been come upon by chance, or even surreptitiously. One eavesdrops on a program that can never entirely be meant for one. One might even see the tendency to think of radio space as mind-space as another kind of listening in, in a more appropriative sense—as a kind of deliberate incorporation or making one's own of what has been come upon.

This may also account for the fact that the radio has been thought of both as the most intimate of communications and the most impersonal. Perhaps we can say that radio is characterized both by the intimacy of its impersonality and the impersonality of its intimacy.

In processing radio space as mind-space, we make it possible to believe in the priority of the latter—to believe, in other words, that radio has the power it does because it happens to resemble the interior auditory dramas we all already experience. This is perhaps an auditory version of what Daniel Dennett has called the fallacy of the "Cartesian theater"—the idea that somewhere inside the mind, behind its mechanical processes of perception, there exists a kind of primal scene or final instance in which everything is played out, for the solitary benefit of a mind's eye, or mind's ear, itself the organ of some homunculus, who is a miniaturized version of the mind itself (101–38). This, of course, simply reinstates the problem of what perception actually is at a deeper level, and would require an infinite series of Cartesian theaters-within-theaters and homunculi-within-homunculi.

Beckett's radio worlds are indeed highly interior, and many critics have been tempted to see the principal use of the sensory deprivation or sensory concentration of radio as affording Beckett an opportunity to focus undistractedly on the interior workings of the mind. For Martin Esslin, this makes possible a kind of immediacy or tuning-together of the experience represented in the radio play and the experience of the listener: "radio can create a subjective reality halfway between the objective events experienced and their subjective reflection within the mind of the character who experiences them" (130–31). Nearly everybody who has written about Beckett's radio plays seems to agree that their ultimate location is the mind, or at any event, somebody's mind—"the mental landscape that radio, unencumbered by visuals, is so good at" (Frost 322).

Beckett's most extended statement on the nature of radio expresses a slightly different perspective. Refusing permission for his first radio play, *All That Fall*, to be adapted for the stage, Beckett wrote to his American publisher Barney Rosset:

> *All That Fall* is a specifically radio play, or rather radio text, for voices, not bodies. . . . Even the reduced visual dimension it will receive from the simplest and most static of readings . . . will be destructive of whatever quality it may have and which depends on the whole thing's *coming out of the dark*. (qtd. in Zilliacus, n.p.)

Here, the emphasis is not upon the space that radio occupies or constitutes but rather on its emergence from nothing and nowhere. It is in radio that Beckett seems to have found the possibility of writing without ground—in which, that is to say, the spoken words are at once figure and ground. Under such conditions, to retire from utterance is to lapse from existence, a point made all the more intensely by Mrs. Rooney's insistence in *All That Fall* that she is indeed still there even when she is not speaking: "Do not imagine, because I am silent, that I am not present, and alive to all that is going on" (*Complete Dramatic Works* [hereinafter *CDW*] 185). Characters in *All That Fall* surge up out of nowhere or rather, perhaps, arise in their words, entering the sound space of the play with no announcement and vacating it just as abruptly. Existence in sound is the only existence possible. And yet, the comic overstatement of certain sounds, like the "*exaggerated station sounds. Falling signals. Bells. Whistles. Crescendo of train whistle approaching*" which mark the passage of the up mail in *All That Fall* also suggests a desperate need to convince, as though sound itself, even in this medium in which sound is everything, could never be enough. (The ostentatiously synthesized sounds of "*Sheep, bird, cow, cock*" that open and punctuate the play [*CDW* 172] also suggest the dubiousness of the sound-background.)

Radio Work

But if radio does appear to come from nowhere, it can never in fact do so, the radiophonic fantasies of mystics and psychotics aside, without any material intermediary or apparatus—even if, like the legendary tooth filling, its radiophonic action is accidental or unwilled. Radio can come out of nowhere only because it passes between. Radio, just like cinema, always requires an apparatus, an array or arrangement of elements that is prepared in advance. To be sure, the material forms and arrangements of the radio are much more variable than the cinematic apparatus, as classically described by theorists like Jean-Louis Baudry.[1] Whereas as a basic condition of cinema one must, however minimally, subtract or absent oneself from involvement in the world (one must at the very least be facing forward), one can nowadays listen to radio as one runs, irons, eats, and makes love. Nevertheless, just as in the cinema, the apparatus is more than the support or technical framework of radio. The array or syntactic disposition of elements of which radio is compounded—including the writer, the speaker, the transmitter, the medium, the receiver, the context of reception, the listener—spreads through the whole of radio, dividing and in the process constituting that homogenous dark or nothingness out of which it seems to come.

The apparatus of radio has slipped out of the picture, as radio has got the reputation of being an immaterial art. This really began in the rise of public broadcasting during the 1930s and with the impetus of war in the 1940s, as listening became an ever more diffuse and involuntary activity. Radio provided more and more of an environment in which to live and sank more and more into the background. And listening became correspondingly less focused, more peripheral, more compounded with other things. Radios themselves became smaller, lighter, and more portable with the development of midget radios during the Second World War, including one that was designed to be operated from within a gas mask (Hill 85).

Beckett's work for and with the idea of radio reactivates an earlier tradition in which listening to radio was an active, absorbing, and laborious undertaking. By the 1950s, all the work of radio had passed across to the production and transmission side, with listening requiring little in the way of preparation or active attention. But in the early days of radio, before the advent of broadcasting, radio was mostly the preserve of hobbyists and adventurers, for whom listening was an intricate and expensive procedure. During the teens of the century and the early 1920s, radio listeners, like early motorists and computer users, had often built their own apparatus, which needed to be carefully maintained. Once the designs of radio had stabilized and been commercialized, the radio set, often disguised as a piece of furniture, was merely a way-station through which sounds and voices could pass on their way to the listener. But before this, the apparatus was no mere accessory to the act of listening. Apparatus and act were closely imbricated and reciprocally transforming. Listeners to crystal sets had to cope with the susceptibility of the apparatus to de-tuning. G. E. Mortley described the fragility of crystal reception in an article in the short-lived *Weather and Wireless Magazine* in 1924:

> a crystal is somewhat "uncertain, coy and hard to please" with regard to location and pressure of contact, and it not infrequently happens that just as one reaches an important point during a communication, some slight vibration caused by traffic or what not can cause the crystal to become displaced, and the signal will be lost. (13)

The arrival of valves freed operators from the problems of adjusting crystals but brought problems of their own:

> The valve has brought many knotty little points with it. The most difficult part of the whole set are the accumulators. They require constant watching. Their importance need not be described in full, since we all know that if they fail "out goes the light!" (Allinson 42)

One listened not only with the ear but also with the vigilant eye and patient, painstaking fingers, and even with the tongue—the author of this article recommended developing the trick of tasting the strength of the charge remaining in the battery by applying the wires to the tongue (43).

Radio listening of this kind was described often and explicitly as "work," requiring active, vigilant, and inventive attention: "The purity of music and speech where crystal rectification is employed is usually considerably greater than with valve rectification, unless the latter is in skilled hands . . . positive reliability is essential when working on weak signals or distant stations" (Mortley 13). Add to this the fact that the radio frequency bands were so sparsely populated with signals to listen to, causing radio enthusiasts to tune eagerly into transmissions from ships and military sources in their search for communications, and one has the sense that the ratio of activity is concentrated firmly on the reception rather than the transmission side. Beckett's work for radio activates this archaic sense, very literally, of the work *of* radio, the strenuous, solitary ardors of audition.

Beckett's work for radio is concentrated into a short period of his writing career. His first play for radio was *All That Fall*, written on invitation for the BBC in late 1956 and broadcast in January 1957. This seemed to trigger an intense period of reflection on and writing for radio, which occupied him from early 1959, when he wrote the play *Embers*, through to 1962, during which period he completed a sequence of closely related radio works: *Rough for Radio I* (written in French in late 1961 and first published as *Esquisse radiophonique*), *Rough for Radio II* (written in French in the early 1960s and published as *Pochade radiophonique*), *Words and Music* (written at the end of 1961, first broadcast by the BBC November 1962), and *Cascando* (written in early 1962 and first broadcast by the French ORTF in October 1963). The last of Beckett's engagements with radio occurred in 1963, when he produced an English version of a play by Robert Pinget, *La Manivelle*, as *The Old Tune*.

I think Stanley Richardson and Jane Alison Hale are right to say that "Beckett's radio plays are not only for radio, they are about radio" (285). Perhaps the most important feature of Beckett's work for the radio is that it can also be thought of as a kind of work *on* radio, a working through of the grounds of possibility for radio and what radio itself makes possible. Although Beckett's work for radio is concentrated into the space of about five years, the forms of radio radiate or diffuse throughout his work for other media. The work on radio works, we may say, on Beckett's work.

Alternating Currents

Gilles Deleuze and Félix Guattari have habituated us to the idea that machines are not merely analogous to the actions of desiring but may also be generative of it—that desiring is no more or no other than a machinery, by which they usually seem to mean a conjuncture of relations. But desiring-machines, like machines in general, are rarely apprehended as such and as a whole, just as the new experiences of "communication," "broadcasting," or "transmission" never present themselves as such. Rather they appear through certain approximations or synecdoches which stand for the entire ensemble of arrangements that makes up the machinery in question, just as Kleinian part-objects are both detached from and stand in for the body in its ungraspable wholeness. Among these mechanical part-objects are the screen, the wire, the lever, the wheel, the joystick, the pedal, and the mouse. Of these, perhaps no object is fuller of power and portent than the switch. Whether in the form of button, rocker, slider, tap, knob, or cord, the switch is the executive means whereby the apparatus is moved abruptly from one state to another—from "off" to "on." In one sense, the switch is part of the apparatus; in another sense, because it has the power to bring the entire apparatus into working configuration, it is a kind of meta-apparatus, a machinery for communicating with the machine and making it work. When the machinery is itself concerned with communication, the means whereby one communicates with it takes on an added significance.

We have become so familiar with the states of being off and on and the patterns of alternation between them that we no longer grasp its strangeness or its newness. I am not suggesting that before there were switches, people had no conception of absolute or strongly counterposed either/or alternative states. In this sense, off is to on as black is to white, death is to life, absence is to presence, and nonbeing is to being. Devices for turning things on and off more or less instantly began to multiply through the mechanical age, and by the beginning of the twentieth century, switches and valves and taps for gas, water, and electricity were common.

The first use of the word to mean a crossing over or redirection was in 1797, to refer to railway points. In 1845, in a reference in the *Annual Register* to "a 'switch' which, when turned in one direction allows the train to pass direct on," the word was still being used in inverted commas, as though to indicate that the usage was still not widespread. During the second half of the nineteenth century, the word itself started to be switched across to other mechanisms and then, increasingly, to various forms of electrical appliances.

Perhaps the most culturally powerful of these was the electric chair, invented as a more humane—because more instant—way to execute felons. This method of execution seems first to have suggested itself in 1881 to a dentist and former steamboat engineer called Albert Southwick, who was surprised by how quickly and apparently painlessly a drunken man died when he touched the terminals of an electrical generator. In that year, discussions began about the use of electrocution to replace hanging. These discussions became caught up in the rivalry that developed between the direct current (DC) service established by Thomas Edison and the system of alternating current (AC) that had been developed by Nikola Tesla and provided by Westinghouse. As part of his efforts to show how dangerous AC was compared with DC, and therefore appropriate for capital punishment but not domestic use, Edison conducted dozens of public electrocutions of dogs and other animals (including an elephant). When execution by electricity passed into law in 1889, George Westinghouse, whose company supplied AC electricity, campaigned against the law and refused to supply generators for the execution process. The fact that electrocution briefly became known as "Westinghousing" shows that his fears were well founded.

Of course, the rapid alternations of AC—at around fifty cycles a second—were not directly apprehensible. But devices like the electric bell seemed to offer an enactment of its power and fluctuating form. Perhaps alternating current proved acceptable in the long run because it seemed to be in accord with the many forms of undulation or oscillation with which people were increasingly made familiar from the late 1890s onward. The pain and danger of oscillation rapidly gave way to forms of pleasure, with the first development of vibrators for medical and then domestic use in the late 1880s (Maines). By the 1940s, the word "buzz" was also being used to describe the pleasurable sense of arousal derived from the use of drugs, as though the organic-chemical world were being electrolized. Increasingly, turning "on" and "off" came to be applied to affective states. "Turning on" to mean experiencing the high of intoxication dates from about the mid-1950s. Turning on sexually followed in short order.

There are two kinds of alternating current in Beckett's work. First, there is the ideal of an alternation between absolute states of on and off. But this itself alternates in Beckett's work with much more unpredictable and capricious comings and goings, which seem to be emblematized in the slapstick reading lamp in *Rough for Theatre II*. Here, two Pinteresque investigators, placed at either end of the stage, each at a table with a reading lamp, are investigating the life and probable suicide of an unnamed subject. Their attempts to make out the documentary evidence of morbid sensitivity in their subject are comically accompanied by a similar sensitivity in one of the reading lamps:

> B: I'll read the whole passage: '... morbidly sensitive to the opinion of others—' [*His lamp goes out.*] Well! The bulb has blown! [*The lamp goes on again.*] No it hasn't! Must be a faulty connection. [*Examines lamp, straightens flex.*] The flex was twisted, now all is well. [*Reading.*] '... morbidly sensitive—' [*The lamp goes out.*] Bugger and shit!
>
> A: Try giving her a shake. [*B shakes the lamp. It goes on again.*] See! I picked up that wrinkle in the Band of Hope. [*Pause.*]
>
> B: }   '... morbidly sensitive—'
>   }[*Together.*]
> A: }   Keep your hands off the table.
>
> B: What?
>
> A: Keep your hands off the table. If it's a connection the least jog can do it.
>
> B: [*Having pulled back his chair a little way.*] '... morbidly sensitive—'

> [*The lamp goes out. B bangs on the table with his fist. The lamp goes on again. Pause.*]
>
> A: Mysterious affair, electricity. (*CDW* 242–43)

In Beckett's work, the states of being on and off are at once starkly counterposed and capriciously unpredictable. If much of his work is dedicated to the effort to go on, to get on, much is also concerned with the effort to turn things off—the "buzzing" doubts in the mind of the speaker in *Not I*, for example, or the strange electronic susurration of the sea in *Embers*.

There is a particular salience to the on/off switch of the radio that makes for a new understanding, a new experience of "offness." For anything to be switched off is for it to be in a state of suspension or abeyance. Offness signifies a certain kind of readiness, an imminently actualizable possibility, rather than a simple negative. "Off" does not mean idle or at rest: it means standing by, being able, even about, at any moment to be turned on.

When words fail on the stage, the stage, characters, and scenery are still visibly, if mutely, there. The stage is like Freud's unconscious, in which, he wrote, "we never discover a 'no'" ("Negation" 238). When words and sounds die away on the radio, there is broadcast silence—what has come to be called "dead air." What one hears during broadcast silence is not exactly the sound of the radio when it is off; rather, it is a kind of radiophonic offness, an offness that is nonetheless on. Interestingly, broadcasting regulations distinguish sharply between being "off-air" and the broadcast of nothing, of "dead air" or what is known as "unmodulated carrier," which latter is nowadays an offense. Under British broadcasting laws, any radio station that transmits more than ten minutes of dead air without any warning announcement or explanation is liable to legal penalty, or a fine of up to £25,000 per minute.

Unspeaking characters are not simply equivalent to characters who are offstage; rather, they resemble Polonius behind the arras in that they are on stage without being evident in the only way in which, after all, one can be evident in radio, namely, by signifying their presence through sound. Where the stage provided a kind of relief, in its palpability, its three-dimensionality, its necessities of space and action, for a Beckett tormented by the uncertainties of his Trilogy, the radio let in something like the opposite, in which absence and presence enter each other's condition. Indeed, we can say that this is part of the demand of radio—that its off condition enter into the broadcast. Later on, Beckett played a variation on this notion in the screenplay for his film *Film*, which specifies that "the film is entirely silent except for the 'sssh!' in part one" (*CDW* 323). The soundtrack is not off, or absent, as it might be said to be in a silent film, but rather full of silence, or offness. For radio differs from other devices for transmitting or reproducing sound. Whereas lifting the telephone or switching on the phonograph itself initiates the sound that is to be heard, in radio, the signal to which one tunes must already be there, unheard, but ready-to-be-heard, and by others beside oneself.

This uncertain condition of the radio switch is dramatized in Freud's famous description of playful alternation, the fort/da game of his grandson, described in his *Beyond the Pleasure Principle*. It is not often remembered that Freud describes two versions of this game. Freud says that, in his game of alternately releasing and retrieving a cotton-reel flung out from his cot, the child gains pleasure from mastering the pain caused to him by the periodic disappearances of his mother. He then adds a footnote relating an episode which, he says, "confirmed this interpretation fully."

> One day the child's mother had been away for several hours and on her return was met with the words "Baby o-o-o-o!" which was at first incomprehensible. It soon turned out, however, that during this long period of solitude the child had found a method of making *himself* disappear. He had discovered his reflection in a full-length mirror which did not quite reach to the ground, so that by crouching down he could make his mirror-image "gone." (14 n.6)

But far from confirming the interpretation of the first game, this seems to be a very different setup from the game that Freud has just interpreted, in which the cotton-reel stands for the mother, whom the child is able in play to treat like a puppet on a string. Whatever motive the child might have for joying in his own disappearance, it seems unrelated to his other game. What is more, where the cotton-reel game seems to depend upon a simple alternation between the visibility and invisibility of the object-toy, with the child continuously present throughout and able to appreciate and enjoy the coming and going of his mother-surrogate, in the mirror game, it is the enjoying subject who makes himself appear and disappear, and derives pleasure from that. All that holds the child together in the intervals of invisibility is the fact that, crouching down, he is able to say that he is "o-o-o-o!"—*fort*, away, or gone. In other words, in the second game, the child accedes to something like the condition of the radio body, which is there only if and when it utters, even as that utterance may testify to the fact that, in spite of all, it is not really or fully "there."

Switchboards

A number of actual switching devices feature in Beckett's work for radio. In *Rough for Radio I*, a woman is given a demonstration of the two "needs" of a man she has come to visit, in the form of two knobs which, when turned to the right, produce the faint sound of music and a faint voice, whether singing or speaking is not made clear (*CDW* 268)). Daniel Albright suggests that, in contrast to the Beckettian stage settings that seem like magnified interiors of a skull, here "he conceives an imaginary theatre space as a magnified version of a radio receiver" (112). This produces strange convolutions. The woman who has come to hear the sounds is astonished by what she finds in this scenario. First, she discovers the asymmetry of transmission and reception and that even though listening may be discontinuous, radio itself is continuous:

> SHE: Is it true the music goes on all the time?
> HE: Yes.
> SHE: Without cease?
> HE: Without cease.
> SHE: It's unthinkable! [*Pause.*] And the words too? All the time too?
> HE: All the time.
> SHE: Without cease?
> HE: Yes.
> SHE: It's unimaginable. So you are here all the time?
> HE: Without cease. (*CDW* 267)

And then, seemingly forgetting that she is on, or perhaps rather in, radio, she asks if it would be possible to see the sources of the sound:

> SHE: May one see them?
> HE: No, madam.
> SHE: I may not go and see them?
> HE: No, madam. (*CDW* 267)

Here, Beckett's English translation adds a little extra detail that is not in his original French version: "May we have a little light?" the woman asks and is refused with the same "No, madam," seeming to indicate that despite the odd specificity of detail relating to the setting (the woman asks if she may squat "on this hassock" and enquires as she leaves whether the carpet is a Turkoman), there is actually nothing to be seen, or to see with, in this eyeless place. When she asks if the sounds she is to hear are live, her French interlocutor wearily replies "Mais bien entendu, madame," but she receives no answer to her query in the English version (*CDW* 268; *Pas, suivi* 90).

The visitor's attention then turns to the apparatus to be used for hearing the sounds. She is told that she must twist the knob to the right rather than pushing it. We hear a click as she activates the sounds of the faint music with one knob and another click as she turns on the sound of a single voice with the other. These knobs seem peculiar in their functioning. First, they do not seem to allow for alteration of volume, so that the voice and music remain distressingly faint, despite the woman's cries of "Louder!" Second, they do not seem to stay on of their own accord but rather to lapse into silence after a few seconds, as though metered, or perhaps like the automatically (but here silently) returning dial of a telephone. So we hear the click as the knobs are turned repeatedly to the right but never an answering click as they are turned off. The knobs are the only audible and executive parts of whatever apparatus is being used to convey and listen to the sounds. In a sense, they control the whole play, which then becomes an apparatus for tuning into the agon of listening to radio.

These switches are unusual in their literalness. But metaphorical switches and switchings also abound in Beckett's work, which is governed by alternation and oscillation. One might say that this is one of the most insistent forms in which the spectral apparatus of the radio radiates through his work, a work that might then be designated not just as literally radiophonic, in that Beckett wrote some of his most significant works for the radio, but also radiophoric, in that there is a kind of warping, or carrying away of the forms of the work by the phantasmal apparatus of radio. The inhabitants of the cylinder in *The Lost Ones* are subject to an artificial climate in which light and temperature rise and fall in regular coordinated cycles. Every now and then, at unpredictable intervals, the fluctuations of both light and temperature cease for a short period, as though both were "connected somewhere to a single commutator" (42). Beckett's odd term is a literal translation of the French "commutateur," which, given the judicial associations of switch-throwing, allows the faint flicker of a suggestion that a judicial sentence is being commuted. After the densely unparagraphed spate of *The Unnamable*, Beckett began to favor writing in short segments, separated by blank spaces. *How*

It Is gives the impression of spasmodic bursts of murmuring, broken up by silences; later prose works like the texts of the *Nohow On* trilogy, *Company*, *Ill Seen Ill Said* and *Worstward Ho* suggest a more measured pacing, with the gaps in the text seeming to be filled more with rumination than desperate, panicked lockjaw. But in all these cases, there is a rhythm of remission and resumption in which the idea and experience of switching between alternate states of silence and utterance are to the fore. The very last words that Beckett wrote, or published, to be spoken in the theater seem to designate a closing down of transmission not just of the particular work in which they feature but of Beckett's work as a whole: "Make sense who may. I switch off," says V at the end of *What Where* (1983).

Often, there is the suggestion that to be switched off and, more especially, on, in this way is very painful. Being suddenly switched into speech is like the awakening suffered by King Lear—"you do me wrong to take me out o' the grave" (*King Lear* IV.7, 51). The harsh bell that wakes Winnie and summons her to another "happy day" of maundering yap is an instance of this kind of on-switch. In *Ohio Impromptu*, a Listener sits opposite a Reader and employs knocks on the table both to activate the reading when it has lapsed and to "rewind" the reading to an earlier point. The most literal form of switching on is perhaps in the radio play *Rough for Radio II*, in which the interrogation of the unfortunate Fox is initiated by the thudding of a ruler and pencil on a desk and then, when he proves too taciturn, the "*swish and thud of pizzle on flesh*" (CDW 278). This may remind us that the principal reference for the word "switch," up until the nineteenth century, was to a whip or lash, usually made of a flexible twig or branch. The early form of the word was *swits* or *switz*, apparently a variant of the Low German *zwuksen*, which means to bend up and down but is also imitative of the swishing noise of the lash.

The experience of switching, or being switched, is not just a matter of being activated or deactivated. In many of Beckett's works, the drama is developed and sustained through a switching between voices, characters, or states. In *Play*, an inquisitory light switches restlessly between the three different witness-narrators, either in order to stitch together the sordid tale of adulterous deception they severally recount or in quest of some truth unspoken by any of them. The second movement of the text has the three enurned characters addressing the light that comes on and off, prodding them into speech. We are to assume that none of the three knows of the presence of the other two, despite the fact that their urns are touching and that they are all contributing to the unfolding of their shared story. Theirs is a condition of non-coincident participation. For both characters and spotlight, existence is a matter of patterned intermittency. For the characters, there is the arbitrary and unintelligible switching on and off of the light. For the light, there is the restless switching between channels, anxious not to let a crucial word be uttered unheard.

Keep That Sound Down

The on/off switch in radios and other such appliances is often combined with a volume control. In Beckett's work, there is an equivalent linkage. Voices can suddenly be amplified, as in the moments in *Embers* in which the character Henry appears to be able to summon and amplify sounds in his mind:

> HENRY: A drip! A drip! [*Sound of drip, rapidly amplified, suddenly cut off.*] Again! [*Drip again. Amplification begins.*] No! [*Drip cut off.*] (CDW 255)
>
> HENRY: Hooves! [Pause. Louder.] Hooves! [*Sound of hooves walking on hard road. They die rapidly away.*] Again! [*Hooves as before.*] (CDW 257)

More usually, they are subject to slow, agonizing diminishment, as at the end of *Eh Joe*. In this play for television, we hear a voice telling Joe of his own efforts to switch off the voices in his head. What the stage directions call "the mounting tension of *listening*," which is all we are given to see, has Joe screwing up his attention to make out the final words of the speaker describing what we presume is the suicide of one of Joe's lovers (perhaps even her own), as the volume diminishes. As the camera moves in more and more tightly on Joe's face and the volume diminishes, it is as though a volume control were being turned up to its maximum to counteract the effect of the fading out that is both dreaded and desired:

> [*Voice drops to whisper, almost inaudible except words in italics.*]. . .
>
> *Breasts* in the stones . . . and the *hands*. . . . Before they go. . . . *Imagine* the hands. . . . What are they at? . . . In the *stones*. . . .
>
> [*Image fades, voice as before.*]
>
> What are they fondling? . . . Till they go. . . . There's love for you. . . . Isn't it Joe? . . . Wasn't it Joe? . . . *Eh Joe?* . . . Wouldn't you say? . . . Compared to us. . . . Compared to Him. . . . *Eh Joe?* . . .
>
> [*Voice and image out. End.*] (CDW 366–67)

An anxiety about the diminishment or augmentation of volume is to be found in other Beckett plays for various media. In *Happy Days*, the earth-bound Winnie tests the reception of her words on her partner Willie through a careful modulation of volume:

> WINNIE: Can you hear me? [*Pause.*] There! [*All these directions loud. Now in her normal voice, still turned towards him.*] Can you hear me? [*Pause.*] I beseech you, Willie, just yes or no, can you hear me, just yes or nothing.
>
> [*Pause.*]
>
> WILLIE: Yes.
>
> WINNIE: [*Turning front, same voice.*] And now?
>
> WILLIE: [*Irritated.*] Yes.
>
> WINNIE: [*Less loud.*] And now?
>
> WILLIE: [*More irritated.*] Yes.
>
> WINNIE: [*Still less loud.*] And now? [*A little louder.*] And now?
>
> WILLIE: [*Violently.*] Yes! (CDW 147–48)

Winnie's concern is that her words should not be wasted—should not, one might say, be broadcast in vain, without a listener or receiving apparatus. For many, the volume control instantiated a world in which the normal physical limitations of distance and audibility can be overridden—in which the sound of the world could in principle be infinitely augmented. For Beckett, volume control is more likely to create inaudibility, or near-inaudibility. This makes it very hard to accept Everett Frost's suggestion that "ontologically speaking, in radio sound not only makes sense, but *essence. Esse est audiri.* . . . To be is to be heard (or, better, to be heard is to be; and not to be heard is not to be). It is significant that Beckett's characters often go blind, but seldom deaf" (316). By contrast, much of his world, and many of his characters and dramatic setups are decidedly hard of hearing, with variability of volume making for a kind of structural deafness in the radio apparatus.

The television play *Ghost Trio* also evidences a concern with the conditions of audibility:

> V: Good evening. Mine is a faint voice. Kindly tune accordingly. [*Pause.*] Good evening. Mine is a faint voice. Kindly tune accordingly. [*Pause.*] It will not be raised or lowered, whatever happens. (CDW 408)

Asking the listener to "tune" suggests that establishing the right volume—a kind of ideal equipoise, perhaps between transmission and reception, neither one predominating—is equivalent to finding the right auditory focus, locking on to the station rather than in between stations. A little later on, the voice menacingly reminds the listener of the slightly uncomfortable optimum that it demands: "Forgive my stating the obvious. [*Pause.*] Keep that sound down" (*CDW* 408).

Tuning

The switch is an executive device, one that puts the listener in a position of control over the machinery that is thereby put into motion or discontinued. But the radio incorporates a more specific and sensitive form of executive control than either the on/off or volume switches. For listening to the radio also requires *tuning*. This makes the machinery of radio—especially early radios in which tuning could be a delicate and troublesome affair, subject to the vicissitudes of atmospherics and the physical condition of the apparatus itself—both more forensic and more volatile than that of other devices such as the gramophone or the telephone. In tuning, the listener to the radio actively and repeatedly constitutes his or her relation to the device and the transmissions to which it gives access. Tuning is perhaps a mechanical version of the phatic function, in which the contact between listener and signal is established, checked, and confirmed. The uncertainty and fragility of Beckett's radiophoric apparatus means that the functions of switching and adjusting volume often in fact approximate that of tuning, or attempting to bring together in the same zone of reception, or frequency band, the listener and the transmitter. Beckett returns this musical metaphor to its source at the beginning of *Words and Music*, in which the controlling or summoning voice attempts to synchronize the two agencies or faculties (Joe and Bob) who represent words and music.

The apparatus of radio also includes the interference or atmospherics that, according to a well-known story, made it difficult for Beckett, listening in Paris, to hear the first BBC broadcast of his play *All That Fall*. Interference, scrambling, fading of signal, detuning, all the vicissitudes that beset the listener to radio, are made part of Beckett's writing for the medium, which features a large number of inchoate or unintelligible sounds. Perhaps the most striking of these is the sound of the sea in *Embers*. As long as it is "the sound of the sea," it is an interpretable signal, emerging from the noise of contingency. But for Henry the sound of the sea does not quite correlate with "the sound of the sea."

That sound you hear is the sea. [*Pause. Louder.*] I say that sound you hear is the sea, we are sitting on the strand. [*Pause.*] I mention it because the sound is strange, so unlike the sound of the sea, that if you didn't see what it was you wouldn't know what it was.

It is an anguished kind of interference, which is both less and more than an identifiable sound or signal. His spectral interlocutor Ada is not at all disturbed by the sound, which she finds peaceful and describes as "like another time, in the same place" (*CDW* 258). But for Henry the sea seems to be the sound of indeterminacy itself, corroding and decaying the clarity of signals: hence his desire for definite sounds that stand clear of their background, rather than including their background in themselves, or being assimilated to it—the thumps of the music-master's ruler, the stabbing of the F-key on the piano, his father's slamming of the door and the clashing of stones:

Thuds, I want thuds! Like this! [*He fumbles in the shingle, catches up two big stones and starts dashing them together.*] Stone! [*Clash.*] Stone! [*Clash. 'Stone!' and clash amplified, shut off. Pause. He throws one stone away. Sound of its fall.*] That's life. [*He throws the other stone away. Sound of its fall.*] Not this ... [*Pause.*] ... sucking! (*CDW* 260–61)

Writing for radio seems to have attuned Beckett to the effects of interference or sonorous murk in his writing for other media. *How It Is* imagines a speaker murmuring his words in the mud, the words strained and slobbered as though they were themselves a kind of primal soup. *Not I* arises out of an inaudible gabble and subsides at the end of the play back into it, as though we had come to rest in a temporary slot of clear reception. *Play* begins with a "chorus" in which all three characters speak unintelligibly all at once, before the spotlight is able to separate the three stations or channels. Part of the point of the repetition of the play is to give the listener a chance to piece together a story that is unlikely to make much sense on first listening, as though signal were emerging from noise.

It has sometimes been noted how oddly and bulkily bodily Beckett's work for this allegedly abstract medium can be. This is especially true of *All That Fall*, with its panting, shoving, straining, sniffling, and shuffling. But, as Daniel Albright has noted, there is another dimension of physicality that is repeatedly evoked in the play—the physicality not of clear and distinct forms, but of soft edges, of the drift into indistinctness: it is, he says "a soft sort of piece, a play about erosion" (110). But the play also correlates softness with declension, with the falling that is alluded to in its title and played with remorselessly throughout the text. Raising bulk upward costs huge and extravagantly audible effort, whether it is Mrs. Rooney being shoved into the seat of Mr. Slocum's van or her purgatorial toilings up the Matterhorn of the station steps. The principle of inertia ensures that these risings are only ever temporary and achieved at great cost, compared with the universal tendency of the material world to sink and settle:

> MRS ROONEY: Suppose I do get up, will I ever get down?
> MR SLOCUM: [*Breathing hard.*] You'll get down, Mrs Rooney, you'll get down. We may not get you up, but I warrant we'll get you down. (*CDW* 178)

Distinctness is correlated with uprightness, while the irresistible lapse and drift of things downward suggests merging, decomposition, the loss of distinguishable form, just as Mrs. Rooney imagines herself flopping down on the road "like a big fat jelly out of a bowl" (*CDW* 174). And this parabolic motion of alternation between up and down has sonorous correlatives. Articulate speech belongs to uprightness, just as descent is accompanied by cacophony and confusion, as in the directions for the sound of the descent of the Rooneys down the station steps—"*Confused noise of their descent. Panting, stumbling, ejaculations, curses. Silence*" (190). These confused or inarticulate sounds are the aural correlative to the "lingering dissolution" evoked by Mrs. Rooney, which is followed directly by her observation that "Now we are white with dust from head to foot" (175). Sound is also an irritant, which has the power to raise the dust that Mrs. Rooney despairs "will not settle in our time. And when it does some great roaring machine will come and whirl it all skyhigh again" (176). The logic here is perhaps that the effect of the roaring sound is as much to pulverize as to lift into distinctness. The subsiding tendency even extends to Mr. Tyler's bicycle: "My back tyre has gone down again. I pumped it hard as iron before I set out. And now I am on the rim" (175). We do not hear the sound of the air escaping from Mr. Tyler's tire, but it is doubled by the general inarticulate windiness of the play, with all its panting, tittering, cackling, and groaning, including Mrs. Rooney blowing her nose "*violently and long*" (185), and the sudden enforced deflation of Tommy: "*Loud titter from TOMMY cut short by MR BARRELL with backhanded blow in the stomach. Appropriate noise from TOMMY*" (184). Of course, Beckett's attraction to the fart and its minor form, the fizzle, is well-known, but there is evidence that on at least one occasion he associated it with the capacities or liabilities of radio in particular. In September

1938, during the anxious period leading up to war, he described in a letter to George Reavey the effect on him of listening to Adolf Hitler: "I heard Adolf the Peacemaker on the wireless last night. And thought I heard the air escaping—a slow puncture" (qtd. in Knowlson 297).

We do not think of sound as having weight, but Beckett's sound-world exhibits a kind of declensive ballistics. If radio is normally a sublimating device, which turns material forms and objects into the events and energies of sound, here, radio sound does not radiate outward, but lapses downward, as though energy were being converted into dead weight, and clarity, like brightness, were falling from the air. In the end, the polyphony of voices and animal cries so comically picked out from their background, like a conductor, by Mrs. Rooney—"the birds—[*Brief chirp.*]—are tired singing. The cows—[*Brief moo.*]—and sheep—[*Brief baa.*]—ruminate in silence" (*CDW* 192)—are swallowed up in the "*Tempest of wind and rain*" that ends the play (199).

The pneumatic entropy of *All That Fall* is matched by *The Old Tune*, Beckett's English, or rather Irish, rendering of Robert Pinget's play *La Manivelle*. This is not usually included in accounts of Beckett's work of radio, though it has some striking continuities with it. The two wheezing old geezers whose rambling, spasmodic gassings by the side of a road are followed out through the play, struggle to make out what each is saying against the deafening roars of traffic. Gorman's complaints about the traffic ("They'd tear you to flitters with their flaming machines" [*CDW* 338]) are reminiscent of the "great roaring machine" that Mrs. Rooney anticipates (176) The other voice scored in the play is an unreliable barrel-organ, which Mr. Gorman's voice is clearly meant to mirror: "*Old man's cracked voice, frequent pauses for breath even in the middle of a word, speech indistinct for want of front teeth, whistling sibilants*" (337). The end of the play replaces their speech with a contest staged between the barrel organ and the traffic noise that threatens to engulf it. Though the victory goes to the tune, it is a tune that is itself made up of noise rather than being wholly distinct from it.

For Marinetti and other early radio enthusiasts, the radio represented the promise of an intoxicating dissolution of boundaries and limits. Where Marinetti projects an "immensification of space" and a "pure organism of sensations" (267), others celebrated the capacity of radio to synthesize sound-worlds, which would no longer, as in the theater, need to be assembled from disparate elements like sound, light, music, movement, and speech. Radio means joyous moreness and exceeding of limit for many of its early practitioners and theorists. It is as though radio were, like radiation, a source of limitless, expansive energy. Even Ezra Pound, who, according to Daniel Tiffany, was suspicious of radio's powers to enchant and fascinate, and interrupt and disfigure the voice, and therefore sought to take control of and channel the new form (280–88), nevertheless recognized the odd affinity between the fluidity and shiftingness of *The Cantos* and the machinery he called "a God damn destructive and dispersive devil of an invention" (*Letters* 441).

Some have seen Beckett taking advantage of the same freedom in his work for radio. Kim Conner, for example, argues that Beckett develops a "radioactive voice," which, freed from the anchors of the body "is procreative precisely because of its disembodiment," and concludes:

> Through the technology of sound recording and broadcasting, the matter of the voice can be separated from the matter of the body, transmuted into energy, stored, and reconverted at will back into the matter of sound. Therefore, so can the multivalent associations and significance of that voice (indeed of all sound) be separated from its context, withdrawn from the passage of time and transported across space. (311)

But there is little sense of anything being done "at will" in the radio work of Beckett. The sound-world he evokes, not just in his works specifically for radio, but also in the ways in which the radio condition is propagated throughout his work is tenuous, infirm, impeded, difficult, discontinuous. For Beckett, radio is projected as lessness, as liability and travail. Focusing on the distributed and distributing body of the radio apparatus, by means of which voices are abruptly terminated and painfully revived, Beckett finds in radio an anguished intermittence of being, in which neither transmitter nor receiver can ever be at peace or in one piece.

Notes

1. Surprisingly few writers have attempted to adapt the idea of cinematic apparatus to radio. One of them is Alan Beck in "The Death of Radio," especially section 4.

BIBLIOGRAPHY

Abraham, Julie. "'We Are Americans': Gertrude, *Brewsie and Willie*." *Modern Fiction Studies* 42.3 (1996): 508–27.

Ackroyd, Peter. *T. S. Eliot*. London: Hamish Hamilton, 1984.

Adorno, Theodor W. *Current of Music: Elements of a Radio Theory*. Ed. Robert Hullot-Kentor. Frankfurt am Main: Suhrkamp, 2006.

———. "Little Heresy." *Essays on Music*. Ed. Richard Leppert. Trans. Susan H. Gillespie. Berkeley: University of California Press, 2002. 288–317.

———. "Memorandum: Music in Radio." June 26, 1938, Lazarsfeld Papers, Columbia University Archives.

———. *Minima Moralia: Reflections from Damaged Life*. Trans. E. F. N. Jephcott. London: Verso, 1974.

———. *Notes to Literature Volume II*. Trans. Shierry Weber Nicholsen. New York: Columbia University Press, 1992.

———. "On the Fetish Character in Music and the Regression in Listening." *Essays on Music*. Ed. Richard Leppert. Trans. Susan H. Gillespie. Berkeley: University of California Press, 2002. 318–26.

———. "Scientific Experiences of a European Scholar in America." *Critical Models: Catchwords and Interventions*. Trans. Henry Pickford. New York: Columbia University Press, 1999. 215–42.

———. "A Social Critique of Radio Music." *Kenyon Review* 7.2 (1945): 208–17.

Aggarwal, Varun. "Jagadish Chandra Bose: The Real Inventor of Marconi's Wireless Receiver." New Delhi, India: Netaji Subhas Institute of Technology. www.geocities.com/mumukshu/bose_real_inventor.pdf.

Aitken, Hugh G. J. *Syntony and Spark: The Origins of Radio*. Princeton, N.J.: Princeton University Press, 1985.

Albright, Daniel. *Beckett and Aesthetics*. Cambridge, UK: Cambridge University Press, 2003.

Allinson, J. Reginald. "The Care of Accumulators." *Weather and Wireless Magazine* 2 (1924): 42–43.

Althusser, Louis. *Lenin and Philosophy and Other Essays*. Trans. Ben Brewster. New York: Monthly Review Press, 1971.

Angell, James Rowland. "Radio and National Morale." *American Journal of Sociology* 47.3 (1941): 352–59.

Armand, Louis. *Techne: James Joyce, Hypertext and Technology*. Prague: Charles University Press, 2003.

Arnheim, Rudolph. *Radio: An Art of Sound*. London: Faber and Faber, 1936.

Arnold, H. F. "The Night Wire." *Weird Tales* September 1926: 380–84.

Arnold, Matthew. *Culture and Anarchy*. London: Macmillan, 1923.

Ashton, Jennifer. "'Rose is a Rose': Gertrude Stein and the Critique of Indeterminacy." *Modernism/modernity* 9.4 (2002): 581–604.

Artaud, Antonin. *Artaud on Theatre*. Trans. Claude Schumacher and Brian Singleton. Chicago: Ivan R. Dee, 2004.

———. "Having Done with the Judgment of God." *Wireless Imagination: Sound, Radio, and the Avant-Garde*. Ed. Douglas Kahn and Gregory Whitehead. Trans. Clayton Eshelman. Cambridge, Mass.: MIT Press, 1992. 309–29.

Attridge, Derek. "Innovation, Literature, Ethics: Relating to the Other." *PMLA* 114:1 (1999): 20–31.

Auden, W. H. "Psychology and Art Today." *The Arts Today*. Ed. Geoffrey Grigson. London: John Lane The Bodley Head, 1935. Rpt. Port Washington, N.Y.: Kennikat Press, 1970. 1–21.

Avery, Todd. *Radio Modernism: Literature, Ethics, and the BBC, 1922–1938*. Aldershot: Ashgate, 2006.

Baker, Russell, ed. *The Norton Book of Light Verse*. New York: Norton, 1986.

Bannerman, R. LeRoy. *Norman Corwin and Radio: The Golden Years*. University: University of Alabama Press, 1986.

Barlow, William. *Voice Over: The Making of Black Radio*. Philadelphia: Temple University Press, 1999.

Barnouw, Erik. *A History of Broadcasting in the United States*. New York: Oxford University Press, 1966–70.

Barthes, Roland. "Listening." *The Responsibility of Forms: Critical Essays on Music, Art, Representation*. Trans. Richard Howard. New York: Hill and Wang, 1985. 245–60.

Barton, J. E. "Will the New City Make New Men?" *Listener* March 23, 1932: 412–14.

Bates, Milton J. "Stevens' Soldier Poems and Historical Possibility." *The Wallace Stevens Journal* 28.2 (2004): 203–9.

Baucom, Ian. "Frantz Fanon's Radio: Solidarity, Diaspora, and the Tactics of Listening." *Contemporary Literature* 42.1 (2001): 15–49.

Baudry, Jean-Louis. "Ideological Effects of the Basic Cinematographic Apparatus." *Movies and Methods: An Anthology: Vol. 2*. Ed. Bill Nichols. Berkeley: University of California Press, 1985. 531–42.

Bazerman, Charles. *The Languages of Edison's Light*. Cambridge, Mass.: MIT Press, 1999.

Beard, George. *American Nervousness*. New York: G. P. Putnam's Sons, 1881.

Beck, Alan. "The Death of Radio: An Essay in Radio-Philosophy for the Digital Age." http://www.savoyhill.co.uk/deathofradio/. Accessed April 30, 2008.

Beckett, Samuel. *Complete Dramatic Works*. London: Faber and Faber, 1986.

———. *The Lost Ones*. London: Calder and Boyars, 1972.

———. *Pas, suivi de quatre esquisses*. Paris: Editions de Minuit, 1978.

Beer, Gillian. "Wireless: Popular Physics, Radio and Modernism." *Cultural Babbage: Technology, Time and Invention*. Ed. Francis Spufford and Jenny Uglow. London: Faber and Faber, 1996. 149–66.
Begnal, Michael H. and Grace Eckley. *Narrator and Character in* Finnegans Wake. Lewisburg, Penn.: Bucknell University Press, 1975.
Bell, Ian F. A. *Critic as Scientist: The Modernist Poetics of Ezra Pound*. 1981. London: Methuen, 2000.
Benjamin, Walter. *Illuminations*. Trans. Harry Zohn. Ed. Hannah Arendt. New York: Schocken, 1986.
———. *One Way Street and Other Writings*. Trans. Edmund Jephcott. London: New Left Books, 1979.
Bernstein, Charles, ed. Introduction. *Close Listening: Poetry and the Performed Word*. New York: Oxford University Press, 1998. 3–26.
Berry, Ellen E. *Curved Thought and Textual Wandering: Gertrude Stein's Postmodernism*. Ann Arbor: University of Michigan Press, 1992.
Binni, Walter. *La poetica del decadentismo italiano*. Firenze: Sansoni, 1938.
Biocca, Frank A. "The Pursuit of Sound: Radio, Perception and Utopia in the Early Twentieth Century." *Media, Culture and Society* 10 (1988): 61–79.
Birkhead, May. "All Paris Thrilled by Radio Invention." *New York Times* December 18, 1927: N16.
Blue, Howard. *Words at War: World War II Era Radio Drama and the Postwar Broadcasting Industry Blacklist*. Lanham, Md.: Scarecrow Press, 2002.
Blum, Cinzia. "Transformations in the Futurist Technological Mythopoeia." *Philological Quarterly* 74.1 (1995): 77–97.
Blythe, Ronald. *The Age of Illusion: Some Glimpses of Britain between the Wars 1919–1940*. 1963. Oxford, UK: Oxford University Press, 1983.
Bo, Carlo. "La nuova poesia." *Il novecento*. Ed. Natalino Sapegno. Milano: Garzanti, 1987.
Booth, Marcella. "The Zukofsky Papers: The Cadence of a Life." *Louis Zukofsky: Man and Poet*. Ed. Carroll F. Terrell. Orono, Maine: National Poetry Foundation, 1979. 393–400.
Brecht, Bertolt. *Brecht on Film and Radio*. Trans. and ed. Marc Silberman. London: Methuen, 2000.
Breiner, Laurence. "Caribbean Voices on the Air: Radio, Poetry, and Nationalism in the Anglophone Caribbean." *Communities of the Air: Radio Century, Radio Culture*. Ed. Susan Merrill Squier. Durham, N.C.: Duke University Press, 2003. 93–108.
Brendon, Piers. *The Dark Valley: A Panorama of the 1930s*. London: Jonathan Cape, 2000.
Breslin, Glenna. "Lorine Niedecker: Composing a Life." *Revealing Lives: Autobiography, Biography, and Gender*. Ed. Susan Groag Bell and Marilyn Yalom. New York: State University of New York Press, 1990. 141–53.
Breuer, Josef and Sigmund Freud. *Studies on Hysteria. The Standard Edition of the Complete Psychological Works of Sigmund Freud*. Ed. James Strachey. London: Hogarth Press, 1953–74. Vol. 2, 1–134.

Bridson, D. G. *Prospero and Ariel: The Rise and Fall of Radio: A Personal Recollection.* London: Gollancz, 1971.

Briggs, Asa. *The Golden Age of Wireless. The History of Broadcasting in the United Kingdom, Vol. II.* London: Oxford University Press, 1965.

Brown, Robert J. *Manipulating the Ether: The Power of Broadcast Radio in Thirties America.* Jefferson, N.C.: McFarland, 1999.

Burke, Kenneth. *Language as Symbolic Action.* Berkeley: University of California Press, 1966.

Burns, C. DeLisle. *Leisure in the Modern World.* New York: Century, 1932.

Calder-Marshall, Arthur. *The Changing Scene.* London: Chapman and Hall, 1937.

Cameron, Evan William. "*Citizen Kane*: The Influence of Radio Drama on Cinematic Design." *Papers of the Radio Literature Conference 1978.* Ed. Peter Lewis. Durham: University of Durham Press, 1978. 85–98.

Campbell, Timothy C. *Wireless Writing in the Age of Marconi.* Minneapolis: University of Minnesota Press, 2006.

Cantril, Hadley. *Invasion from Mars: A Study in the Psychology of Panic.* Princeton, N.J.: Princeton University Press, 1940.

Cantril, Hadley and Gordon W. Allport. *The Psychology of Radio.* New York: P. Smith, 1941.

Cardiff, David. "The Serious and the Popular: Aspects of the Evolution of the Radio Talk, 1928-1939." *Media, Culture and Society* 2 (1980): 29–47.

———. "Time, Money and Culture: BBC Programme Finances, 1927–1939." *Media, Culture and Society* 5 (1983): 379–80.

Carpenter, Humphrey. *A Serious Character: The Life of Ezra Pound.* Boston: Houghton Mifflin, 1988.

Carpignano, Paolo and Robin Andersen, Stanley Aronowitz, and William DiFazio. "Chatter in the Age of Electronic Reproduction: Talk Television and the 'Public Mind.'" *The Phantom Public Sphere.* Ed. Bruce Robbins. Minneapolis: University of Minnesota Press, 1993. 93–120.

Chavez, Carlos. *Toward a New Music: Music and Electricity.* New York: Norton, 1927.

Cheney, Margaret. *Nikola Tesla: Man Out of Time.* Englewood Cliffs, N.J.: Prentice Hall, 1981.

Chessman, Harriet. *The Public Is Invited to Dance: Representation, the Body, and Dialogue in Gertrude Stein.* Stanford, Calif.: Stanford University Press, 1989.

Clark, Suzanne. *Sentimental Modernism: Women Writers and the Revolution of the Word.* Bloomington: Indiana University Press, 1991.

———. "Uncanny Millay." *Millay at 100: A Critical Reappraisal.* Ed. Diane P. Freedman. Carbondale: Southern Illinois University Press, 1995. 3–26.

Clark, T. J. *Farewell to an Idea: Episodes from a History of Modernism.* New Haven: Yale University Press, 1999.

Clarke, Bruce. "Allegories of Victorian Thermodynamics." *Configurations* 4 (1996): 67–90.

Cockburn, Claud. *Bestseller: The Books that Everyone Read, 1900-1939.* 1972. Harmondsworth, UK: Penguin, 1975.

Codel, Martin. Introduction. *Radio and Its Future*. Ed. Martin Codel. 1930. Rpt. New York: Arno Press and the *New York Times*, 1972.
Conner, Kim. "Beckett and Radio: The Radioactive Voice." *Samuel Beckett Today/Aujourd'hui* 6 (1997): 303–12.
Connolly, Cyril. "Writers and Society, 1940–3." *The Condemned Playground: Essays: 1927–1944*. London: Hogarth, 1985. 260–87.
Connor, James A. "Radio Free Joyce: *Wake* Language and the Experience of Radio." *Sound States: Innovative Poetics and Acoustical Technologies*. Ed. Adalaide Morris. Chapel Hill: University of North Carolina Press, 1997. 17–31.
Connor, Steven. *Dumbstruck: A Cultural History of Ventriloquism*. New York: Oxford University Press, 2000.
Conrad, Bryce. "Gertrude Stein in the American Marketplace." *Journal of Modern Literature* 19.2 (1995): 215–33.
Conrad, Joseph. *The Nigger of the 'Narcissus.'* 1897. Oxford, UK: Oxford University Press, 1984.
Contini, Gianfranco. "Innovazioni Metriche Italiane fra Otto e Novecento." *La Letteratura italiana Otto-Novecento, Vol. 4*. Firenze: Sansoni, 1974. 185–95.
———. *Letteratura dell'Italia Unita 1861–1968*. Firenze: Sansoni, 1968.
Cornell, Julien. *The Trial of Ezra Pound*. London: Faber and Faber, 1966.
Cortelazzo, Manlio and Paolo Zolli. "Sorprendere." *Dizionario etimologico della lingua italiana*. Vol. 5. Bologna: Zanichelli, 1988. 1232.
Corwin, Norman. *On a Note of Triumph*. New York: Simon and Schuster, 1945.
———. *Seems Radio Is Here to Stay*. *Radiotext(e)*. Ed. Neil Strauss. New York: Semiotext(e), 1993. 137–46.
———. *Untitled and Other Radio Dramas*. New York: Henry Holt, 1947.
Cory, Mark. "Soundplay: The Polyphonous Tradition of German Radio Art." *Wireless Imagination: Sound, Radio, and the Avant-Garde*. Ed. Douglas Kahn and Gregory Whitehead. Cambridge, Mass.: MIT Press, 1992. 331–72.
Costello, Brannon. "Richard Wright's *Lawd Today!* and the Political Uses of Modernism." *African American Review* 37.1 (2003): 39–52.
Coyle, Michael. "Checklist of the Radio Broadcasts of T. S. Eliot." *T. S. Eliot and the Turning World*. Ed. Jewel Spears Brooker. London: Macmillan, 2001. 205–13.
———. "Eliot on the Air: 'Culture' and the Challenges of Mass Communication." *T. S. Eliot and the Turning World*. Ed. Jewel Spears Brooker. London: Macmillan, 2001. 141–54.
———. "The European Radio Broadcasts of T. S. Eliot." *Miscelánea: A Journal of English and American Studies* 20 (1999): 341–53.
———. *Ezra Pound, Popular Genres, and the Discourse of Culture*. University Park: Pennsylvania State University Press, 1995.
———. "'This rather elusory broadcast technique': T. S. Eliot and the Genre of the Radio Talk." *ANQ* 11.4 (1998): 32–42.
"Creating a Demand." *Listener* January 30, 1929: 98.
Crisell, Andrew. *An Introductory History of British Broadcasting*. 2d ed. London: Routledge, 1997.

Croft, Andy. *Red Letter Days: British Fiction in the 1930s*. London: Lawrence and Wishart, 1990.

Cuddy-Keane, Melba. "Virginia Woolf, Sound Technology and the New Orality." *Virginia Woolf in the Age of Mechanical Reproduction*. Ed. Pamela Caughie. New York: Garland, 2000. 69–96.

cummings, e.e. *The Selected Letters of e.e.cummings*. Ed. Frederick W. Dupree. New York: Harcourt Brace, 1969.

Curnutt, Kirk. "Inside and Outside: Gertrude Stein on Identity, Celebrity, and Authenticity." *Journal of Modern Literature* 23.2 (1999): 291–308.

Curry, Elizabeth R. "Rex Warner on the Allegorical Novel, Power Politics, and the Contemporary Scene: A Personal Interview." *Genre* 5 (1972): 404–15.

Curry, Tom. "The Soul Snatcher." *Astounding Stories* April 1930: 101–11.

Cuthbert, Margaret, ed. *Adventure in Radio*. New York: Howell, Soskin, 1945.

Czitrom, Daniel J. *Media and the American Mind: From Morse to McLuhan*. Chapel Hill: University of North Carolina Press, 1983.

Danius, Sara. *The Senses of Modernism: Technology, Perception, and Aesthetics*. Ithaca, N.Y.: Cornell University Press, 2002.

Davidson, Michael. "Technologies of Presence: Orality and the Tapevoice of Contemporary Poetics." *Sound States: Innovative Poetics and Acoustical Technologies*. Ed. Adalaide Morris. Chapel Hill: University of North Carolina Press, 1997. 97–125.

Day Lewis, C. *The Buried Day*. New York: Harper, 1960.

———. "The Revolution in Literature." *Listener* March 27, 1935: 511–12, 537.

———. *Starting Point*. New York: Harper, 1938.

Day Lewis, C., ed. *The Mind in Chains: Socialism and the Cultural Revolution*. London: Frederick Muller, 1937.

De Certeau, Michel. "Walking in the City." *The Cultural Studies Reader*. Ed. Simon During. London: Routledge, 1993. 151–60.

de Gourmont, Remy. *The Natural Philosophy of Love*. Trans. Ezra Pound. London: Boni and Liveright, 1922.

Deane, Patrick. *History in Our Hands: A Critical Anthology of Writings on Literature, Culture and Politics from the 1930s*. London: Leicester University Press, 1998.

Deleuze, Gilles. "Ethics without Morality." *The Deleuze Reader*. Ed. Constantin V. Boundas. New York: Columbia University Press, 1993. 69–77.

Dennett, Daniel C. *Consciousness Explained*. Harmondsworth, UK: Penguin, 1993.

Denny, George V., Jr. "Radio Builds Democracy." *Journal of Educational Sociology* 14.6 (1941): 370–77.

Dent, Peter, ed. *The Full Note: Lorine Niedecker*. Budleigh Salterton, Devon: Interim Press, 1983.

Derrida, Jacques. "Living On/Border Lines." *Deconstruction and Criticism*. Ed. H. Bloom. New York: Continuum, 1979.

Dery, Marc. "Jammers, Spookers, and Scramblers: Information War in the Ether." *Radiotext(e)*. Ed. Neil Strauss. New York: Semiotext(e), 1993. 253–58.

Deutsch, Helene. "Occult Processes Occurring during Psychoanalysis." *Imago* 12 (1926): 418–33.

Devereux, George. "A Summary of Istvan Hollos' Theories." *Psychoanalysis and the Occult*. Ed. George Devereux. New York: International Universities Press, 1953. 199–203.

"Discussion Groups." *Listener* January 23, 1929: 60.

Doane, Mary Anne. "Information, Crisis, Catastrophe." *Logics of Television: Essays in Cultural Criticism*. Ed. Patricia Mellencamp. Bloomington: Indiana University Press, 1990. 222–39.

"Does the B.B.C. Care for Its Listeners?" *Listener* July 3, 1935: 1–2, 38–37.

Doob, Leonard, ed. *Ezra Pound Speaking: Radio Speeches of World War II*. Westport, Conn.: Greenwood Press, 1978.

Dos Passos, John. *Number One*. New York: Houghton Mifflin, 1943.

Douglas, Susan. *Inventing American Broadcasting, 1899–1922*. Baltimore: Johns Hopkins University Press, 1989.

———. *Listening In: Radio and the American Imagination from Amos 'n' Andy and Edward R. Murrow to Wolfman Jack and Howard Stern*. New York: Times Books, 1999.

Dunham, Franklin. "Democracy and the Radio." *Public Opinion Quarterly* 2.1 (1938): 77–79.

DuPlessis, Rachel Blau. "Lorine Niedecker, the Anonymous: Gender, Class, Genre and Resistances." *Lorine Niedecker: Woman and Poet*. Ed. Jenny Penberthy. Orono: National Poetry Foundation, 1996. 113–37.

DuPlessis, Rachel Blau and Peter Quartermain, eds. *The Objectivist Nexus: Essays in Cultural Poetics*. Tuscaloosa: University of Alabama Press, 1999.

Eastman, Max. *Great Companions: Critical Memories of Some Famous Friends*. New York: Farrar, Straus and Cudahy, 1959.

Eliot, T. S. *Christianity and Culture. Two Noted Books Complete in One Volume: The Idea of a Christian Society, and Notes towards the Definition of Culture*. New York: Harvest, 1968.

———. "In Praise of Kipling's Verse." *Harper's* 184.1106 (1942): 149–57.

———. "Last Words." *Criterion* 18.71 (1939): 269–70.

———. "Literature." *The Unity of European Culture: A Series of Broadcasts given over the B.B.C. Foreign Service July to October 1953*. Ed. Richard Law. London: William Clowes, 1953. 19–21.

———. "Notes . . . from T. S. Eliot." *University of Chicago Magazine* 43.3 (1950): 11.

———. *On Poetry and Poets*. London: Faber and Faber, 1957.

———. "The Problem of Education." *Harvard Advocate* 121.1 (1934): 11–12.

———. *Selected Essays*. New York: Harcourt, 1964.

———. "T. S. Eliot on Poetry in Wartime." *Common Sense* 11.10 (October 1942): 351.

———. "The Television Habit." *London Times* December 20, 1950: 7.

———. "Television Is Not Friendly Enough." *City Press* [London] November 28, 1958: 12.

———. *The Use of Poetry and the Use of Criticism*. Cambridge, Mass.: Harvard University Press, 1961.

Ellmann, Maud. *The Poetics of Impersonality: T. S. Eliot and Ezra Pound*. Brighton: Harvester, 1987.

Ely, Melvin Patrick. *The Adventures of Amos 'n' Andy: A Social History of an American Phenomenon*. New York: Free Press, 1991.

Esposito, Roberto. *Immunitas. Protezione e negazione della vita*. Torino: Einaudi, 2002.

Esslin, Martin. "Samuel Beckett and the Art of Broadcasting." *Mediations: Essays on Brecht, Beckett and the Media*. New York: Grove Press, 1982. 125–54.

Faranda, Lisa Pater, ed. *"Between Your House and Mine": The Letters of Lorine Niedecker to Cid Corman, 1960–1970*. Durham, N.C.: Duke University Press, 1986.

"Farewell to Savoy Hill." *Listener* May 4, 1932: 632.

Farman, Irvin. *Tandy's Money Machine: How Charles Tandy Built Radio Shack into the World's Largest Electronics Chain*. Chicago: Mobium, 1992.

Fearing, Kenneth. *Clark Gifford's Body*. New York: Random House, 1942.

Fisher, Margaret. *Ezra Pound's Radio Operas: The BBC Experiments, 1931-33*. Cambridge, Mass.: MIT Press, 2002.

Fisher, Sterling. "The Radio and Public Opinion." *Public Opinion Quarterly* 2.1 (1938): 79–82.

Fleay, Clive and M. L. Sanders. "Looking into the Abyss: George Orwell at the BBC." *Journal of Contemporary History* 24 (1989): 503–18.

Flint, R. W., ed. *Marinetti: Selected Writings*. New York: Farrar, Straus and Giroux, 1972.

Flory, Wendy Stallard. *Ezra Pound and the Cantos: A Record of Struggle*. New Haven, Conn.: Yale University Press, 1980.

Forrester, John. *The Seductions of Psychoanalysis: Freud, Lacan, and Derrida*. Cambridge, UK: Cambridge University Press, 1992.

Forster, E. M. *Commonplace Book*. Stanford, Calif.: Stanford University Press, 1985.

———. "In My Library." *A Bloomsbury Group Reader*. Ed. S. P. Rosenbaum. Oxford: Blackwell, 1993. 292–95.

Foucault, Michel. *Discipline and Punish: The Birth of the Prison*. New York: Vintage, 1995.

Fraser, Nancy. "Rethinking the Public Sphere: A Contribution to the Critique of Actually Existing Democracy." *The Phantom Public Sphere*. Ed. Bruce Robbins. Minneapolis: University of Minnesota Press, 1993. 1–32.

Freedman, Diane P., ed. *Millay at 100: A Critical Reappraisal*. Carbondale: Southern Illinois University Press, 1995.

Freud, Sigmund. *Beyond the Pleasure Principle*. 1920. New York: Norton, 1961.

———. *Civilization and Its Discontents*. 1930. New York: Norton, 1989.

———. *The Complete Correspondence of Sigmund Freud and Ernest Jones, 1908–1939*. Ed. R. Andrew Paskauskas. Cambridge, Mass.: Harvard University Press, 1993.

———. "Dreams and the Occult." *Psychoanalysis and the Occult*. Ed. George Devereux. New York: International Press, 1953. 91–112.

———. "Dreams and Telepathy." *The Standard Edition of the Complete Psychological*

Works of Sigmund Freud. Ed. James Strachey. London: Hogarth Press, 1953–74. Vol. 18, 197–220.

———. "Negation." *The Standard Edition of the Complete Psychological Works of Sigmund Freud.* Ed. James Strachey. London: Hogarth Press, 1953–74. Vol. 19, 233–38.

———. "The Occult Significance of Dreams." *The Standard Edition of the Complete Psychological Works of Sigmund Freud.* Ed. James Strachey. London: Hogarth Press, 1953–74. Vol. 19, 127–38.

———. "Project for a Scientific Psychology." *The Standard Edition of the Complete Psychological Works of Sigmund Freud.* Ed. James Strachey. London: Hogarth Press, 1953–74. Vol. 1, 283–388.

———. "Psychoanalysis and Telepathy." *The Standard Edition of the Complete Psychological Works of Sigmund Freud.* Ed. James Strachey. London: Hogarth Press, 1953–74. Vol. 18, 177–93.

———. "Psycho-Analytic Notes on an Autobiographical Account of a Case of Paranoia (Dementia Paranoides)." *The Standard Edition of the Complete Psychological Works of Sigmund Freud.* Ed. James Strachey. London: Hogarth Press, 1953–74. Vol. 12, 3–82.

———. *The Standard Edition of the Complete Psychological Works of Sigmund Freud.* Ed. James Strachey. London: Hogarth Press, 1953–74.

———. "Totem and Taboo." *The Standard Edition of the Complete Psychological Works of Sigmund Freud.* Ed. James Strachey. London: Hogarth Press, 1953–74. Vol. 13, 1–161.

———. "The Uncanny." *The Standard Edition of the Complete Psychological Works of Sigmund Freud.* Ed. James Strachey. London: Hogarth Press, 1953–74. Vol. 17, 219–56.

———. "Victor Tausk." *The Standard Edition of the Complete Psychological Works of Sigmund Freud.* Ed. James Strachey. London: Hogarth Press, 1953–74. Vol. 17, 275.

Frost, Everett C. "Mediatating on Beckett, *Embers* and Radio Theory." *Beckett and the Arts: Music, Visual Arts, and Non-Print Media.* Ed. Lois Oppenheim. New York: Garland, 1999. 311–31.

Froula, Christine. *A Guide to Ezra Pound's Selected Poems.* New York: New Directions, 1982.

Frye, Northrop. *Anatomy of Criticism.* Princeton, N.J.: Princeton University Press, 1957.

Furr, Derek. "Listening to Millay." *Journal of Modern Literature* 29.2 (2006): 94–110.

"Futurismo." *Dizionario critico della letteratura italiana.* 2d ed. Vol. 2. Torino: Unione Tipografico Editrice, 1986.

Gallup, Donald. *T. S. Eliot: A Bibliography—Revised and Extended Edition.* New York: Harcourt, 1969.

Giddings, Robert. "John Reith and the Rise of Radio." *Literature and Culture in Modern Britain, Volume 1: 1900– 1929.* Ed. Clive Bloom. London: Longman, 1993. 146–66.

———. "Radio in Peace and War." *Literature and Culture in Modern Britain Volume 2: 1930–1955.* Ed. Gary Day. Harlow: Longman, 1997. 132–57.

Gilbert, Susan. "Female Female Impersonator: Millay and the Theatre of Personality."

Critical Essays on Edna St. Vincent Millay. Ed. William B. Thesing. New York: G. K. Hall, 1993. 293–313.

———. *Millay at 100: A Critical Reappraisal*. Ed. Diane P. Freedman. Carbondale: Southern Illinois University Press, 1995. 163–81.

Gitelman, Lisa. *Scripts, Grooves and Writing Machines*. Stanford, Calif.: Stanford University Press, 1999.

Glancey, Jonathan. "Through the Round Window." *The Guardian* online, Monday, July 28, 2003. http://www.guardian.co.uk/print/0%2C3858%2C4721184-110428%2C00.html.

Goldman, Martin. *The Demon in the Aether: The Story of James Clerk Maxwell*. Edinburgh: Paul Harris, 1983.

Gordon, David. "Meeting E. P. and Then . . ." *Paideuma* 1.13 (1974). 112–18.

Gould, Jack. "A Minority Report." *New York Times*. May 20, 1945: x5.1.

Gould, Jean. *Amy: The World of Amy Lowell and the Imagist Movement*. New York: Dodd, Mead, 1975.

Hansen, Miriam Bratu. "The Mass Production of the Senses." 6.2 (1999): 59–77.

Hanssen, Beatrice. *Walter Benjamin's Other History*. Berkeley: University of California Press, 1998.

Haraway, Donna. "A Cyborg Manifesto: Science, Technology, and Socialist-Feminism in the Late Twentieth Century." *Simians, Cyborgs, and Women: The Reinvention of Nature*. London: Routledge, 1991. 149–81.

Harrington, Joseph. "Wallace Stevens and the Poetics of National Insurance." *American Literature*. 67.1 (1995): 95–114.

Harris, Percy W. "The Maintenance of Wireless Telegraph Apparatus." 1917. www.earlyradiohistory.us/1917ship.htm.

Harrison, Ian. *The Book of Inventions*. New York: National Geographic, 2004.

Hayles, N. Katherine. *Chaos Bound: Orderly Disorder in Contemporary Literature and Science*. Ithaca, N.Y.: Cornell University Press, 1990.

———. "Voices out of Bodies, Bodies out of Voices: Audiotape and the Production of Subjectivity." *Sound States: Innovative Poetics and Acoustical Technologies*. Ed. Adalaide Morris. Chapel Hill: University of North Carolina Press, 1997. 74–96.

Helleman, Frank. "Towards Techno-Poetics and Beyond: The Emergence of Modernism/Avant-Garde Poetics out of Science and Media-Technology." *The Turn of the Century: Modernism and Modernity in Literature and the Arts*. European Cultures: Studies in Literature and the Arts, no. 3. Ed. Christian Berg and Frank Durieux. Berlin: de Gruyter, 1995. 291–301.

Heyman, C. David. *Ezra Pound: The Last Rower: A Political Profile*. New York: Richard Seaver/Viking, 1976.

Hill, Jonathan. *The Cat's Whisker: 50 Years of Radio Design*. London: Oresko Books, 1978.

Hilmes, Michele. *Radio Voices: American Broadcasting, 1922–1952*. Minneapolis: University of Minnesota Press, 1997.

Holley, Margaret. *The Poetry of Marianne Moore: A Study in Voice and Value*. New York: Cambridge University Press, 1987.

Holroyd, Michael. *Lytton Strachey and the Bloomsbury Group: His Work, Their Influence*. Harmondsworth, UK: Penguin, 1971.

Hong, Sungook. *Wireless: From Marconi's Black-Box to the Audio*. Cambridge, Mass.: MIT Press, 2001.

Horkheimer, Max and Theodor W. Adorno. "The Culture Industry." *Dialectic of Enlightenment*. Trans. Edmund Jephcott. 1947. Rpt. Stanford, Calif.: Stanford University Press, 2002.

Hullot-Kentor, Robert. "Right Listening and a New Type of Human Being." *The Cambridge Companion to Adorno*. Ed. Tom Huhn, Cambridge, UK: Cambridge University Press, 2004. 181–97.

———. "Second Salvage: Prolegomenon to a Reconstruction of *Current of Music*." *Cultural Critique* 60 (Spring 2005): 134–69.

"Human Radio Emanations." *New York Times*. September 28, 1927: 27.

Huyssen, Andreas. *After the Great Divide: Modernism, Mass Culture, Postmodernism*. Bloomington: Indiana University Press, 1987.

Hynes, Samuel. *The Auden Generation: Literature and Politics in England in the 1930s*. New York: Viking, 1977.

Jaffe, Aaron. *Modernism and the Culture of Celebrity*. New York: Cambridge University Press, 2005.

Jameson, Fredric. *Postmodernism, or, the Cultural Logic of Late Capitalism*. Durham, N.C.: Duke University Press, 1991.

Jameson, Storm. "Documents." *Writing in Revolt: Theory and Examples*. Fact 4 (1937): 9–17.

Jay, Martin. *Downcast Eyes: The Denigration of Vision in Twentieth Century French Thought*. Berkeley: University of California Press, 1993.

Jaynes, Julian. *The Origin of Consciousness in the Breakdown of the Bicameral Mind*. Boston: Houghton Mifflin, 1976.

Jenemann, David. *Adorno in America 1938–1953*. Minneapolis: University of Minnesota Press, 2007.

Johnston, John. "Friedrich Kittler: Media Theory after Poststructuralism." *Friedrich A. Kittler Essays: Literature Media Information Systems*. Ed. John Johnston. Amsterdam: OPA, 1997. 2–26.

———. "Mediality in *Vineland* and *Neuromancer*." *Reading Matters: Narratives in the New Media Ecology*. Ithaca, N.Y.: Cornell University Press, 1997. 173–92.

Johnstone, Richard. *The Will to Believe: Novelists of the Nineteen-Thirties*. Oxford: Oxford University Press, 1982.

Joyce, James. *Finnegans Wake*. London: Faber and Faber, 1975.

———. *Ulysses*. London: Penguin, 1992.

Kahn, Douglas. "Death in Light of the Phonograph: Raymond Roussel's *Locus Solus*." *Wireless Imagination: Sound, Radio, and the Avant-Garde*. Ed. Douglas Kahn and Gregory Whitehead. Cambridge, Mass.: MIT Press, 1992. 69–104.

———. "Introduction: Histories of Sound Once Removed." *Wireless Imagination: Sound, Radio, and the Avant-Garde*. Ed. Douglas Kahn and Gregory Whitehead. Cambridge, Mass.: MIT Press, 1992. 1–29.

———. *Noise Water Meat: A History of Sound in the Arts*. Cambridge, Mass.: MIT Press, 1999.

Kahn, Douglas and Gregory Whitehead, eds. *Wireless Imagination: Sound, Radio, and the Avant-Garde*. Cambridge, Mass.: MIT Press, 1992.

Kaplan, Milton Allen. *Radio and Poetry*. New York: Columbia University Press, 1949.

Kavina, Lydia. "My Experience with the Theremin." *Leonardo Music Journal* 6 (1996): 51–56.

Kayman, Martin. *The Modernism of Ezra Pound: The Science of Poetry*. London: Macmillan, 1986.

Kearns, George. *A Guide to Ezra Pound's Selected Cantos*. New Brunswick, N.J.: Rutgers University Press, 1980.

Kennedy, David M. *Freedom from Fear: The American People in Depression and War, 1929–1945*. New York: Oxford University Press, 1999.

Kenner, Hugh. *The Mechanic Muse*. Oxford: Oxford University Press, 1987.

———. *The Pound Era*. Berkeley: University of California Press, 1973.

———. "The Sound of Sense." *Paideuma* 9.3 (1980): 9–12.

Kermode, Frank. *History and Value*. Oxford: Oxford University Press, 1988.

Kern, Stephen. *The Culture of Time and Space, 1880–1918*. Cambridge, Mass.: Harvard University Press, 1983.

Kipling, Rudyard. "Wireless." *Traffics and Discoveries*. London: Macmillan, 1904. 197–223.

Kittler, Friedrich A. *Discourse Networks, 1800/1900*. Trans. Michael Metteer. Stanford, Calif.: Stanford University Press, 1990.

———. *Gramophone, Film, Typewriter*. Trans. Geoffrey Winthrop-Young and Michael Wutz. Stanford, Calif.: Stanford University Press, 1999.

Knowlson, James. *Damned to Fame: The Life of Samuel Beckett*. London: Bloomsbury, 1996.

Koch, Howard. *The Panic Broadcast*. New York: Avon, 1970.

Lacan, Jacques. "The Circuit." *The Seminar of Jacques Lacan: Book II: The Ego in Freud's Theory and in the Technique of Psychoanalysis 1954–1955*. Trans. Jacques-Alain Miller. New York: Norton, 1991. 73–85.

Lambert, R. S. *Ariel and All His Quality: An Impression of the BBC from Within*. London: Gollancz, 1940.

Landini, Adelmo. *Marconi sulle vie dell'etere: la storica impresa narrata dell'Ufficiale Marconista dell'Elettra*. Torino: Società Editrice Internazionale, 1955.

Laplanche, Jean. *Life and Death in Psychoanalysis*. Baltimore: Johns Hopkins University Press, 1976.

Latour, Bruno. *Pandora's Hope*. Cambridge, Mass.: Harvard University Press, 1999.

———. *Science in Action*. Cambridge, Mass.: Harvard University Press, 1987.

Law, Richard, ed. *The Unity of European Culture: A Series of Broadcasts given over the B.B.C. Foreign Service July to October 1953*. London: William Clowes, 1953.

Lazarsfeld, Paul F. "An Episode in the History of Social Research: A Memoir." *The Intellectual Migration: Europe and America, 1930–1960*. Ed. Donald Fleming and

Bernard Bailyn. Cambridge, Mass.: Belknap Press of Harvard University Press, 1969. 270–337.

Leavis, F. R. "What's Wrong with Criticism?" *Scrutiny* 1.2 (1932): 132–46.

Leavis, Q. D. "Leslie Stephen: Cambridge Critic." *Scrutiny* 7.4 (1939): 404–15.

LeMahieu, D. L. *A Culture for Democracy: Mass Communication and the Cultivated Mind in Britain between the Wars*. Oxford, UK: Clarendon, 1988.

Levin, Harry. *James Joyce: A Critical Introduction*. Norfolk: New Directions, 1941.

Levine, George. *Realism and Representation: Essays on the Problem of Realism in Relation to Science, Literature, and Culture*. Madison: University of Wisconsin Press, 1993.

Levy, Paul. *Moore: G. E. Moore and the Cambridge Apostles*. Oxford: Oxford University Press, 1981.

Lewis, Percy Wyndham. *Time and Western Man*. Santa Rosa, Calif.: Black Sparrow, 1993.

Lewis, Sinclair. *It Can't Happen Here*. New York: Doubleday, 1935.

Lewty, Jane. "Virginia Woolf and the Synapses of Radio." *Locating Woolf: The Politics of Space and Place*. Ed. Anna Snaith and Michael Whitworth. London: Palgrave Macmillan, 2007. 148–63.

Lippmann, Walter. *Public Opinion*. New York: Free Press, 1997.

"Literary Values." *Listener* 14 May 1930: 844.

Lodge, Sir Oliver. *Ether and Reality*. London: Hodder and Stoughton, 1925.

Lomas, Robert. *The Man Who Invented the Twentieth Century: Nikola Tesla, Forgotten Genius of the Twentieth Century*. London: Headline, 1999.

Longenbach, James. *Wallace Stevens: The Plain Sense of Things*. New York: Oxford University Press, 1991.

Lott, Eric. "Double V, Double-Time: Bebop's Politics of Style." *Callaloo* 11.3 (1988): 597–605. Rpt. in *The Jazz Cadence of American Culture*. Ed. Robert G. O'Meally. New York: Columbia University Press, 1998. 457–68.

———. *Love and Theft: Blackface Minstrelsy and the American Working Class*. New York: Oxford University Press, 1993.

Lowenthal, Leo. "Biographies in Popular Magazines." *Radio Research 1942–1943*. Ed. Paul Lazarsfeld and Frank N. Stanton. New York: Sloan, Duell and Pearce, 1943. 507–48.

Luckhurst, Roger. *The Invention of Telepathy: 1870–1901*. London: Oxford University Press, 2002.

MacCarthy, Desmond. "The Art of Reading." Desmond and Mary MacCarthy Papers. Lilly Library, Bloomington, Ind.

———. "Henry James." *Portraits*. New York: Oxford University Press, 1955. 149–69.

———. "The Magnifying Glass on Modern Literature." *Listener* September 23, 1931: 479–80.

———. "Prophets, Priests, and Purveyors." *Criticism*. 1932. Freeport, N.Y.: Books for Libraries, 1969. 115–18.

Macdonell, A. G. *England, Their England*. 1933. London: Macmillan, 1957.

MacLeish, Archibald. *The Fall of the City: A Verse Play for Radio.* New York: Farrar and Rinehart, 1937.

Madge, Charles. "Press, Radio, and Social Consciousness." *The Mind in Chains: Socialism and the Cultural Revolution.* Ed. C. Day Lewis. London: Frederick Muller, 1937. 147–63.

Maines, Rachel P. *The Technology of Orgasm: "Hysteria," the Vibrator, and Women's Sexual Satisfaction.* Baltimore: Johns Hopkins University Press, 1999.

Marinetti, F. T. and Pino Masnata. "Multiplied Man and the Reign of the Machine." *Marinetti: Selected Writings.* Ed. R. W. Flint. New York: Farrar, Straus and Giroux, 1972. 90–93.

———. "La Radia." *Gazetta del Popolo* Oct. 1933. Rpt. in *Wireless Imagination: Sound, Radio, and the Avant-Garde.* Ed. Douglas Kahn and Gregory Whitehead. Cambridge, Mass.: MIT Press, 1992. 265–68.

———. "Risposte alle obiezioni." *Teoria e invenzione futurista.* Ed. Luciano De Maria. Milano: Mondadori, 1968.

———. "Technical Manifesto of Futurist Literature." *Marinetti: Selected Writings.* Ed. R. W. Flint. New York: Farrar, Straus and Giroux, 1972. 84–89.

Marks, Peter. "Illusion and Reality: The Spectre of Socialist Realism in Thirties Literature." *Rewriting the Thirties: Modernism and After.* Ed. Keith Williams and Stephen Matthews. London: Longman, 1997. 23–36.

Marvin, Carolyn. *When Old Technologies Were New: Thinking about Electric Communication in the Late Nineteenth Century.* New York: Oxford University Press, 1988.

Masini, Giancarlo. *Marconi.* New York: Marsilio, 1995.

Matheson, Hilda. *Broadcasting.* The Home University Library of Modern Knowledge. London: Thornton Butterworth, 1933.

———. "The Record of the B.B.C: Programme of Speech and Entertainment." *Political Quarterly* 6 (1935): 506–18.

Mattelart, Armand. *Mapping World Communication.* Trans. Susan Emanuel and James A. Cohen. Minneapolis: University of Minnesota Press, 1994.

Matthews, William. "Radio Plays as Literature." *Hollywood Quarterly* 1.1 (1945): 41–42.

McChesney, Robert. *Telecommunications, Mass Media and Democracy.* New York: Oxford University Press, 1993.

McLuhan, Eric. *The Role of Thunder in* Finnegans Wake. Toronto: University of Toronto Press, 1997.

McLuhan, Marshall. *The Gutenberg Galaxy.* Toronto: Toronto University Press, 1962.

———. *Understanding Media: The Extensions of Man.* 1964. Rpt. Boston: MIT Press, 1994.

Mengaldo, Pier Vicenzo. *Il Novecento.* Milano: Il Mulino, 1991.

Menser, Michael. "Becoming-Heterarch: On Technocultural Theory, Minor Science, and the Production of Space." *Technoscience and Cyberculture.* Ed. Stanley Aronowitz et al. London: Routledge, 1996. 293–316.

Middleton, Peter. *Distant Reading: Performance, Readership and Consumption in Contemporary Poetry.* Tuscaloosa: University of Alabama Press, 2005.

———. "Folk Poetry and the American Avant-Garde." *Journal of American Studies*. 31.2 (1997): 203–18.
Milesi, Laurent. "Joyce, Language and Languages." *Palgrave Advances in James Joyce Studies*. Ed. Jean-Michel Rabaté. London: Palgrave Macmillan, 2004. 144–61.
Milford, Nancy. *Savage Beauty: The Life of Edna St. Vincent Millay*. New York: Random House, 2001.
Millay, Edna St. Vincent. *Collected Poems*. New York: Harper Collins, 1956.
———. [Edna St. Vincent Millay reads several of her poems.] Rec. 193–? Audiotape. Brander Matthews Dramatic Museum Collection (Library of Congress). RXA 5652 B1–4.
———. *Letters of Edna St. Vincent Millay*. Ed. Alan Ross Macdougall. New York: Harper, 1952.
———. *The Voice of the Poet: Five American Women*. Series ed. J. D. McClatchy. New York: Random House, 2001.
Miller, Nina. *Making Love Modern: The Intimate Public Worlds of New York's Literary Women*. New York: Oxford University Press, 1999.
Milutis, Joe. *Ether: The Nothing that Connects Everything*. Minneapolis: University of Minnesota Press, 2006.
"The Minstrel and the Microphone." *Listener* October 2, 1929: 436.
Monroe, Harriet. "Comment: The Radio and the Poets." *Poetry* 36.1 (1930): 32–35.
Montague, Stephen. "Rediscovering Leon Theremin." *Tempo* 177 (1991): 18–23.
Montefiore, Janet. *Men and Women Writers of the 1930s: The Dangerous Flood of History*. London: Routledge, 1996.
Moore, G. E. *Principia Ethica*. Cambridge: Cambridge University Press, 1903.
Morris, Adalaide. Introduction. *Sound States: Innovative Poetics and Acoustical Technologies*. Ed. Adalaide Morris. Chapel Hill: University of North Carolina Press, 1997. 1–14.
———. "Sound Technologies and the Modernist Epic: H.D. on the Air." *Sound States: Innovative Poetics and Acoustical Technologies*. Ed. Adalaide Morris. Chapel Hill: University of North Carolina Press, 1997. 32–55.
———, ed. *Sound States: Innovative Poetics and Acoustical Technologies*. Chapel Hill: University of North Carolina Press, 1997.
Morrison, David E. "Kultur and Culture: The Case of Theodor W. Adorno and Paul F. Lazarsfeld." *Social Research* 45.2 (1978): 334.
———. *The Search for a Method: Focus Groups and the Development of Mass Communication Research*. London: University of Luton Press, 1998.
Mortley, G. E. "Crystal Rectification." *Weather and Wireless Magazine* 2 (1924): 13–14.
Muggeridge, Malcolm. *The Thirties*. London: Hamish Hamilton, 1940.
Munton, Alan and Alan Young. "Edward Upward: A Conversation." *PN Review* 19 (1980): 41–45.
"'Music from Ether' Again." *New York Times*, February 15, 1928, 21.
Niedecker, Lorine. *Collected Works*. Ed. Jenny Penberthy. Berkeley: University of California Press, 2002.

―――. "Extracts from Letters to Kenneth Cox." *The Full Note: Lorine Niedecker.* Ed. Peter Dent. Budleigh Salterton, Devon: Interim Press, 1983. 36–42.

―――. "Local Letters." *Lorine Niedecker: Woman and Poet.* Ed. Jenny Penberthy. Orono: National Poetry Foundation, 1996. 87–107.

Oliver, Owen. "The Soul Machine." *Pall Mall Magazine* 48.223 (1911): 744.

Olson, Tillie. *Yonnondio: From the Thirties.* 1934. London: Virago, 1980.

O'Meally, Robert G., ed. *The Jazz Cadence of American Culture.* New York: Columbia University Press, 1998.

Ong, Walter J. *Orality and Literacy: The Technologizing of the Word.* New York: Methuen, 1982.

Oppenheim, Janet. *The Other World: Spiritualism and Psychical Research in England, 1850–1914.* Cambridge, UK: Cambridge University Press, 1985.

"The Oracle from the Microphone." *Listener* July 10, 1929: 48.

Orton, Richard and Hugh Davies. "Theremin." *The New Grove Dictionary of Music and Musicians* 25. London: Macmillan, 2001. 386–87.

Orwell, George. *Poetry and the Microphone.* New Saxon Pamphlet No. 3 (March 1945).

Otis, Laura. "The Other End of the Wire: Uncertainties of Organic and Telegraphic Communication." *Configurations* 9 (2001): 181–206.

Overstreet, Harry A. and Bonaro W. Overstreet. *Town Meeting Comes to Town.* New York: Harper and Bros., 1938.

Owen, Alex. *The Place of Enchantment: British Occultism and the Culture of the Modern.* Chicago: University of Chicago Press, 2004.

Packard, Winthrop. "The Work of a Wireless Telegraph Man." 1904. *The World's Work* (February 1904): 4467–70. http://earlyradiohistory.us/1904work.htm.

Paulu, Burton. *British Broadcasting: Radio and Television in the United Kingdom.* Minneapolis: University of Minnesota Press, 1956.

Pawley, Edward. *BBC Engineering, 1922–72.* London: BBC, 1972.

Penberthy, Jenny. "Life and Writing." *Collected Works.* By Lorine Niedecker. Ed. Jenny Penberthy. Berkeley: University of California Press, 2003. 1–11.

―――, ed. *Lorine Niedecker: Woman and Poet.* Orono: National Poetry Foundation, 1996.

―――. *Niedecker and the Correspondence with Zukofsky, 1931–1970.* Cambridge, UK: Cambridge University Press, 1993.

Perez, Vincent. "Movies, Marxism, and Jim Crow: Richard Wright's Cultural Criticism." *Texas Studies in Literature and Language* 43.2 (2001): 142–68.

Peters, John Durham. *Speaking into the Air: A History of the Idea of Communication.* Chicago: University of Chicago Press, 1999.

Pierce, M. S., John. "Pre-Vision." *Astounding Stories* March 1936: 105–14.

"A Place in the Sun." *Listener* December 4, 1929: 748.

"Points of View." *Listener* November 13, 1929: 640.

Pore, Jarod. "Do-it-yourself Radio and TV." *The Happy Mutant Handbook.* Ed. Mark Frauenfelder, Clara Sinclair, and Gareth Branwyn. New York: Riverhead, 1995. 26–28.

Postgate, Raymond. *What to Do with the B.B.C.* Day to Day Pamphlets No. 28. London: Hogarth Press, 1935.

Pound, Ezra. "A Few Don'ts." *Poetry* I.6 (March 1913).

———. "Antheil and the Treatise on Harmony." *Ezra Pound and Music: The Complete Criticism.* Ed. R. Murray Schafer. New York: New Directions, 1977. 296–306.

———. *The Cantos of Ezra Pound.* New York: New Directions, 1996.

———. *Drafts and Fragments of Cantos CX–CXVII.* London: Faber and Faber, 1970.

———. "e. e. cummings Alive." *New English Weekly* 6.10 (Dec. 20, 1934): 210–11.

———. *Gaudier-Brzeska: A Memoir.* New York: New Directions, 1970.

———. *Guide to Kulchur.* London: Faber and Faber, 1954.

———. *The Letters of Ezra Pound 1907–1941.* Ed. D. D. Paige. London: Faber and Faber, 1951.

———. *Literary Essays of Ezra Pound.* Ed. T. S. Eliot. London: Faber and Faber, 1954.

———. *Personae: Collected Shorter Poems.* Ed. Lea Baechler and A. Walton Litz. London: Faber and Faber, 2001.

———. *Selected Prose 1910–1965.* Ed. William Cookson. New York: New Directions, 1973.

———. *The Spirit of Romance.* New York: New Directions, 1968.

———. *Translations.* Ed. Hugh Kenner. London: Faber and Faber, 1953.

"Prejudice and Education." *Listener* November 6, 1929: 608.

Quartermain, Peter. "Reading Niedecker." *Lorine Niedecker: Woman and Poet.* Ed. Jenny Penberthy. Orono: National Poetry Foundation, 1996. 219–227.

"Radio Listeners in Panic, Taking War Drama as Fact." *New York Times.* October 31, 1938: 1.

"Radio's Aid is Invoked to Explore Telepathy." *New York Times.* August 30, 1925: XX3.

Rasula, Jed. "Understanding the Sound of Not Understanding." *Close Listening: Poetry and the Performed Word.* Ed. Charles Bernstein. New York: Oxford University Press, 1998. 233–61.

Read, Forrest, ed. *The Letters of Ezra Pound to James Joyce.* London: Faber and Faber, 1967.

Reddick, L. D. "Educational Programs for the Improvement of Race Relations: Motion Pictures, Radio, the Press, and Libraries." *Journal of Negro Education* 13.3 (1944): 367–89.

Redman, Tim. *Ezra Pound and Fascism.* Cambridge UK: Cambridge University Press, 1991.

Reed, Thomas H. "Commercial Broadcasting and Civic Education." *Public Opinion Quarterly* 1.3 (1937): 57–67.

Reeve, N. H. *The Novels of Rex Warner.* New York: St. Martin's Press, 1989.

Reith, John. *Broadcast over Britain.* London: Hodder and Stoughton, 1924.

———. Foreword. *All about Your Wireless Set.* By P. P. Eckersley. London: Hodder and Stoughton, [1930]. 5–6.

———. *Into the Wind.* London: Hodder and Stoughton, 1949.

———. *The Reith Diaries.* Ed. Charles Stuart. London: Collins, 1975.

Richardson, Stanley and Jane Alison Hale. "Working Wireless: Beckett's Radio Writing." *Samuel Beckett and the Arts: Music, Visual Arts, and Non-Print Media.* Ed. Lois Oppenheim. New York: Garland, 1999. 269–94.

Rilke, Rainer Maria. *Sonnets to Orpheus.* Trans. David Young. Middletown, Conn.: Wesleyan University Press, 1987.

Robertson, Lisa. "'In Phonographic Deep Song': Sounding Niedecker." *Poetry Project Newsletter* 198 (2004): 11–12.

Rogin, Michael. *Blackface, White Noise: Jewish Immigrants in the Hollywood Melting Pot.* Berkeley: University of California Press, 1996.

Rosenbaum, S. P., ed. *A Bloomsbury Group Reader.* Cambridge, Mass.: Blackwell, 1993.

Rouse, William Merriam. "The Dead Man's Thoughts." *Munsey's Magazine* June 1921: 641–51.

Russell, Eric Frank. "The Great Radio Peril." *Astounding Stories* April 1937: 47–55.

Russolo, Luigi. *The Art of Noise (Futurist Manifesto, 1913).* Trans. Robert Filliou. New York: Something Else Press, 1967.

Rutzky, R. L. *High Techne.* Minneapolis: University of Minnesota Press, 1999.

Saerchinger, César. *Hello America! Radio Adventures in Europe.* Boston: Houghton Mifflin, 1938.

Said, Edward. *Representations of the Intellectual.* New York: Vintage, 1994.

Salaris, Claudia and Lawrence Rainey. "Marketing Modernism: Marinetti as Publisher." *Modernism/modernity* 1.3 (1994): 109–27.

Savage, Barbara Dianne. *Broadcasting Freedom: Radio, War, and the Politics of Race, 1938–1948.* Chapel Hill: University of North Carolina Press, 1999.

Sayre, Jeanette. "Progress in Radio Fan-Mail Analysis." *Public Opinion Quarterly* 3.2 (1939): 272–78.

"Says Human Brain Emits Radio Waves," *New York Times* August 21, 1925: 1.

Scannell, Paddy and David Cardiff. *A Social History of British Broadcasting, Volume One 1929–1939: Serving the Nation.* London: Basil Blackwell, 1991.

Schachterle, Lance. "Information Entropy in Pynchon's Fiction." *Configurations* 4 (1996): 185–214.

Schafer, Murray. "Open Ears." *The Auditory Culture Reader.* Ed. Michael Bull and Les Back. Oxford, UK: Berg, 2003. 25–39.

Schmidt, Leigh Eric. *Hearing Things: Religion, Illusion, and the American Enlightenment.* Cambridge, Mass.: Harvard University Press, 2002.

Schnapp, Jeffrey T. "Propeller Talk." *Modernism/modernity* 1.3 (1994): 153–78.

Sconce, Jeffrey. *Haunted Media: Electronic Presence from Telegraphy to Television.* Durham, N.C.: Duke University Press, 2000.

Seifer, Marc J. *Wizard: The Life and Times of Nikolas Tesla.* New York: Citadel, 1996.

Sieveking, Lance. *The Stuff of Radio.* London: Cassell, 1934.

Simons, David. "Radio Galaxy." *Radiotext(e).* Ed. Neil Strauss. New York: Semiotext(e), 1993. 346–48.

Sinclair, Upton. *Mental Radio: Does It Work, and How?* London: T. Werner Laurie, 1930.

Singer, Ben. "Modernity, Hyperstimulus, and the Rise of Popular Sensationalism."

Cinema and the Invention of Modern Life. Ed. Leo Charney and Vanessa Schwartz. Berkeley: University of California Press, 1995. 72–102.

Sklaroff, Lauren. "Variety for the Servicemen: The Jubilee Show and the Paradox of Racializing Radio in World War II." *American Quarterly* 56.4 (2004): 945–73.

Small, Ian, ed. *The Aesthetes: A Sourcebook*. London: Routledge, 1979.

Smulyan, Susan. *Selling Radio: The Commercialization of American Broadcasting 1920–1934*. Washington, D.C.: Smithsonian Institution Press, 1994.

Solms, Mark. "Sigmund Freud's Drawings." *From Neurology to Psychoanalysis: Sigmund Freud's Neurological Drawings and Diagrams of the Mind*. Ed. Lynn Gamwell and Mark Solms. Binghamton: State University of New York Press, 2006. 13–18.

Spann, Marcella. "Through the Smoke Hole: Ezra Pound's Last Year at St. Elizabeths." *Paideuma* 3.1 (1974): 158–62.

Sprague, Rosemary. *Imaginary Gardens: A Study of Five American Poets*. Philadelphia: Chilton, 1969.

"The Speaker on the Hearth." *Listener* September 11, 1929: 354–55, 358.

Spinelli, Martin. "Not Hearing Poetry on Public Radio." *Communities of the Air: Radio Century, Radio Culture*. Ed. Susan Merrill Squier. Durham, N.C.: Duke University Press, 2003. 195–216.

———. *Radio Radio*. Ubu Web. Ed. Kenneth Goldsmith. November 20, 2005. http://www.ubu.com/radio.

Squier, Susan Merrill, ed. *Communities of the Air: Radio Century, Radio Culture*. Durham, N.C.: Duke University Press, 2003.

"Stabilising Speech." *Listener* July 24, 1929: 120.

Stansky, Peter. *On or About December 1910: Early Bloomsbury and Its Intimate World*. Cambridge, Mass.: Harvard University Press, 1996.

Stein, Gertrude. *Brewsie and Willie*. Writings 1932–1946. Ed. Catharine R. Stimpson and Harriet Chessman. New York: Library of America, 1998. 713–78.

———. "Broadcast at Lyon." Yale Collection of American Literature, Beinecke Library. MSS 76 Series I, Box 9, folder 172.

———. "I Came and Here I Am." *Cosmopolitan*, February 1936. *How Writing Is Written: Volume II of the Previously Uncollected Writings of Gertrude Stein*. Ed. Robert Bartlett Haas. Los Angeles: Black Sparrow Press, 1974. 71–72.

———. *Ida*. Writings 1932–1946. Ed. Catharine R. Stimpson and Harriet Chessman. New York: Library of America, 1998. 609–704.

———. "The New Hope in Our 'Sad Young Men.'" *New York Times Magazine*, June 3, 1945. *How Writing Is Written: Volume II of the Previously Uncollected Writings of Gertrude Stein*. Ed. Robert Bartlett Haas. Los Angeles: Black Sparrow Press, 1974. 143.

———. "Off We All Went to See Germany." *Life*, August 6, 1945. *How Writing Is Written: Volume II of the Previously Uncollected Writings of Gertrude Stein*. Ed. Robert Bartlett Haas. Los Angeles: Black Sparrow Press, 1974. 140.

———. "A Radio Interview." With William Lundell. November 12, 1934, WJZ and NET. *Paris Review* 116 (1990): 95.

———. *Wars I Have Seen*. New York: Random House, 1945.

Sterne, Jonathan. *The Audible Past: Cultural Origins of Sound Reproduction.* Durham, N.C.: Duke University Press, 2003.

Stevens, Wallace. *The Collected Poems.* New York: Vintage, 1990.

———. *Letters of Wallace Stevens.* Ed. Holly Stevens. Berkeley: University of California Press, 1996.

———. *The Necessary Angel: Essays on Reality and the Imagination.* New York: Vintage, 1951.

———. *Opus Posthumous.* Ed. Milton Bates. New York: Vintage, 1990.

Stewart, Garrett. *Reading Voices: Literature and the Phonotext.* Berkeley: University of California Press, 1990.

Strauss, Neil, ed. *Radiotext(e).* New York: Semiotext(e), 1993.

Streeter, Thomas. *Selling the Air: A Critique of the Policy of Commercial Broadcasting in the United States.* Chicago: University of Chicago Press, 1996.

Studebaker, J. W. "Scaling Cultural Frontiers." *Journal of Educational Sociology* 12.8 (1939): 487–91.

Surette, Leon. *The Birth of Modernism: Ezra Pound, T. S. Eliot, W.B. Yeats and the Occult.* Montreal: McGill Queen's University Press, 1993.

Tabachnick, Stephen. *Fiercer than Tigers: The Life and Work of Rex Warner.* East Lansing: Michigan State University Press, 2002.

Tate, Allen. "Ezra Pound." *An Examination of Ezra Pound: A Collection of Essays.* Ed. Peter Russell. Norfolk: New Directions, 1950. 60–72.

Tausk, Victor. "On the Origins of the Influencing Machine." 1918. *Incorporations.* Ed. Jonathan Crary and Sanford Kwinter. New York: Zone, 1992. 542–69.

Tesla, Nikola. *My Inventions: The Autobiography of Nikola Tesla.* New York: Barnes and Noble, 1995.

———. "The Problem of Increasing Human Energy." *Century*, June 1900. http://www.tfcbooks.com/tesla/1919-05-00.htm.

Theall, Donald F. *James Joyce's Techno-Poetics.* Toronto: University of Toronto Press, 1997.

Theremin, Leon S. "The Design of a Musical Instrument Based on Cathode Relays." Trans. Oleg Petrishev. *Leonardo Music Journal* 6 (1996): 49–50.

Thesing, William B. Introduction. *Critical Essays on Edna St. Vincent Millay.* Ed. William B. Thesing. New York: G. K. Hall, 1993. 1–25.

Tichi, Cecelia. *Shifting Gears: Technology, Literature, Culture in Modernist America.* Chapel Hill: University of North Carolina Press, 1987.

Tiffany, Daniel. *Radio Corpse: Imagism and the Cryptaesthetic of Ezra Pound.* Cambridge, Mass.: Harvard University Press, 1995.

Tomlinson, Charles. "Introduction: A Rich Sitter." *The Full Note: Lorine Niedecker.* Ed. Peter Dent. Budleigh Salterton, Devon: Interim Press, 1983. 7–10.

Torrey, E. Fuller. *The Roots of Treason: Ezra Pound and the Secret of St. Elizabeths.* London: Sidgewick and Jackson, 1984.

Troyen, Carol and Erica E. Hirshler. *Charles Sheeler: Paintings and Drawings.* Boston: Little, Brown, 1987.

Tytell, John. *Ezra Pound: The Solitary Volcano.* London: Bloomsbury, 1987.

Ulmer, Gregory. *Heuristics: The Logic of Invention*. Baltimore: Johns Hopkins University Press, 1994.

Upward, Edward. *Journey to the Border*. London: Hogarth Press, 1938.

———. "A Marxist Interpretation of Literature." *The Mind in Chains: Socialism and the Cultural Revolution*. Ed. C. Day Lewis. London: Frederick Muller, 1937. 147–63.

———. "Statement for the Literature/Sociology Conference on '1936' at Essex University, July 1978." *1936, The Sociology of Literature: Proceedings of the Essex Conference on the Sociology of Literature, July 1978*. 197–217.

Utell, Janine. "The Loss of History: The Publishing of 30s Documentary, Word and Image." *Working Papers on the Web* 6 (2003). http://www.shu.ac.uk/wpw/thirties/thirties%20utell%20html.html.

Vaillant, Derek W. "Sounds of Whiteness: Local Radio, Racial Formation, and Public Culture in Chicago, 1921–1935." *American Quarterly* 54.1 (2002): 25–66.

Villiers de l'Isle Adam, Auguste. *Tomorrow's Eve*. [*L'Eve Future*.] Trans. Robert Martin Adams. Urbana: University of Illinois Press, 1982.

Viswanathan, Gauri. *Masks of Conquest: Literary Study and British Rule in India*. New York: Columbia University Press, 1989.

"Voices from the Past." *Listener* May 8, 1929: 634.

Vološinov, V. N. *Marxism and the Philosophy of Language*. Trans. Ladislav Matejka and I. R. Titunik. Cambridge, Mass.: Harvard University Press, 1986.

Walker, Cheryl. "The Female Body as Icon: Edna Millay Wears a Plaid Dress." *Millay at 100: A Critical Reappraisal*. Ed. Diane P. Freedman. Carbondale: Southern Illinois University Press, 1995. 85–99.

Warner, Rex. "The Allegorical Method." *The Cult of Power*. 1947. Port Washington, N.Y.: Kennikat Press, 1969. 130–49.

———. *The Professor*. 1938. New York: Knopf, 1939.

Watkins, Mel. *On the Real Side*. New York: Simon and Schuster, 1994.

Watson, Emily. *The Soundscape of Modernity: Architectural Acoustics and the Culture of Listening in America 1900–1933*. Cambridge, Mass.: MIT Press, 2002.

Weaver, Warren. "Some Recent Contributions to the Mathematical Theory of Communication." *The Mathematical Theory of Communication*. By Claude Shannon and Warren Weaver. 1949. Urbana: University of Illinois Press, 1998.

Weber, Samuel. *Mass Mediauras*. Stanford, Calif.: Stanford University Press, 1996.

"Week by Week." *Listener* May 21, 1930: 888–89.

Weightman, Gavin. *Signor Marconi's Magic Box: How an Amateur Inventor Defied Scientists and Began the Radio Revolution*. London: HarperCollins, 2003.

Weiss, Allen S. *Phantasmic Radio*. Durham, N.C.: Duke University Press, 1995.

Wellek, Rene. *A History of Modern Criticism: 1750–1950*. Vol. 5. New Haven, Conn.: Yale University Press, 1986.

Welles, Orson and Peter Bogdanovich. *This Is Orson Welles*. New York: HarperCollins, 1992.

"What the Public Wants." *Listener* February 5, 1930: 232.

Wheeler, Lesley. *Voicing American Poetry: Sound and Performance from the 1920s to the Present*. Ithaca, N.Y.: Cornell University Press, 2008.

White, E. B. "Comment." *New Yorker* May 21, 1938: 13.

——. *One Man's Meat*. New York: HarperCollins, 1983.

Whitehead, Kate. "Broadcasting Bloomsbury." *The Yearbook of English Studies. Literature in the Modern Media: Radio, Film, and Television Special Number*. Ed. Andrew Gurr. London: Modern Humanities Research Association, 1990. 121–31.

Whitworth, Michael. *Einstein's Wake: Relativity, Metaphor and Modernist Literature*. Oxford, UK: Oxford University Press, 2001.

Wilde, Oscar. "The Soul of Man under Socialism." *The Works of Oscar Wilde*. New York: Walter J. Black, 1927.

Williams, Keith. *British Writers and the Media 1930–45*. Houndsmills, UK: Manchester University Press, 1996.

Williams, Raymond. *The Politics of Modernism: Against the New Conformists*. Ed. Tony Pinkney. London: Verso, 1989.

——. "The Significance of 'Bloomsbury' as a Social and Cultural Group." *Keynes and the Bloomsbury Group*. Ed. Derek Crabtree and A. P. Thirlwall. London: Macmillan, 1980. 40–67.

Williams, William Carlos. *The Collected Poems of William Carlos Williams*. Vol. 2. New York: New Directions, 1986.

Willis, Elizabeth. "Possessing Possession: Lorine Niedecker, Folk, and the Allegory of Making." *XCP: Cross-Cultural Poetics*. 9 (2001): 97–106.

Wilson, Edmund. *The Shores of Light: A Literary Chronicle of the Twenties and Thirties*. New York: Farrar, Straus and Young, 1952.

Wisconsin Historical Society Archives. University of Wisconsin, Madison. Register for Writers Program: Wisconsin Writings and Research Notes, 1936–1942. Series 1762. Wis Mis MM. Box 6, Folder 3–Box 8, Folder 7.

Woodward, Anthony. *Ezra Pound and the Pisan Cantos*. London: Routledge, 1965.

Woolf, Virginia. "The Leaning Tower." *Collected Essays*. Vol. 2. London: Hogarth Press, 1966. 162–76.

——. *Letters Vol. II*. Ed. Nigel Nicolson. London: Hogarth Press, 1977.

——. *Three Guineas*. New York: Harcourt Brace Jovanovich, 1966.

——. *A Writer's Diary: Extracts from the Diary of Virginia Woolf*. Ed. Leonard Woolf. London: Hogarth Press, 1953.

Worrell, W. H. "Do Brains or Dollars Operate Your Set?" *Radio Broadcast* 2 (November 1922): 70.

Wright, Richard. *Lawd Today!* 1963. New York: Library of America, 1991.

Yaeger, Patricia. "Consuming Trauma; or, the Pleasures of Merely Circulating." *Journal X: A Journal in Culture and Criticism* 1.2 (1997): 225–51.

Zilliacus, Clas. *Beckett and Broadcasting: A Study of the Works of Samuel Beckett For and In Radio and Television*. Abo: Abo Akademi, 1976.

Zukofsky, Louis. "Sincerity and Objectivity: With Special Reference to the Work of Charles Reznikoff." *Poetry* 37.5(1931): 272–88.

CONTRIBUTORS

TODD AVERY is an associate professor of English at the University of Massachusetts Lowell; his recent publications include *Radio Modernism: Literature, Ethics, and the BBC, 1922–1938* (2006).

J. STAN BARRETT completed his Ph.D. in English at the University of Michigan in 2005 and is currently attending the University of Pennsylvania Law School, from which he will graduate in 2010.

TIMOTHY C. CAMPBELL teaches in the Department of Romance Studies at Cornell University. He is the author of *Wireless Writing in the Age of Marconi* (2006) as well as the translator of Roberto Esposito's *Bios: Biopolitics and Philosophy* (2008) and *Communitas: The Origin and Destiny of Community* (2009).

DEBRA RAE COHEN is assistant professor of English at the University of South Carolina. She is the author of *Remapping the Home Front: Locating Citizenship in British Women's Great War Fiction* (2002).

STEVEN CONNOR is professor of modern literature and theory at Birkbeck College, London. He is the author of Dumbstruck: A Cultural History of Ventriloquism (2000), The Book of Skin (2004), and Fly (2006).

Founding president of the Modernist Studies Association, MICHAEL COYLE is professor of English at Colgate University. He has published widely on T. S. Eliot, Ezra Pound, and the persistence of Modernist theoretical principles.

BROOK HOUGLUM holds a Social Sciences and Humanities Research Council postdoctoral fellowship at the University of California, San Diego.

AARON JAFFE is associate professor of English at the University of Louisville. He is the author of *Modernism and the Culture of Celebrity* (2005) and a co-editor of two forthcoming essay collections, *Modernist Star Maps*, with Jonathan E. Goldman (2009), and *The Year's Work in Lebowski Studies*, with Edward Comentale (2009).

DAVID JENEMANN is assistant professor of English and film and television studies at the University of Vermont. He is the author of *Adorno in America* (2007) as well as a number of essays on Modernism and media.

JANE LEWTY studies poetry at the Iowa Writers' Workshop; she has published several articles on radio and the work of Joyce, Woolf, and Pound.

JEFFREY SCONCE is associate professor in the Screen Cultures program at Northwestern University and the author of *Haunted Media: Electronic Presence from Telegraphy to Television* (2000).

MARTIN SPINELLI is senior lecturer in media and film at the University of Sussex, UK. He has produced numerous internationally broadcast innovative radio series including Radio Radio and LINEbreak.

LESLEY WHEELER'S most recent books are *Voicing American Poetry: Sound and Performance from the 1920s to the Present* (2008) and *Scholarship Girl* (poems; 2007). She is professor and chair of English at Washington and Lee University in Lexington, Virginia.

JONAH WILLIHNGANZ is a lecturer in the Program in Writing and Rhetoric at Stanford University and director of the Stanford Storytelling Project.

SARAH WILSON is assistant professor in the Department of English at the University of Toronto. Her book *Melting-Pot Modernism,* is forthcoming in 2010 from Cornell University Press.

INDEX

ABC (American Broadcasting Company), 86
Adam, Villiers de l'Isle, 4
Adams, John, 202
Adler, Alfred, 34
Adorno, Theodor W., 5, 89, 91–101, 116, 140–41n3, 192–93; aesthetics of, 95, 100; and "The Culture Industry," 166, 173, 193; and *Current of Music*, 89, 93, 95, 98, 102; in *Minima Moralia*, 101–2; in "On the Fetish Character," 93, 100. *See also* Frankfurt School
Aesthetics, 69, 81, 84–85; and Adorno, 95, 100; of Bloomsbury Group, 158–59, 161, 164–67, 169–73; and Modernism, 25, 101; of radio, 51, 125, 156, 250–51, 274; of Stein, 107
African Americans, 117; and blackness, 119, 120; and black power, 133; disempowerment of, 126, 131; and forms of communication, 129; and vernacular, 134; voices of, 119–20, 123n19, 138. *See also* National Association for the Advancement of Colored People; race; Universal Negro Improvement Association
Agency, 94, 127, 164; of authors, 14–15; of individuals, 90, 174; and the occult, 34, 48; and race, 131, 139; of radio, 3, 146
Akron Beacon Journal, 84
Albright, Daniel, 284, 290
Alice in Sponsor-land, 95

Allport, Gordon, 259–60
Althusser, Louis, 130
American Armed Forces Radio, 191
American Nervousness (Beard), 35
America's Town Meeting of the Air, 110–11, 114, 118, 120, 122n8, 123n8
Amos 'n' Andy (radio), 118, 120
Angell, James Rowland, 108
Annual Register, 280
Antenna, 14, 16, 17, 19, 20, 26, 29, 41, 43, 53, 210
Antin, David, 253
Anti-Semitism, 202, 214
Anxiety, 95, 212, 257, 259; and authority, 72; and technology, 44–45, 91, 233, 264, 288
Apollinaire, Guillaume, 199
Aristotle, 202, 212
Armand, Louis, 207
Armstrong, Edwin H., 19
Arnheim, Rudolph, 199
Arnold, Matthew, 161, 162, 169, 176, 188, 190
Art for Your Sake, 92
Artaud, Antonin, 69–70, 77–78, 81, 84–85. *See also* Theater of Cruelty
Attridge, Derek, 163–64, 170–71
Auden, W. H., 5, 149, 151, 263
Auditory, 57, 60–61, 275
Aurality, 107, 149, 154, 254n1; and collage, 222; and confusion, 120; and perception, 213, 222–23, 234; and reception, 223, 228, 234; texts of, 239

319

Austen, Jane, 263
Authoritarianism, 92, 94, 98, 100, 103n6
Avery, Todd, 145, 193

Barney, Natalie, 201
Barnouw, Eric, 240, 251
Barthes, Roland, 225, 228
Barton, J. E., 1
Battle of the Bulge, 185
Baudelaire, Charles, 257, 259, 264, 265, 273n4
Baudry, Jean-Louis, 277
Bazerman, Charles, 26
BBC (British Broadcasting Corporation), 38, 142–55, 156n8, 158, 160–63, 165, 173–74, 203; Eastern Service of, 176; French Service of, 185; influence of, 191; Written Archives Center of, 178. *See also* Listener
Beard, George, 35–36, 43
Beckett, Samuel, 2, 274–93; and *All That Fall*, 276, 278, 289, 290–92; and *Cascando*, 279; in *Company*, 286; in *Eh Joe*, 287; and *Embers*, 279, 282, 287, 289–90; in *Film*, 283; in *Ghost Trio*, 288; in *Happy Days*, 288; in *How It Is*, 285–86, 290; in *Ill Seen Ill Said*, 286; in *The Lost Ones*, 285; in *Nohow On*, 286; in *Not I*, 282, 290; in *Ohio Impromptu*, 286; and *The Old Tune*, 279, 292; in *Play*, 286, 290; and radio, 275–76; and *Rough for Radio I*, 279, 284–85; and *Rough for Radio II*, 279, 286; in *Rough for Theatre II*, 281; sound-world of, 292; in *The Unnamable*, 285; and *Words and Music*, 279, 289; in *Worstword Ho*, 286
Beer, Gillian, 143
Begnal, Michael, 207
Bell, Clive, 164
Bell, Ian F. A., 220n1
Benjamin, Walter, 25, 173, 210; in "Artwork," 28; in *Illuminations*, 263–64; and technologies of reproduction, 6, 155; and "Theses on the Philosophy of History," 23. *See also* Frankfurt School
Bentham, Jeremy, 126
Bergen, Edgar, 239, 252
Bernstein, Charles, 244, 254n1
Beveridge, William, 144
Biddle, Francis, 202
Biocca, Frank, 154
Black-boxing, 16–17, 22
Blackface, 118, 120, 123n19
Blair, Eric. *See* Orwell, George
Bloomsbury Group, 158–74; aesthetics of, 158–59, 161, 164–67, 169–73. *See also* Forster, E. M.; Keynes, John Maynard; MacCarthy, Desmond; Strachey, Lytton; Woolf, Leonard; and Woolf, Virginia
Bokhari, Zulfiqar, 176, 180–81, 192
Bose, J. C., 19, 20
Boswell, John, 168
Bozart-Westminster (magazine), 226
Branly, Edouard, 18, 19, 65n4
Brecht, Bertolt, 5, 11, 96–98, 100, 102
Brendon, Piers, 268
Breuer, Marcel, 43–44, 50n8; and metaphor of electricity, 36; 43–44, 50n8; and *Studies in Hysteria*, 35–36
Bridson, D. G., 144
British Broadcasting Corporation. *See* BBC
Broadcasting, 91, 277; archives of, 2; commercialization of, 165; as cultural practice, 3; ethics of, 158; for the masses, 38, 165; as public service, 165, 167, 173; and reading, 240; regulation of, 20–21. *See also* ABC; CBS; NBC; radio; television; wireless
Broun, Heyward, 77
Brücke, Ernst, 35
Bunting, Basil, 233
Burke, Kenneth, 126

Burns, C. DeLisle, 1
Byron, George Gordon (Lord), 169

Calder-Marshall, Arthur, 147
Cambridge Conversazione Society, 160
Campbell, Timothy, 5, 210
Cantril, Hadley, 72, 73, 85, 87, 259–60,
Capek, Karel, 23
Capitalism, 12, 100, 125, 129, 150
Cardiff, David, 145
Carpenter, Humphrey, 215, 216
Cathexis, 34–37
Cazzamali, Ferdinando, 38–39
CBS (Columbia Broadcasting System), 38, 44, 69, 75, 77–78, 92, 95
Century (magazine), 21
Chavez, Carlos, 200
Cheney, Margaret, 65n4
Churchill, Winston, 143
Church Looks Ahead, The, 179
Cinema, 4, 14, 77, 142, 191, 277
Civil War (U.S.), 33, 128, 133
Clark Gifford's Body (Fearing), 125
Clark, Suzanne, 239, 252
Clark, T. J., 272
Class, 99, 152, 243
Clear Channel, 12
Cohen, Debra Rae, 193
Coherence, 20, 206
Coleridge, Samuel Taylor, 263
Columbia Workshop, 78
Common Sense (journal), 182
Communism, 110
Communist Party, 148, 152
Conner, Kim, 293
Connolly, Cyril, 177
Connor, James A., 205, 253
Connor, Steven, 5, 7
Conrad, Joseph, 14, 25
Consciousness, 4, 32, 38–40, 43–44, 47–49, 61, 131
Consumer electronics, 16
Conversation, 2, 109, 113–16, 160, 163

Corman, Cid, 224, 233, 234
Corwin, Norman, 79–80, 82–84, 88n16, 221; and *On a Note of Triumph*, 68–69, 78, 81, 83; and *Seems Radio Is Here to Stay*, 78, 80
Cory, Mark, 96
Cosmopolitan (magazine), 108
Costello, Brannon, 129
Coughlin, Charles, 108
Cox, Kenneth, 233
Coyle, Michael, 148
Crawford Committee, 160
Crisell, Andrew, 166
Criterion (magazine), 186
Crossley service, 71
Culture, 95, 111, 116, 129, 143, 160, 188; administration of, 93; and Arnold, 161, 169, 189, 193; and Eliot, 176–79, 182–83, 185–86, 189–93, 194n14; of leisure, 117; of Modernism, 6, 107; radio's effect on, 1–2, 12, 65, 124, 161. *See also* Arnold, Matthew; "Culture Industry, The"; mass culture
"Culture Industry, The" (Horkheimer & Adano), 5, 92, 98, 165, 193
cummings, e. e., 212
Curry, Tom, 39–40
Cuthbert, Margaret, 252–53
Czitrom, David, 260, 273n2

Danius, Sarah, 7
Dante, 211, 215
Davidson, Michael, 253
Day Lewis, Cecil, 155–56n8; and attitudes toward broadcasting, 148; in "Revolution in Literature," 154; and *Starting Point*, 147–48, 149, 152, 154
Deane, Patrick, 145
Deb, Mohan Singh, 180
de Certeau, Michel, 160, 174
Defoe, Daniel, 168, 169
DeForest, Lee, 19
Deleuze, Gilles, 170, 171, 279

Index 321

Dennett, Daniel, 275
Denny, George, 110, 111
Derrida, Jacques, 163, 210
Desire, 26, 40, 42, 45
Deutsch, Helene, 36, 39
Dewey, John, 112
Dickens, Charles, 171
Dictation, 46, 52, 55–56, 57, 59, 61, 63
Disciplinary Training Center (Italy), 217, 218
Discursivity, 12, 14, 26, 42, 116, 122–23n8
Dispossession, 15, 126, 129
Diversity, 111, 113–15
Domination, 92, 97
Donne, John, 85
Dos Passos, John, 125
Douglas, Susan, 87
Dow, Caroline B., 243
Dryden, John, 181
Du Maurier, George, 158
Duncan, Ronald, 201, 203
Dunham, Franklin, 111, 112, 114
Dust Bowl, 268

Ears, 43, 55, 80, 85, 90, 97, 217
Eavesdropping, 75, 275
Edgar Bergen–Charlie McCarthy Show, The, 72
Edison, Thomas Alva, 18, 22, 96, 103n6, 280
Efflorescence, 24–27
Einstein, Albert, 32
Electric chair, 39, 280
Electricity, 4, 22, 32, 36, 40, 205, 209, 211, 280
Electromagnetic radiation, 12, 20, 53
Eliot, T. S., 2, 14, 125, 139, 162, 170, 176–93, 212; and Arnoldian aesthetics, 186, 189, 190, 193; in *After Strange Gods*, 189; as cultural critic, 184–85, 188–90, 192–93, 194n14; and *Four Quartets*, 179, 181, 192; and *Notes toward the Definition of Culture*, 185, 189; radio talks of, 177–79, 189; and *Use of Poetry and the Use of Criticism*, 170; and *Use of Poetry and the Use of Culture*, 189–90; war poetry of, 182–83; in *Waste Land, The*, 139, 200
Ellmann, Maud, 211
Entropy, 61–63, 292
Esslin, Martin, 275
Ethics, 45, 150, 159, 160, 163–64, 167, 170–72
Evangelism, 108, 161, 163, 204

Famous Contemporaries, 185
Fascism, 110, 176, 210; in Germany, 103n6; and race, 126–27, 129, 138, 140; rise of, 5. See also Hitler, Adolph; Mussolini, Benito; Nazism
Faulkner, William, 228
Fearing, Kenneth, 125
Federal Communications Act, 107
Federal Communications Commission (FCC), 21
Federal Writers' Project, 228
Fenollosa, Ernest, 213
Fessenden, Reginald, 19, 253
Finley, Ian Hamilton 232
Fireside Chats (Roosevelt), 110, 241
Fisher, Sterling, 112
Fleay, Clive, 180
Fleming, John Ambrose, 19
Flory, Wendy, 219
Folk poetry, 223, 228–29, 231, 235n1
Folk songs, 79–80, 119
Ford, Ford Madox, 212
Forrester, John, 36–37
Forster, E. M., 5, 164–65, 170. See also Bloomsbury Group
Foucault, Michel, 14, 125
Framing, 15, 70, 72, 77, 82, 130
France, 182, 185, 268
Frank, Joseph, 210
Frankenstein (Shelley), 40
Frankfurt School, 5, 116, 125, 148. See also Adorno, Theodor W.; Benjamin, Walter; Horkheimer, Max

322 Index

Fraser, Nancy, 112
Freedom, 52, 56–58, 60, 63–64, 82–83, 97
Freedom's People, 119
Freud, Sigmund, 23, 33–49, 49n4, 62, 282; in *Beyond the Pleasure Principle*, 42–43, 47, 263–64; in *Civilization and Its Discontents*, 33, 261; in "Dreams and the Occult," 48; in *Studies in Hysteria*, 35–36; and telepathy, 34 , 37, 39, 44, 48–49
Frost, Everett, 288
Froula, Christine, 2, 214
Fry, Roger, 164
Futurism, 4, 51–52, 55, 58–59, 62, 64, 66n8, 97. *See also* Marinetti, Filippo Tommaso

Gale, Zona, 228
Galvani, Luigi, 35, 40
Gandhi, Mohandas K., 185
Garvey, Marcus, 133
Geertz, Clifford, 6
Germany, 182, 185–87, 190, 241, 267–68
Gernsback, Hugo, 43
Giddings, Robert, 145
Ginsberg, Allen, 253
Gitelman, Lisa, 7
Glossolalia, 69
Goebbels, Joseph, 202
Gordon, David, 214, 215
Gould, Glenn, 85, 86
Gramophone, 6, 289
Great Depression, 257, 267–68
Green, T. H., 169
Guattari, Felix, 279

Habermas, Jürgen, 112
Hale, Jane Alison, 279
Hallucination, 60, 217, 220
Hansen, Miriam, 14
Harrington, Joseph, 267, 270
H.D. (Hilda Doolittle), 125, 219
Heard, Gerald, 191
Hearing, 52, 56–58, 101, 107, 226, 249

Hertz, Heinrich, 12, 18, 52–53, 65n4
Hilmes, Michele, 167, 241, 243, 254n5
Hindemith, Paul, 96
Hitler, Adolph, 71, 79, 144, 186, 241, 292. *See also* fascism; Nazism
Hoffmann, E. T. A., 23
Hollos, Istvan, 37, 39
Holroyd, Michael, 158
Homer, 205, 214, 217; *Iliad*, 217; *Odyssey*, 214
Homogenization, 5, 142
Hoover, Herbert, 268
Hope, Victor Alexander John, 180
Horkheimer, Max, 5, 165, 173, 192–93. *See also* Frankfurt School
Howe, Elias, 18
Hughes, David Edward, 65n4
Hughes, Langston, 118, 120
Hullot-Kentor, Robert, 95–96
Huxley, Julian, 177
Huxley, Thomas, 169
Huyssen, Andreas, 140–41n3, 178
Hynes, Samuel, 149, 152
Hypnosis, 38, 124

Iliad (Homer), 217. *See also* Homer; *Odyssey*
Imagism, 64, 220. *See also* Pound, Ezra
Imperialism, 163, 177, 183, 185
Incandescence, 24, 26–27
India, 182–85
Indian National Congress, 185
Inscription, 2, 48, 53, 207, 219
Internationalism, 163, 175
International Radio-telegraphic Convention, 20
Internet, 15
Intuition, 42, 56, 57, 60–63, 202
Iron Curtain, 189
Isherwood, Christopher, 5, 149

James, Alice, 230, 231
James, Henry, 230, 231
James, William, 230, 231

Jameson, Storm, 154
Jay, Martin, 60
Jaynes, Julian, 217
Jazz, 92, 101, 118, 119, 120, 241
Jeans, James, 191
Jenemann, David, 5
Jones, Ernest, 34, 37
Joyce, James, 6, 139, 154, 162, 181, 199–220; *Finnegans Wake*, 154, 203–5, 206–10, 214, 218; *Ulysses*, 139, 203, 219
Jubilee, 119
Jung, Carl, 34

Kafka, Franz, 153
Kahn, Douglas, 7, 51, 96, 155, 215
Kant, Immanuel, 47
Kaplan, Milton, 242
Karloff, Boris, 39
Kavina, Lydia, 99
Kearns, George, 216
Kennedy, David, 268
Kenner, Hugh, 205, 210–11, 215–16, 219, 220n 1
Keynes, John Maynard, 164–65. *See also* Bloomsbury Group
King Lear (Shakespeare), 286
Kipling, Rudyard, 32, 181, 183, 185
Kittler, Friedrich, 3, 7, 60, 65n4, 111–12, 155
Korzeniowski, Konrad. *See* Conrad, Joseph
Ku Klux Klan, 46. *See also* white power
Kumlien, Thure, 224

Labor, 21, 27, 28, 91, 135
Lacan, Jacques, 62–63
Ladwig, Walter, 230
Lapham, Increase, 228
Laplanche, Jean, 42
"La Radia" (Marinetti & Masnata), 274
Latimer, Ronald, 257
Latour, Bruno, 16, 17. *See also* black-boxing

Laverty, Maura, 177
Lawrence, D. H., 162
Leavis, F. R., 161, 170
Leavis, Q. D., 161, 170
Le Bon, Gustave, 49
Lee, Vernon, 171
Leisure, 21, 28, 263
LeMahieu, D. L., 145
Levin, Harry, 204
Levinas, Emmanuel, 163–64
Lewis, Sinclair, 125
Lewis, Wyndham, 64, 200, 214
Lewty, Jane, 7, 187
Life (magazine), 121
Limbaugh, Rush, 20
Lincoln, Abraham, 128, 129, 133
Lippmann, Walter, 261–62
Lips, 215, 244
Listener (newspaper), 144, 145, 150, 161, 162, 175n1, 194n10; and "Literary Values," 161, 162; and "The Oracle from the Microphone," 146; and "Prejudice and Education," 146; and "Points of View," 146
Listening, 52, 57, 71, 73–74, 77–80, 275, 278
Literary Review (magazine), 219
Lodge, Oliver, 18, 19, 32, 48, 65n4
London Times, 168
Longenbach, James, 266, 269
Lowenthal, Leo, 3
Luckhurst, Roger, 35

MacCarthy, Desmond: Arnoldian mission of, 160–62, 170, 173; and broadcasting, 163–65, 170–72; as cultural arbiter, 161–62, 168–69; literary values of, 159–63; and *New Spirit in Literature, The*, 162; radio talks of, 169, 171. *See also* Bloomsbury Group
Macdonnell, A. G., 171
MacLeish, Archibald, 124, 216, 221, 241
MacNeice, Louis, 263

324 Index

Madge, Charles, 144
Madison Square Garden, 22
Mann, Thomas, 91
Man Who Changed His Mind, The (film). *See* "Soul Snatcher, The"
Marconi, Guglielmo, 12, 18, 32, 41, 52, 205, 210, 220
Marinetti, Filippo Tommaso, 4, 51–65, 103n6, 274, 292. *See also* Futurism
Marvin, Carolyn, 3
Marx, Karl, 141n4
Marxism and Language (*Vološinov*), 270
Marxism, 151, 152, 156n15
Masefield, John, 241
Masnata, Pino, 4, 103n6, 274
Mass culture, 79, 125, 127, 129, 148, 240; and communication, 127; and consumption, 12, 25
Mass media, 127
Mass mediaura, 14
Mass Observation, 144
Matheson, Hilda, 143
Mattelart, Armand, 19, 21
Matthews, William, 84–85
Maxwell, James C., 52–53, 63
McLuhan, Eric, 207–8
McLuhan, Marshall, 3, 67n16, 253; and *Gutenberg Galaxy, The*, 3; and *Understanding Media*, 47, 262, 271
Mearns, Hughes, 253
Menlo Park, N.J., 22
Middleton, Peter, 222, 251
Migone, Christof, 86
Milesi, Laurent, 207
Milford, Nancy, 243
Mill, John Stuart, 169, 253
Millay, Edna St. Vincent, 238–54, 256n22; in *The Buck in the Snow*, 25; and *Fatal Interview*, 245, 247, 248, 249; and *First Figs from Thistles*, 245; in *The Harp Weaver*, 245; and lyric poetry, 253, 254; as performer, 244–49, 255n14; and radio, 238, 242, 246–49; and *Renascence*, 245; in

Savage Beauty, 250; in *Second April*, 245; and sexuality, 238, 243
Millay, Vincent, 243
Milton, John, 167, 168, 172
Minculpop (fascist Italian Ministry of Popular Culture), 187.
Modernism, 1, 51, 107–8, 125, 139, 154–55, 178; and assemblage, 226; definitions of, 252; literature of, 69, 145, 200; and music, 222; and theater, 81; vernacular of, 14, 91
Modernity, 91, 178; discourses of, 48; in the nineteenth century, 259
Monologues, 199–200
Monroe, Harriet, 241. *See also* Poetry
Montefiore, Janet, 152
Moore, G. E., 160, 163–65, 167–70
Morgan, J. P., 22
Morris, Adelaide, 7, 208, 210, 253, 254
Morse code, 19, 52, 53, 54
Mortley, G. E., 278
Muggeridge, Malcolm, 147
Muir, John, 228
Munich Crisis, 71
Music and You, 92
"Music in Radio" (memo), 98
Mussolini, Benito, 144, 201, 202. *See also* fascism

Nash, Ogden, 85
National Association for the Advancement of Colored People (NAACP), 118. *See also* African Americans; race
Nationalism, 163, 174, 187
Naturalism, 34
Nazism, 118, 165, 184; and Buro Concordia, 202. *See also* fascism; Hitler, Adolph
NBC (National Broadcasting Company), 38, 72, 92, 111
Nero, Bob, 233
Neurasthenia, 36
New Criticism, 125

New York Times, 38, 83, 99, 100
New York Tribune, 73
New York World Telegram, 77
New Yorker, The, 1
Newman, John Henry, 176
Newsweek (magazine), 84
Nicholson, Harold, 161–62
Niedecker, Lorine, 6, 221–35, 236n 6; and *As I Lay Dying* adaptation, 228, 230, 236n 7; in "Letter for Ian," 232; in *New Democracy*, 226; in *New Directions*, 226; in *New Goose*, 229; radio talks of, 231–32; in "Taste and Tenderness," 221
Noise, 51, 66n7, 206, 246, 253, 292. *See also* white noise
Norton, Alice, 231

Occult, 4, 33–34, 36, 40–42, 48, 50n7
Odyssey (Homer), 214. *See also* Homer; *Illiad*
Oliver, Owen, 32
Olson, Tillie, 199
Ong, Walter, 3, 253
Oppenheim, James, 40
Oppenheim, Janet, 40
Oracular voice, 149, 152, 153
Orwell, George, 2, 145, 180–81, 192, 222, 255n16
Overholser, Winfred, 217
Overstreet, Bonaro, 111, 122n8
Overstreet, Harry, 111, 122n8
Owen, Alex, 50n7

Pater, Walter, 158, 170
Pea, Enrico, 202
Penberthy, Jenny, 223, 225–26, 229, 231–32
Perez, Vincent, 128–29
Peters, John Durham, 7, 200
Phil Hendrie Show, The, 86
Phonograph, 3, 51, 141n5, 206, 275
Phosphorescence, 25
Physiognomics, 93–94, 97–99
Picabia, Francis, 219

Pictorialism, 25
Pierce, John, 45
Pinget, Robert, 279
Pleasure, 42–45, 62, 160, 169–72, 264, 268, 283
Pocock, G. N., 155
Podcasting, 12
Poe, Edgar Allan, 181
Poetry (magazine), 241. *See also* Monroe, Harriet
Popov, Alexander, 19
Pores, Jerod, 20
Postgate, Raymond, 145, 153
Pound, Ezra, 2, 6, 64, 125, 187–88, 191, 194n15, 199–220; broadcasts of, 201–4, 208–10, 212, 214, 216–20; in *Cantos*, 200, 205–6, 210, 213–16, 219, 293; and critique of Joyce, 203–4, 220; in *Natural Philosophy of Love*, 218; and *Pisan Cantos*, 218, 219; radio talks of, 219; in *Spirit of Romance*, 211, 218; as translator, 213–14
Poussin, Nicolas, 233
Preece, William, 29
Presence, 132, 136, 152, 154, 217, 280, 286; and human voice, 141n4, 213, 245, 248; of Modernist values, 2; and physicality, 244, 247, 253; of radio, 33, 77, 129, 148–49, 203, 238–39, 246, 253; and sonics, 6; and spectrals, 32
Princeton Radio Research Project (PRRP), 89, 93, 94, 95, 98, 111
Printing press, 3
Propaganda, 73, 187, 201–2
Prosthesis, 261–62
Proximity, 17, 28, 249, 262, 265
Psychoanalysis, 11, 31–50
Public Opinion Quarterly (periodical), 112
Publicists, 12, 58
Pulp fiction, 39, 48

Quantum physics, 32
Quartermain, Peter, 223

326 Index

Race, 126–27; agendas of, 93–94; and broadcasting, 117–22; and paternalism, 118; and ventriloquism, 118. *See also* African Americans; National Association for the Advancement of Colored People; white power
Radar, 22
Radiant mediation, 13
Radio: aesthetics of, 51, 125, 156, 250–51, 274; and audience, 71, 72, 74, 77, 79, 87, 89–90, 95; commercialism of, 15, 21–22, 143; as cultural accelerant, 1; culture of, 12; and democracy, 143, 166–67; and emotional appeals, 108; history of, 32, 140n1, 277; as idea, 6; and the imaginary, 5–6; as information source, 114; intimacy of, 122n2, 275; lyricism of, 253; and the radiogenic, 143, 154; and semantics, 72; social effects of, 1, 125, 258, 260. *See also* broadcasting; radio-shacking; radio-space; radio talks; and wireless
Radio Shack, 15–16
Radio-shacking, 16–17
Radio-space, 80–81, 202, 207, 215, 274–75
Radio Studies, 7
Radio talks, 149, 154, 160, 175; of Eliot, 177–79, 189; of MacCarthy, 169, 171; and Niedecker, 231–32; of Pound, 219; of Stein, 121
Rainey, Laurence, 210
Raquello, Ramón, 71
Read, Forrest, 200–201, 204
Reading, 168, 171–73
Reavey, George, 292
Recapitulation, 43, 147, 149
Reception, 13–15, 20–21, 146, 154, 221, 288
Reddick, L. D., 119
Reich, Wilhelm, 46
Reith, John, 5, 142, 150, 166; Arnoldian mission of, 4, 143, 146, 167, 170, 173; and *Broadcast Over Britain*, 143; broadcast theories of, 146; criticisms of, 144–45, 147–48, 154, 159, 162–63; Scottish accent of, 144; and views on public radio, 143, 160, 165–68, 173–174, 191, 193
Repetition, 59, 80, 205, 269–70, 290
Richards, I. A., 170, 264
Richardson, Stanley, 279
Righi, Augusto, 18
Rilke, Ranier Maria, 215
Robertson, Lisa, 226
Rogers, William G., 109
Romanticism, 14, 16, 52, 60
Rome Radio, 201, 210, 218. *See also* Minculpop
Roosevelt, Franklin D., 109–10, 187, 201, 240–41, 268
Ross, Harold, 1
Rosset, Barney, 276
Roth, Henry, 125
Rouse, William, 41–42
Royal Mail (UK), 29n5
Russell, Eric Frank, 45–46
Russia, 186
Rutzky, R. L., 7

Sackville-West, Vita, 162
Saerchinger, César, 241, 255n6
Said, Edward, 174
Sanders, M. L., 180
Sayers, Dorothy L., 179
Sayre, Jeanette, 111
Scannell, Paddy, 145
Schafer, Murray, 217
Schizophrenia, 50 n. 14, 86, 217
Schnapp, Jeffrey T., 51, 66n14
Schreber, Daniel, 35
Sconce, Jeffrey, 4, 7, 85,
Scott, Walter, 169, 263
Scripts, 69, 167, 222, 228
Scrutiny (journal), 161
Sensory concentration, 275
Sensory deprivation, 275
Shakespeare, William, 182, 183, 199
Shannon, Claude E., 61–63

Index   327

Sheeler, Charles, 90–92, 102
Sidgwick, Henry, 160
Sieveking, Lance, 155
Silberman, Mark, 96
Silence, 140, 167, 276, 285
Sinclair, Upton, 4
Slaby, Adolf, 65n4
Smoot–Hawley Tariff, 268
Smulyan, Susan, 239–40, 251–52
Socialism, 110–11
Socialist Realism, 149, 152, 157n15
"Soul Snatcher, The" (*The Man Who Changed His Mind*), 39
Sounds, 56–58, 62, 64, 154, 285, 287; electronic transmission of, 96; and listening, 85, 224, 231; mediation of, 91; theory of, 7; of white voices, 135–36
Southick, Albert, 280
Spann, Marcella, 217
Speech, 3, 132, 134, 150, 208, 214–15, 270; disembodiment of, 124, 228; and instability of language, 86; as multilateral, 85; as performance, 250–51; and poetry, 222–24, 227, 229–34, 265; and power, 138–39, 291; and race, 129, 131, 134–36; on the radio, 202–3, 221–22, 224–26, 228–29, 231; styles of, 123n19; and voice, 126
Spencer, Herbert, 169
Spiritualism, 33, 35
Spirituals, 119
Sprague, Rosemary, 244
S.S. Titanic, 54
Stalin, Josef, 186
Stansky, Peter, 165
Stanton, Frank, 95
Stein, Gertrude, 107–22, 124; aesthetics of, 107; and aurality, 108, 111–12; and *Autobiography of Alice B. Toklas*, 111; and *Brewsie and Willie*, 114–18, 119–20; and *Everybody's Autobiography*, 108, 110; in "I Came and Here I Am," 108; in *Ida*, 109; radio talks of, 121; in *Wars I Have Seen*, 114

Stephen, Leslie, 169
Stevens, Wallace, 6, 257–72; in "Adagia," 265; attitudes toward radio, 259, 262, 263, 271, 272n1; in *Ideas of Order*, 257, 269; and "The Irrational Elements of Poetry," 258; in "The Noble Rider and the Sound of Words," 258, 260–61, 262, 264–65, 270, 272; in "The Pleasure of Merely Circulating," 258, 266–71; in "A Postcard from the Volcano," 261; in "Surety and Fidelity Claims," 260; in "The Man with the Blue Guitar," 272
Stevenson, Robert Louis, 171
Stewart, Garrett, 240
Strachey, James, 50n8
Strachey, Lytton, 158, 164. See also Bloomsbury Group
Stream of consciousness, 200, 222
Studebaker, J. W., 121
Subsumption, 97, 100, 211
Surette, Leon, 214
Sweden, 182, 183, 267
Swedish News Talks, 182

Talk radio, 2, 241
Tate, Allen, 213
Tausk, Victor, 35
Telegraphy, 273n3; and Marconi, as mental process, 32, 35, 53; and Marinetti, 64; and Tesla, 65n4; as wireless process, 16–17, 19, 21, 51–53
Telepathy, 33–35, 37, 39, 44, 48–49, 59
Telephone, 90–91, 92, 141n5, 200, 225, 228, 275, 285
Television, 46, 86, 122–23n8, 192, 287
Tennyson, Alfred (Lord), 181
Tesla, Nikola, 12, 52, 65n4, 280
Theall, Donald, 206–7
Theater of Cruelty, 69, 73, 82. See also Artaud, Antonin
Theremin, Leon, 98–100, 102
Thompson, Dorothy, 73
Tichi, Cecilia, 7

Tiffany, Daniel, 13, 209, 293
Toledo Blade (newspaper), 84
Tolstoy, Leo, 168
Tongues, 215, 278
Town Meeting Comes to Town (Overstreet), 111
Translation, 210–11, 212–13
Truman, Harry S., 79
Tull, Jethro, 14
Turning Over a New Leaf, 176
Typewriter, 6

Ulmer, Gregory, 12
Unity of European Culture, The, 188
Universal Negro Improvement Association, 133. See also African Americans
University of Chicago Round Table, 110
Untermeyer, Louis, 258
Upward, Edward, 153, 154; in *Journey to the Border*, 152, 156–57n15; and socialist realism, 152, 156–57n15

Van Dyck, Anthony, 233
Variety (newspaper), 77, 84
Vernacular, 73, 83, 129. See also under African Americans
Virgil, 233
Virilio, Paul, 21
Viswanathan, Gauri, 177
Voice, 97, 126, 140, 141n4, 153, 203, 219, 287, 292; disembodiment of, 145, 260; dispossession of, 129; and experimentalism, 222, 225–28; and hailing, 130; migration of, 51; of the oracle, 149, 152, 153; and performance, 120; of radio, 130–31, 133, 136, 138, 141n5, 252; and space, 227; and univocality, 145. See also Oracular voice
Vološinov, V. N., 270
Vorticism, 11

Warner, Rex, 154; in *The Professor*, 149–52

Watson, Emily, 7
Watt, James, 18
We Hold These Truths, 78
We Speak to India, 176, 178, 181
Weather and Wireless Magazine, 278
Weber, Samuel, 14, 25
Weill, Kurt, 96
Wellek, René, 161
Welles, Orson, 87n8, 87–89n9; and *War of the Worlds*, 44, 68–77
Wells, H. G., 69–70, 84–86; and *The Time Machine*, 45; and *War of the Worlds*, 44, 70, 76
Westinghouse, George, 280
Westinghouse Electric, 22
What Goes on Behind Your Radio Dial, 95
White power, 126, 131, 138. See also Ku Klux Klan
White, E. B., 1, 140n2
White, Walter, 118, 120
Whitehead, Gregory, 7, 51, 86,
Whitehead, Kate, 158, 160
Whitman, Walt, 3
Whitworth, Michael, 199
WiFi, 12
Wilde, Oscar, 158, 170, 174–75
Wilkie, Wendell, 219
Williams, Bernard, 170, 174
Williams, Keith, 144, 147
Williams, Raymond, 165
Williams, William Carlos, 140n2
Willis, Elizabeth, 229
Wilson, Edmund, 243
Wireless, 22, 57; and imagination, 51–52, 56, 58–61, 63–64; invention of, 65n4; and media, 65; operators of, 52, 54; and telephony, 22, 52; and writing, 52
Wisconsin Council of Defense, 228
Woodward, Anthony, 219
Woolf, Leonard, 165. See also Bloomsbury Group
Woolf, Virginia, 2, 5, 158, 162, 164–65, 169, 170, 200; in *Between the*

Acts, 200; in *Waves*, 200. *See also* Bloomsbury Group
"Word of God, The," 95. *See also* Oracular voice
Wordsworth, William, 168, 263
Works Progress Administration (WPA), 228
World War I, 21, 33, 44, 183
World War II, 29, 178, 185, 202, 242, 269, 277

Worrell, W. H., 4
Wright, Richard, 118, 120, 123n19, 124–40; and *Lawd Today!*, 125–39

XM satellite radio, 12

Yeats, William Butler, 212

Zola, Emile, 141n4
Zukofsky, Louis, 221, 224, 230–31, 235, 235n1